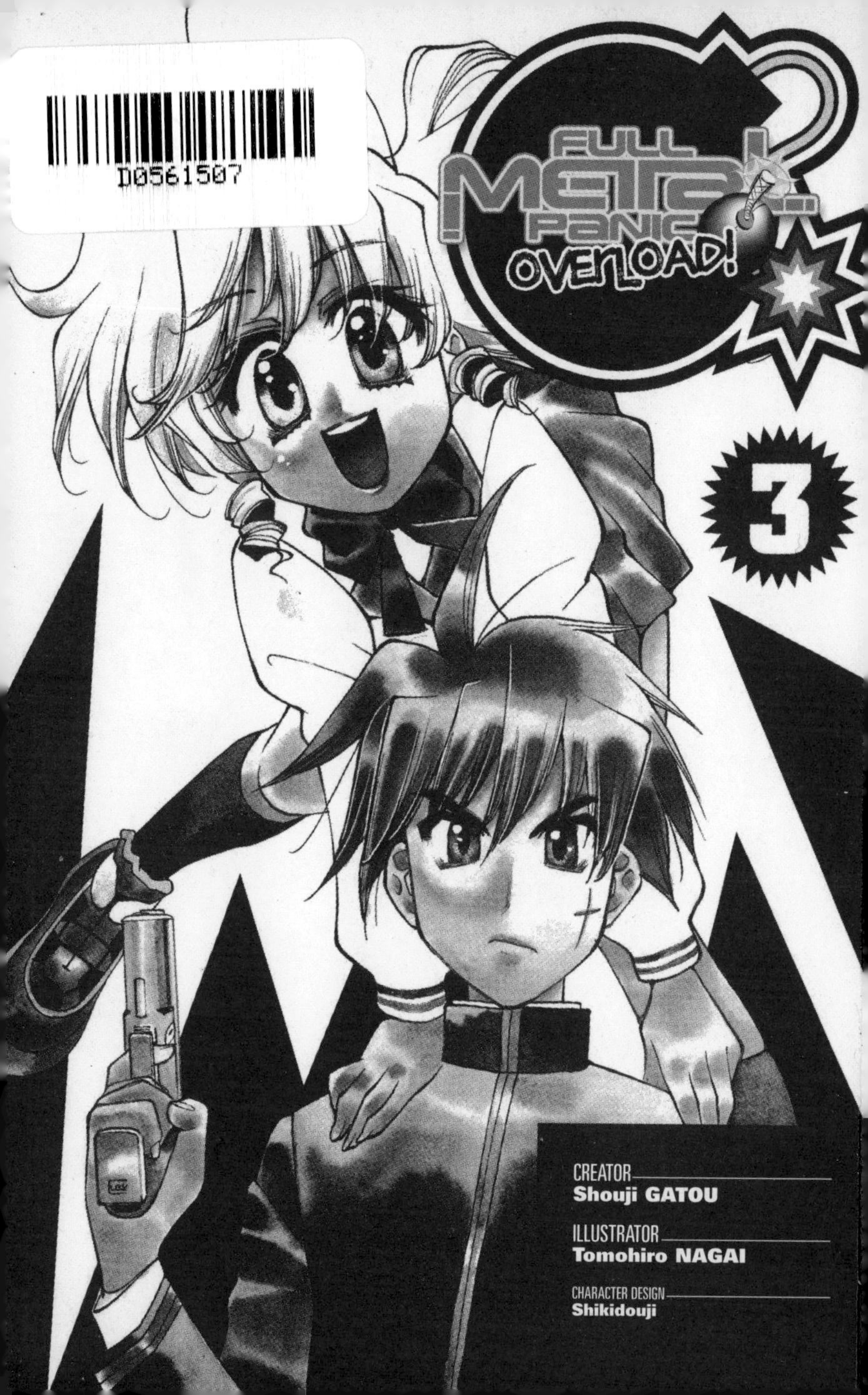
FULL METAL PANIC! OVERLOAD!
3

CREATOR
Shouji GATOU

ILLUSTRATOR
Tomohiro NAGAI

CHARACTER DESIGN
Shikidouji

CONTENTS

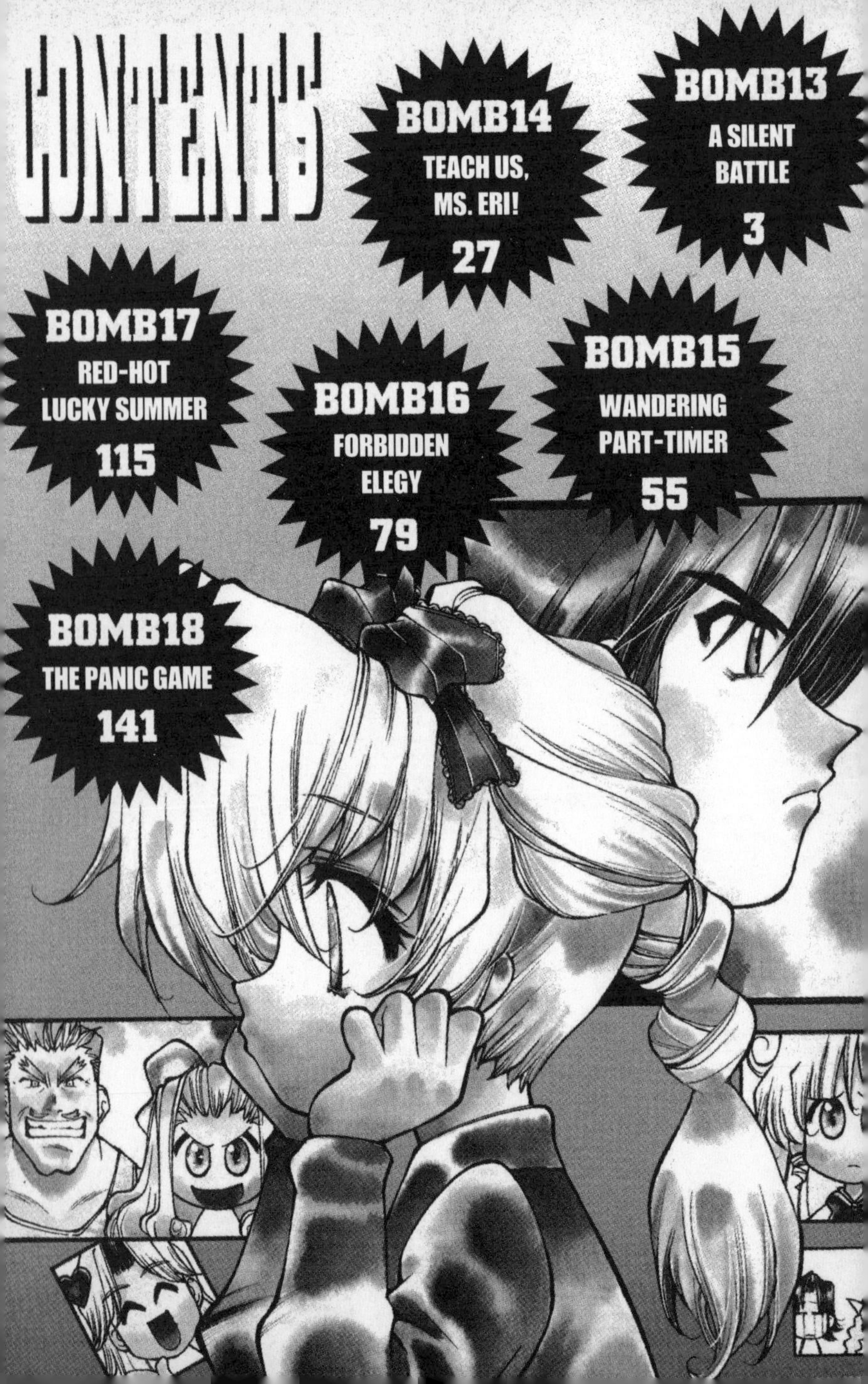

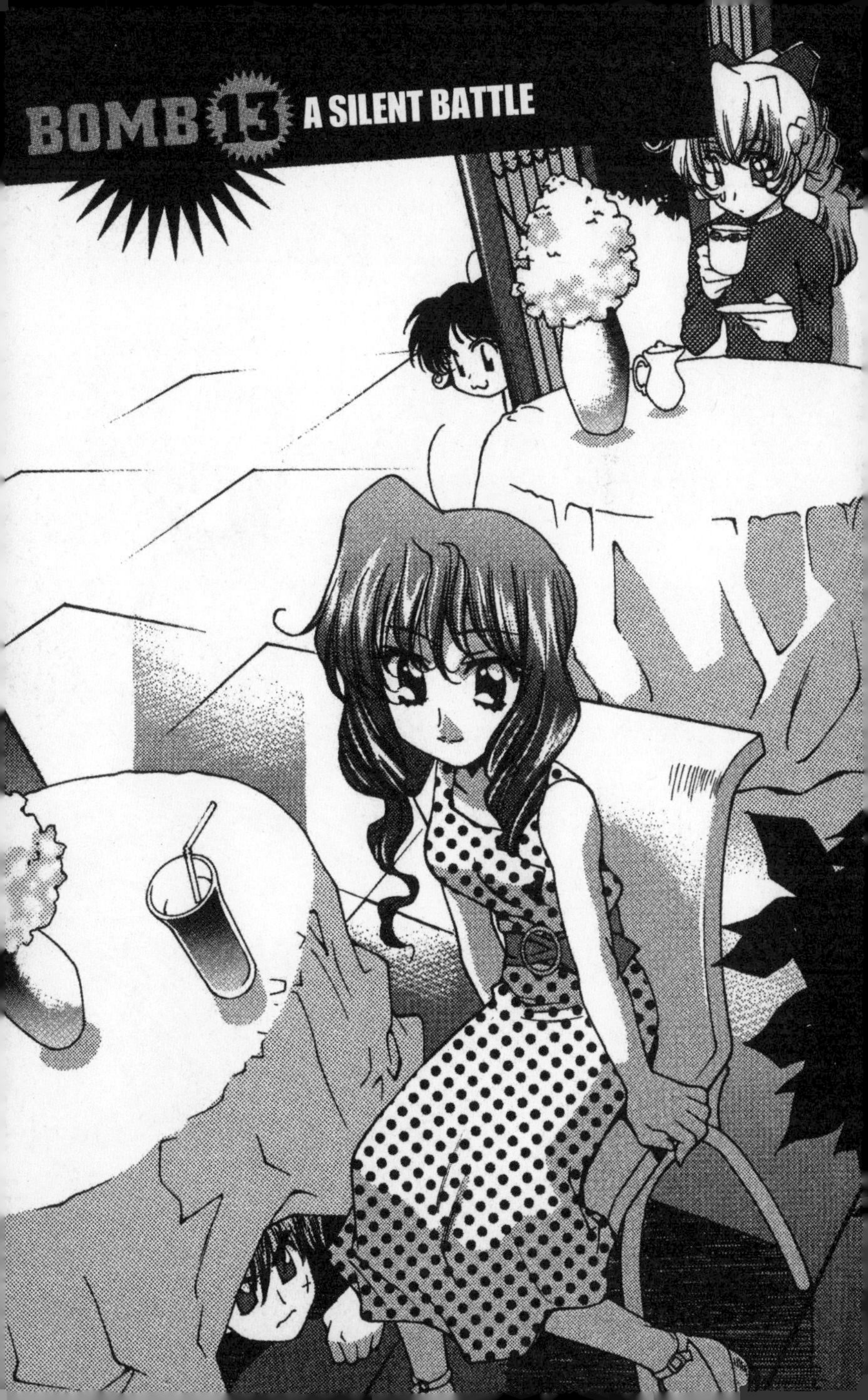
BOMB 13
A SILENT BATTLE

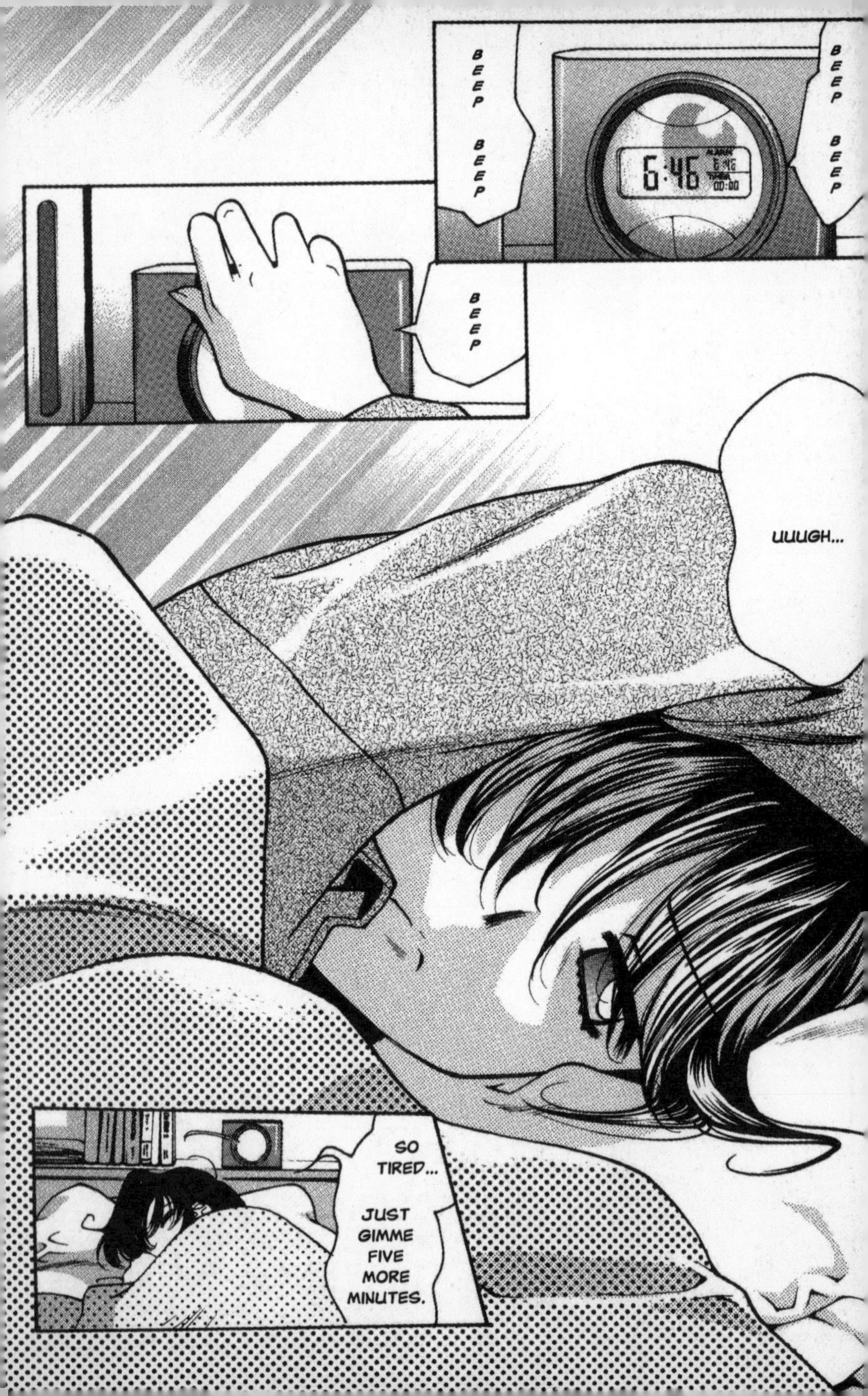
BEEP BEEP BEEP BEEP
BEEP BEEP BEEP BEEP
6:46
BEEP
UUUGH...
SO TIRED...
JUST GIMME FIVE MORE MINUTES.

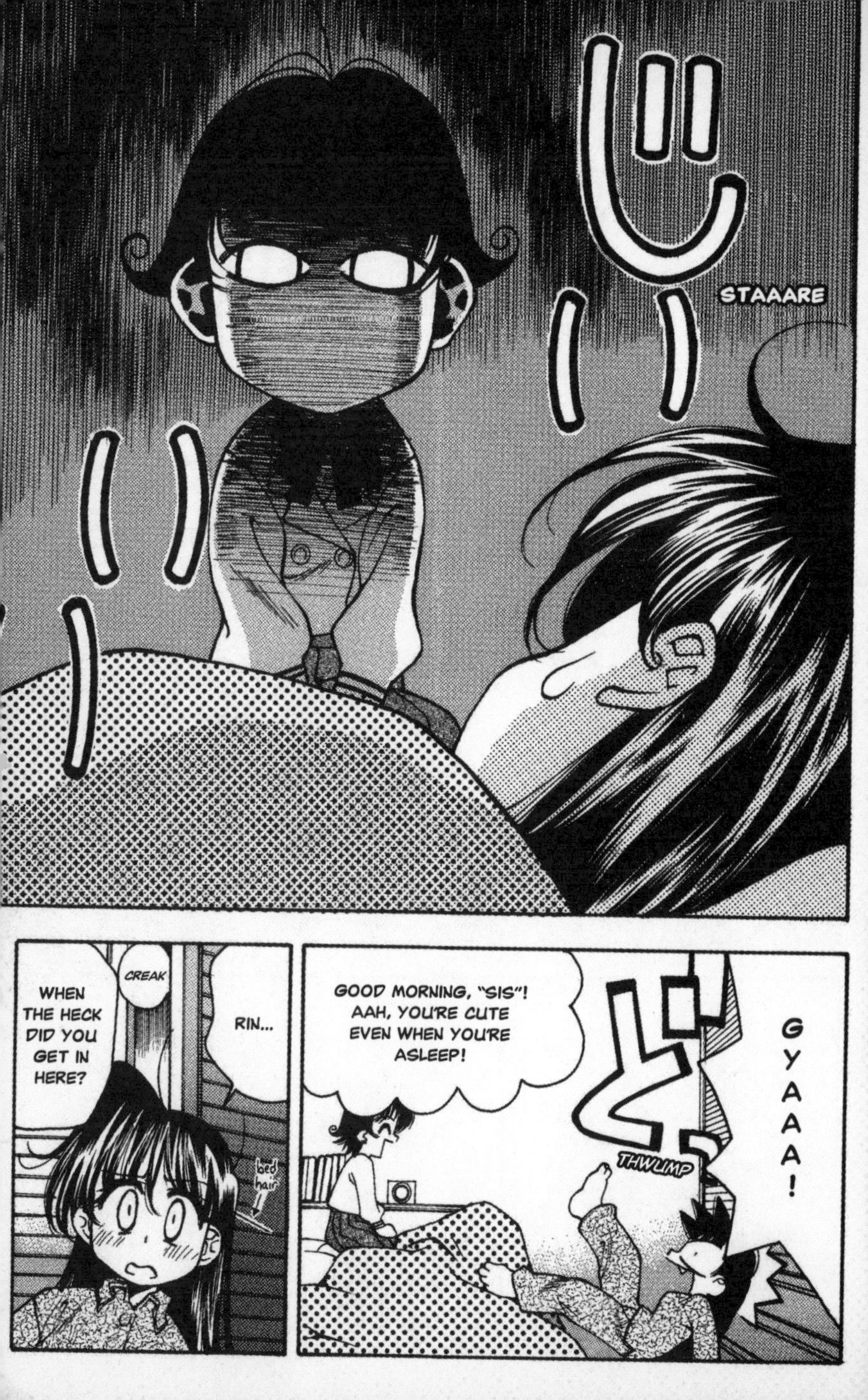
STAAARE
GYAAAA!
THWUMP
GOOD MORNING, "SIS"! AAH, YOU'RE CUTE EVEN WHEN YOU'RE ASLEEP!
RIN...
CREAK
WHEN THE HECK DID YOU GET IN HERE?
bed hair

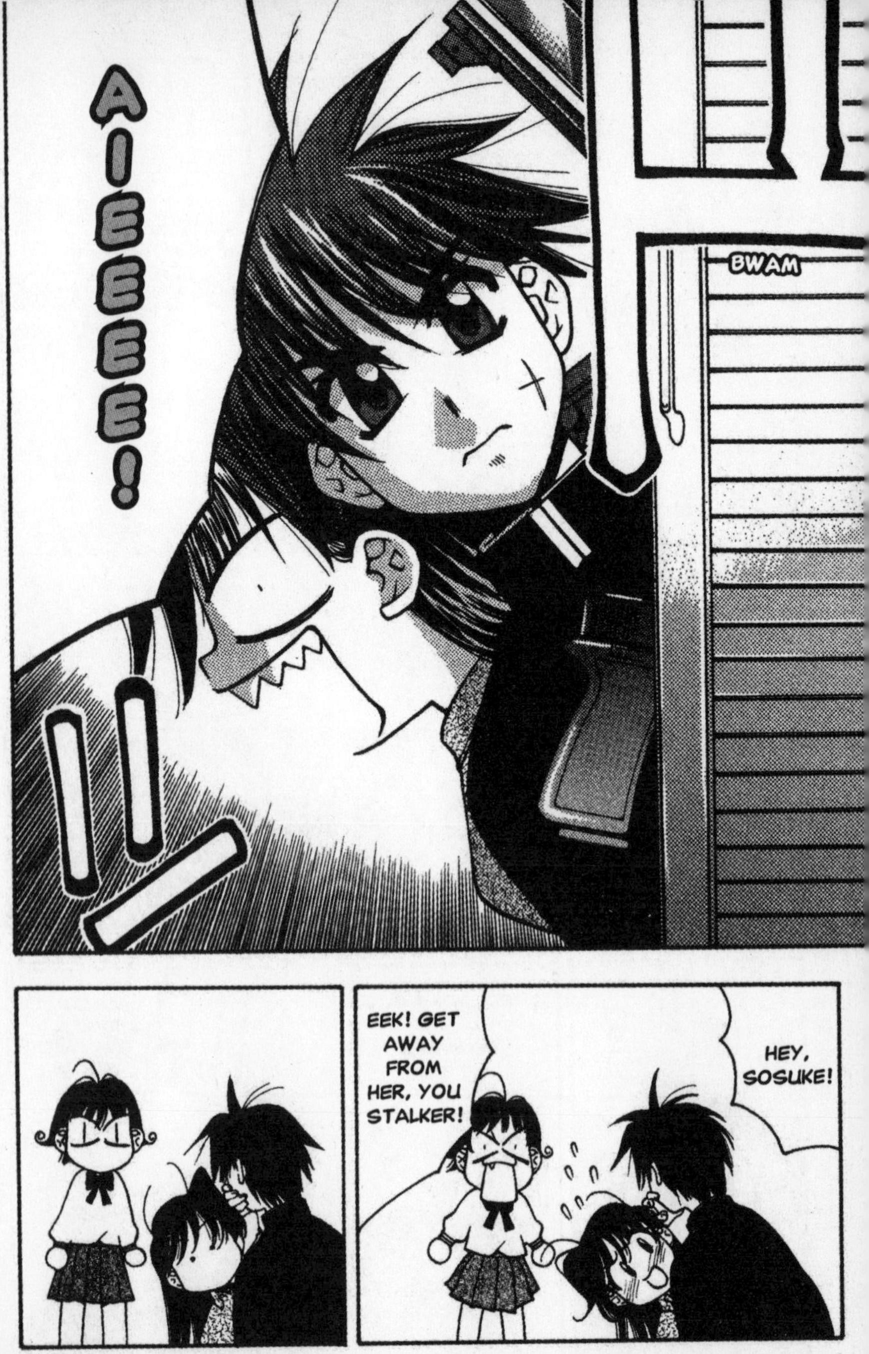
BWAM
AIEEEEE!
HEY, SOSUKE!
EEK! GET AWAY FROM HER, YOU STALKER!

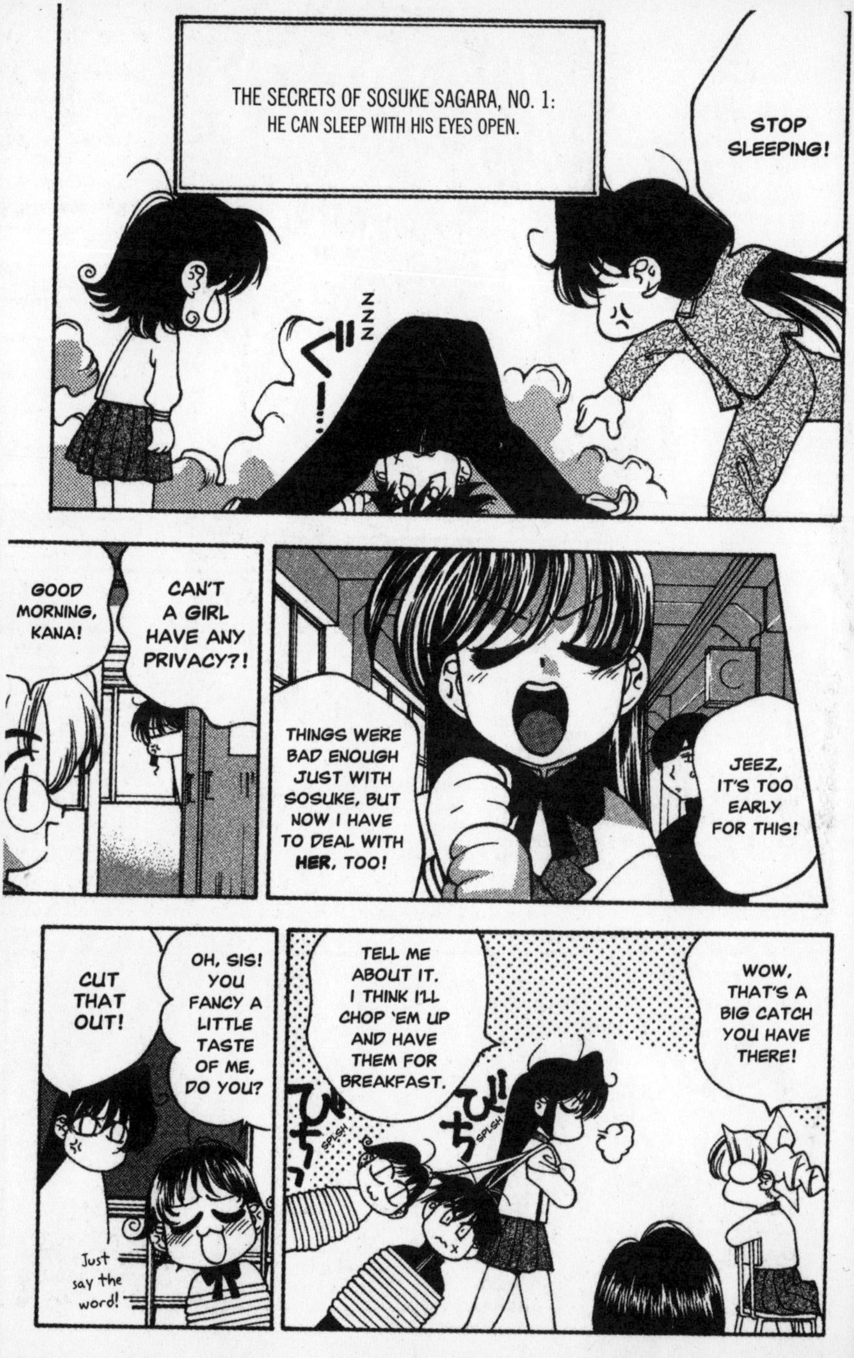
THE SECRETS OF SOSUKE SAGARA, NO. 1:
HE CAN SLEEP WITH HIS EYES OPEN.
STOP SLEEPING!
ZZZ
JEEZ, IT'S TOO EARLY FOR THIS!
THINGS WERE BAD ENOUGH JUST WITH SOSUKE, BUT NOW I HAVE TO DEAL WITH **HER**, TOO!
CAN'T A GIRL HAVE ANY PRIVACY?!
GOOD MORNING, KANA!
WOW, THAT'S A BIG CATCH YOU HAVE THERE!
TELL ME ABOUT IT. I THINK I'LL CHOP 'EM UP AND HAVE THEM FOR BREAKFAST.
SPLSH
SPLSH
OH, SIS! YOU FANCY A LITTLE TASTE OF ME, DO YOU?
CUT THAT OUT!
Just say the word!

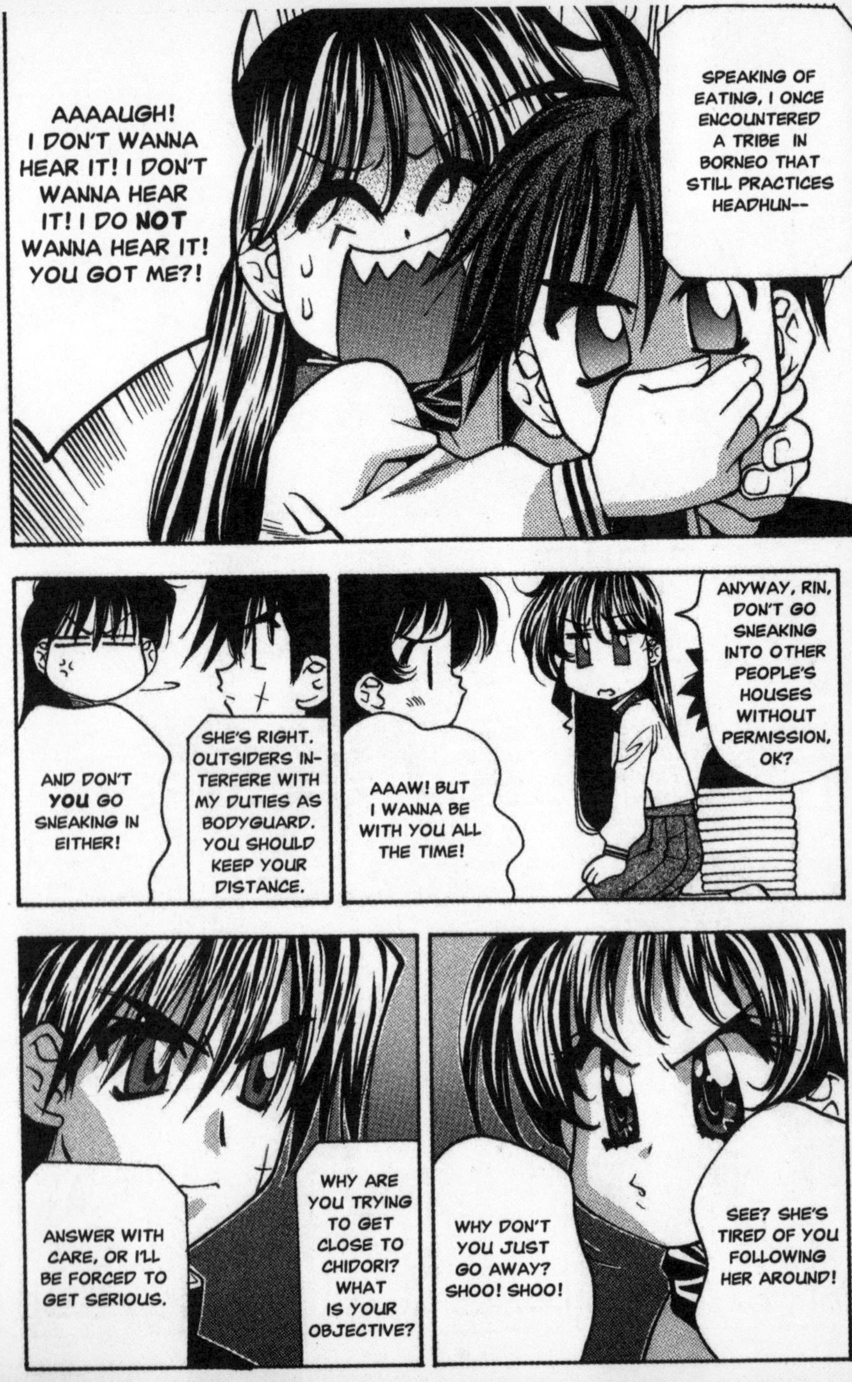
SPEAKING OF EATING, I ONCE ENCOUNTERED A TRIBE IN BORNEO THAT STILL PRACTICES HEADHUN--
AAAAUGH! I DON'T WANNA HEAR IT! I DON'T WANNA HEAR IT! I DO **NOT** WANNA HEAR IT! YOU GOT ME?!
ANYWAY, RIN, DON'T GO SNEAKING INTO OTHER PEOPLE'S HOUSES WITHOUT PERMISSION, OK?
AAAW! BUT I WANNA BE WITH YOU ALL THE TIME!
SHE'S RIGHT. OUTSIDERS INTERFERE WITH MY DUTIES AS BODYGUARD. YOU SHOULD KEEP YOUR DISTANCE.
AND DON'T **YOU** GO SNEAKING IN EITHER!
SEE? SHE'S TIRED OF YOU FOLLOWING HER AROUND!
WHY DON'T YOU JUST GO AWAY? SHOO! SHOO!
WHY ARE YOU TRYING TO GET CLOSE TO CHIDORI? WHAT IS YOUR OBJECTIVE?
ANSWER WITH CARE, OR I'LL BE FORCED TO GET SERIOUS.

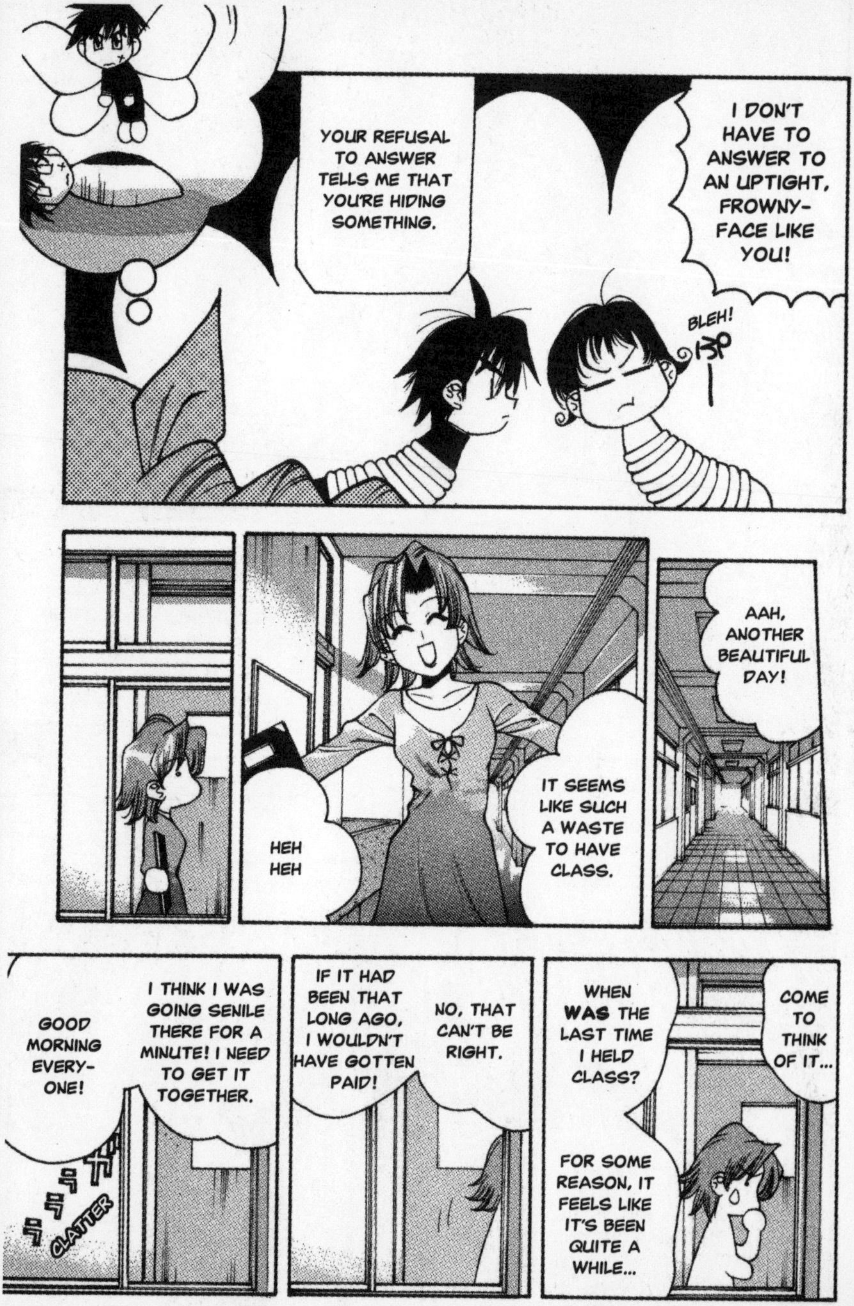
I DON'T HAVE TO ANSWER TO AN UPTIGHT, FROWNY-FACE LIKE YOU!
BLEH!
YOUR REFUSAL TO ANSWER TELLS ME THAT YOU'RE HIDING SOMETHING.
AAH, ANOTHER BEAUTIFUL DAY!
IT SEEMS LIKE SUCH A WASTE TO HAVE CLASS.
HEH HEH
COME TO THINK OF IT...
WHEN WAS THE LAST TIME I HELD CLASS?
FOR SOME REASON, IT FEELS LIKE IT'S BEEN QUITE A WHILE...
NO, THAT CAN'T BE RIGHT.
IF IT HAD BEEN THAT LONG AGO, I WOULDN'T HAVE GOTTEN PAID!
I THINK I WAS GOING SENILE THERE FOR A MINUTE! I NEED TO GET IT TOGETHER.
GOOD MORNING EVERY-ONE!
CLATTER

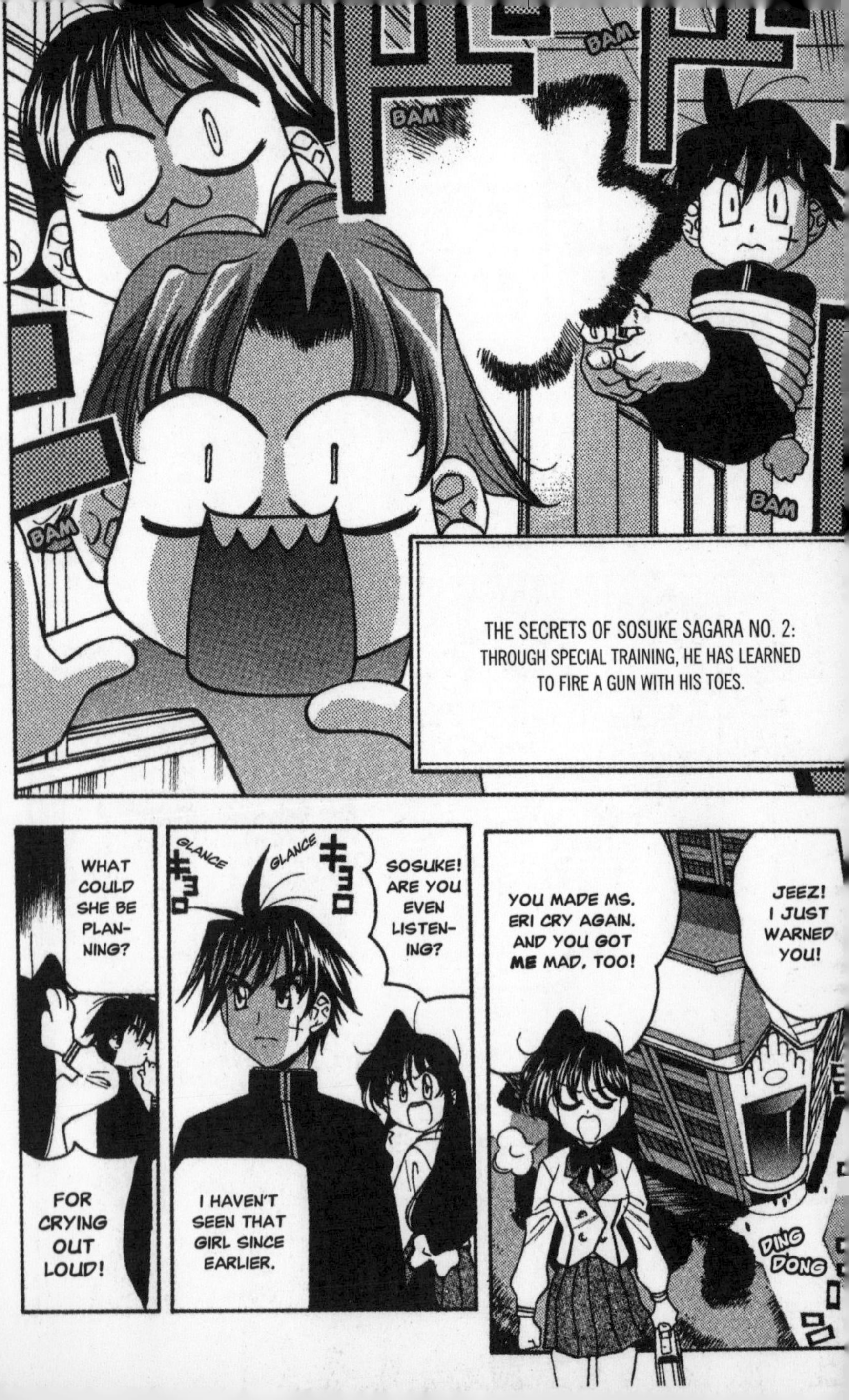
BAM
BAM
BAM
BAM
THE SECRETS OF SOSUKE SAGARA NO. 2: THROUGH SPECIAL TRAINING, HE HAS LEARNED TO FIRE A GUN WITH HIS TOES.
JEEZ! I JUST WARNED YOU!
YOU MADE MS. ERI CRY AGAIN. AND YOU GOT ME MAD, TOO!
DING DONG
SOSUKE! ARE YOU EVEN LISTENING?
GLANCE
GLANCE
I HAVEN'T SEEN THAT GIRL SINCE EARLIER.
WHAT COULD SHE BE PLANNING?
FOR CRYING OUT LOUD!

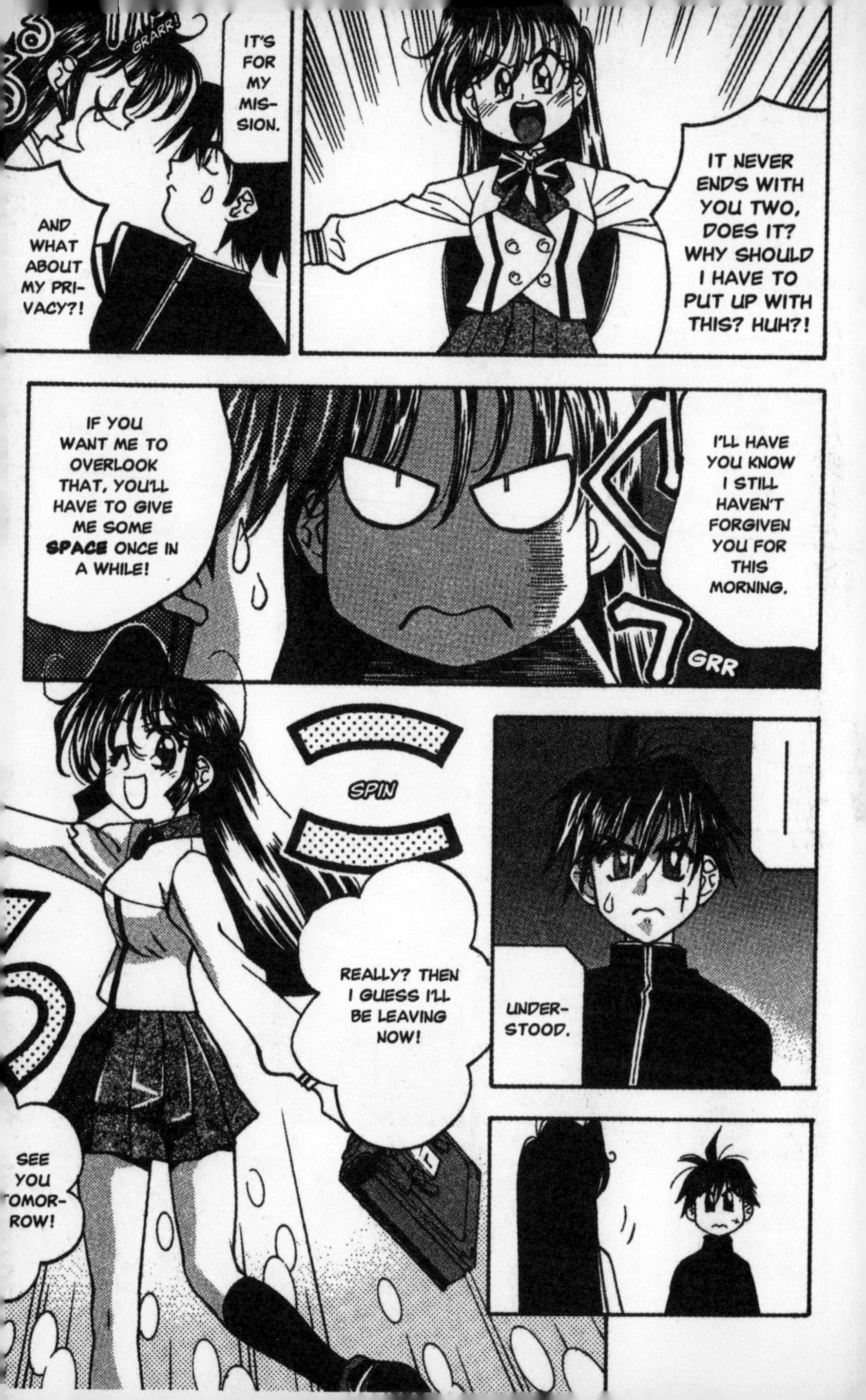
GRARR!
IT'S FOR MY MISSION.
AND WHAT ABOUT MY PRIVACY?!
IT NEVER ENDS WITH YOU TWO, DOES IT? WHY SHOULD I HAVE TO PUT UP WITH THIS? HUH?!
IF YOU WANT ME TO OVERLOOK THAT, YOU'LL HAVE TO GIVE ME SOME SPACE ONCE IN A WHILE!
I'LL HAVE YOU KNOW I STILL HAVEN'T FORGIVEN YOU FOR THIS MORNING.
GRR
SPIN
UNDERSTOOD.
REALLY? THEN I GUESS I'LL BE LEAVING NOW!
SEE YOU TOMORROW!

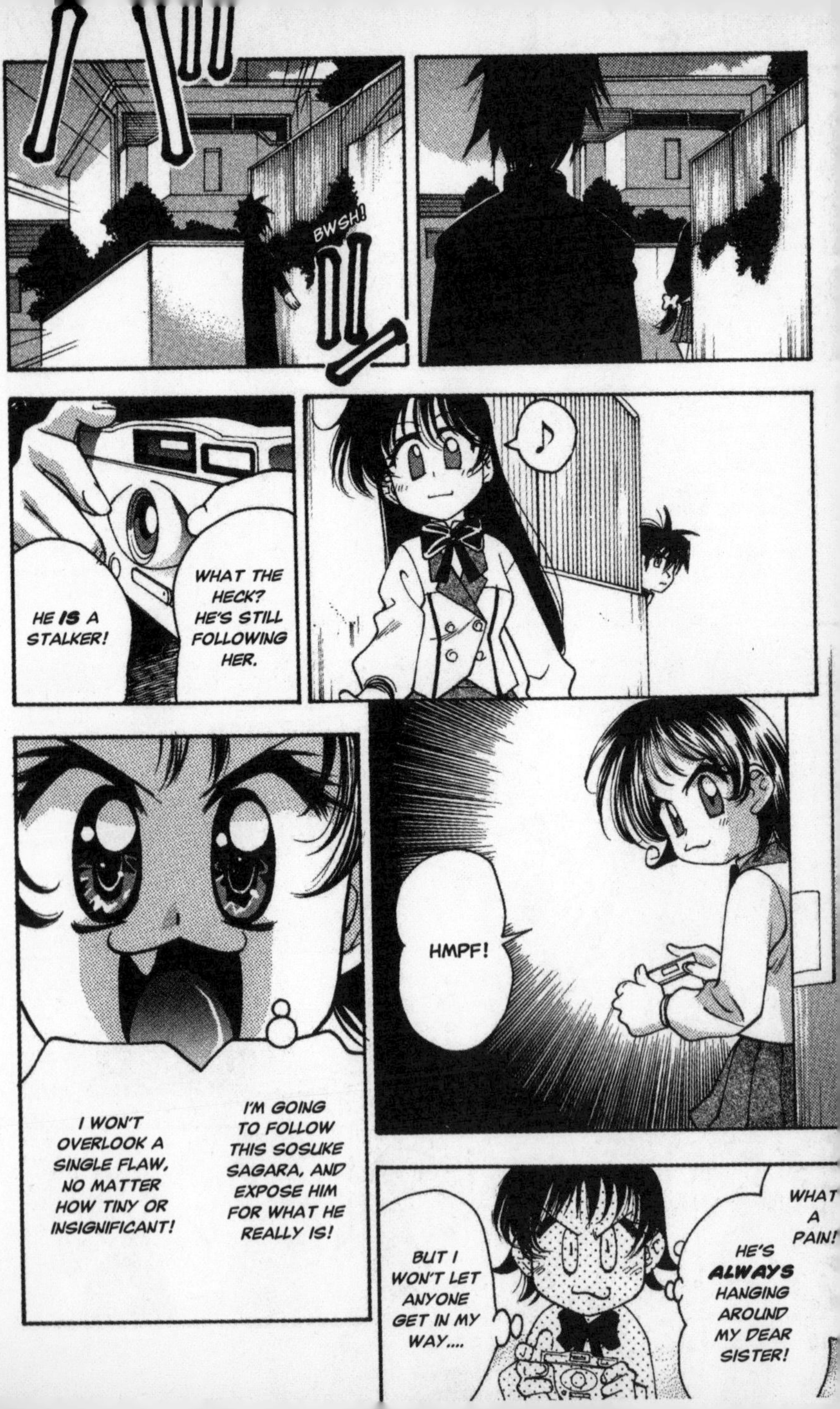
BWSH!
♪
WHAT THE HECK? HE'S STILL FOLLOWING HER.
HE IS A STALKER!
HMPF!
I'M GOING TO FOLLOW THIS SOSUKE SAGARA, AND EXPOSE HIM FOR WHAT HE REALLY IS!
I WON'T OVERLOOK A SINGLE FLAW, NO MATTER HOW TINY OR INSIGNIFICANT!
WHAT A PAIN! HE'S ALWAYS HANGING AROUND MY DEAR SISTER!
BUT I WON'T LET ANYONE GET IN MY WAY....

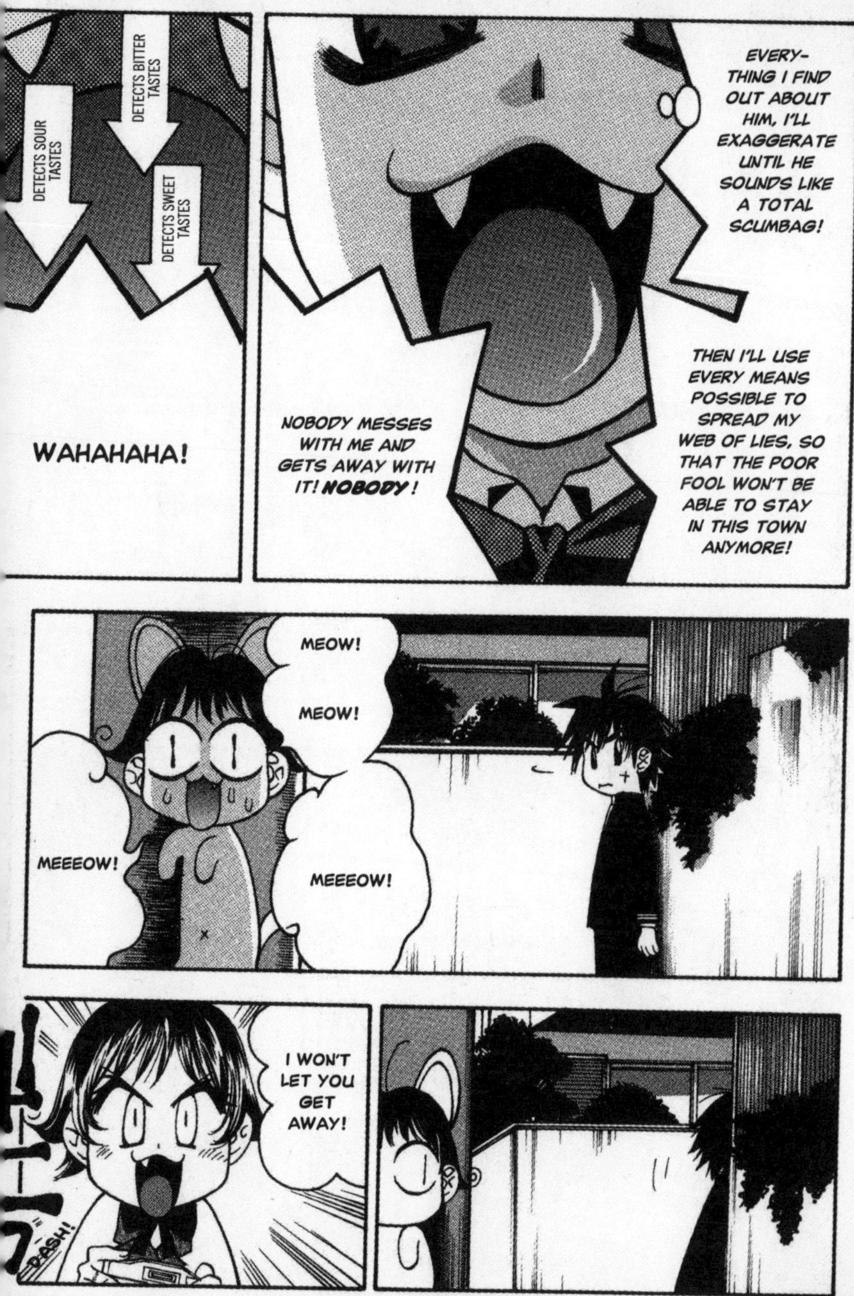
EVERY-THING I FIND OUT ABOUT HIM, I'LL EXAGGERATE UNTIL HE SOUNDS LIKE A TOTAL SCUMBAG!
THEN I'LL USE EVERY MEANS POSSIBLE TO SPREAD MY WEB OF LIES, SO THAT THE POOR FOOL WON'T BE ABLE TO STAY IN THIS TOWN ANYMORE!
NOBODY MESSES WITH ME AND GETS AWAY WITH IT! NOBODY!
DETECTS BITTER TASTES
DETECTS SOUR TASTES
DETECTS SWEET TASTES
WAHAHAHA!
MEOW!
MEOW!
MEEEOW!
MEEEOW!
I WON'T LET YOU GET AWAY!
DASH!

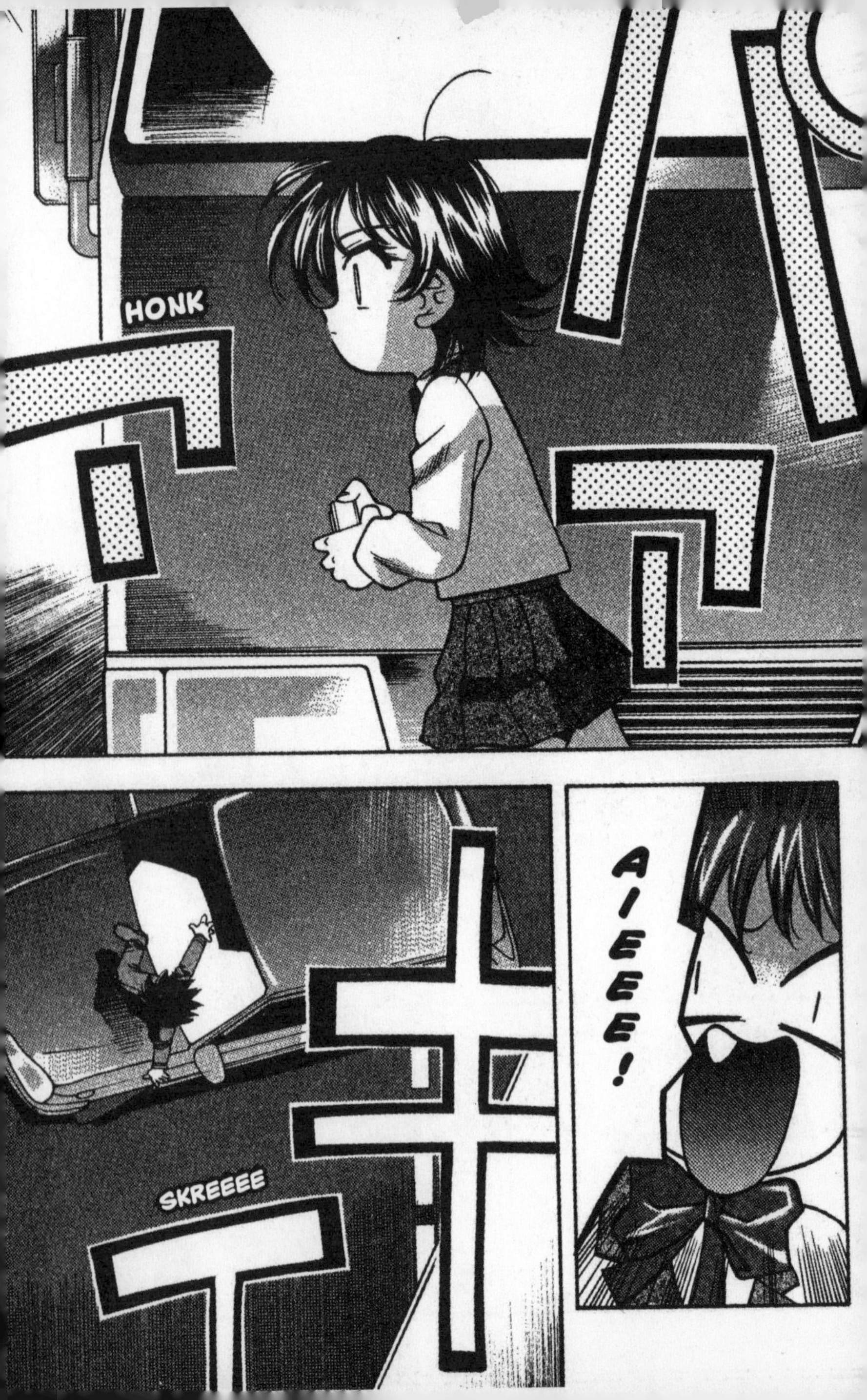
HONK
AIEEE!
SKREEEE

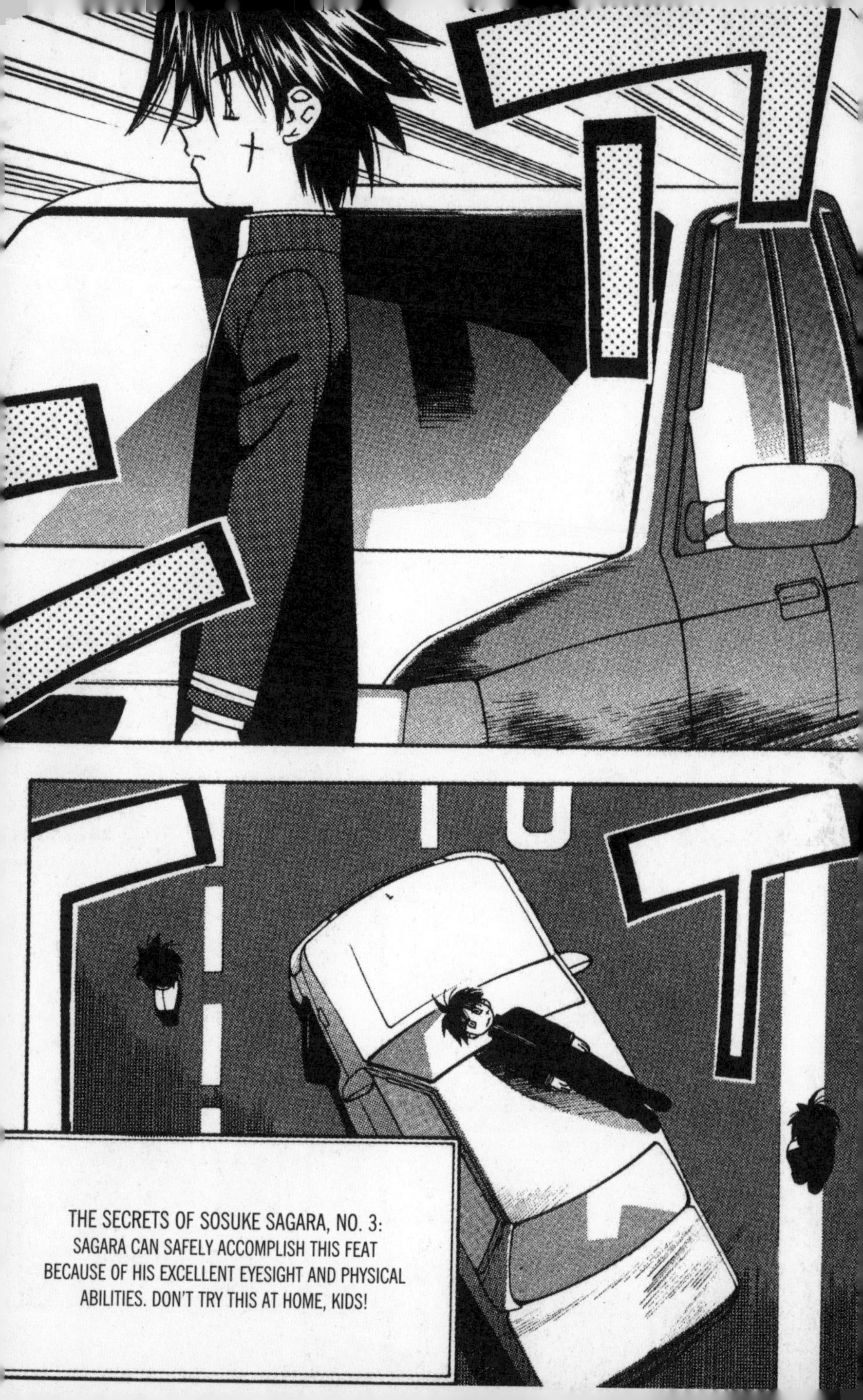
THE SECRETS OF SOSUKE SAGARA, NO. 3:
SAGARA CAN SAFELY ACCOMPLISH THIS FEAT BECAUSE OF HIS EXCELLENT EYESIGHT AND PHYSICAL ABILITIES. DON'T TRY THIS AT HOME, KIDS!

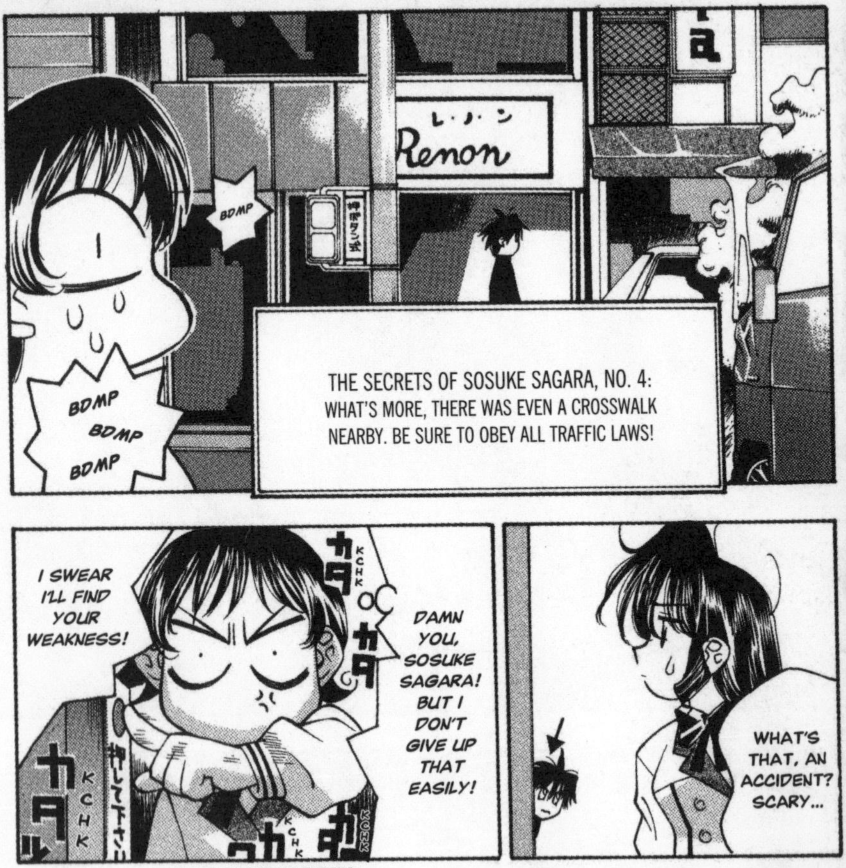
BDMP
BDMP
BDMP
BDMP
THE SECRETS OF SOSUKE SAGARA, NO. 4: WHAT'S MORE, THERE WAS EVEN A CROSSWALK NEARBY. BE SURE TO OBEY ALL TRAFFIC LAWS!
I SWEAR I'LL FIND YOUR WEAKNESS!
KCHK
DAMN YOU, SOSUKE SAGARA! BUT I DON'T GIVE UP THAT EASILY!
KCHK
KCHK
KCHK
WHAT'S THAT, AN ACCIDENT? SCARY...

*ON SIGN: "PLEASE PUSH BUTTON."

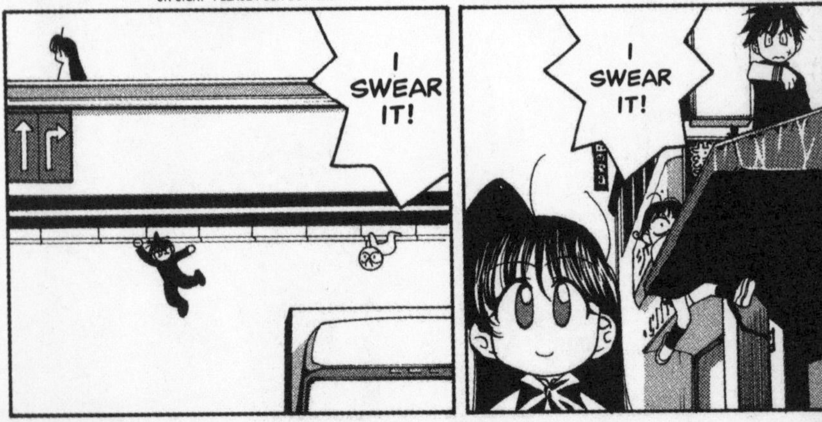
I SWEAR IT!
I SWEAR IT!

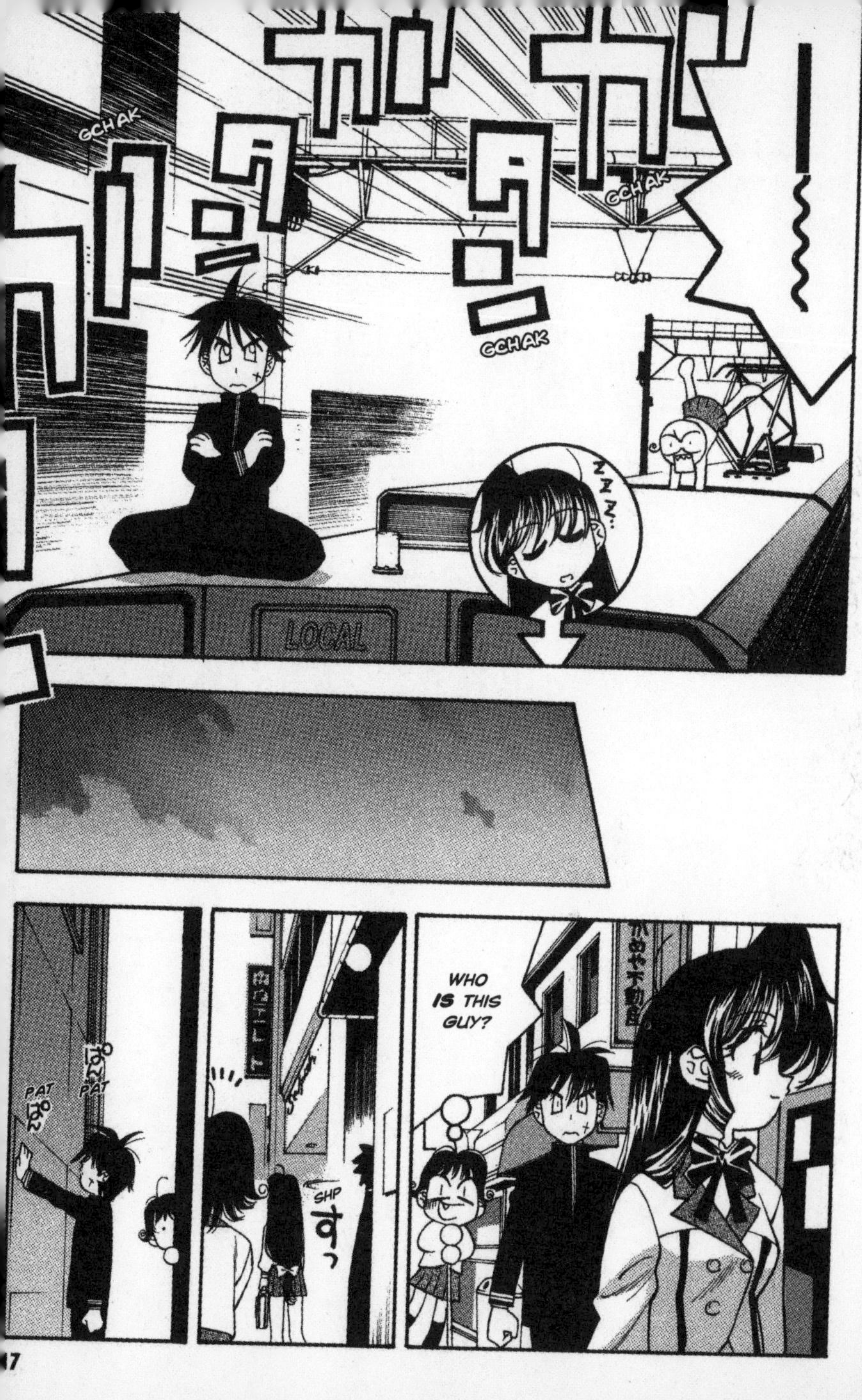
GCHAK
GCHAK
GCHAK
Z Z Z..
LOCAL
WHO IS THIS GUY?
SHP
すっ
ぱん
PAT
ぱん
PAT

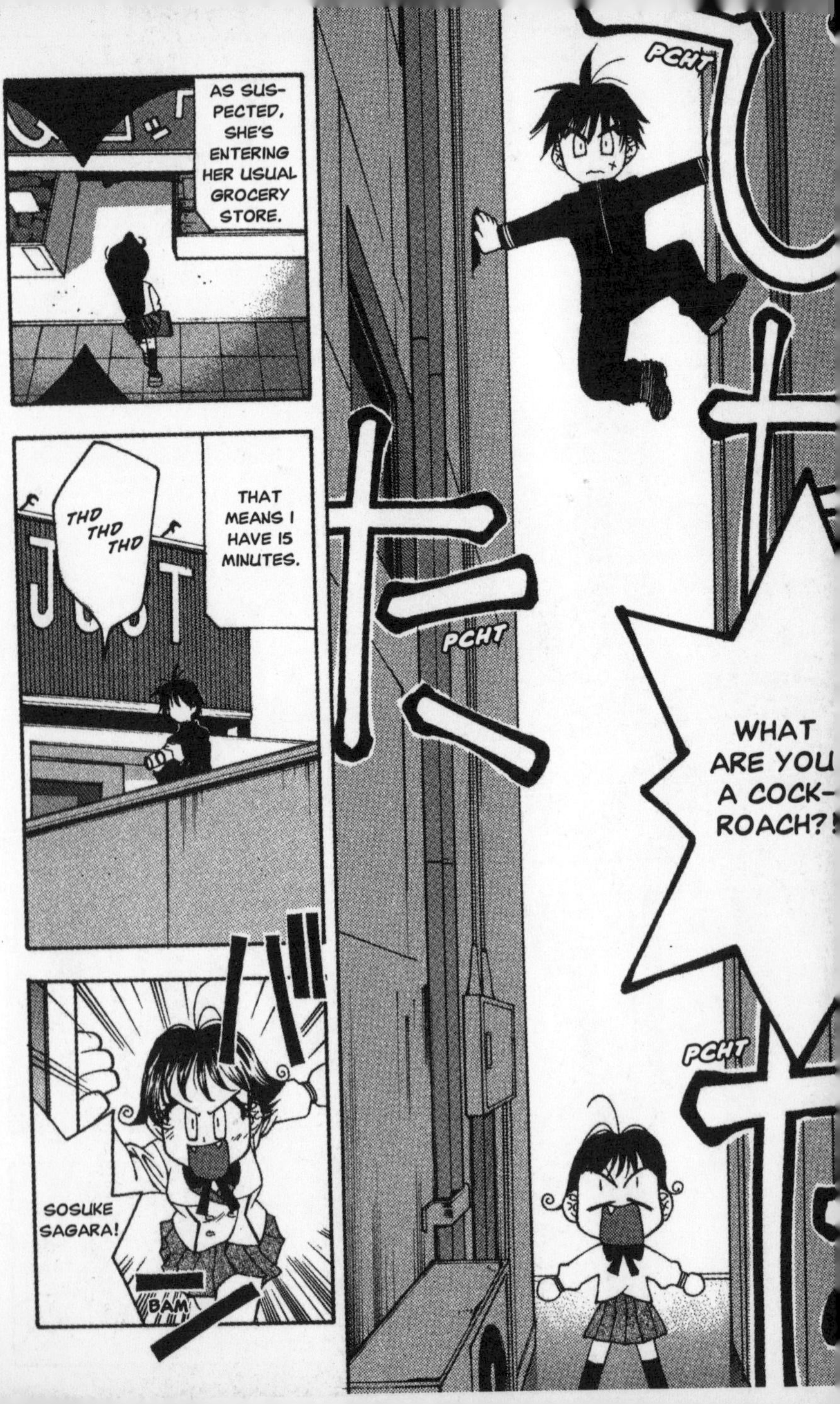
AS SUS-PECTED, SHE'S ENTERING HER USUAL GROCERY STORE.
THD THD THD
THAT MEANS I HAVE 15 MINUTES.
SOSUKE SAGARA!
BAM
PCHT
PCHT
PCHT
WHAT ARE YOU A COCK-ROACH?!

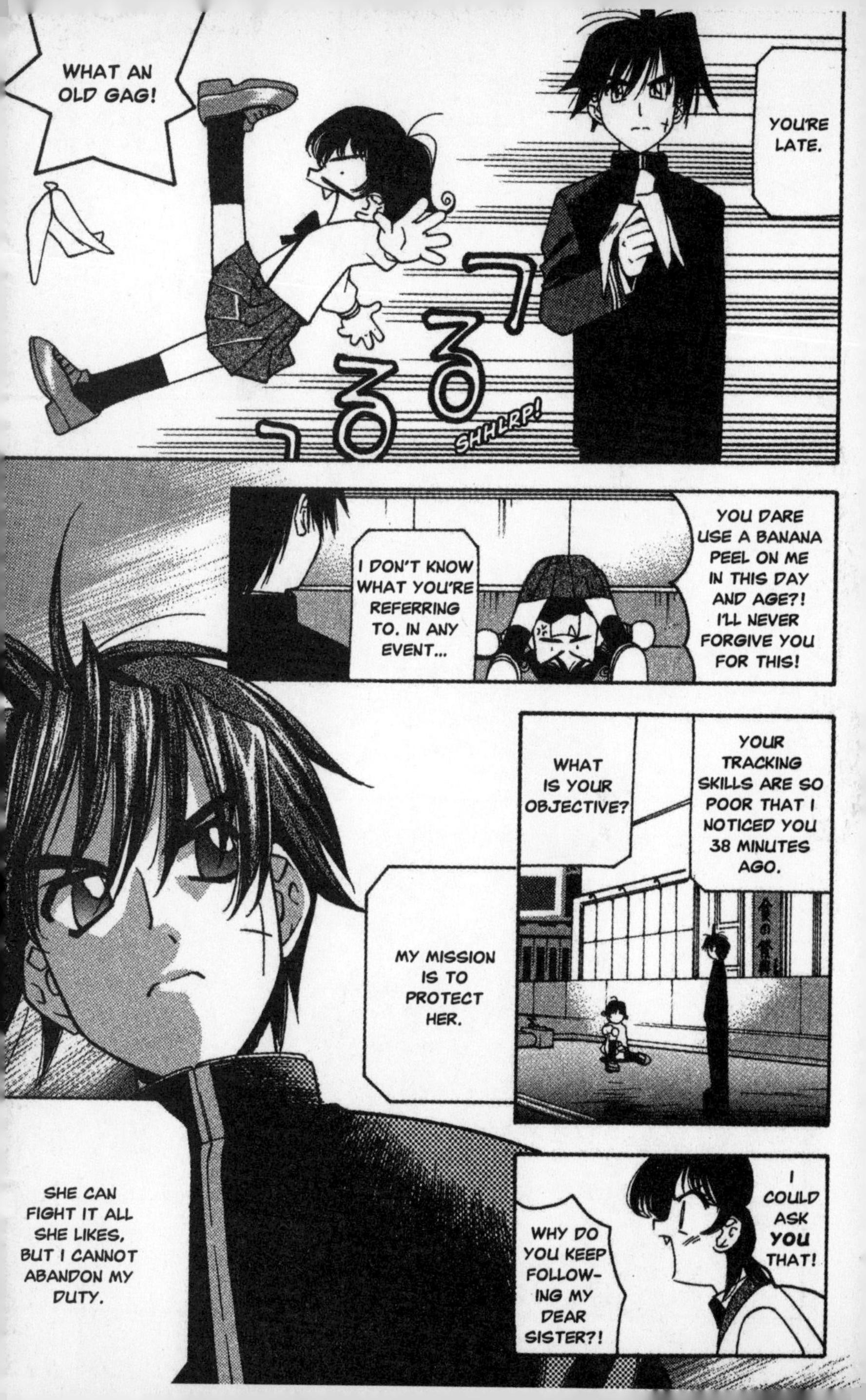

YOU'RE LATE.
SHHLRP!
WHAT AN OLD GAG!
YOU DARE USE A BANANA PEEL ON ME IN THIS DAY AND AGE?! I'LL NEVER FORGIVE YOU FOR THIS!
I DON'T KNOW WHAT YOU'RE REFERRING TO. IN ANY EVENT...
YOUR TRACKING SKILLS ARE SO POOR THAT I NOTICED YOU 38 MINUTES AGO.
WHAT IS YOUR OBJECTIVE?
MY MISSION IS TO PROTECT HER.
I COULD ASK YOU THAT!
WHY DO YOU KEEP FOLLOW-ING MY DEAR SISTER?!
SHE CAN FIGHT IT ALL SHE LIKES, BUT I CANNOT ABANDON MY DUTY.

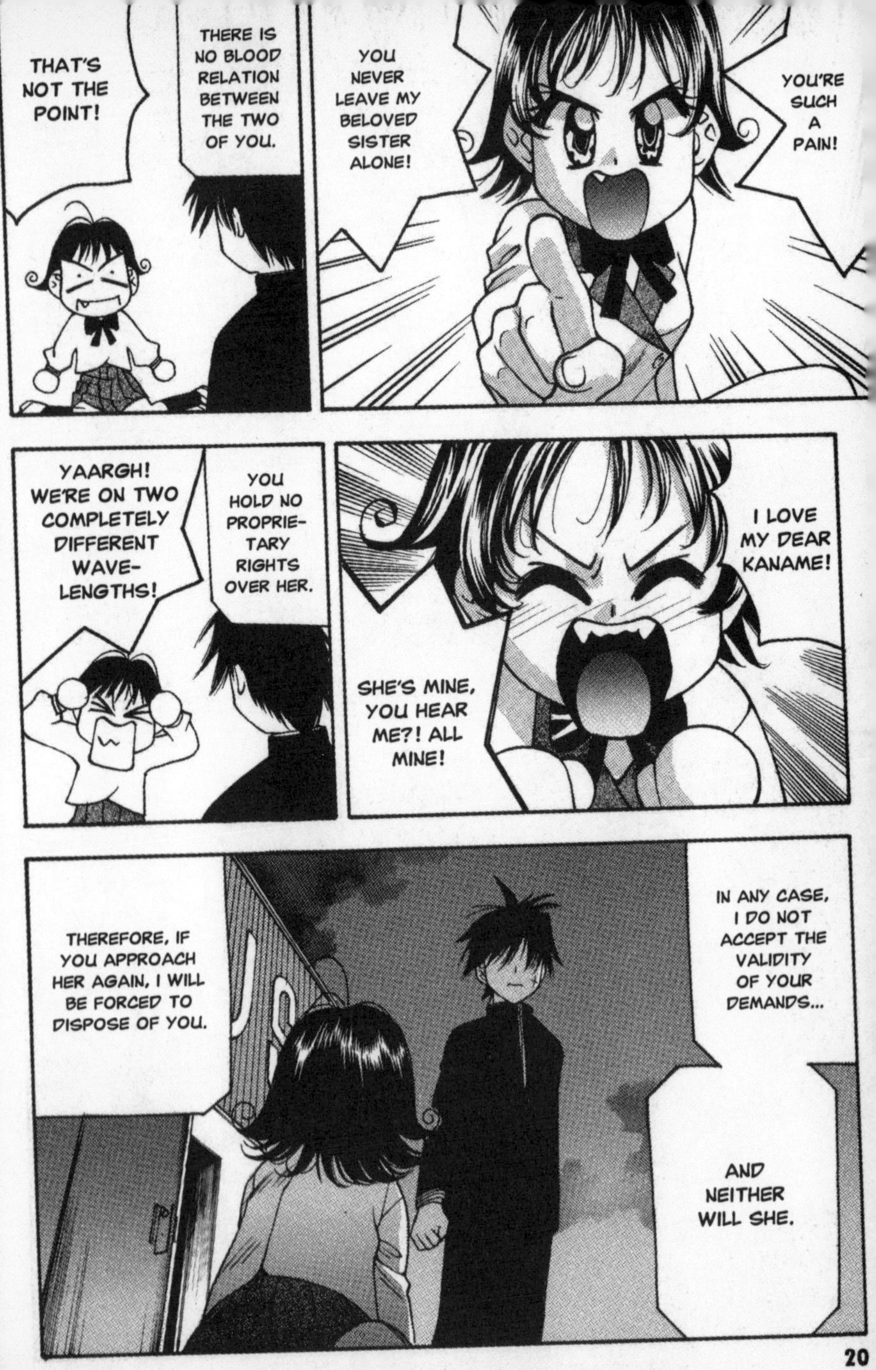
YOU'RE SUCH A PAIN!
YOU NEVER LEAVE MY BELOVED SISTER ALONE!
THERE IS NO BLOOD RELATION BETWEEN THE TWO OF YOU.
THAT'S NOT THE POINT!
I LOVE MY DEAR KANAME!
SHE'S MINE, YOU HEAR ME?! ALL MINE!
YOU HOLD NO PROPRIE-TARY RIGHTS OVER HER.
YAARGH! WE'RE ON TWO COMPLETELY DIFFERENT WAVE-LENGTHS!
IN ANY CASE, I DO NOT ACCEPT THE VALIDITY OF YOUR DEMANDS...
AND NEITHER WILL SHE.
THEREFORE, IF YOU APPROACH HER AGAIN, I WILL BE FORCED TO DISPOSE OF YOU.

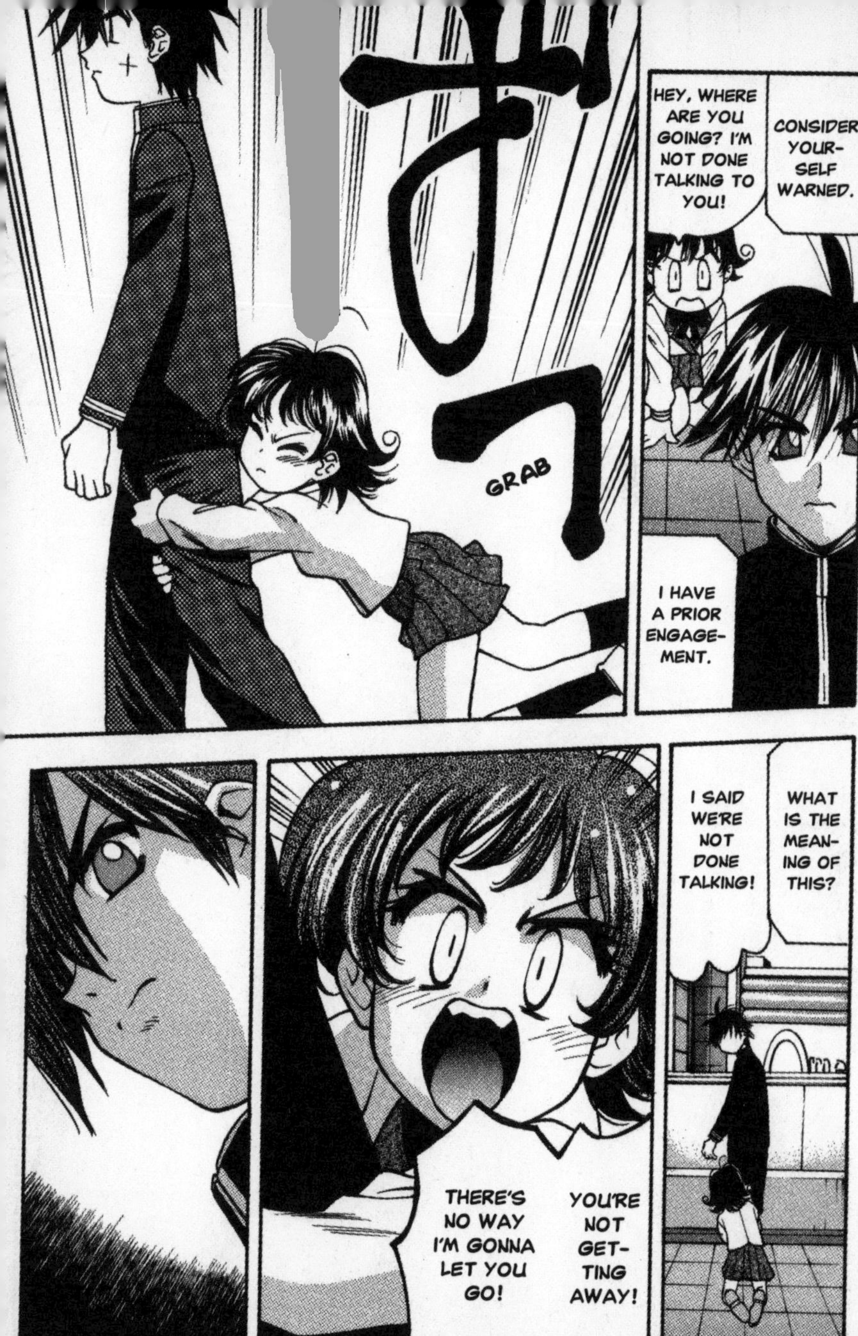
CONSIDER YOUR-SELF WARNED.
HEY, WHERE ARE YOU GOING? I'M NOT DONE TALKING TO YOU!
I HAVE A PRIOR ENGAGE-MENT.
GRAB
WHAT IS THE MEAN-ING OF THIS?
I SAID WE'RE NOT DONE TALKING!
YOU'RE NOT GET-TING AWAY!
THERE'S NO WAY I'M GONNA LET YOU GO!

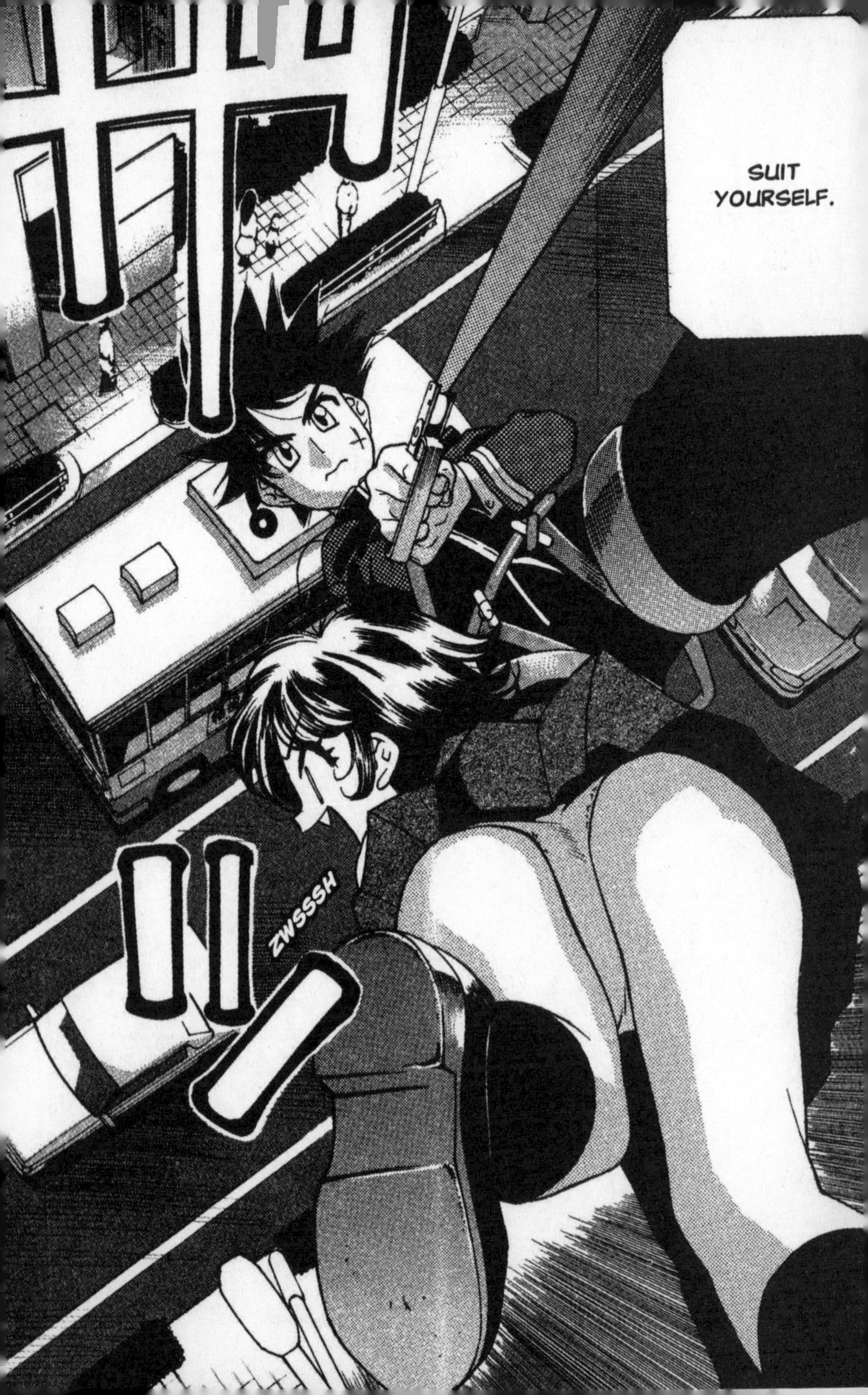
SUIT YOURSELF.
ZWSSSH

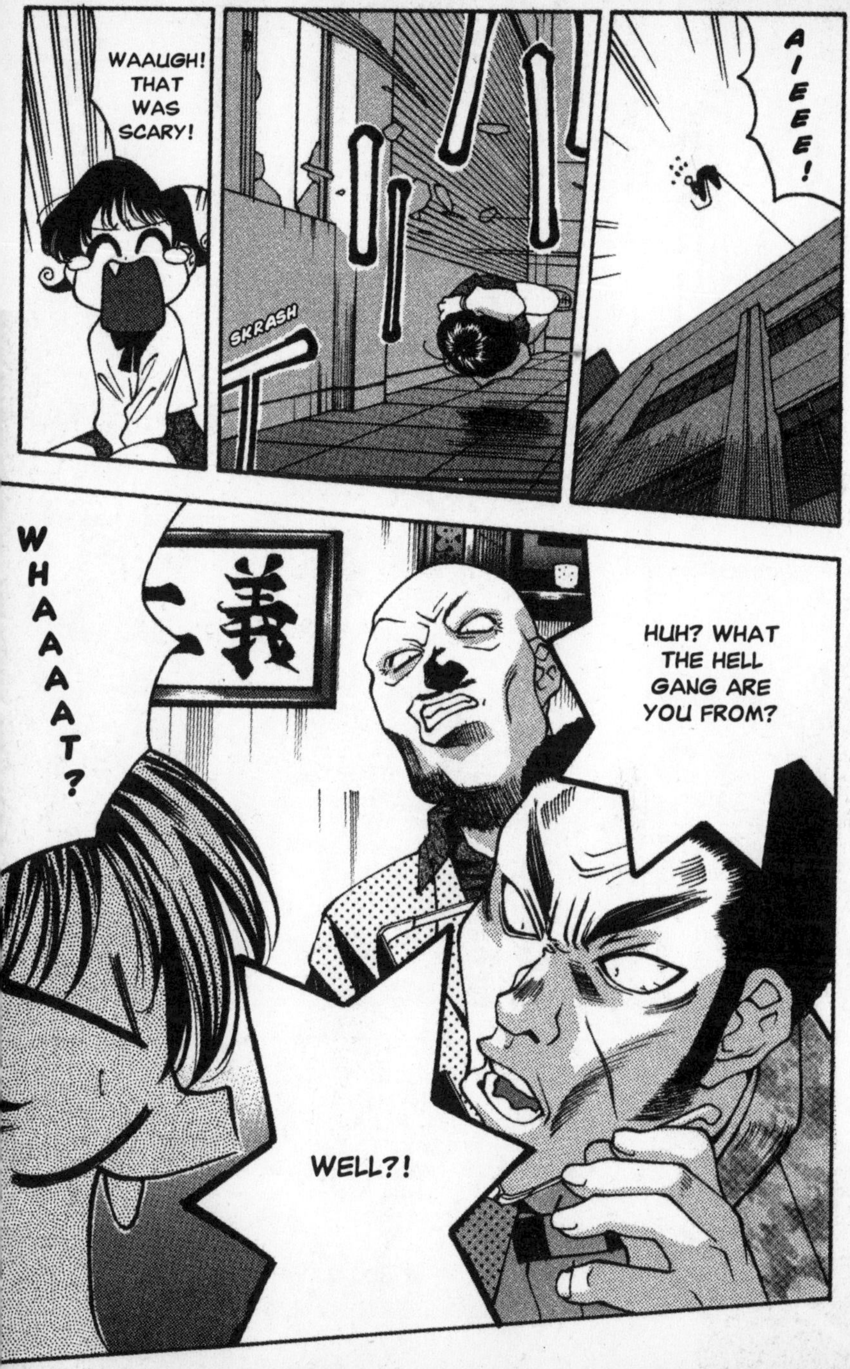
AIEEE!
SKRASH
WAAUGH! THAT WAS SCARY!
義
HUH? WHAT THE HELL GANG ARE YOU FROM?
WELL?!
WHAAAAT?

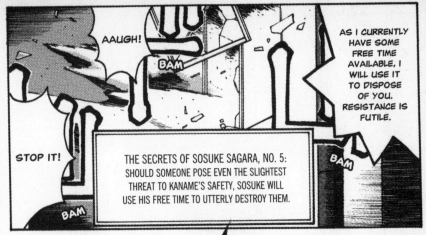

AAUGH!

BAM

AS I CURRENTLY HAVE SOME FREE TIME AVAILABLE, I WILL USE IT TO DISPOSE OF YOU. RESISTANCE IS FUTILE.

STOP IT!

BAM

THE SECRETS OF SOSUKE SAGARA, NO. 5: SHOULD SOMEONE POSE EVEN THE SLIGHTEST THREAT TO KANAME'S SAFETY, SOSUKE WILL USE HIS FREE TIME TO UTTERLY DESTROY THEM.

BAM

I'VE COMPLETED MY ERRAND. IS THERE SOMETHING YOU WISHED TO DISCUSS?

BWAAAH!

HMPF.

PAT
ぱん

PAT
ぱん

BWAAAH!

I'LL REMEMBER THIS DAY! NEXT TIME, YOU'LL BE THE ONE CRYING!

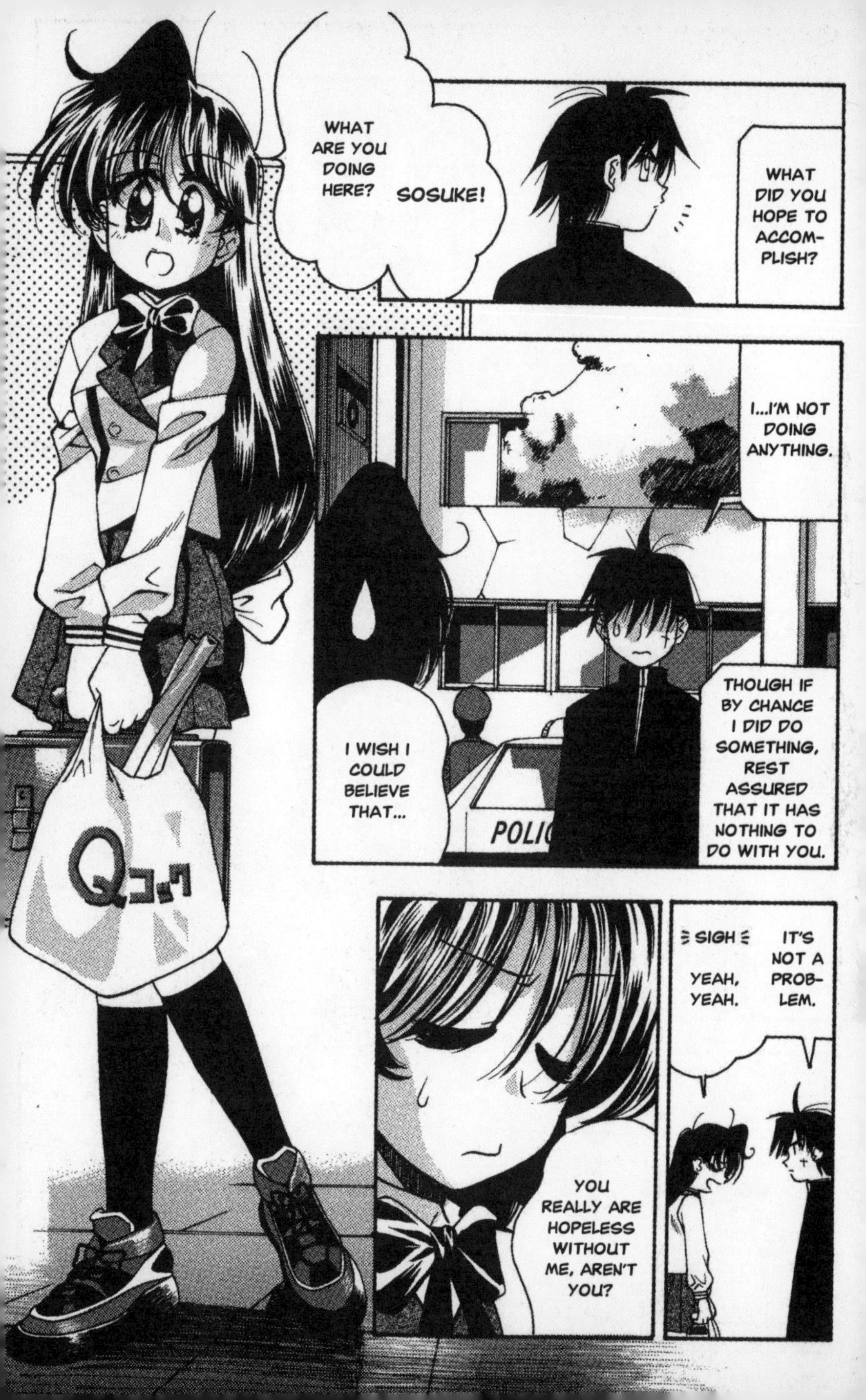
SOSUKE!
WHAT ARE YOU DOING HERE?
WHAT DID YOU HOPE TO ACCOMPLISH?
I...I'M NOT DOING ANYTHING.
THOUGH IF BY CHANCE I DID DO SOMETHING, REST ASSURED THAT IT HAS NOTHING TO DO WITH YOU.
POLIC
I WISH I COULD BELIEVE THAT...
IT'S NOT A PROB-LEM.
≡ SIGH ≡
YEAH, YEAH.
YOU REALLY ARE HOPELESS WITHOUT ME, AREN'T YOU?

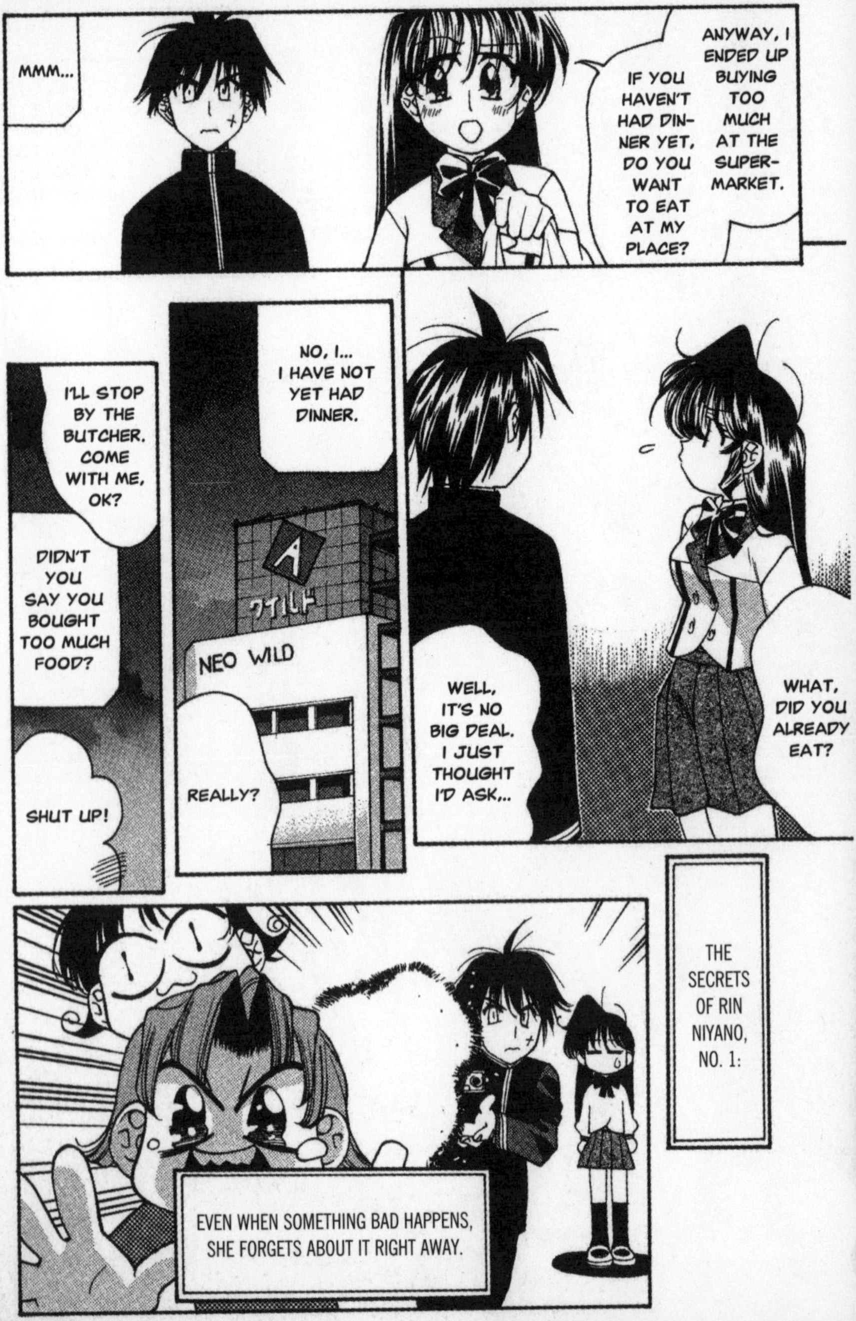
ANYWAY, I ENDED UP BUYING TOO MUCH AT THE SUPERMARKET.
IF YOU HAVEN'T HAD DIN-NER YET, DO YOU WANT TO EAT AT MY PLACE?
MMM...
WHAT, DID YOU ALREADY EAT?
WELL, IT'S NO BIG DEAL. I JUST THOUGHT I'D ASK...
NO, I... I HAVE NOT YET HAD DINNER.
ワイルド
NEO WILD
REALLY?
I'LL STOP BY THE BUTCHER. COME WITH ME, OK?
DIDN'T YOU SAY YOU BOUGHT TOO MUCH FOOD?
SHUT UP!
THE SECRETS OF RIN NIYANO, NO. 1:
EVEN WHEN SOMETHING BAD HAPPENS, SHE FORGETS ABOUT IT RIGHT AWAY.

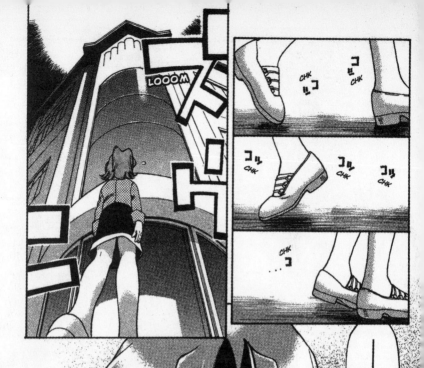

LOOOM

CHK
CHK

CHK
CHK
CHK

...CHK

SIGH

BOMB 14 TEACH US, MS. ERI!

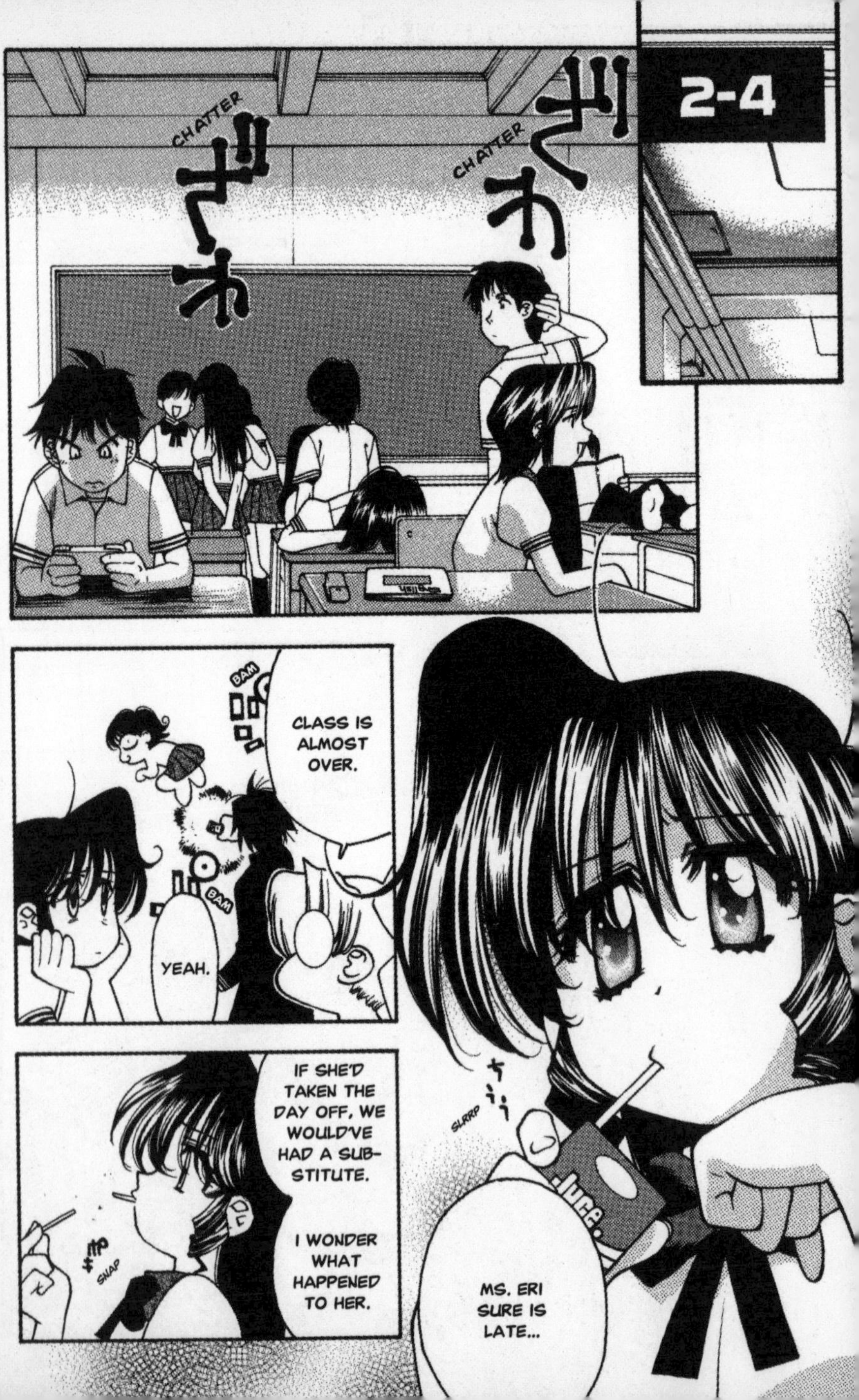

2-4
CHATTER
CHATTER
MS. ERI SURE IS LATE...
SLRRP
Juce.
CLASS IS ALMOST OVER.
BAM
BAM
YEAH.
IF SHE'D TAKEN THE DAY OFF, WE WOULD'VE HAD A SUB-STITUTE.
I WONDER WHAT HAPPENED TO HER.
SNAP

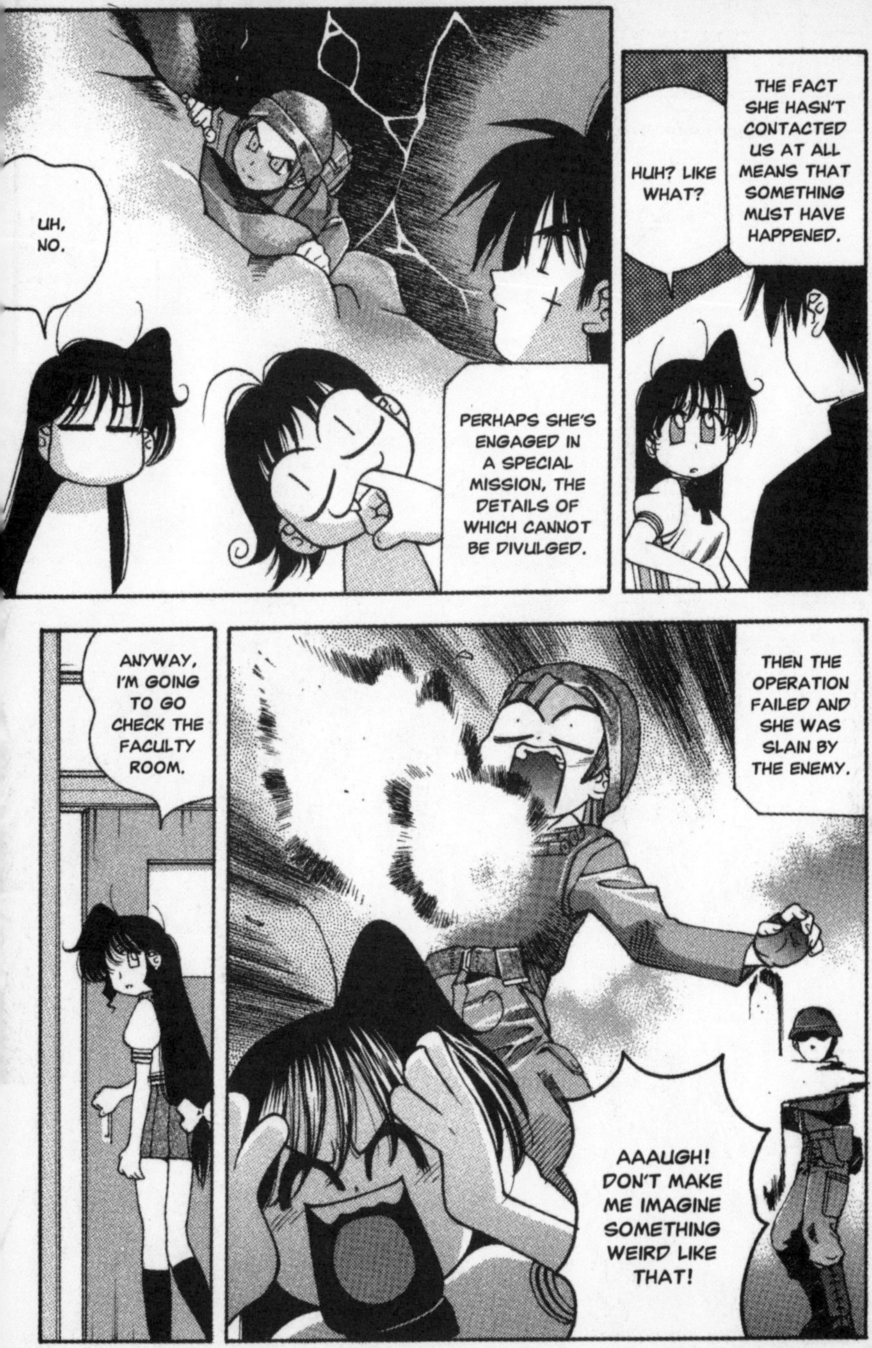
THE FACT SHE HASN'T CONTACTED US AT ALL MEANS THAT SOMETHING MUST HAVE HAPPENED.
HUH? LIKE WHAT?
PERHAPS SHE'S ENGAGED IN A SPECIAL MISSION, THE DETAILS OF WHICH CANNOT BE DIVULGED.
UH, NO.
THEN THE OPERATION FAILED AND SHE WAS SLAIN BY THE ENEMY.
AAAUGH! DON'T MAKE ME IMAGINE SOMETHING WEIRD LIKE THAT!
ANYWAY, I'M GOING TO GO CHECK THE FACULTY ROOM.

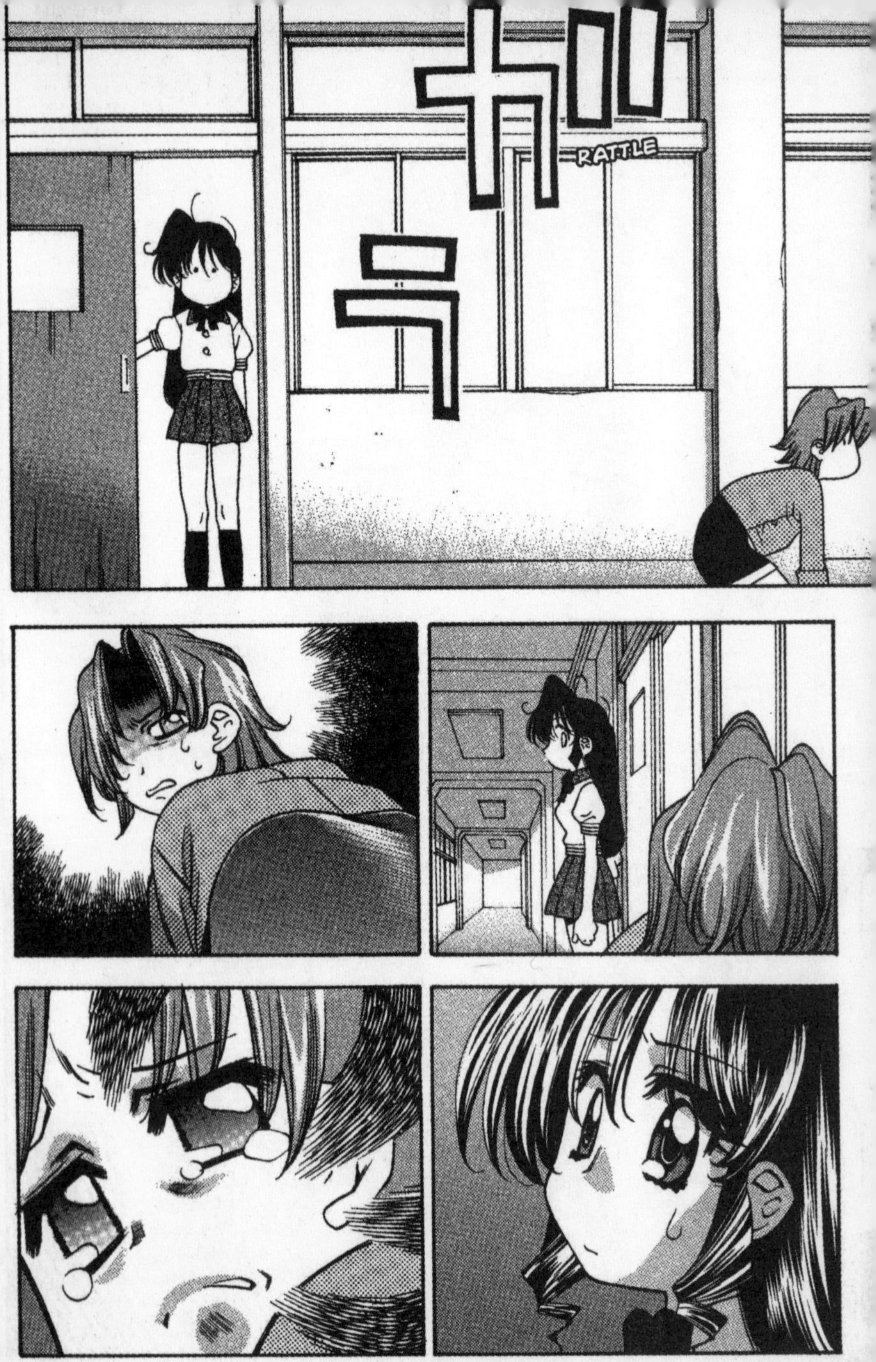
RATTLE

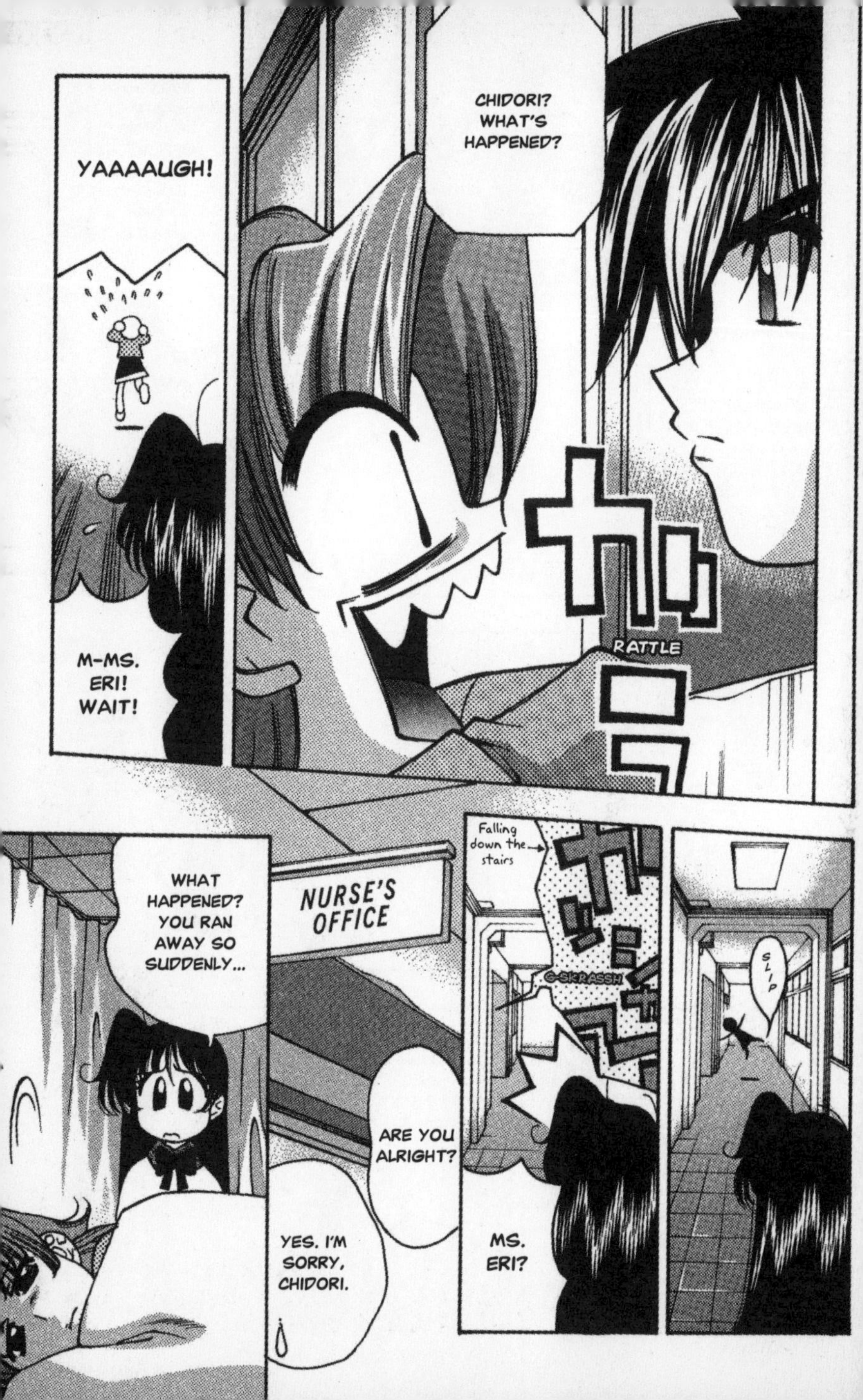
CHIDORI? WHAT'S HAPPENED?
RATTLE
YAAAAUGH!
M-MS. ERI! WAIT!
SLIP
MS. ERI?
Falling down the stairs
G-SKRASSH
NURSE'S OFFICE
WHAT HAPPENED? YOU RAN AWAY SO SUDDENLY...
ARE YOU ALRIGHT?
YES. I'M SORRY, CHIDORI.

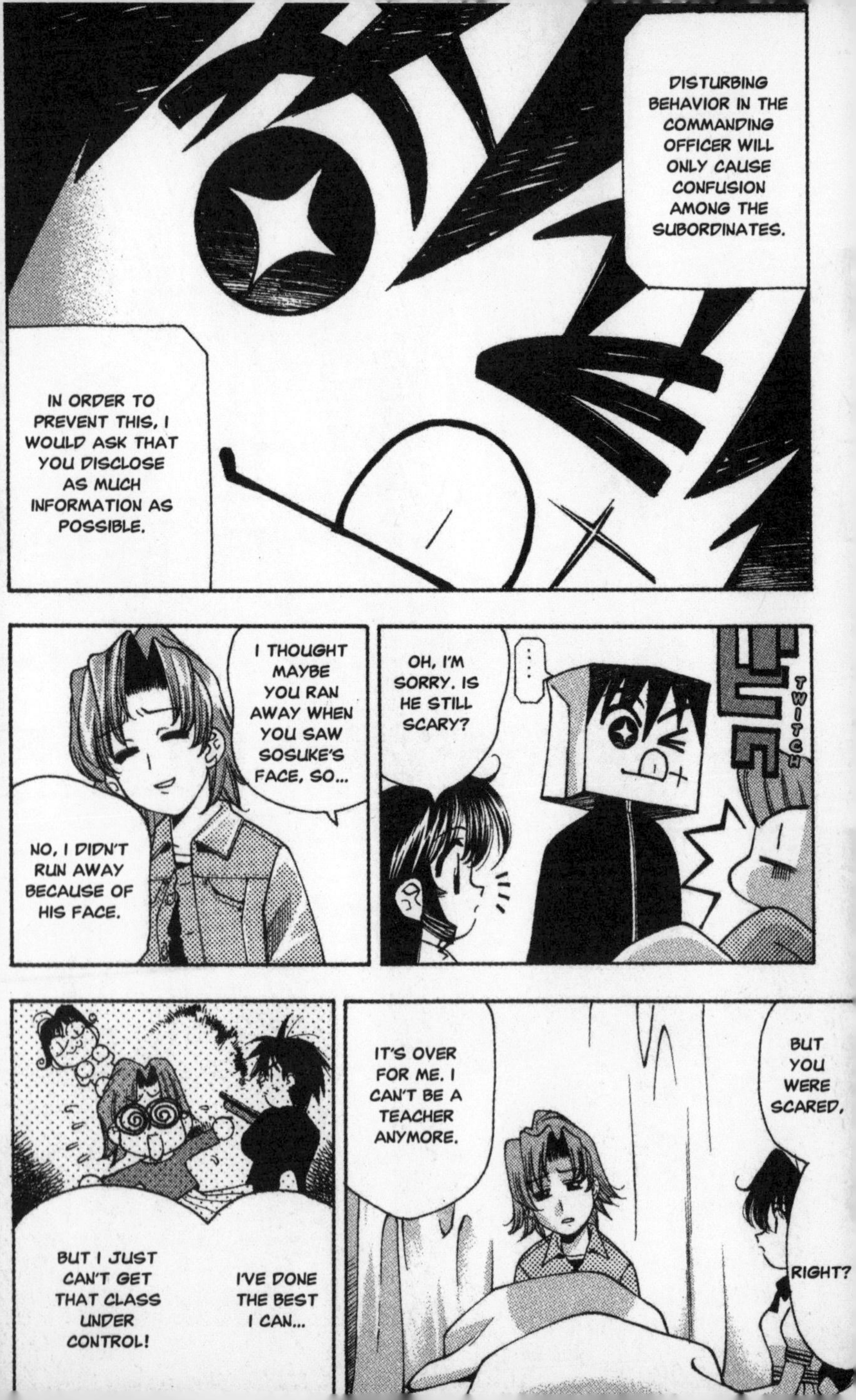
DISTURBING BEHAVIOR IN THE COMMANDING OFFICER WILL ONLY CAUSE CONFUSION AMONG THE SUBORDINATES.
IN ORDER TO PREVENT THIS, I WOULD ASK THAT YOU DISCLOSE AS MUCH INFORMATION AS POSSIBLE.
....
OH, I'M SORRY. IS HE STILL SCARY?
TWITCH
I THOUGHT MAYBE YOU RAN AWAY WHEN YOU SAW SOSUKE'S FACE, SO...
NO, I DIDN'T RUN AWAY BECAUSE OF HIS FACE.
BUT YOU WERE SCARED.
RIGHT?
IT'S OVER FOR ME. I CAN'T BE A TEACHER ANYMORE.
I'VE DONE THE BEST I CAN...
BUT I JUST CAN'T GET THAT CLASS UNDER CONTROL!

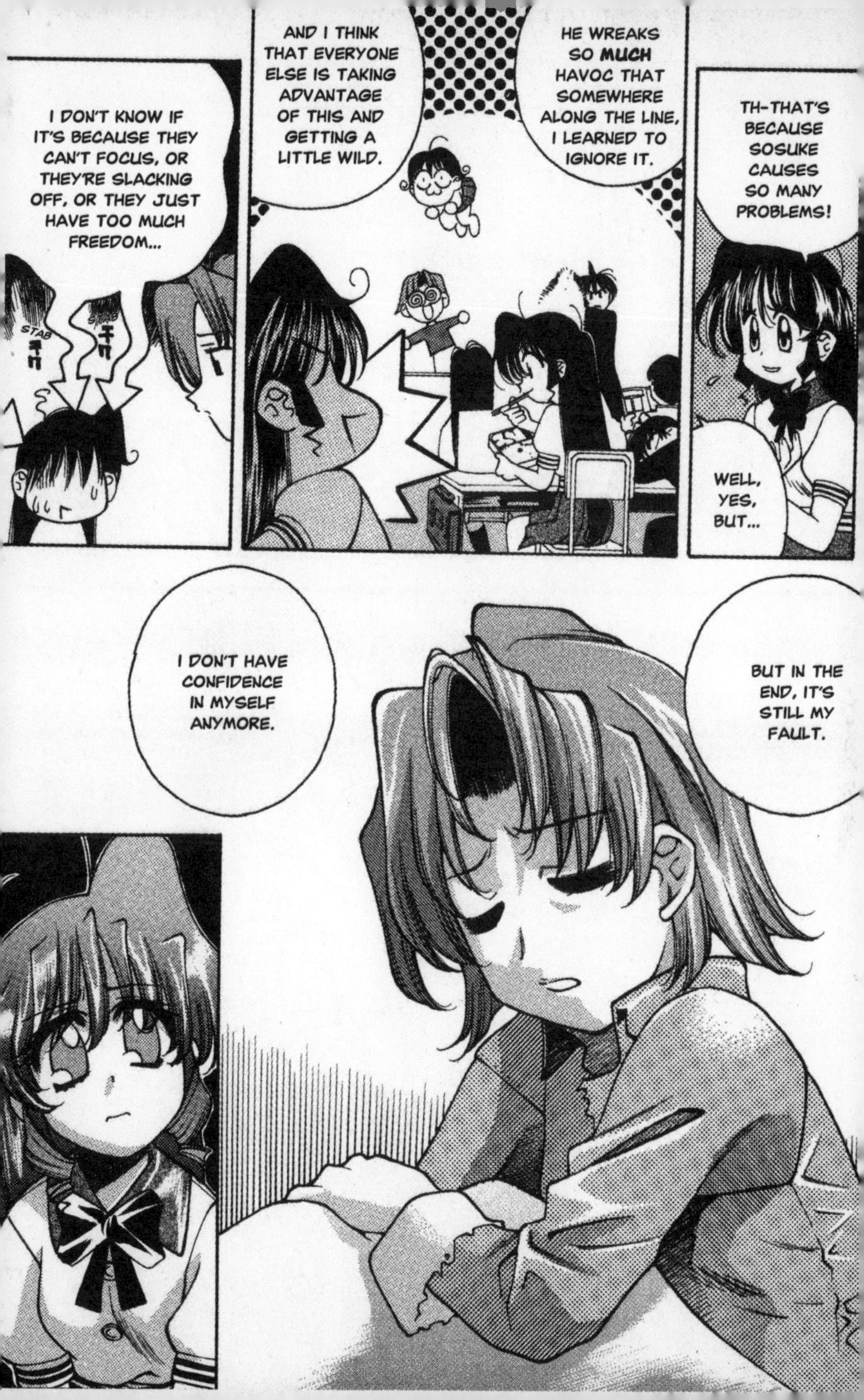
TH-THAT'S BECAUSE SOSUKE CAUSES SO MANY PROBLEMS!
WELL, YES, BUT...
HE WREAKS SO MUCH HAVOC THAT SOMEWHERE ALONG THE LINE, I LEARNED TO IGNORE IT.
AND I THINK THAT EVERYONE ELSE IS TAKING ADVANTAGE OF THIS AND GETTING A LITTLE WILD.
I DON'T KNOW IF IT'S BECAUSE THEY CAN'T FOCUS, OR THEY'RE SLACKING OFF, OR THEY JUST HAVE TOO MUCH FREEDOM...
STAB
STAB
BUT IN THE END, IT'S STILL MY FAULT.
I DON'T HAVE CONFIDENCE IN MYSELF ANYMORE.

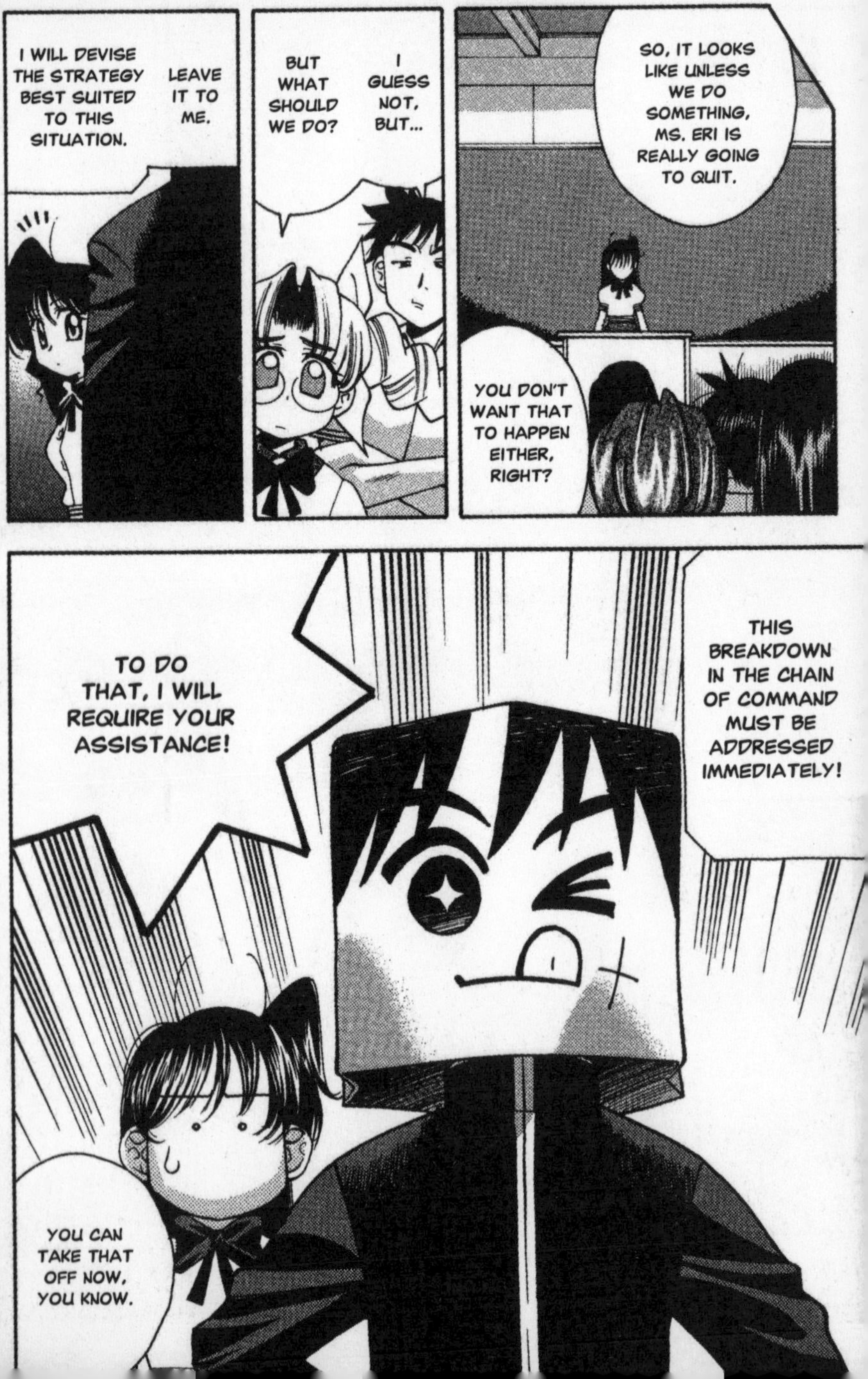
SO, IT LOOKS LIKE UNLESS WE DO SOMETHING, MS. ERI IS REALLY GOING TO QUIT.
YOU DON'T WANT THAT TO HAPPEN EITHER, RIGHT?
I GUESS NOT, BUT...
BUT WHAT SHOULD WE DO?
LEAVE IT TO ME.
I WILL DEVISE THE STRATEGY BEST SUITED TO THIS SITUATION.
THIS BREAKDOWN IN THE CHAIN OF COMMAND MUST BE ADDRESSED IMMEDIATELY!
TO DO THAT, I WILL REQUIRE YOUR ASSISTANCE!
YOU CAN TAKE THAT OFF NOW, YOU KNOW.

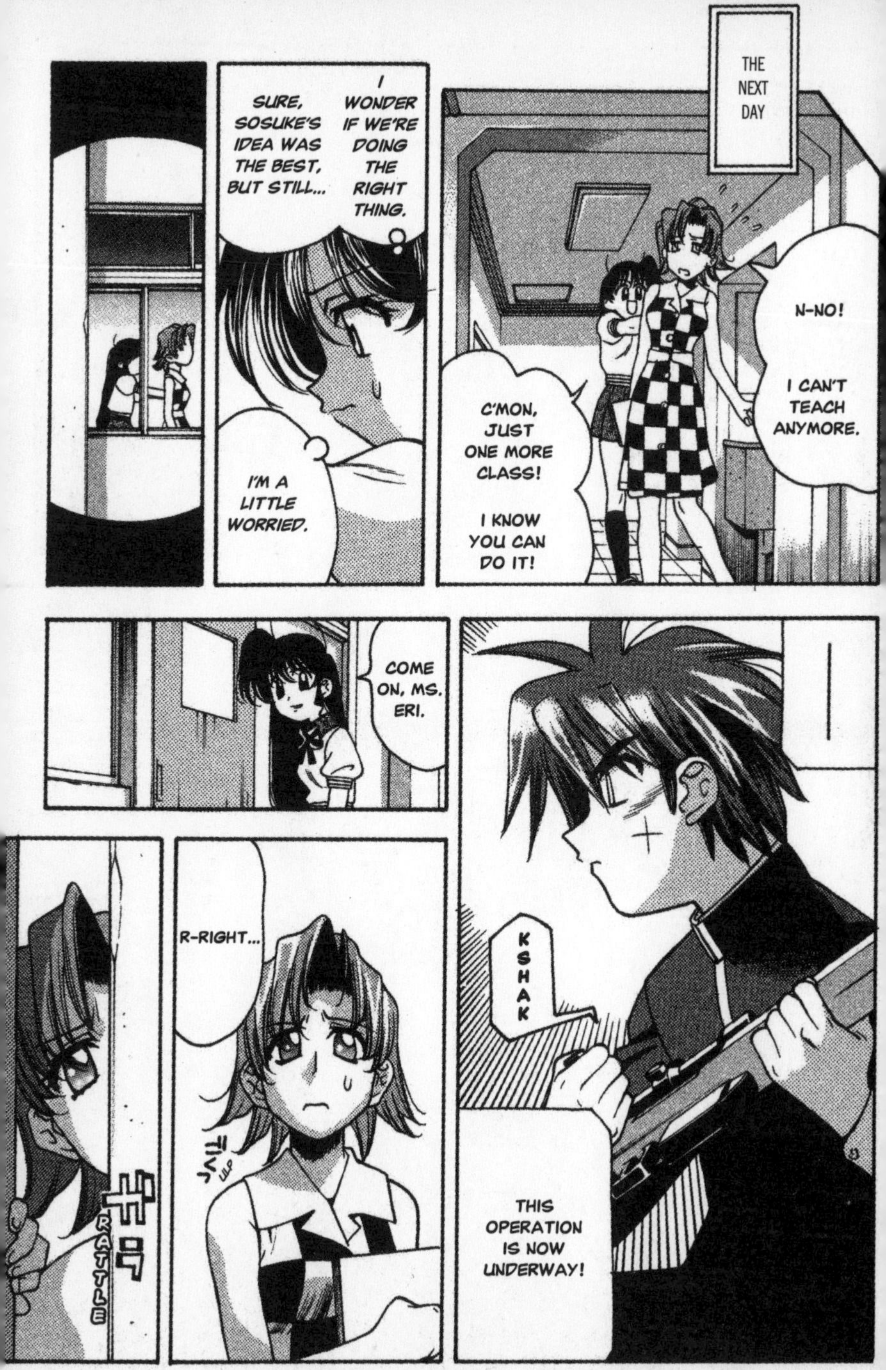

THE NEXT DAY
N-NO!
I CAN'T TEACH ANYMORE.
C'MON, JUST ONE MORE CLASS!
I KNOW YOU CAN DO IT!
I WONDER IF WE'RE DOING THE RIGHT THING.
SURE, SOSUKE'S IDEA WAS THE BEST, BUT STILL...
I'M A LITTLE WORRIED.
KSHAK
THIS OPERATION IS NOW UNDERWAY!
COME ON, MS. ERI.
R-RIGHT...
GULP
RATTLE

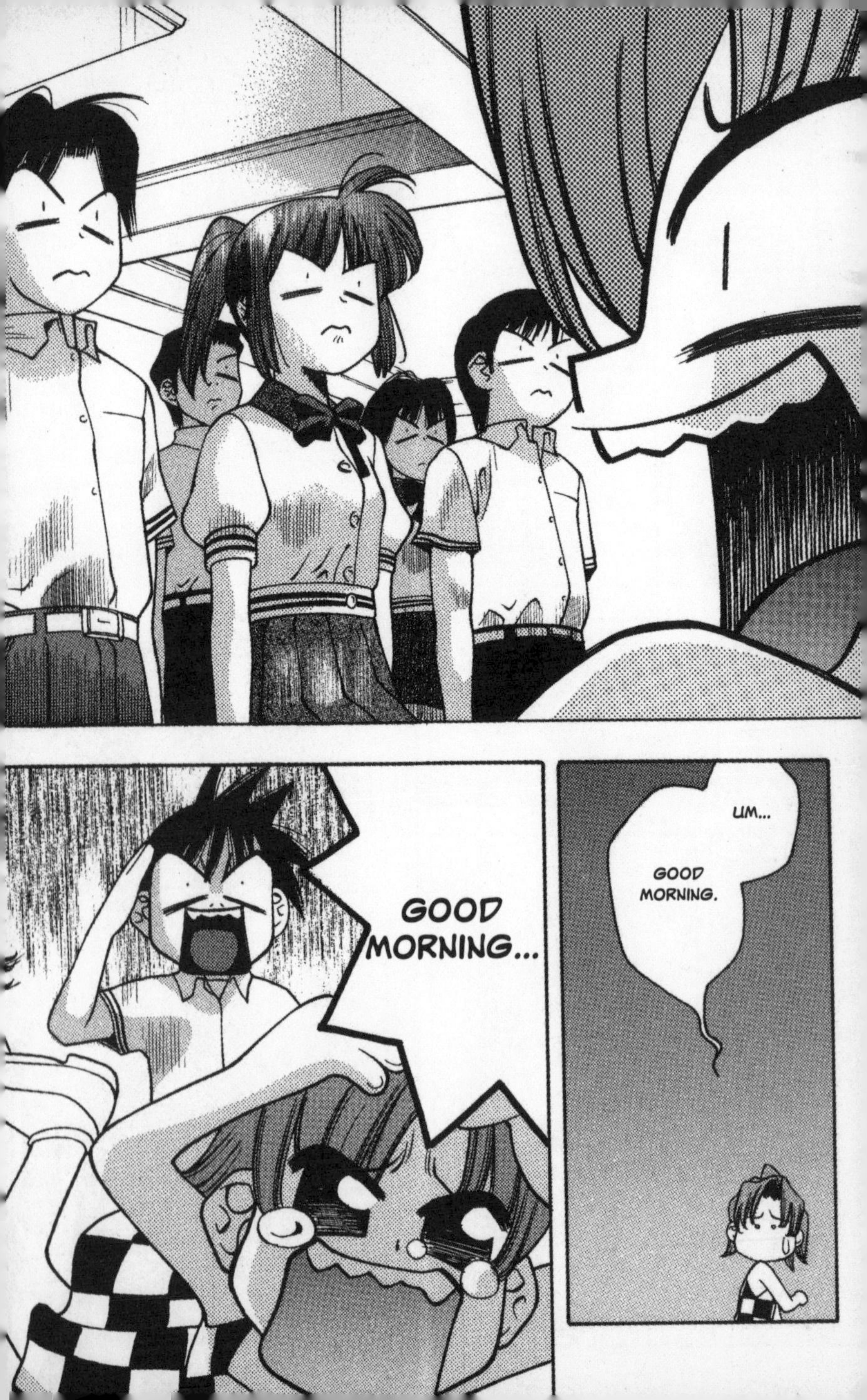
UM...
GOOD MORNING.
GOOD MORNING...

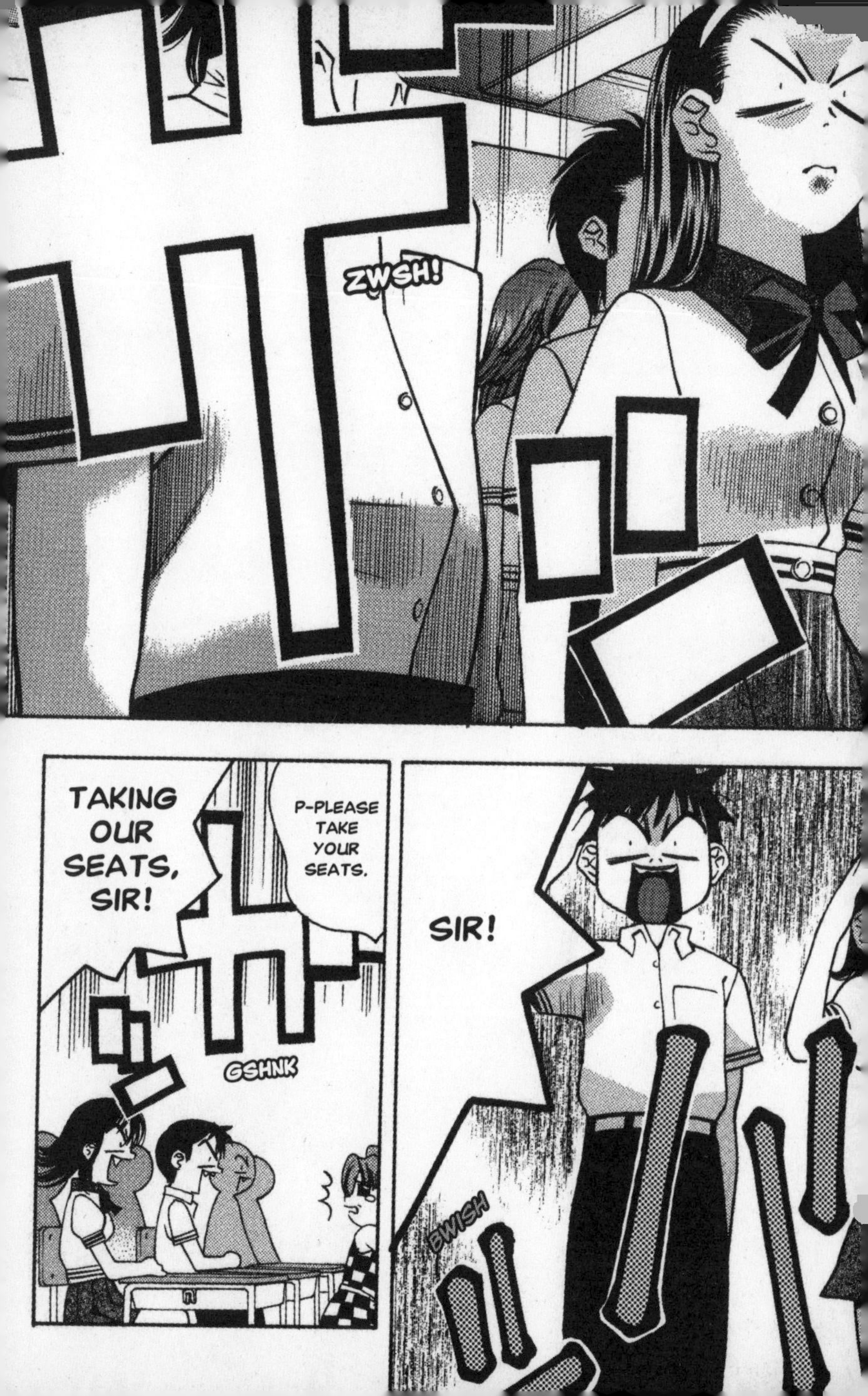
ZWSH!
SIR!
BWISH
P-PLEASE TAKE YOUR SEATS.
TAKING OUR SEATS, SIR!
GSHNK

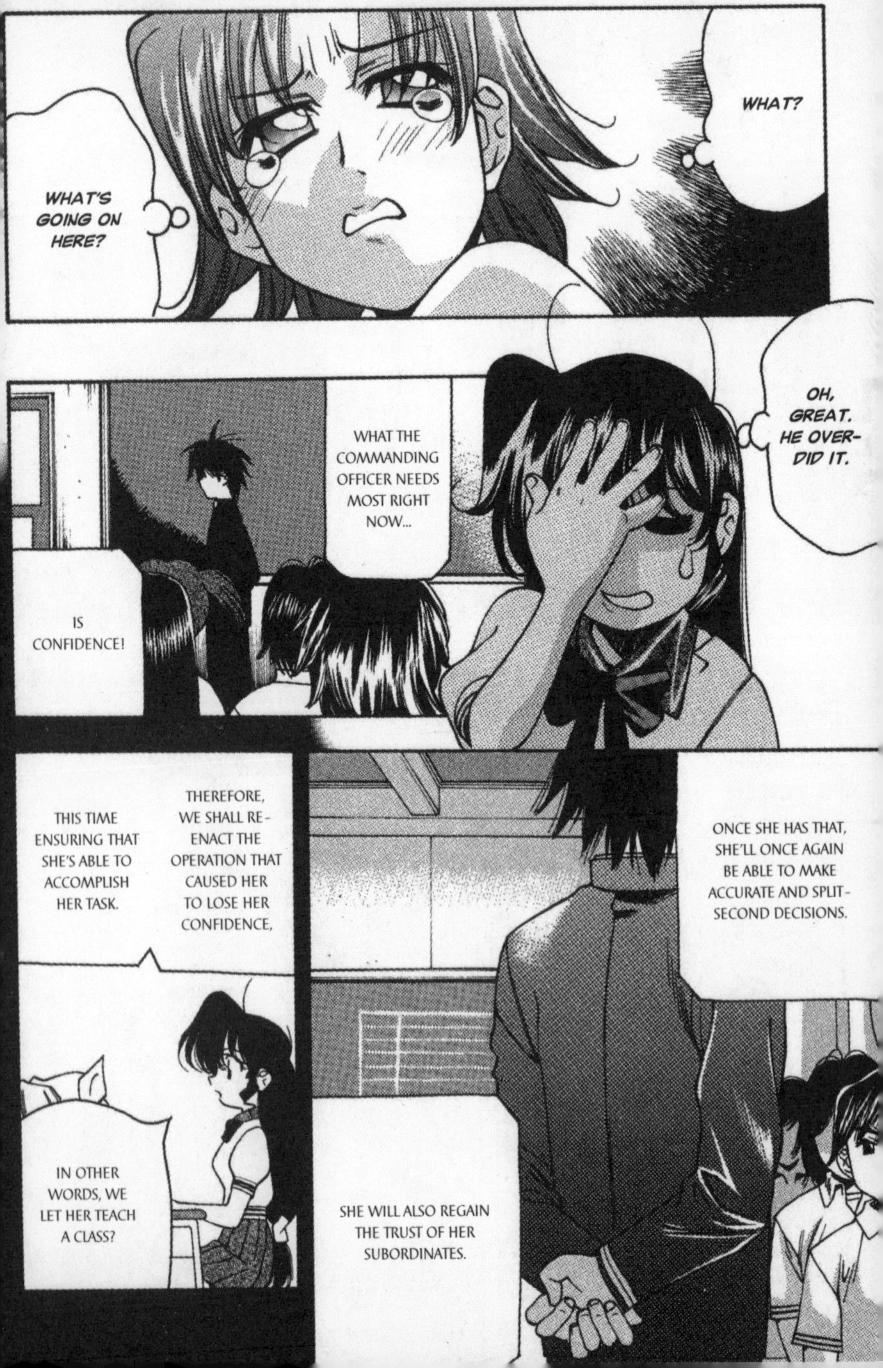

WHAT?
WHAT'S GOING ON HERE?
OH, GREAT. HE OVER-DID IT.
WHAT THE COMMANDING OFFICER NEEDS MOST RIGHT NOW...
IS CONFIDENCE!
ONCE SHE HAS THAT, SHE'LL ONCE AGAIN BE ABLE TO MAKE ACCURATE AND SPLIT-SECOND DECISIONS.
SHE WILL ALSO REGAIN THE TRUST OF HER SUBORDINATES.
THEREFORE, WE SHALL RE-ENACT THE OPERATION THAT CAUSED HER TO LOSE HER CONFIDENCE,
THIS TIME ENSURING THAT SHE'S ABLE TO ACCOMPLISH HER TASK.
IN OTHER WORDS, WE LET HER TEACH A CLASS?

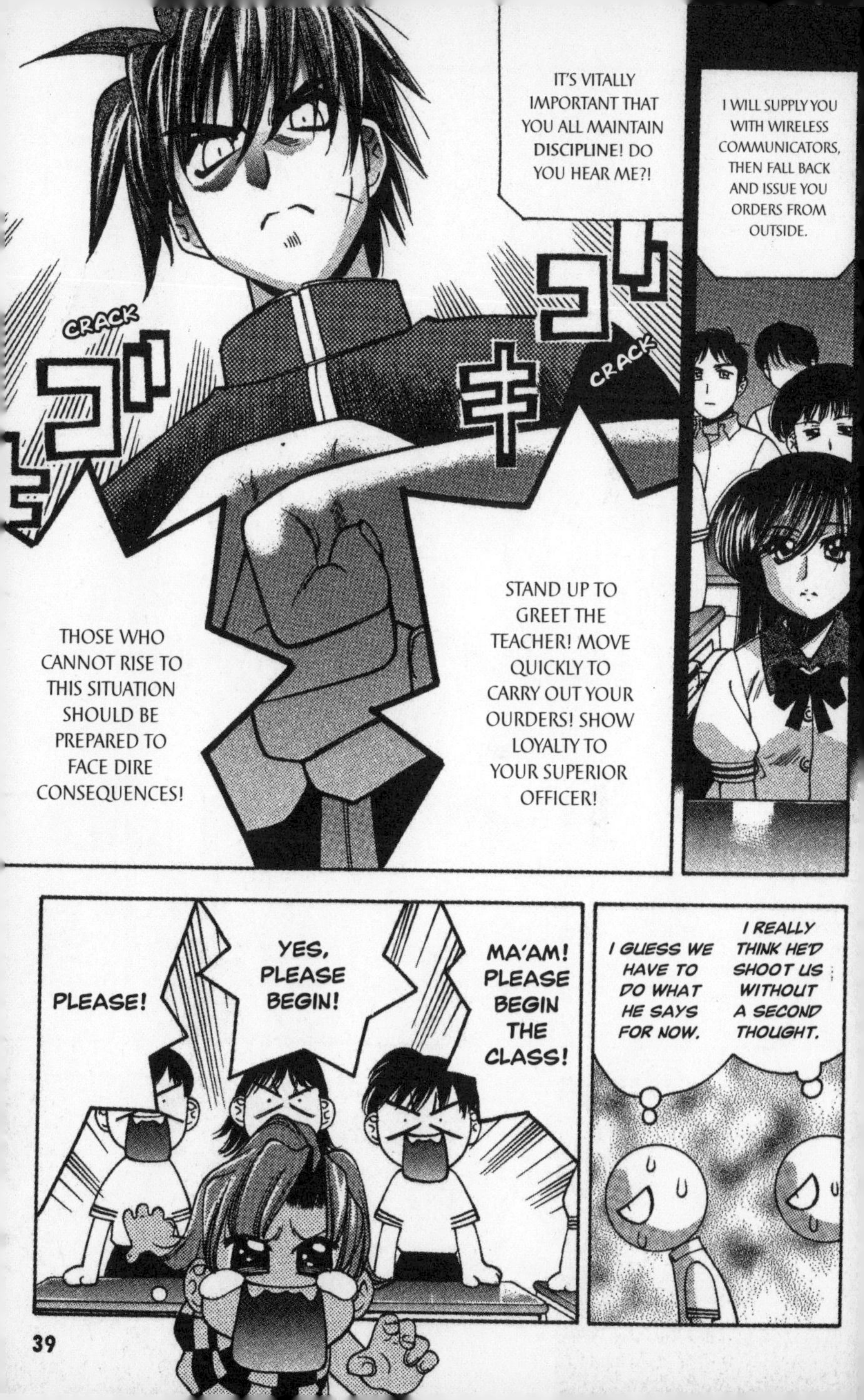
I WILL SUPPLY YOU WITH WIRELESS COMMUNICATORS, THEN FALL BACK AND ISSUE YOU ORDERS FROM OUTSIDE.
IT'S VITALLY IMPORTANT THAT YOU ALL MAINTAIN DISCIPLINE! DO YOU HEAR ME?!
CRACK
CRACK
STAND UP TO GREET THE TEACHER! MOVE QUICKLY TO CARRY OUT YOUR OURDERS! SHOW LOYALTY TO YOUR SUPERIOR OFFICER!
THOSE WHO CANNOT RISE TO THIS SITUATION SHOULD BE PREPARED TO FACE DIRE CONSEQUENCES!
I REALLY THINK HE'D SHOOT US WITHOUT A SECOND THOUGHT.
I GUESS WE HAVE TO DO WHAT HE SAYS FOR NOW.
MA'AM! PLEASE BEGIN THE CLASS!
YES, PLEASE BEGIN!
PLEASE!

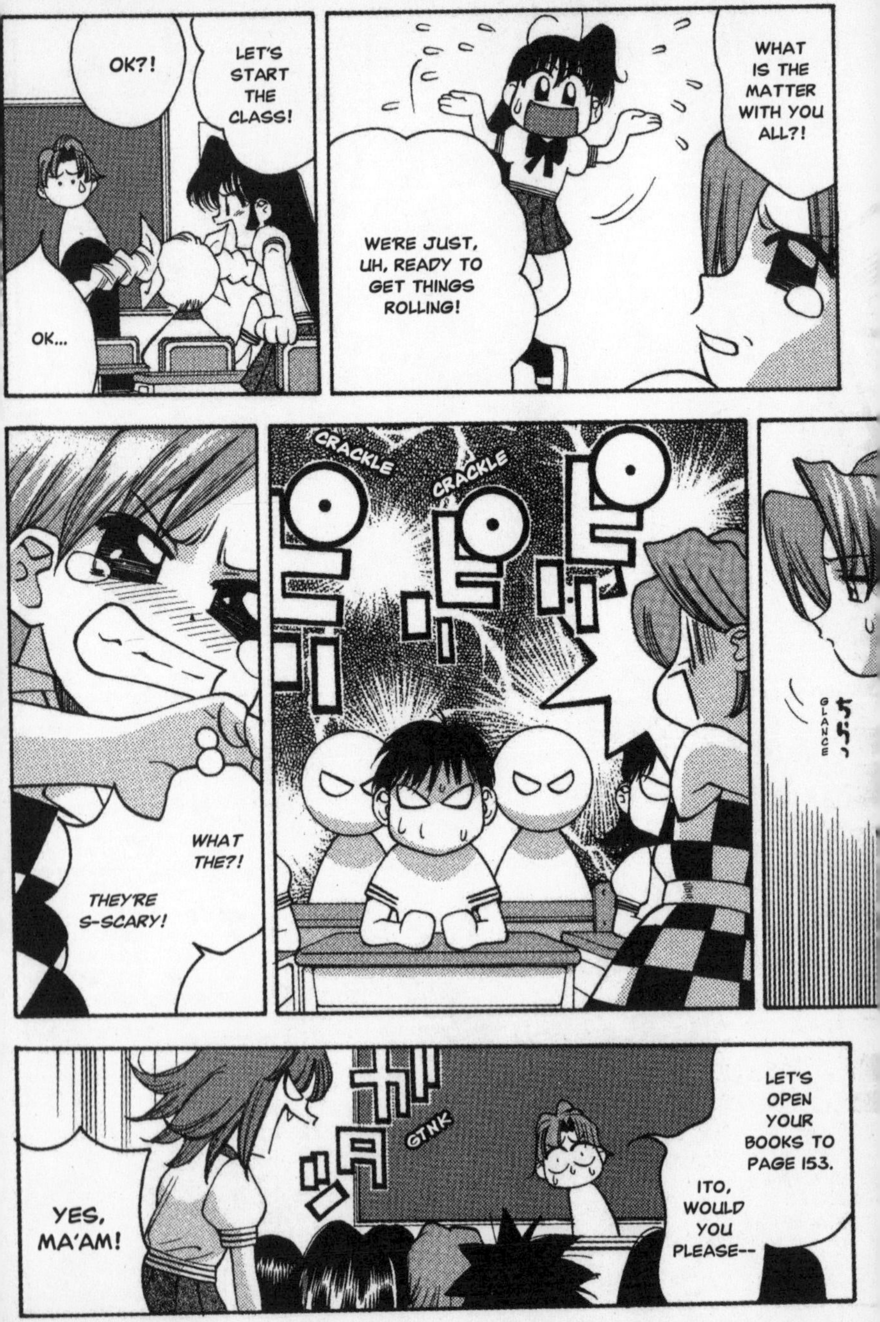

WHAT IS THE MATTER WITH YOU ALL?!
WE'RE JUST, UH, READY TO GET THINGS ROLLING!
LET'S START THE CLASS!
OK?!
OK...
GLANCE
CRACKLE
CRACKLE
WHAT THE?!
THEY'RE S-SCARY!
LET'S OPEN YOUR BOOKS TO PAGE 153.
ITO, WOULD YOU PLEASE--
GTNK
YES, MA'AM!

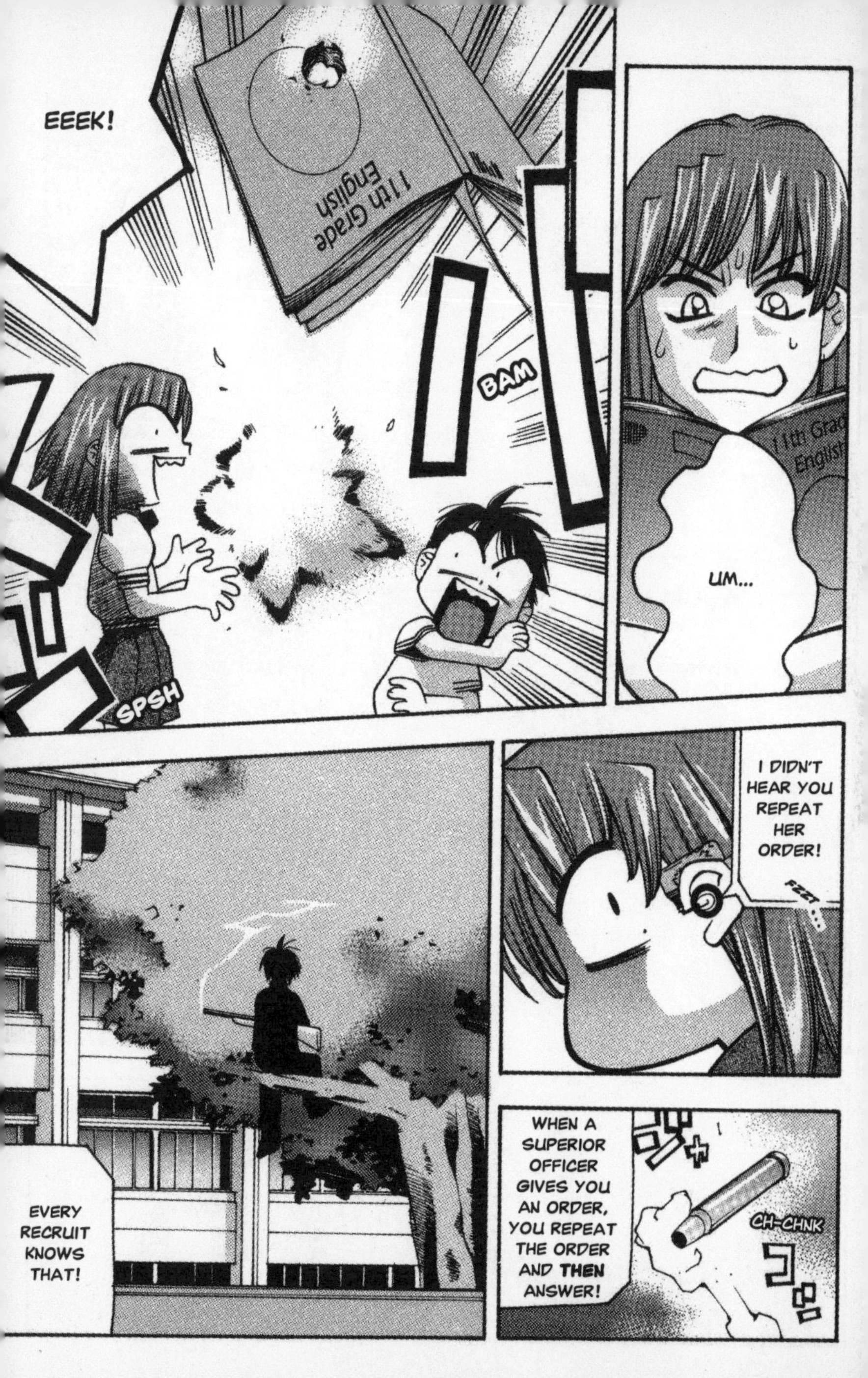

11th Grade English
UM...
EEEK!
11th Grade English
BAM
SPSH
I DIDN'T HEAR YOU REPEAT HER ORDER!
FZZT...
WHEN A SUPERIOR OFFICER GIVES YOU AN ORDER, YOU REPEAT THE ORDER AND **THEN** ANSWER!
CH-CHNK
EVERY RECRUIT KNOWS THAT!

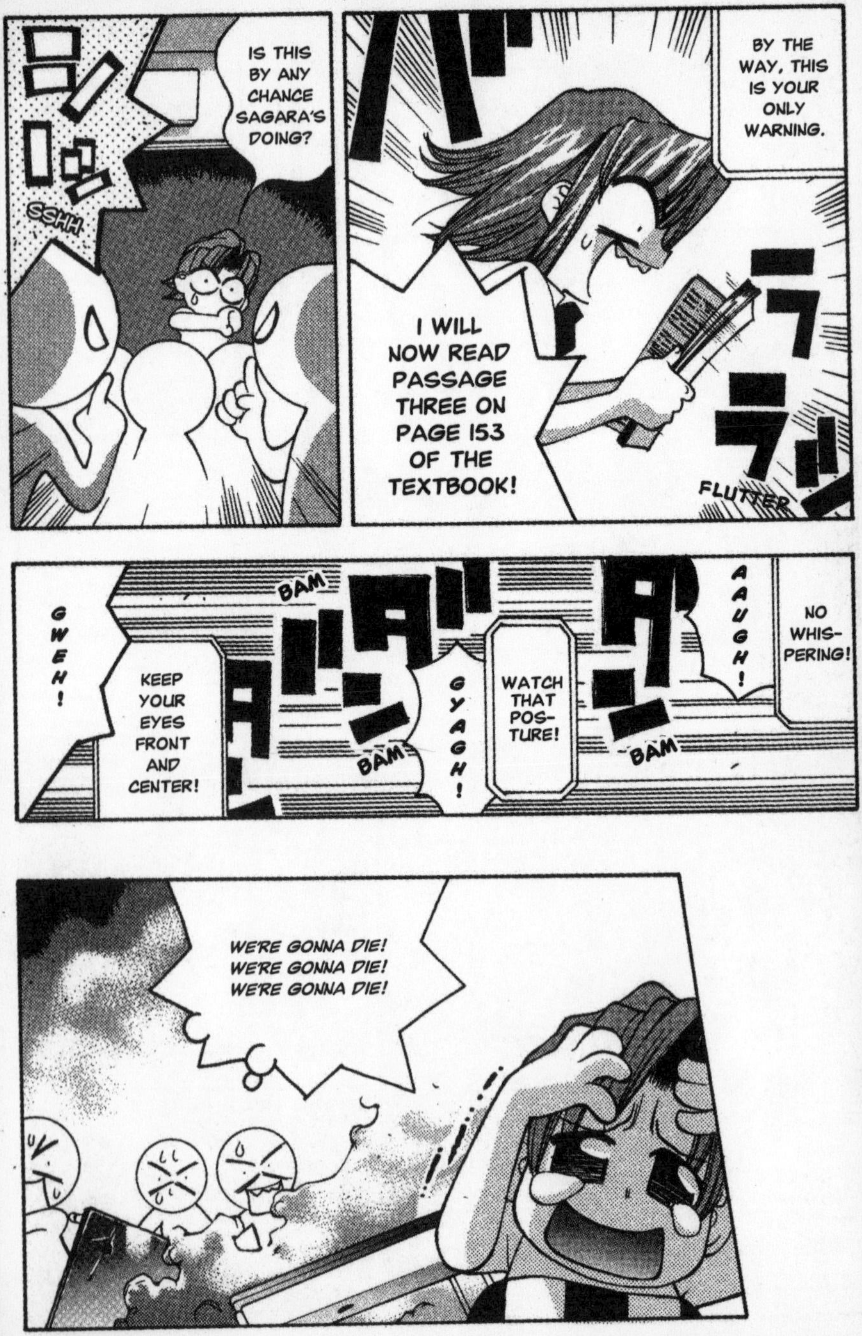
BY THE WAY, THIS IS YOUR ONLY WARNING.
I WILL NOW READ PASSAGE THREE ON PAGE 153 OF THE TEXTBOOK!
FLUTTER
IS THIS BY ANY CHANCE SAGARA'S DOING?
SSHH
NO WHIS-PERING!
AAUGH!
BAM
WATCH THAT POS-TURE!
GYAGH!
BAM
BAM
KEEP YOUR EYES FRONT AND CENTER!
GWEH!
WE'RE GONNA DIE!
WE'RE GONNA DIE!
WE'RE GONNA DIE!

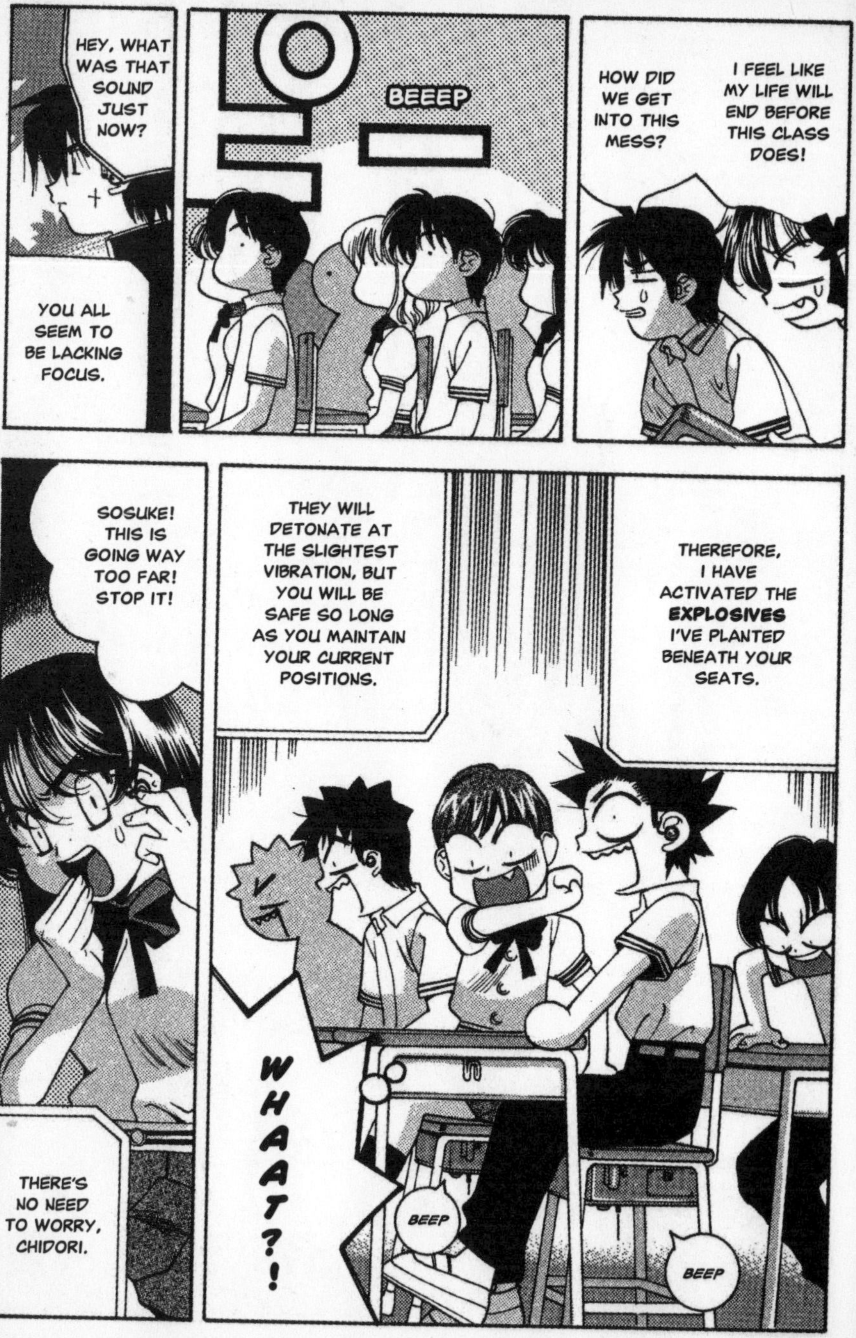
I FEEL LIKE MY LIFE WILL END BEFORE THIS CLASS DOES!
HOW DID WE GET INTO THIS MESS?
BEEEP
HEY, WHAT WAS THAT SOUND JUST NOW?
YOU ALL SEEM TO BE LACKING FOCUS.
THEREFORE, I HAVE ACTIVATED THE EXPLOSIVES I'VE PLANTED BENEATH YOUR SEATS.
THEY WILL DETONATE AT THE SLIGHTEST VIBRATION, BUT YOU WILL BE SAFE SO LONG AS YOU MAINTAIN YOUR CURRENT POSITIONS.
WHAAAT?!
BEEP
BEEP
SOSUKE! THIS IS GOING WAY TOO FAR! STOP IT!
THERE'S NO NEED TO WORRY, CHIDORI.

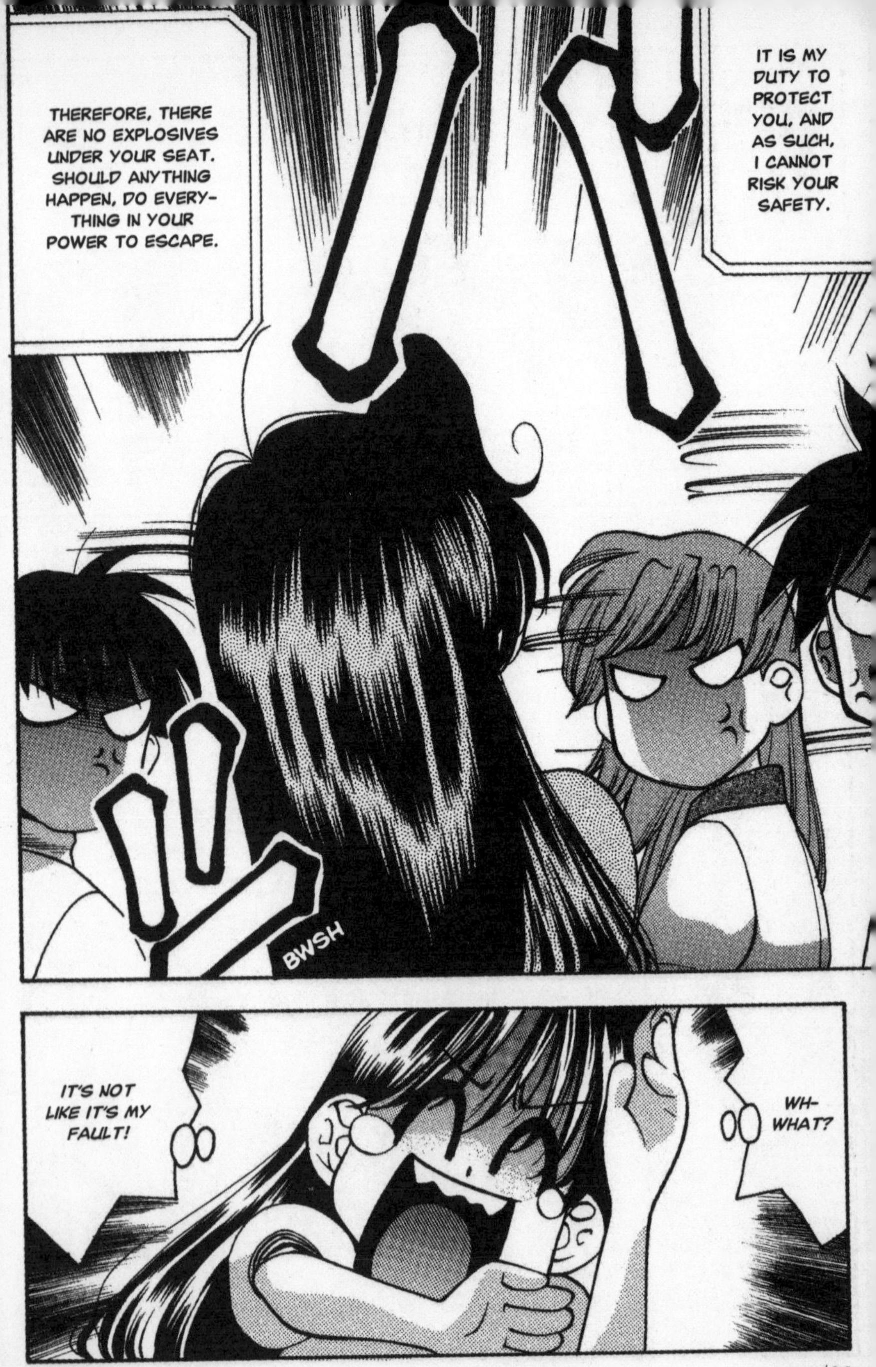
IT IS MY DUTY TO PROTECT YOU, AND AS SUCH, I CANNOT RISK YOUR SAFETY.
THEREFORE, THERE ARE NO EXPLOSIVES UNDER YOUR SEAT. SHOULD ANYTHING HAPPEN, DO EVERY-THING IN YOUR POWER TO ESCAPE.
BWSH
WH- WHAT?
IT'S NOT LIKE IT'S MY FAULT!

TOKIWA.

YEAH...

KANA, WE HAVE TO STOP SAGARA!

EH?!

GLOOOM

I'M SORRY TO INTERRUPT YOU WHILE YOU'RE TALKING, BUT WOULD YOU MIND PLEASE TRANSLATING THIS FOR ME?

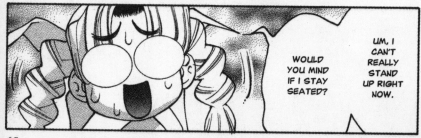

WOULD YOU MIND IF I STAY SEATED?

UM, I CAN'T REALLY STAND UP RIGHT NOW.

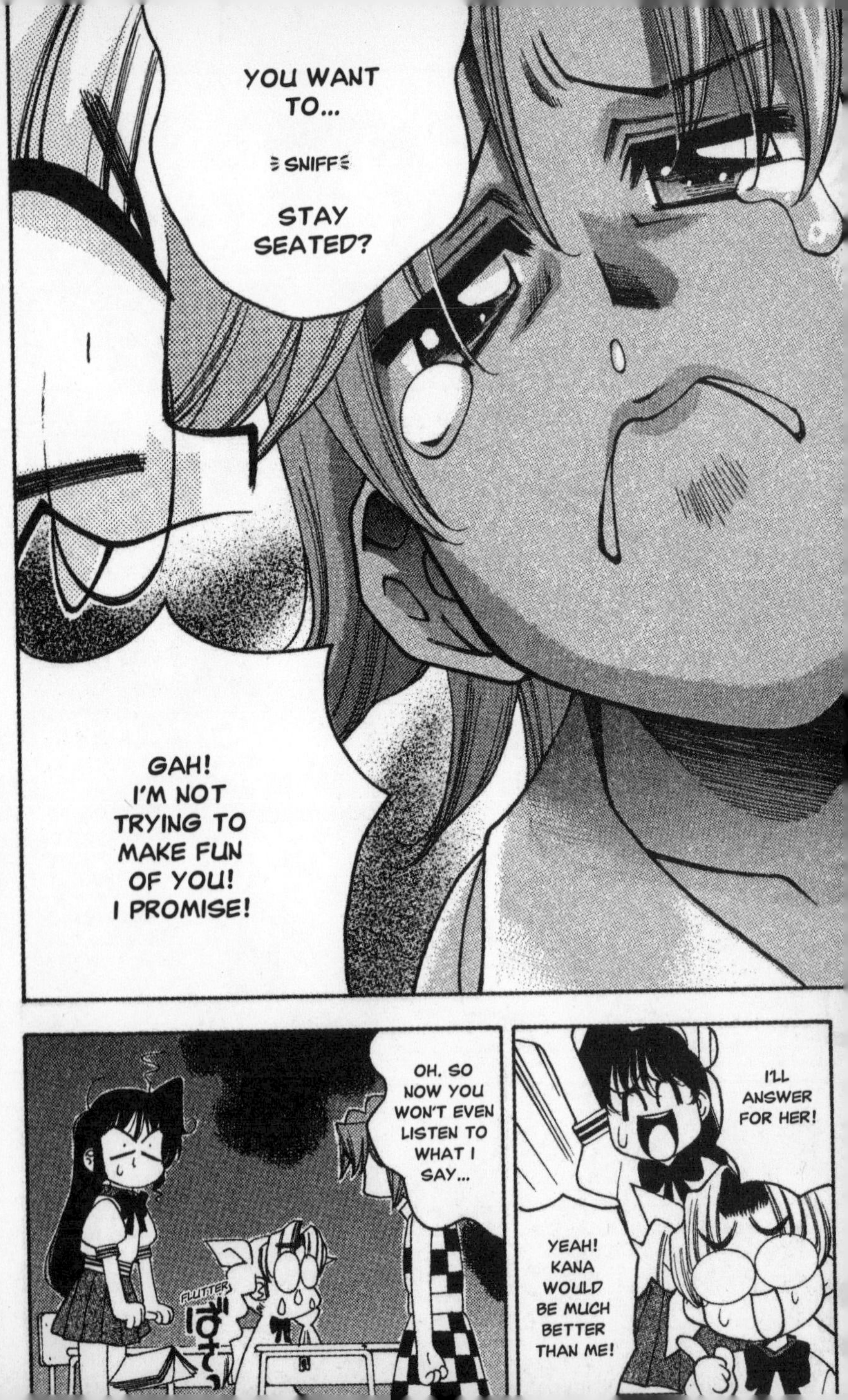
YOU WANT TO...
SNIFF
STAY SEATED?
GAH! I'M NOT TRYING TO MAKE FUN OF YOU! I PROMISE!
I'LL ANSWER FOR HER!
YEAH! KANA WOULD BE MUCH BETTER THAN ME!
OH. SO NOW YOU WON'T EVEN LISTEN TO WHAT I SAY...
FLUTTER

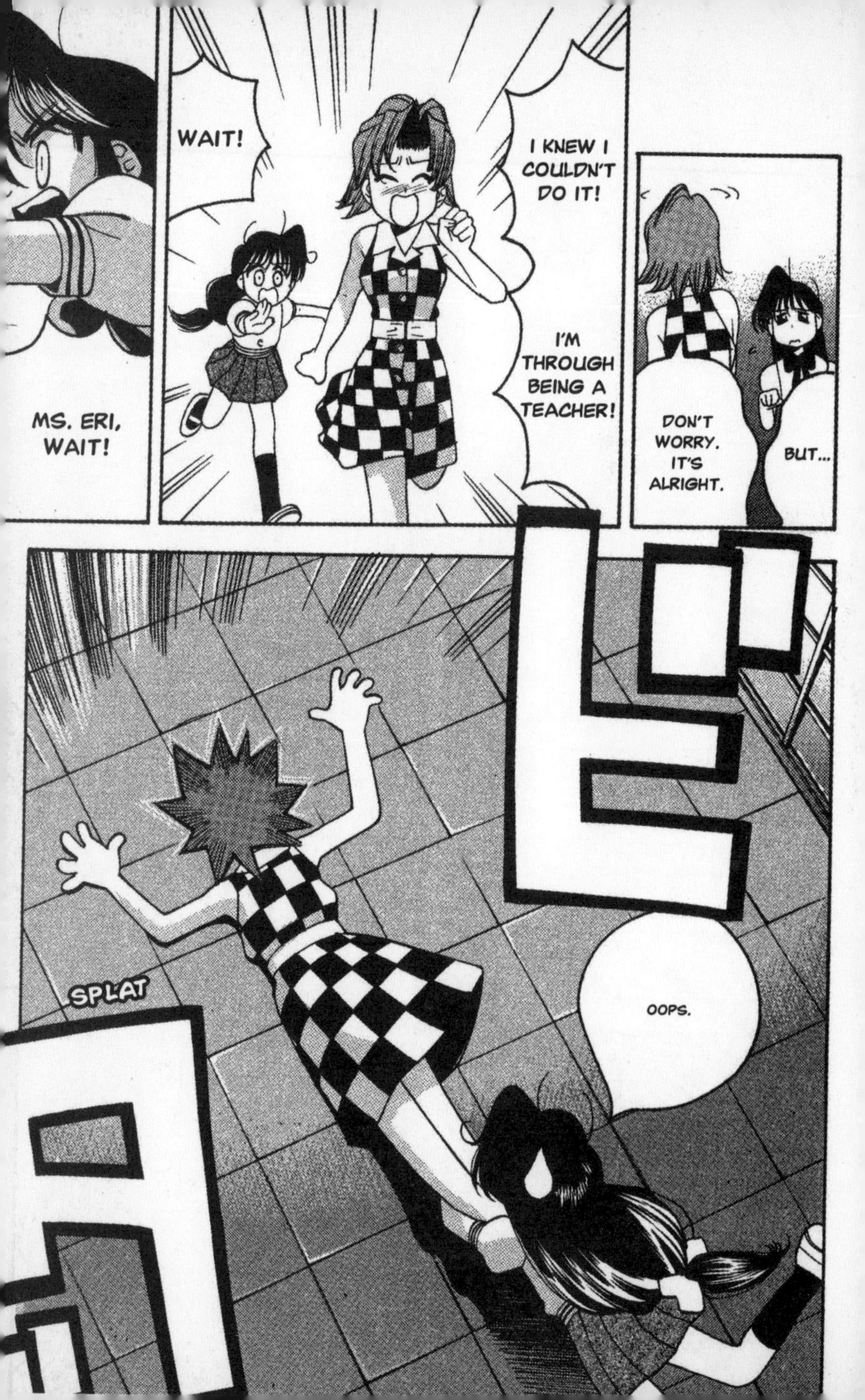
BUT...
DON'T WORRY. IT'S ALRIGHT.
I KNEW I COULDN'T DO IT!
I'M THROUGH BEING A TEACHER!
WAIT!
MS. ERI, WAIT!
OOPS.
SPLAT

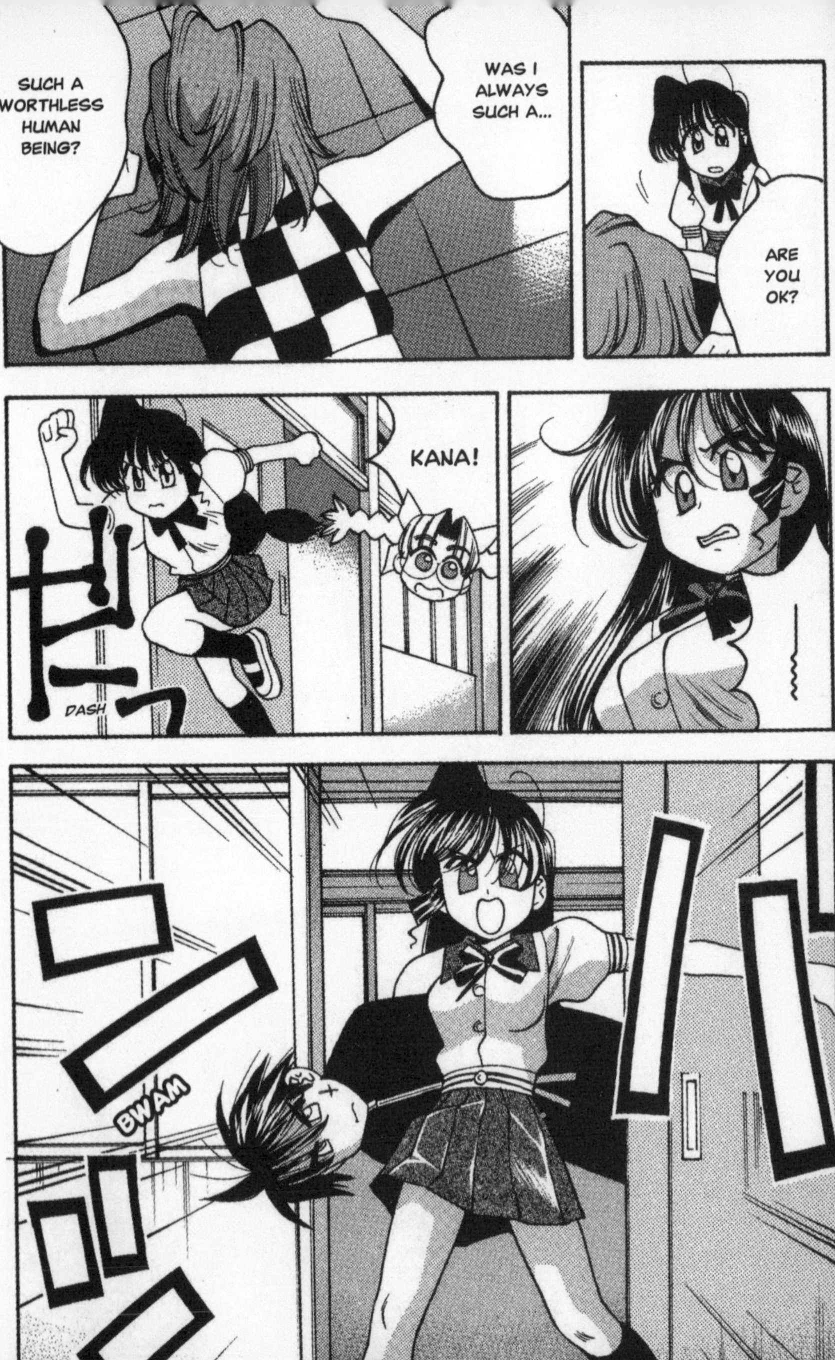
WAS I
ALWAYS
SUCH A...
SUCH A
WORTHLESS
HUMAN
BEING?
ARE
YOU
OK?
KANA!
DASH
BWAM

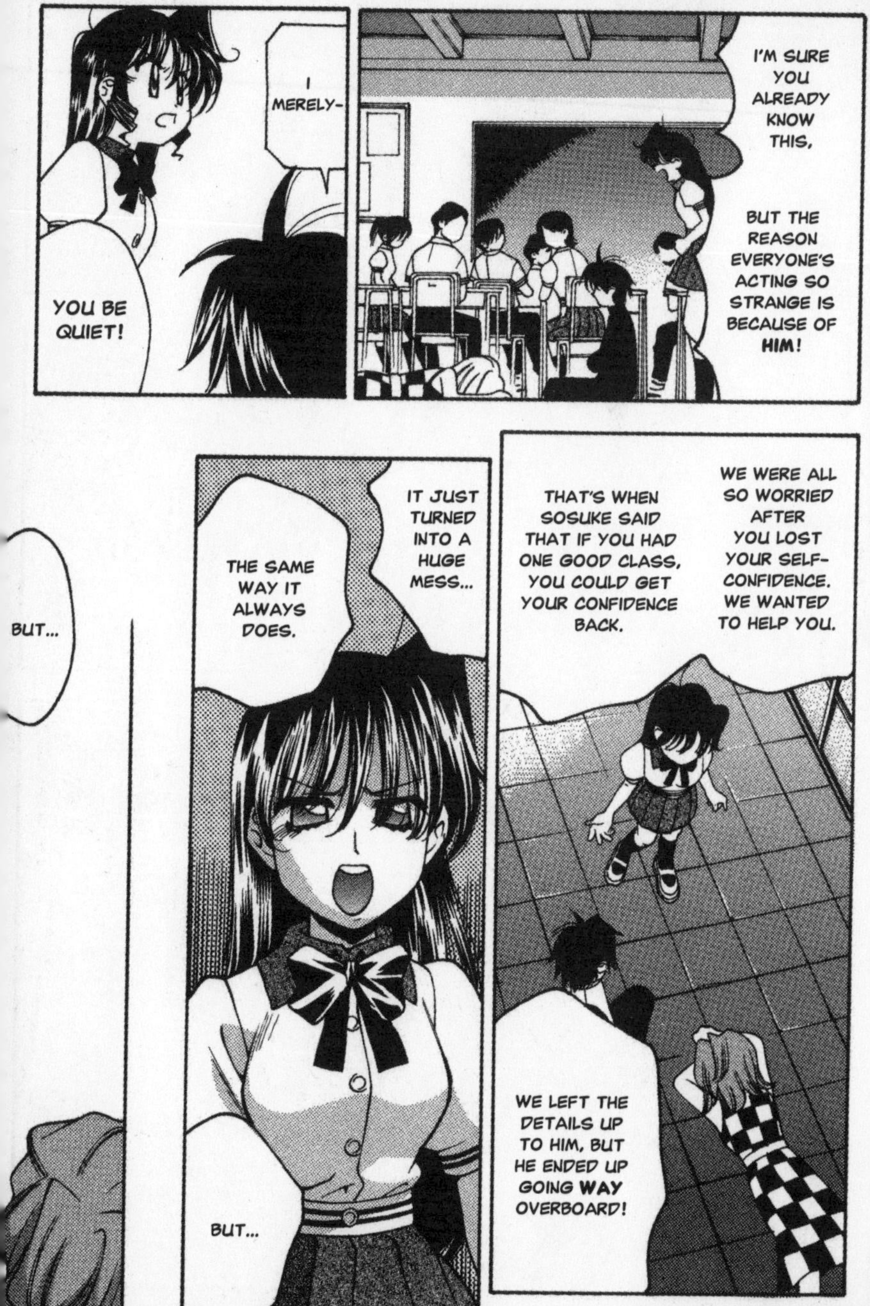
I'M SURE YOU ALREADY KNOW THIS,
BUT THE REASON EVERYONE'S ACTING SO STRANGE IS BECAUSE OF **HIM**!
I MERELY-
YOU BE QUIET!
WE WERE ALL SO WORRIED AFTER YOU LOST YOUR SELF-CONFIDENCE. WE WANTED TO HELP YOU.
THAT'S WHEN SOSUKE SAID THAT IF YOU HAD ONE GOOD CLASS, YOU COULD GET YOUR CONFIDENCE BACK.
WE LEFT THE DETAILS UP TO HIM, BUT HE ENDED UP GOING **WAY** OVERBOARD!
IT JUST TURNED INTO A HUGE MESS...
THE SAME WAY IT ALWAYS DOES.
BUT...
BUT...

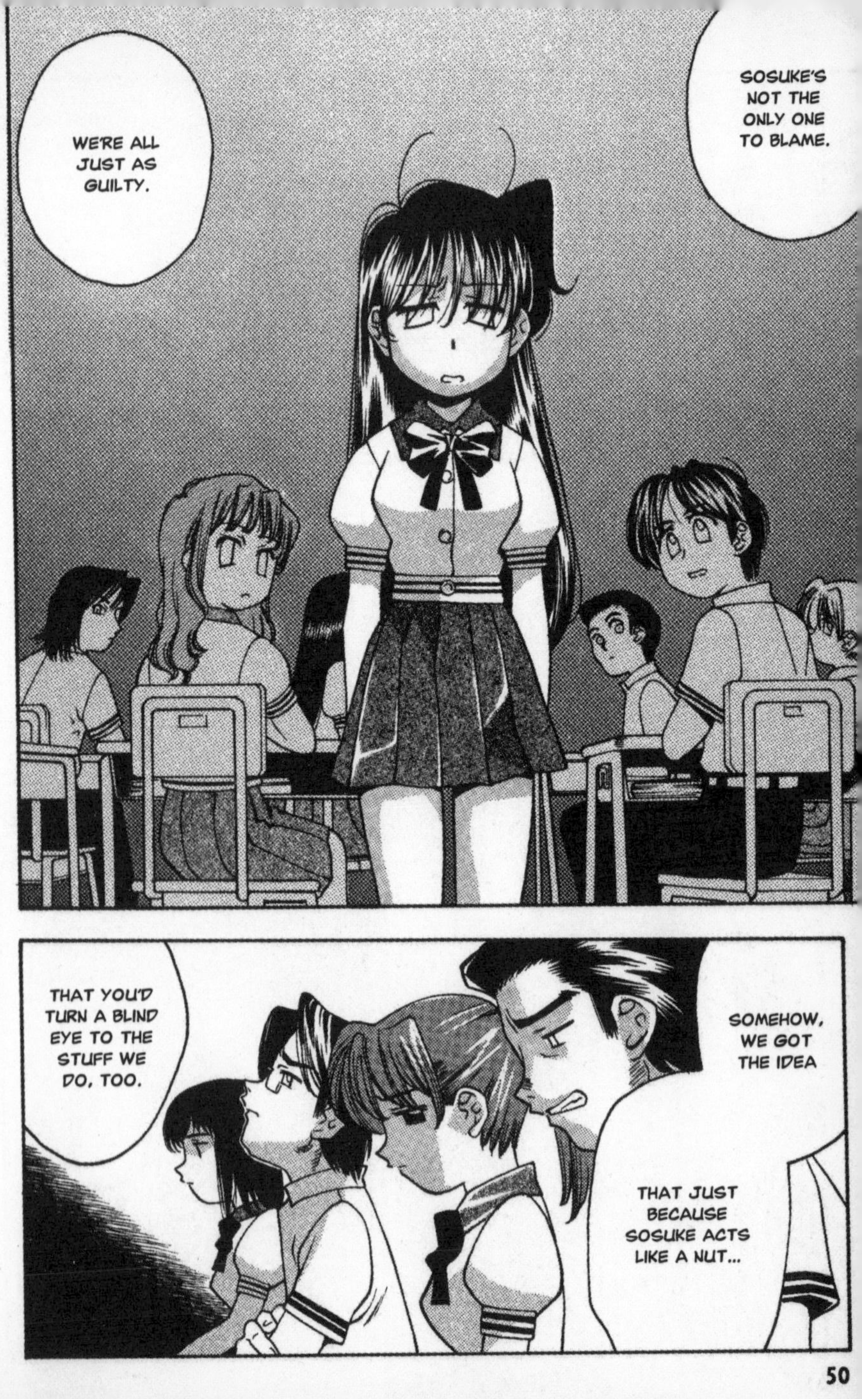
SOSUKE'S NOT THE ONLY ONE TO BLAME.
WE'RE ALL JUST AS GUILTY.
SOMEHOW, WE GOT THE IDEA
THAT JUST BECAUSE SOSUKE ACTS LIKE A NUT...
THAT YOU'D TURN A BLIND EYE TO THE STUFF WE DO, TOO.

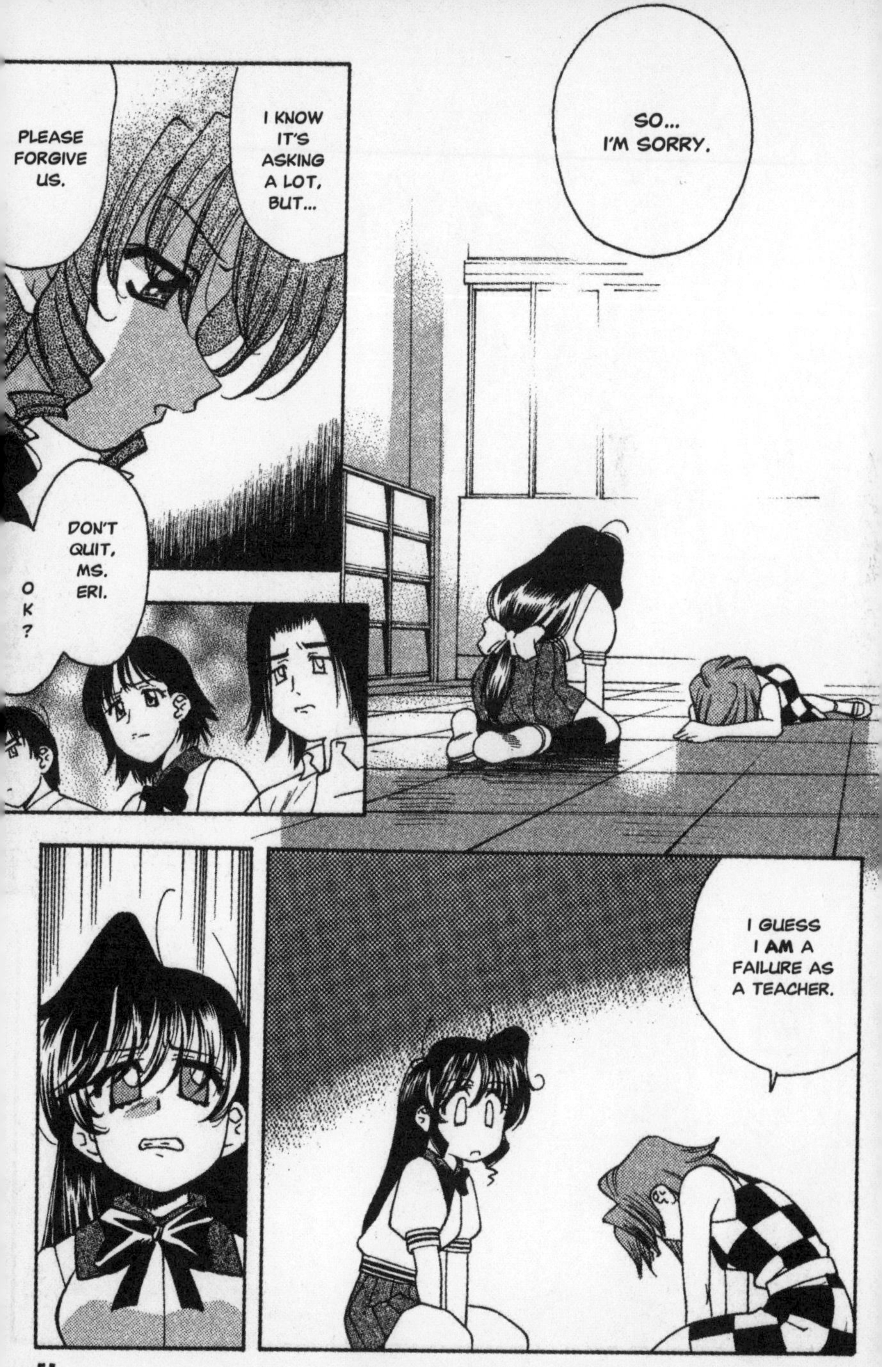
SO... I'M SORRY.
I KNOW IT'S ASKING A LOT, BUT...
PLEASE FORGIVE US.
DON'T QUIT, MS. ERI.
OK?
I GUESS I **AM** A FAILURE AS A TEACHER.

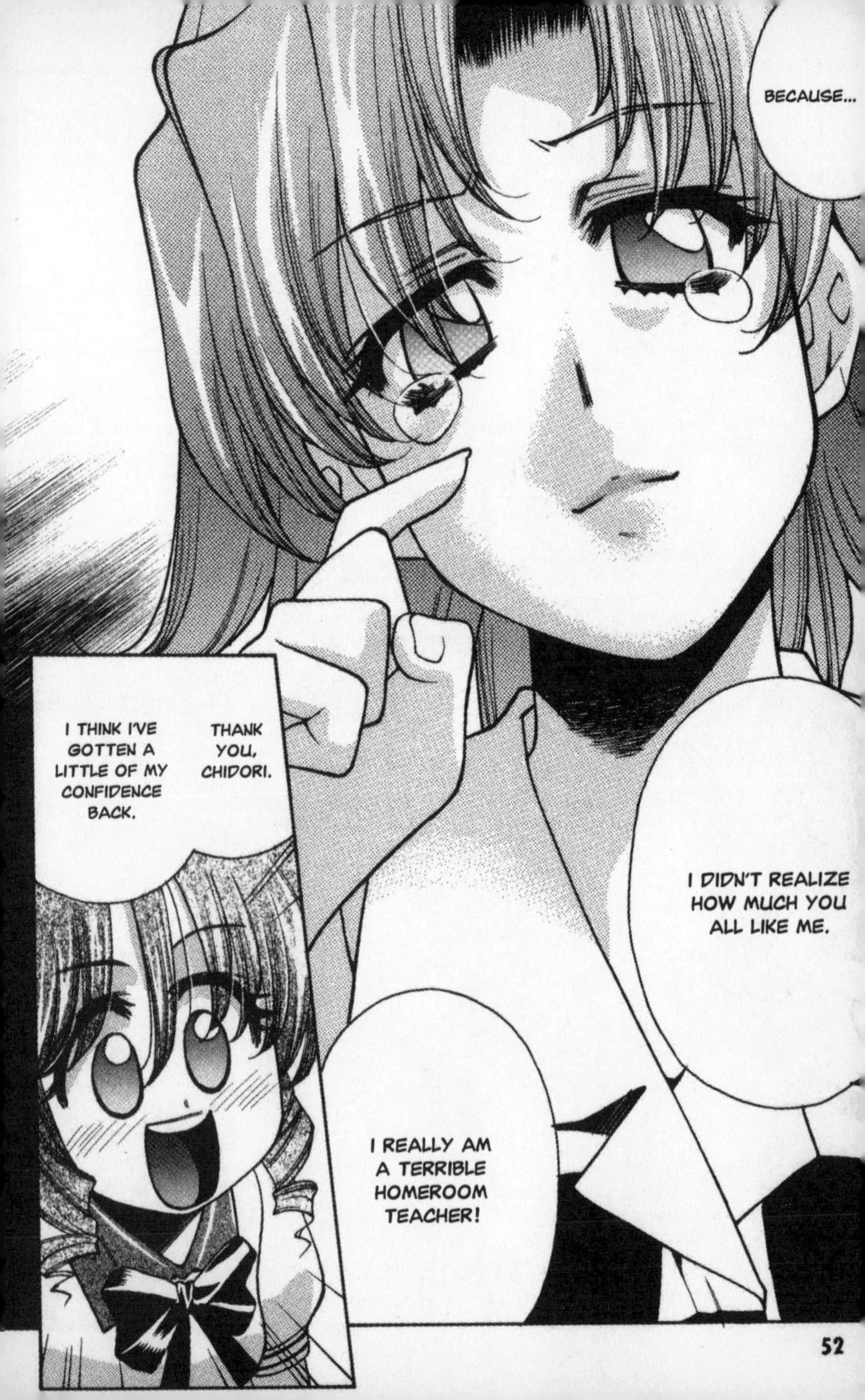
BECAUSE...
I DIDN'T REALIZE HOW MUCH YOU ALL LIKE ME.
I REALLY AM A TERRIBLE HOMEROOM TEACHER!
THANK YOU, CHIDORI.
I THINK I'VE GOTTEN A LITTLE OF MY CONFIDENCE BACK.

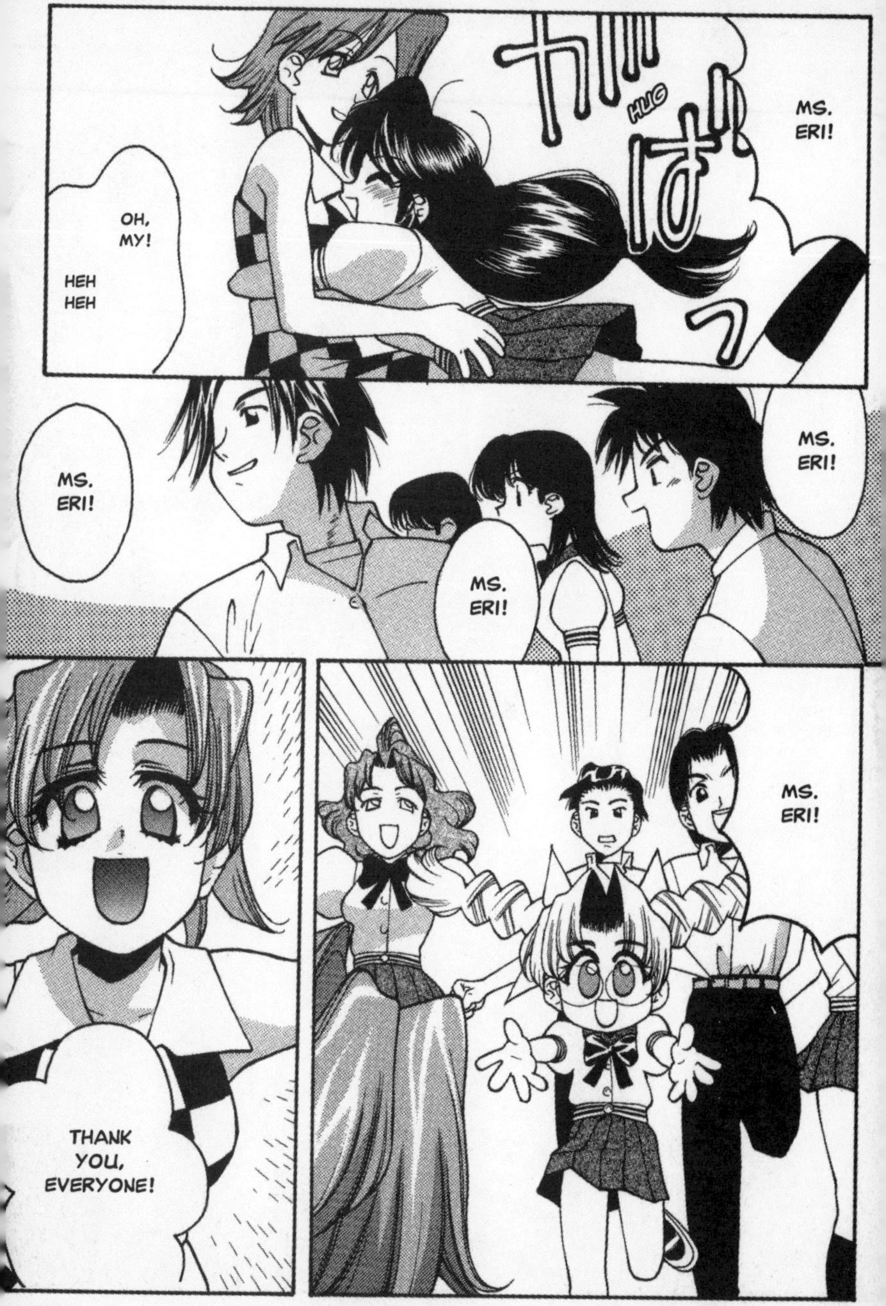
MS. ERI!
HUG
OH, MY!
HEH HEH
MS. ERI!
MS. ERI!
MS. ERI!
MS. ERI!
THANK YOU, EVERYONE!

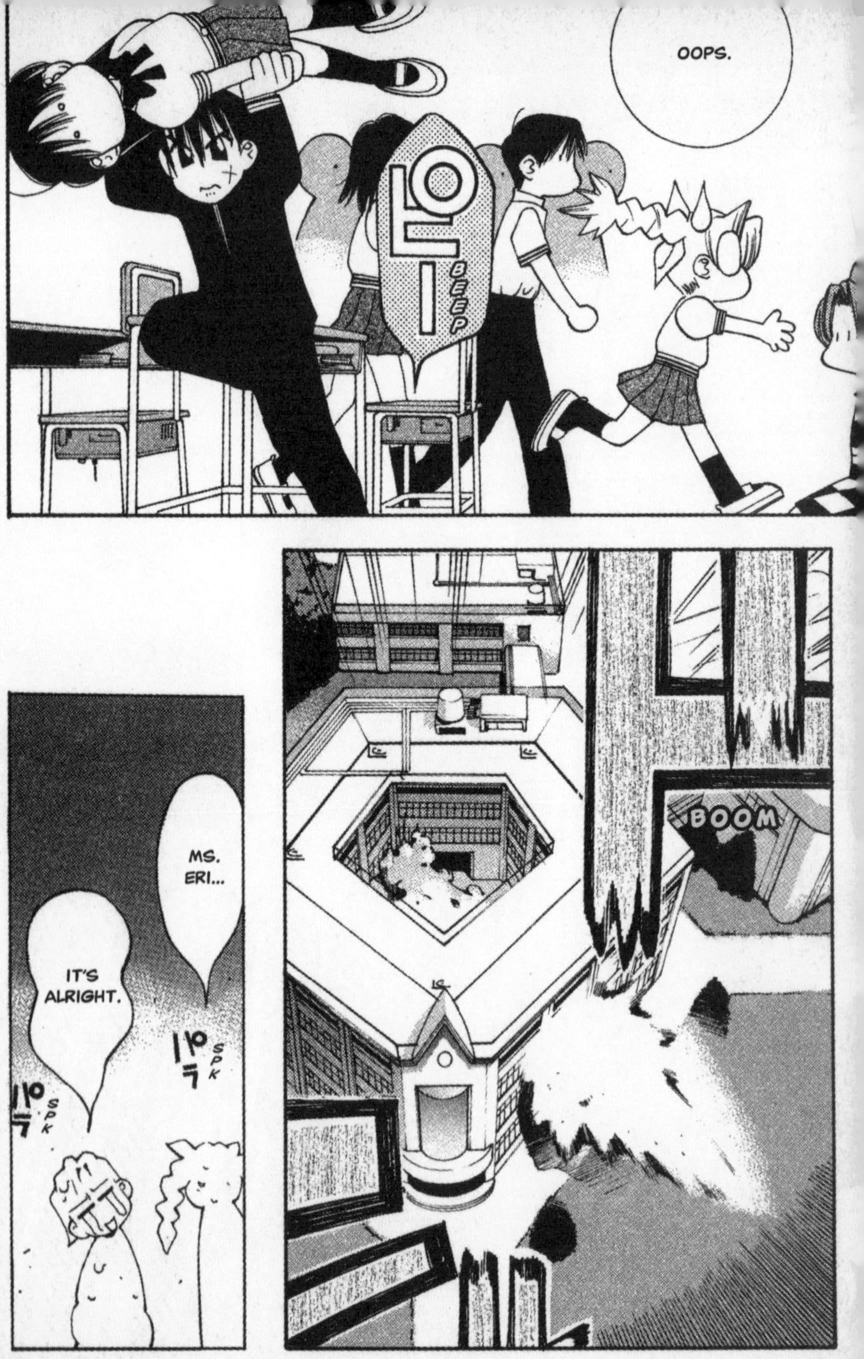

OOPS.
BEEP
BOOM
MS. ERI...
IT'S ALRIGHT.
SPK
SPK

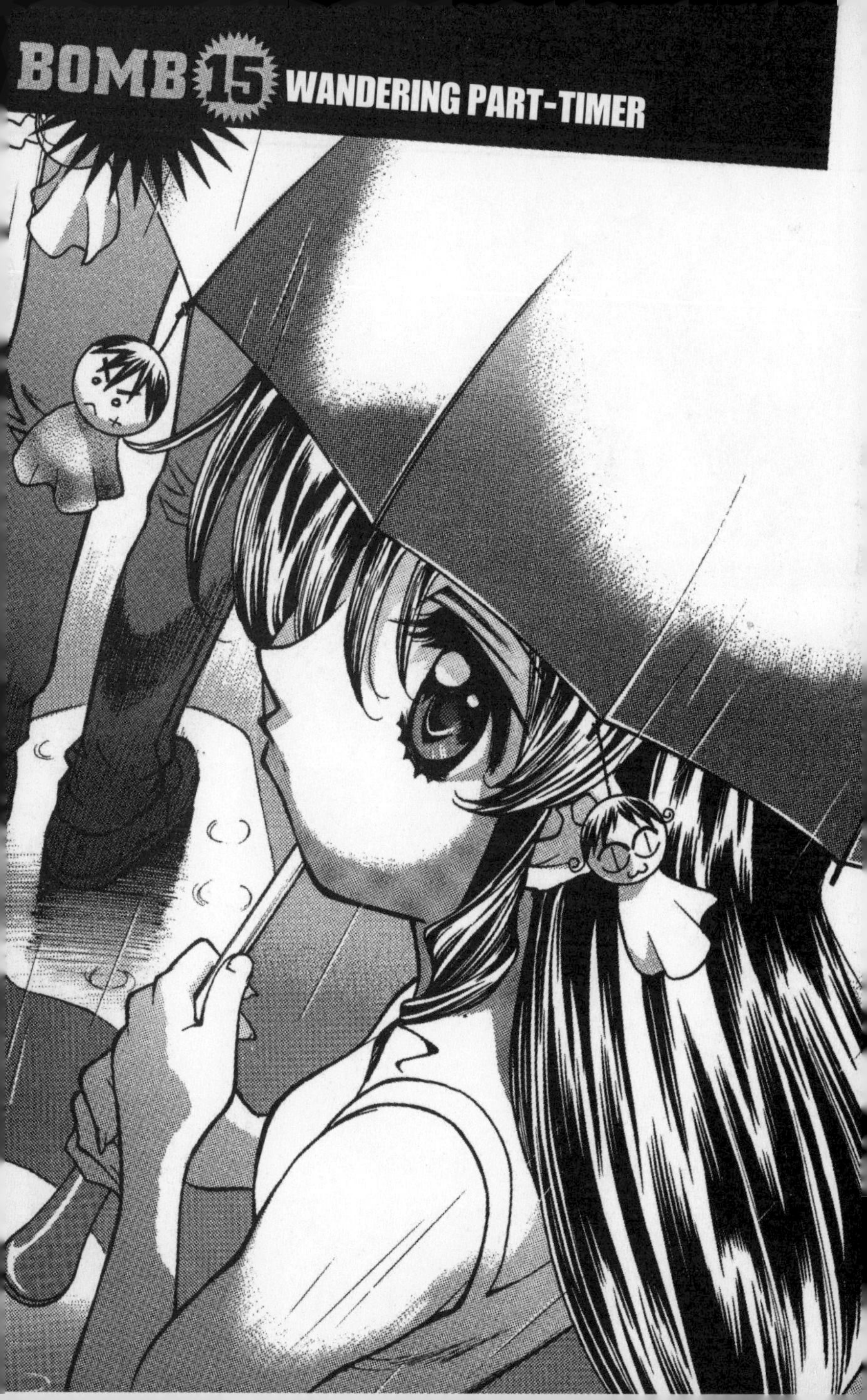
BOMB 15
WANDERING PART-TIMER

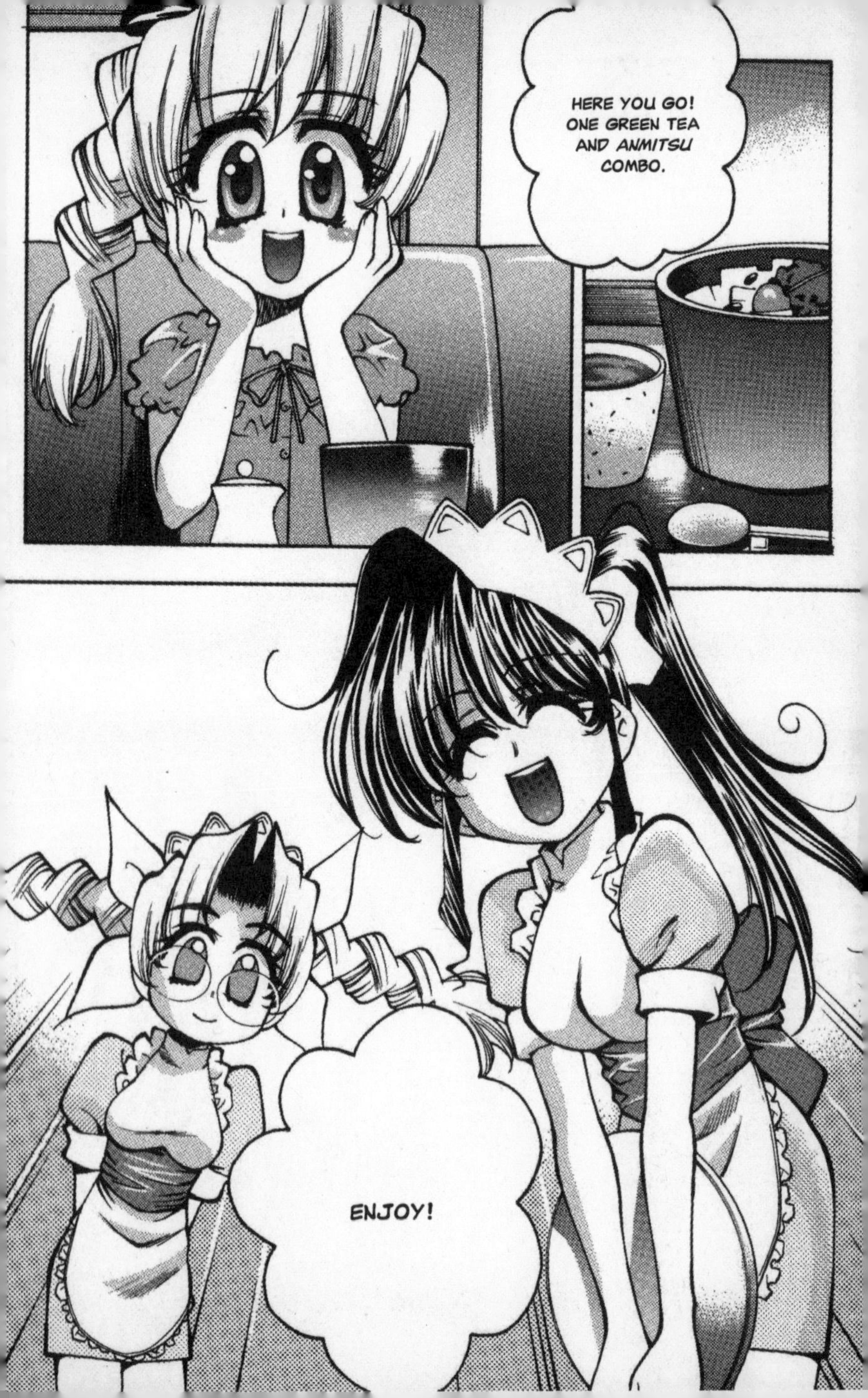
HERE YOU GO! ONE GREEN TEA AND ANMITSU COMBO.
ENJOY!

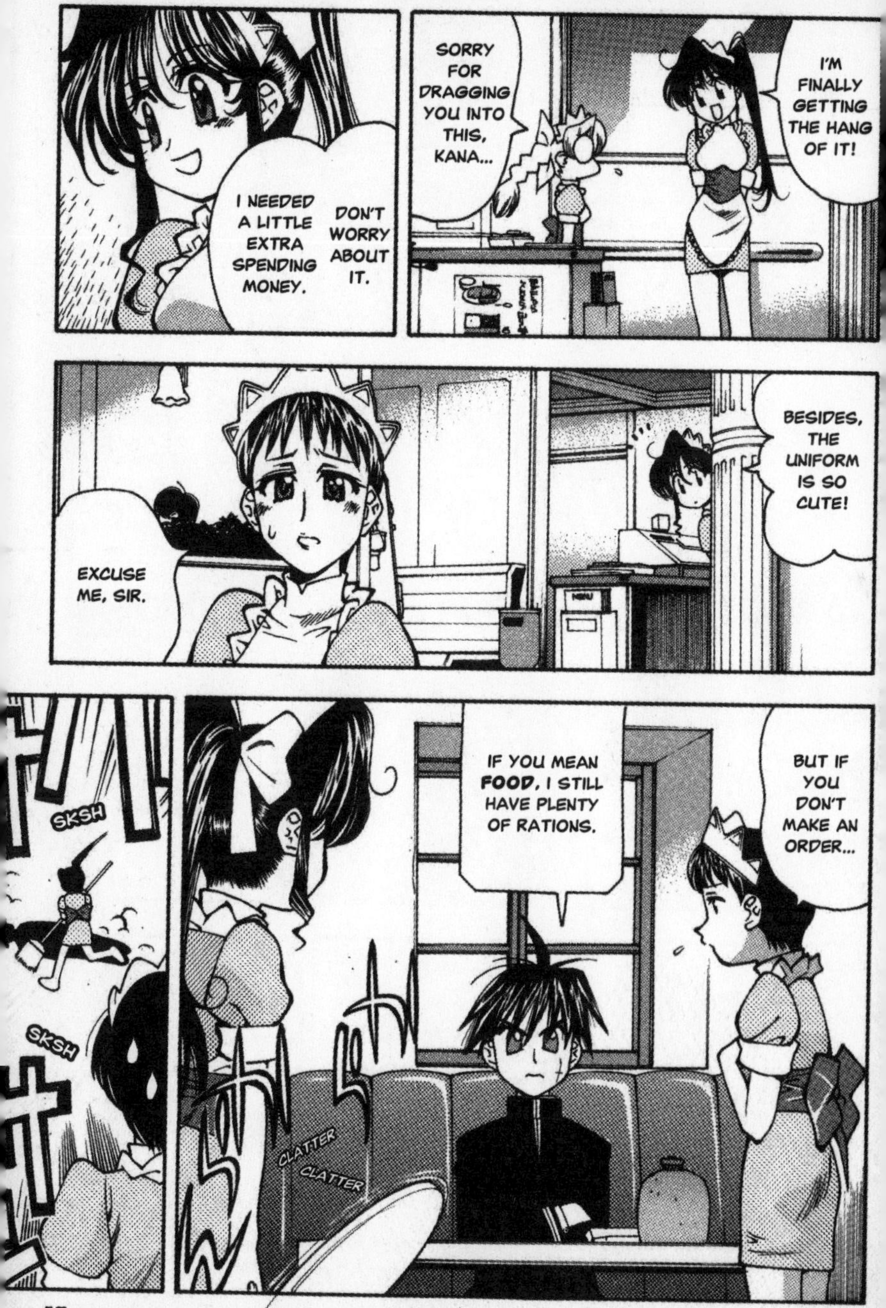
I'M FINALLY GETTING THE HANG OF IT!
SORRY FOR DRAGGING YOU INTO THIS, KANA...
DON'T WORRY ABOUT IT.
I NEEDED A LITTLE EXTRA SPENDING MONEY.
BESIDES, THE UNIFORM IS SO CUTE!
EXCUSE ME, SIR.
BUT IF YOU DON'T MAKE AN ORDER...
IF YOU MEAN FOOD, I STILL HAVE PLENTY OF RATIONS.
CLATTER
CLATTER
SKSH
SKSH

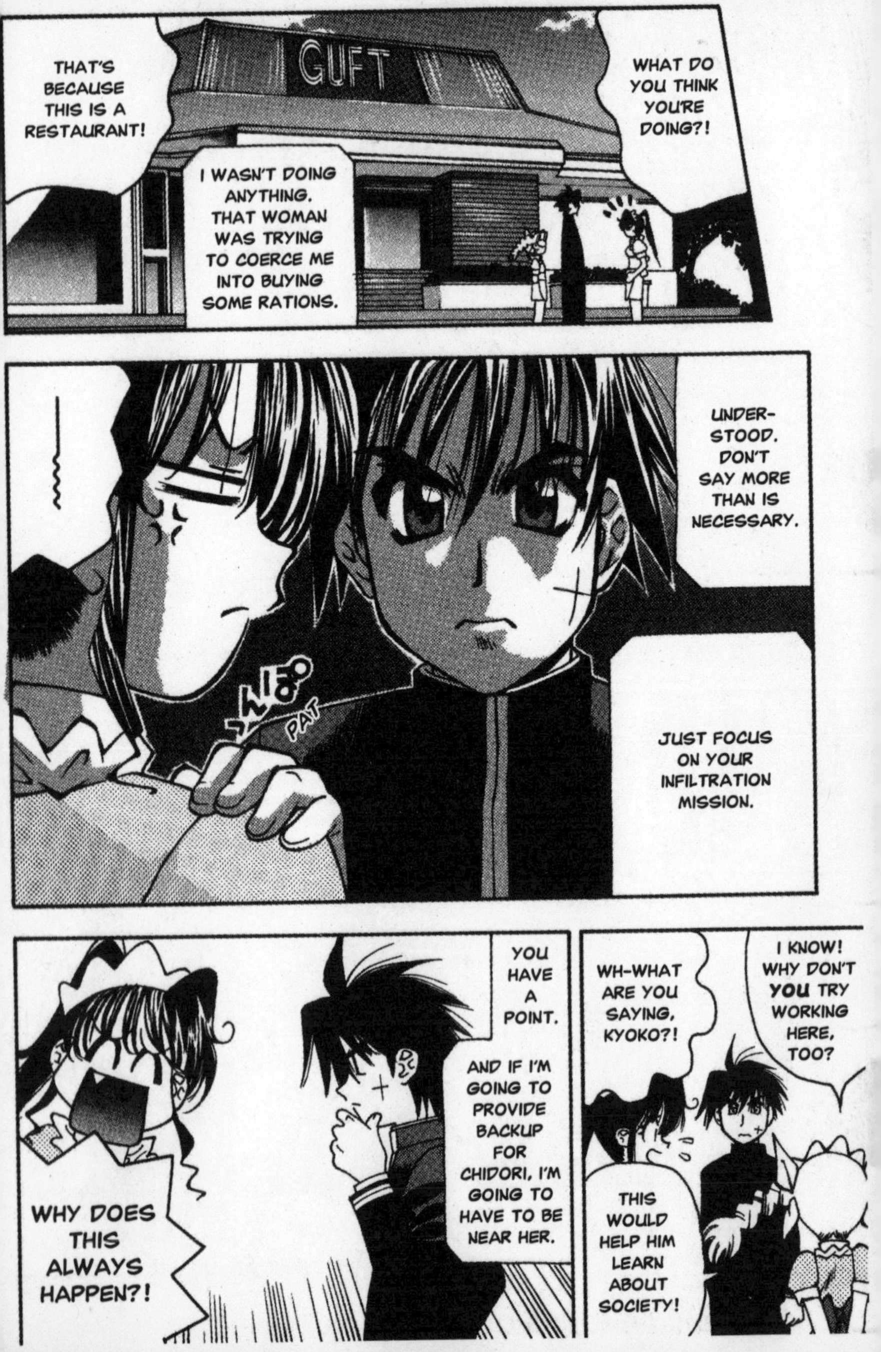
GUFT
WHAT DO YOU THINK YOU'RE DOING?!
I WASN'T DOING ANYTHING. THAT WOMAN WAS TRYING TO COERCE ME INTO BUYING SOME RATIONS.
THAT'S BECAUSE THIS IS A RESTAURANT!
UNDER-STOOD. DON'T SAY MORE THAN IS NECESSARY.
JUST FOCUS ON YOUR INFILTRATION MISSION.
PAT
I KNOW! WHY DON'T **YOU** TRY WORKING HERE, TOO?
WH-WHAT ARE YOU SAYING, KYOKO?!
THIS WOULD HELP HIM LEARN ABOUT SOCIETY!
YOU HAVE A POINT.
AND IF I'M GOING TO PROVIDE BACKUP FOR CHIDORI, I'M GOING TO HAVE TO BE NEAR HER.
WHY DOES THIS ALWAYS HAPPEN?!

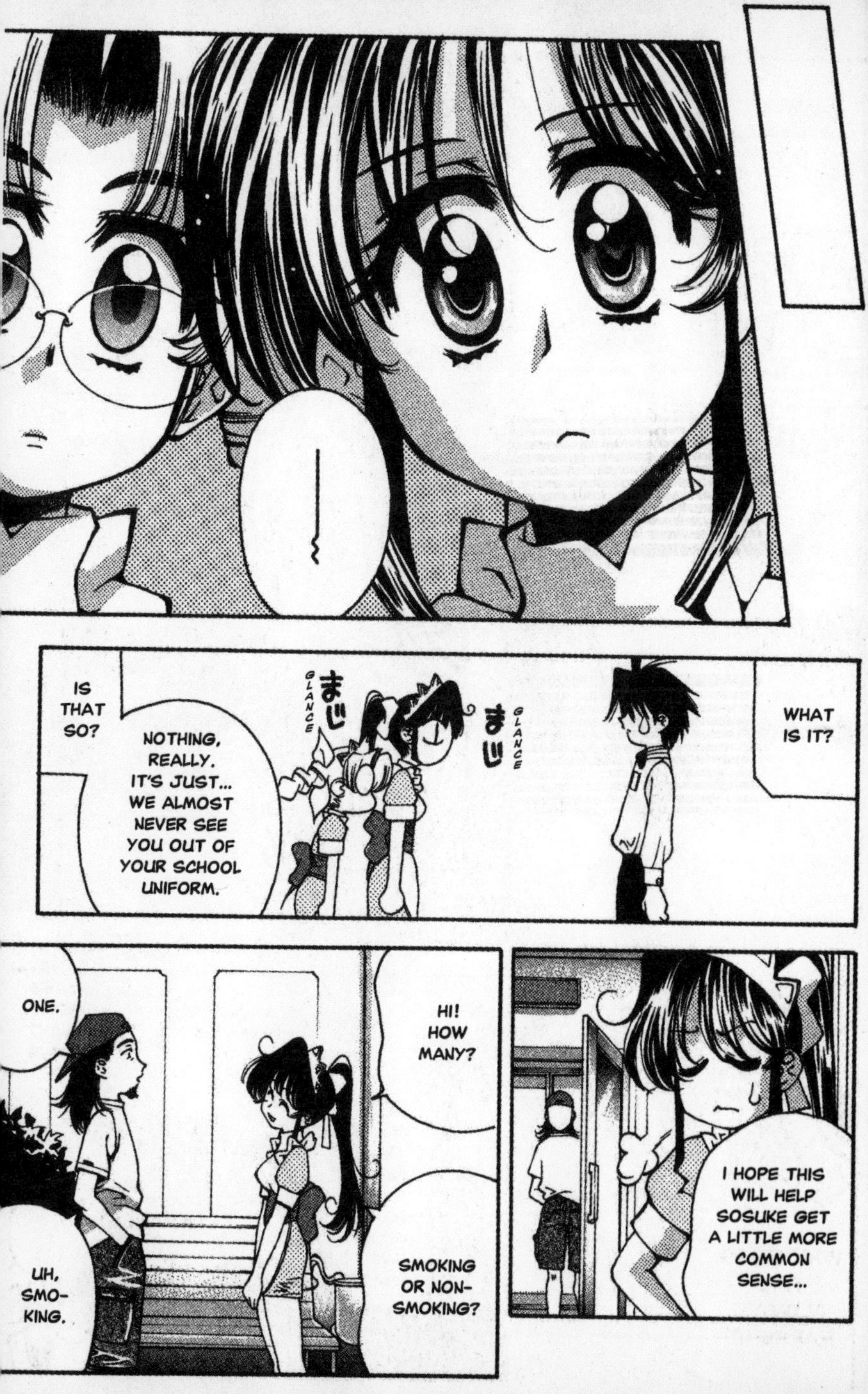
WHAT IS IT?
まじ GLANCE
まじ GLANCE
NOTHING, REALLY. IT'S JUST... WE ALMOST NEVER SEE YOU OUT OF YOUR SCHOOL UNIFORM.
IS THAT SO?
I HOPE THIS WILL HELP SOSUKE GET A LITTLE MORE COMMON SENSE...
HI! HOW MANY?
ONE.
SMOKING OR NON-SMOKING?
UH, SMO-KING.

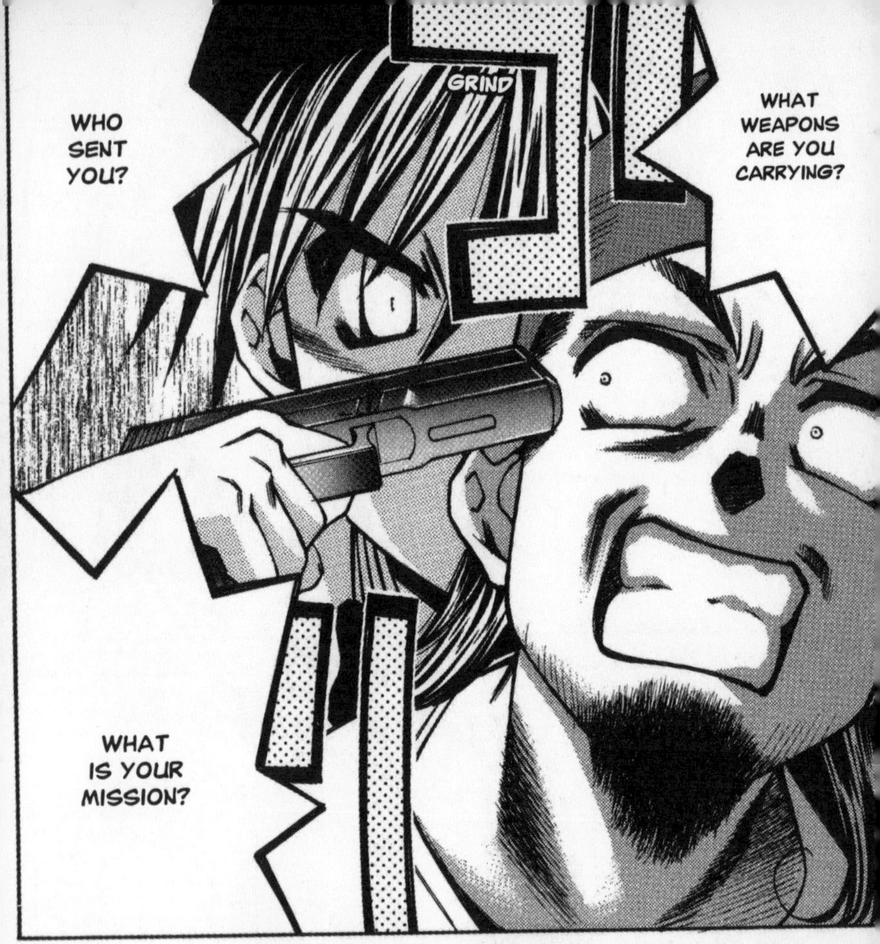
GRIND
WHO SENT YOU?
WHAT WEAPONS ARE YOU CARRYING?
WHAT IS YOUR MISSION?

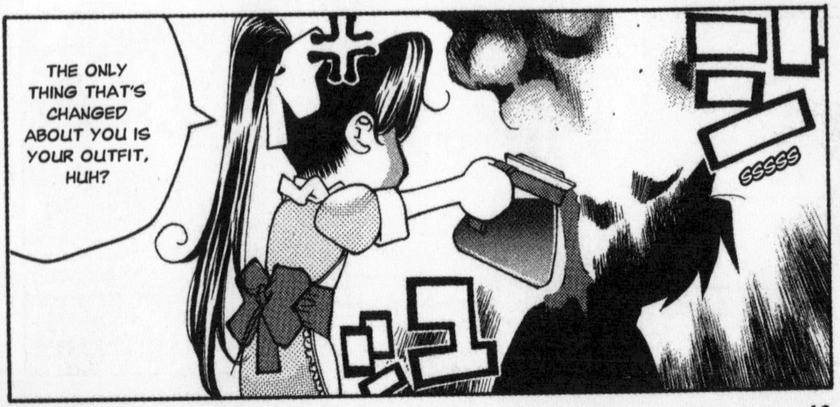
SSSSS
THE ONLY THING THAT'S CHANGED ABOUT YOU IS YOUR OUTFIT, HUH?

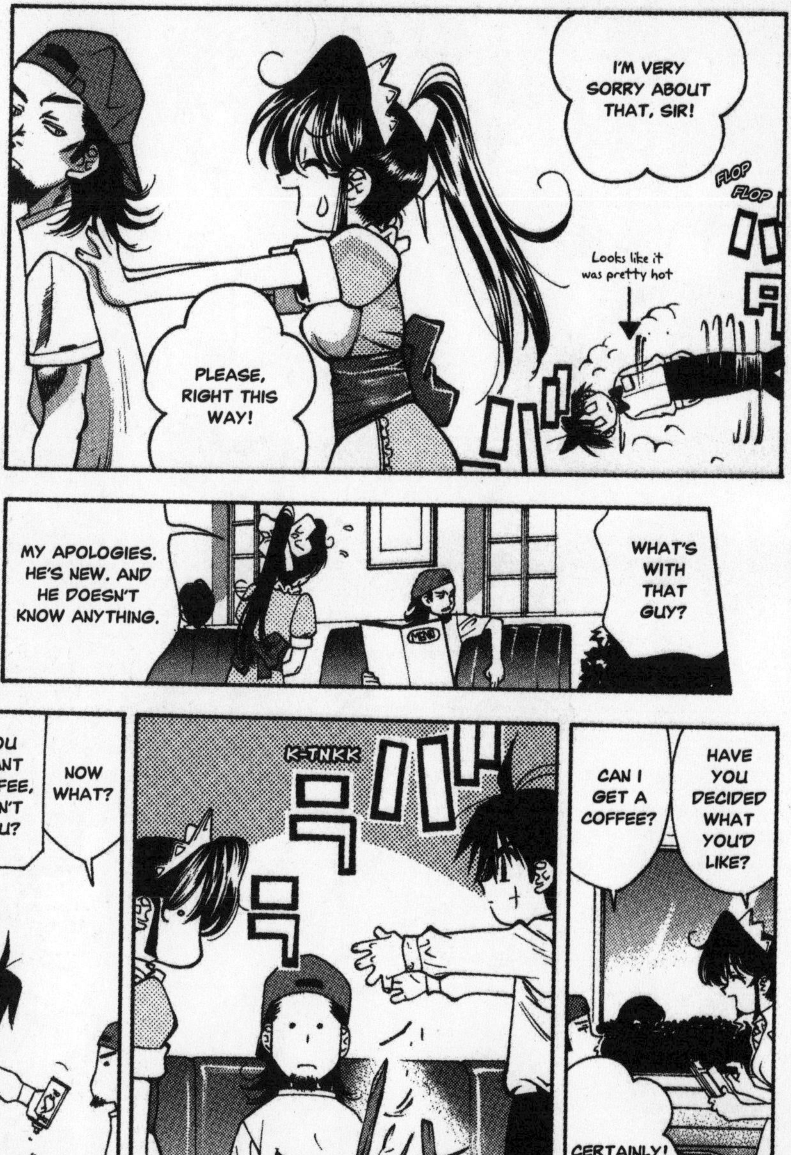
I'M VERY SORRY ABOUT THAT, SIR!
FLOP FLOP
Looks like it was pretty hot
PLEASE, RIGHT THIS WAY!
WHAT'S WITH THAT GUY?
MY APOLOGIES. HE'S NEW. AND HE DOESN'T KNOW ANYTHING.
HAVE YOU DECIDED WHAT YOU'D LIKE?
CAN I GET A COFFEE?
CERTAINLY!
K-TNKK
NOW WHAT?
YOU WANT COFFEE, DON'T YOU?

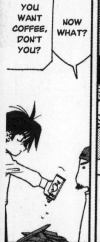

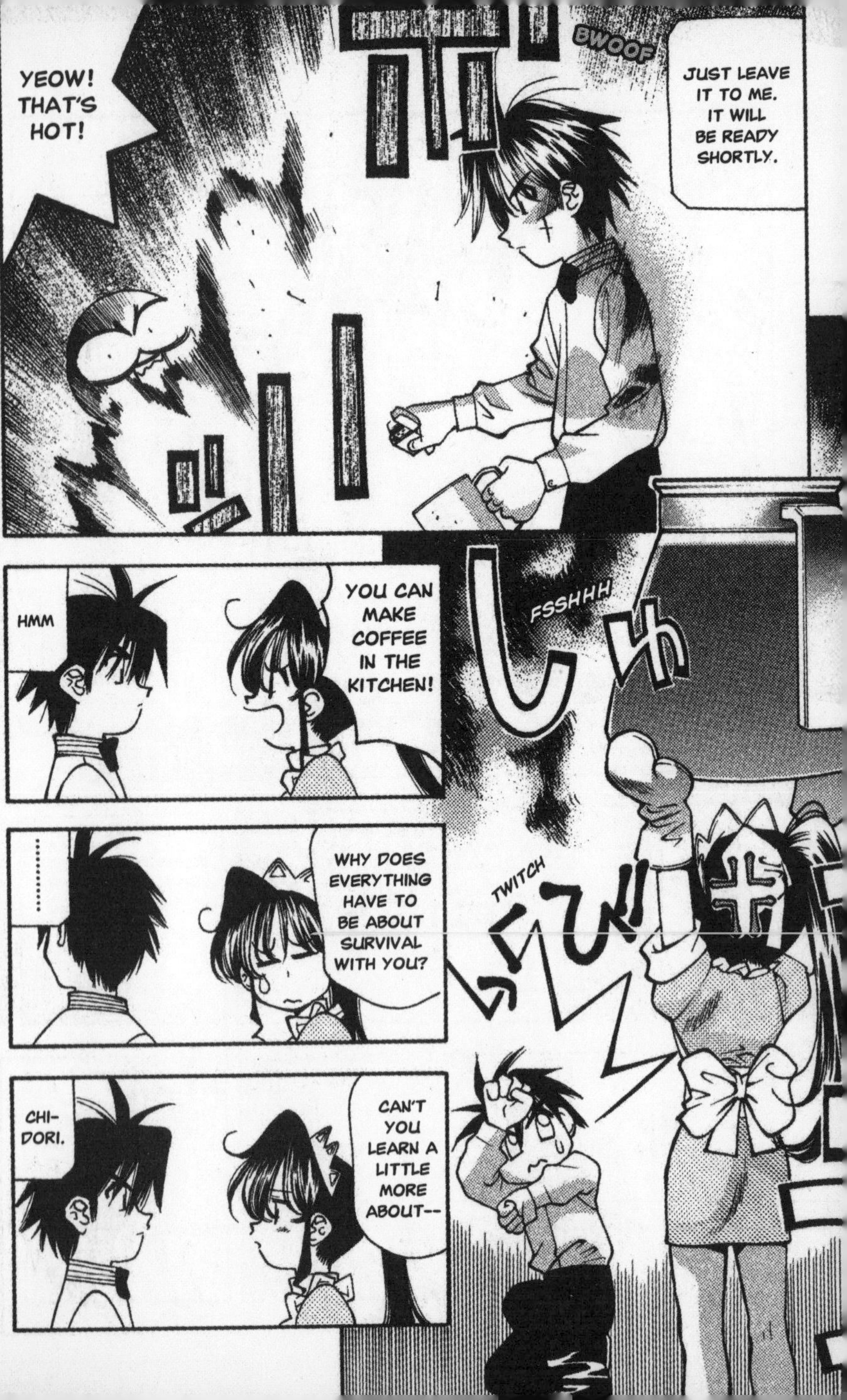
JUST LEAVE IT TO ME. IT WILL BE READY SHORTLY.
BWOOF
YEOW! THAT'S HOT!
YOU CAN MAKE COFFEE IN THE KITCHEN!
HMM
WHY DOES EVERYTHING HAVE TO BE ABOUT SURVIVAL WITH YOU?
....
CAN'T YOU LEARN A LITTLE MORE ABOUT--
CHI-DORI.
FSSHHH
TWITCH

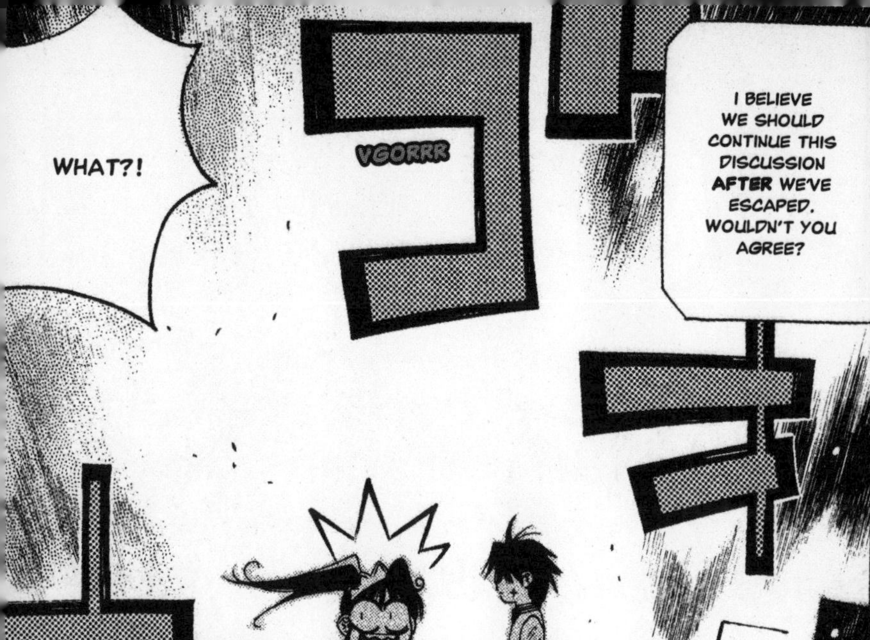
I BELIEVE WE SHOULD CONTINUE THIS DISCUSSION **AFTER** WE'VE ESCAPED. WOULDN'T YOU AGREE?
VGORRR
WHAT?!

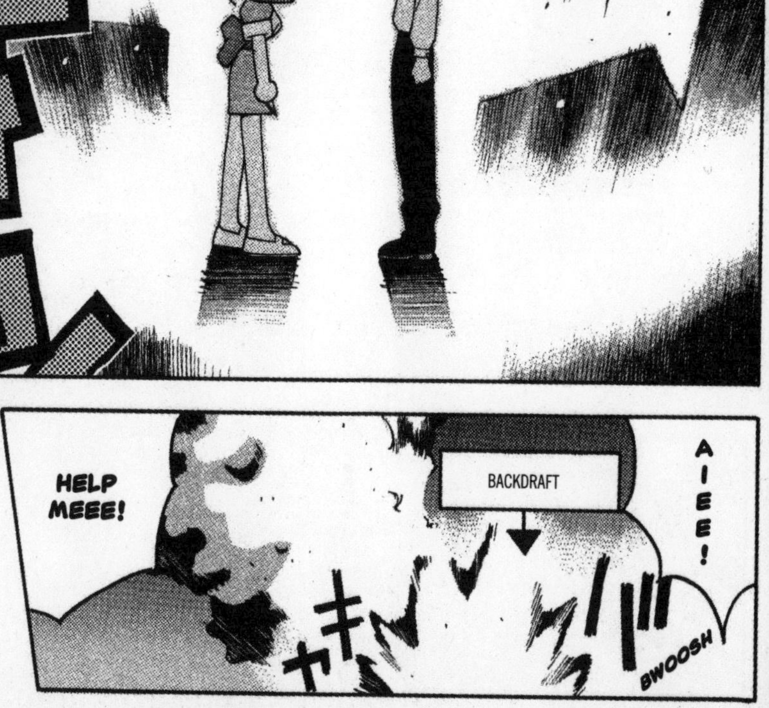
AIEEE!
BACKDRAFT
HELP MEEE!
BWOOSH

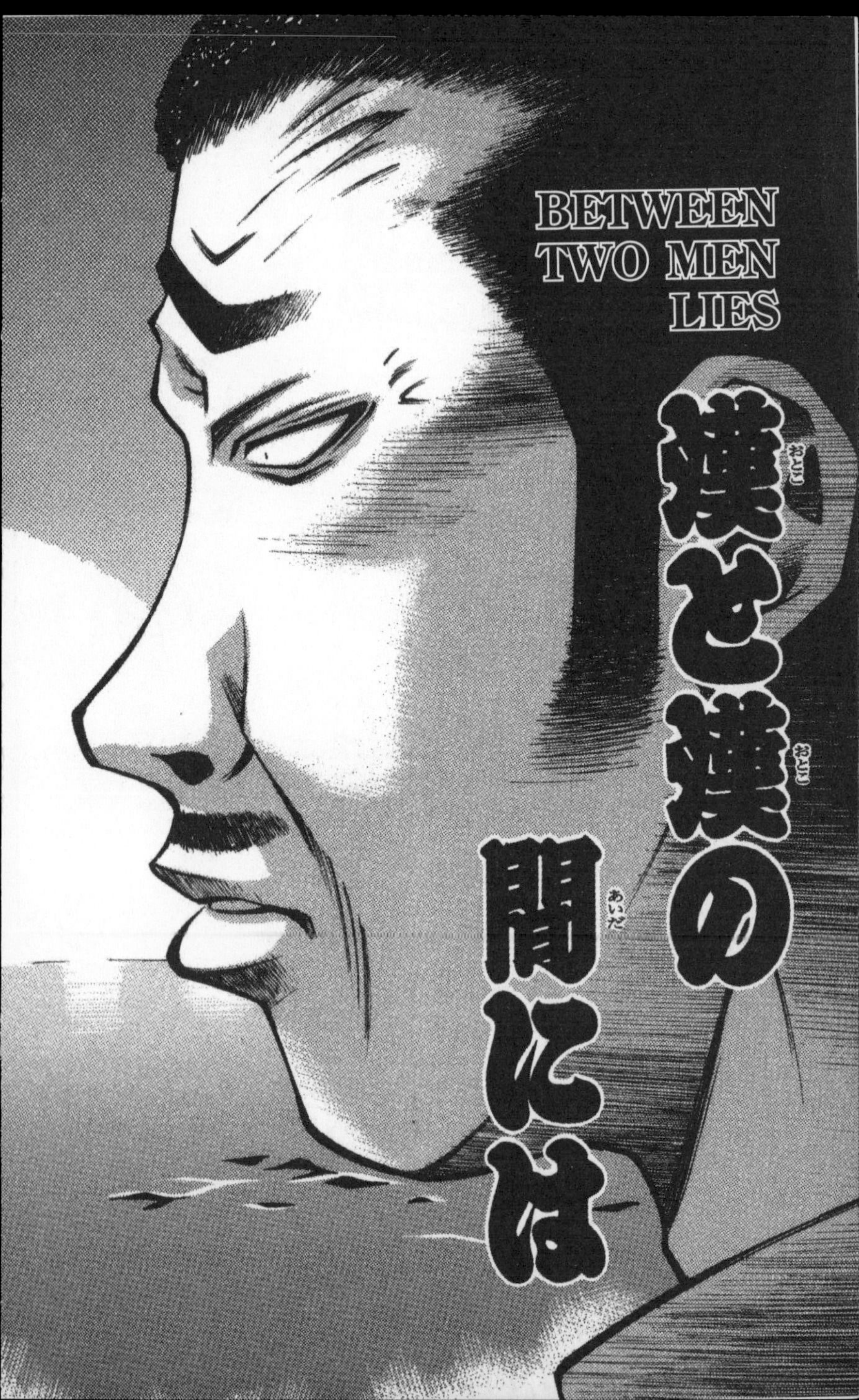
BETWEEN
TWO MEN
LIES
漢と漢の間には

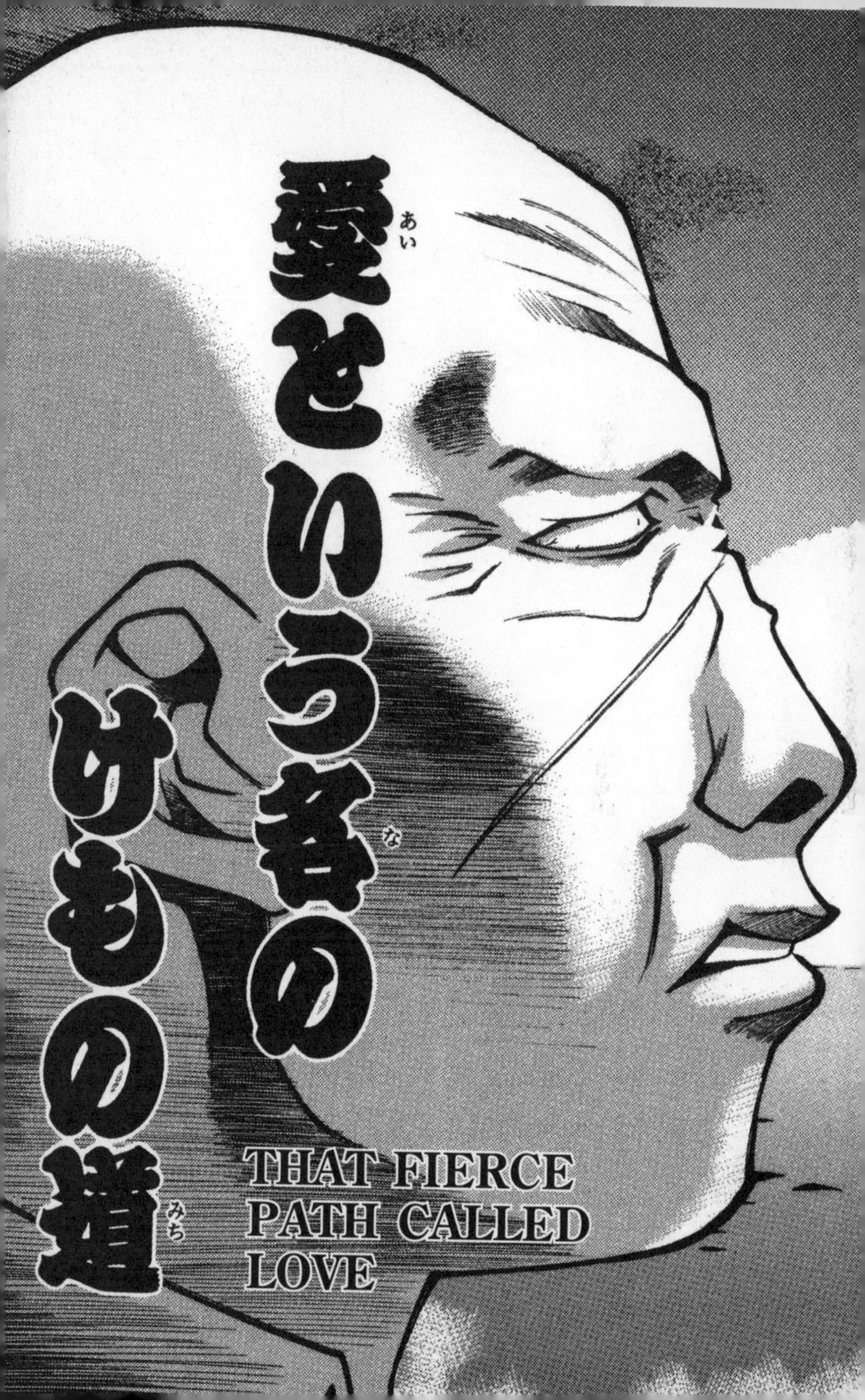
愛という名のけものの道
THAT FIERCE PATH CALLED LOVE

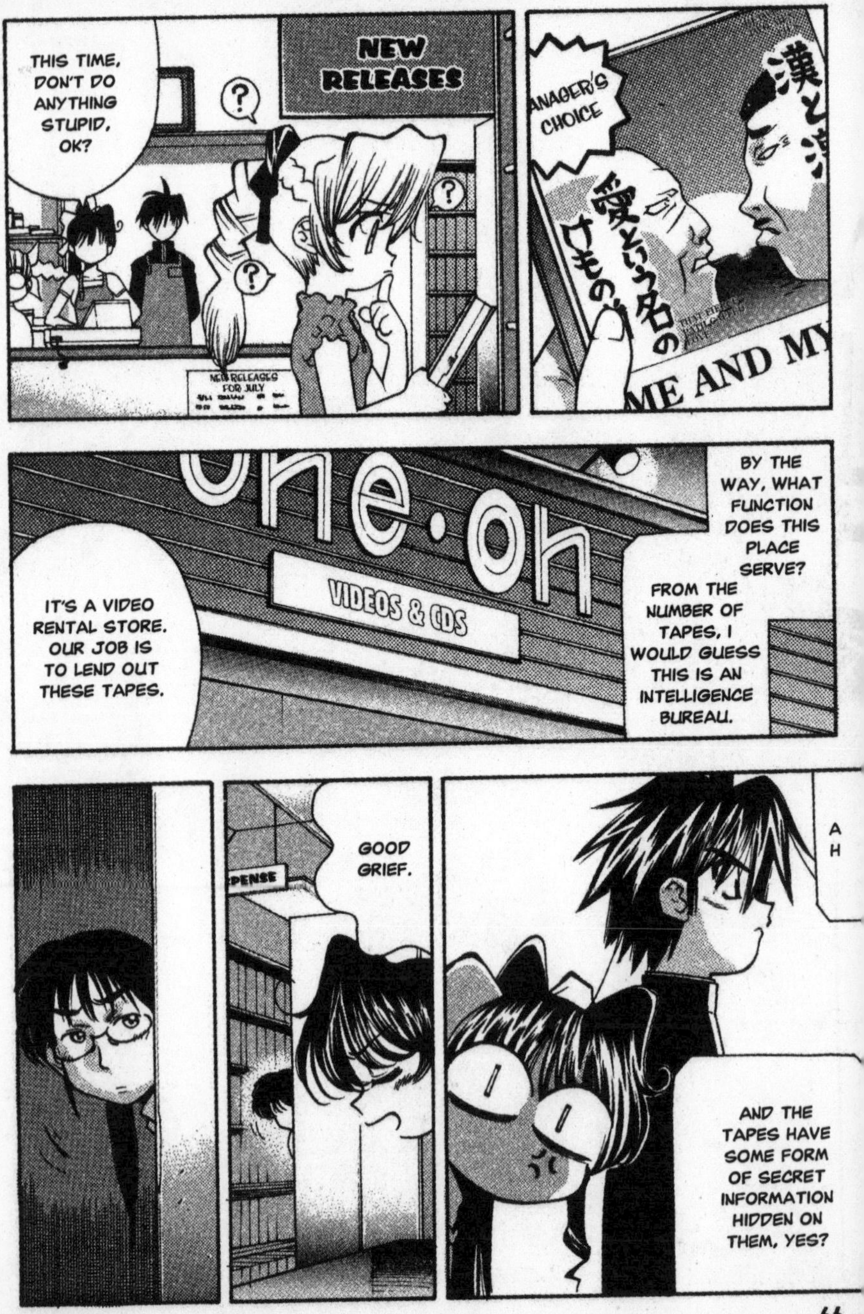
THIS TIME, DON'T DO ANYTHING STUPID, OK?
NEW RELEASES
?
?
?
NEW RELEASES FOR JULY
ANAGER'S CHOICE
漢と
愛という名の
ME AND MY
BY THE WAY, WHAT FUNCTION DOES THIS PLACE SERVE?
IT'S A VIDEO RENTAL STORE. OUR JOB IS TO LEND OUT THESE TAPES.
VIDEOS & CDS
FROM THE NUMBER OF TAPES, I WOULD GUESS THIS IS AN INTELLIGENCE BUREAU.
GOOD GRIEF.
AH
AND THE TAPES HAVE SOME FORM OF SECRET INFORMATION HIDDEN ON THEM, YES?

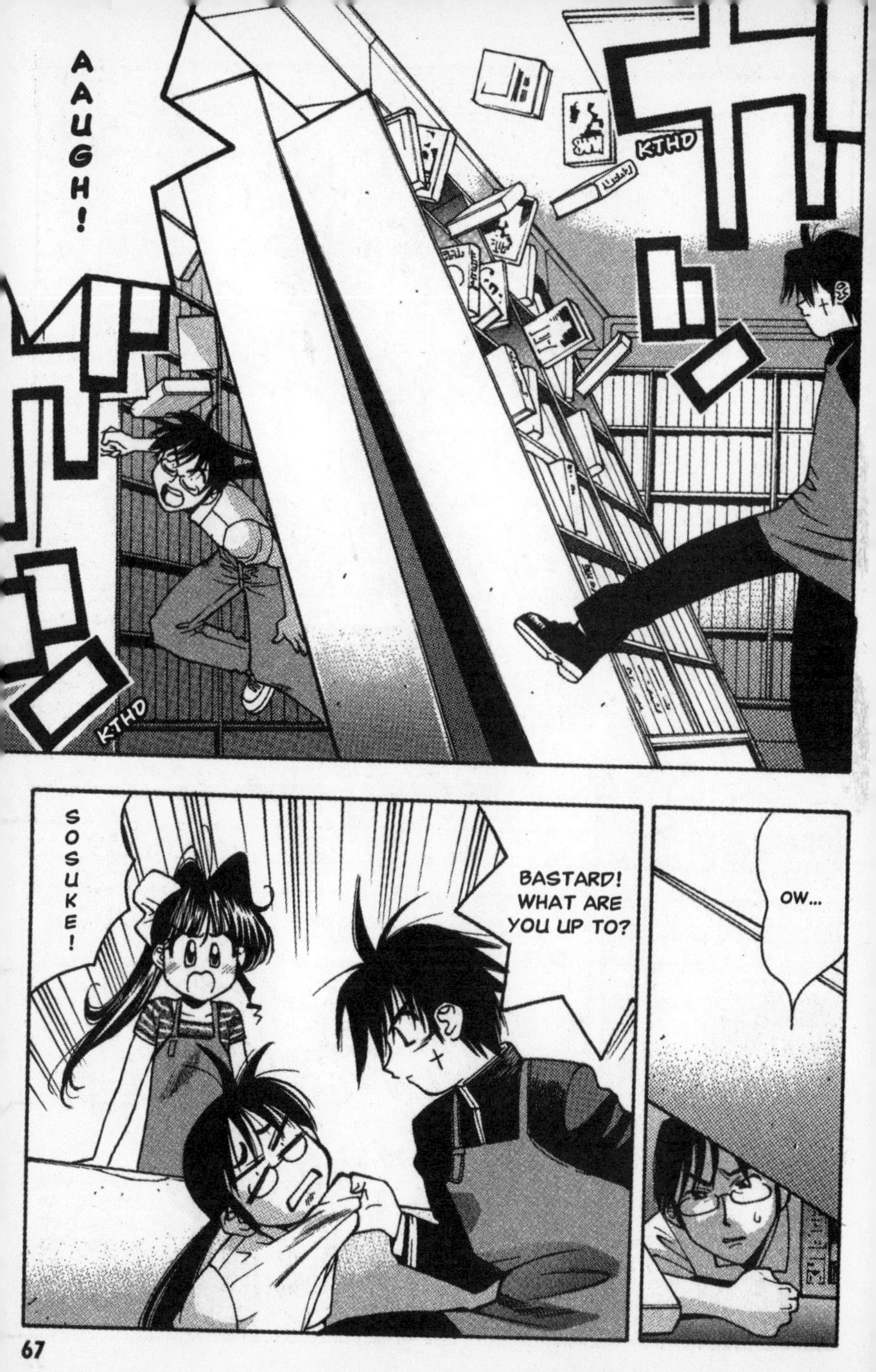
KTHD
AAUGH!
KTHD
OW...
BASTARD! WHAT ARE YOU UP TO?
SOSUKE!

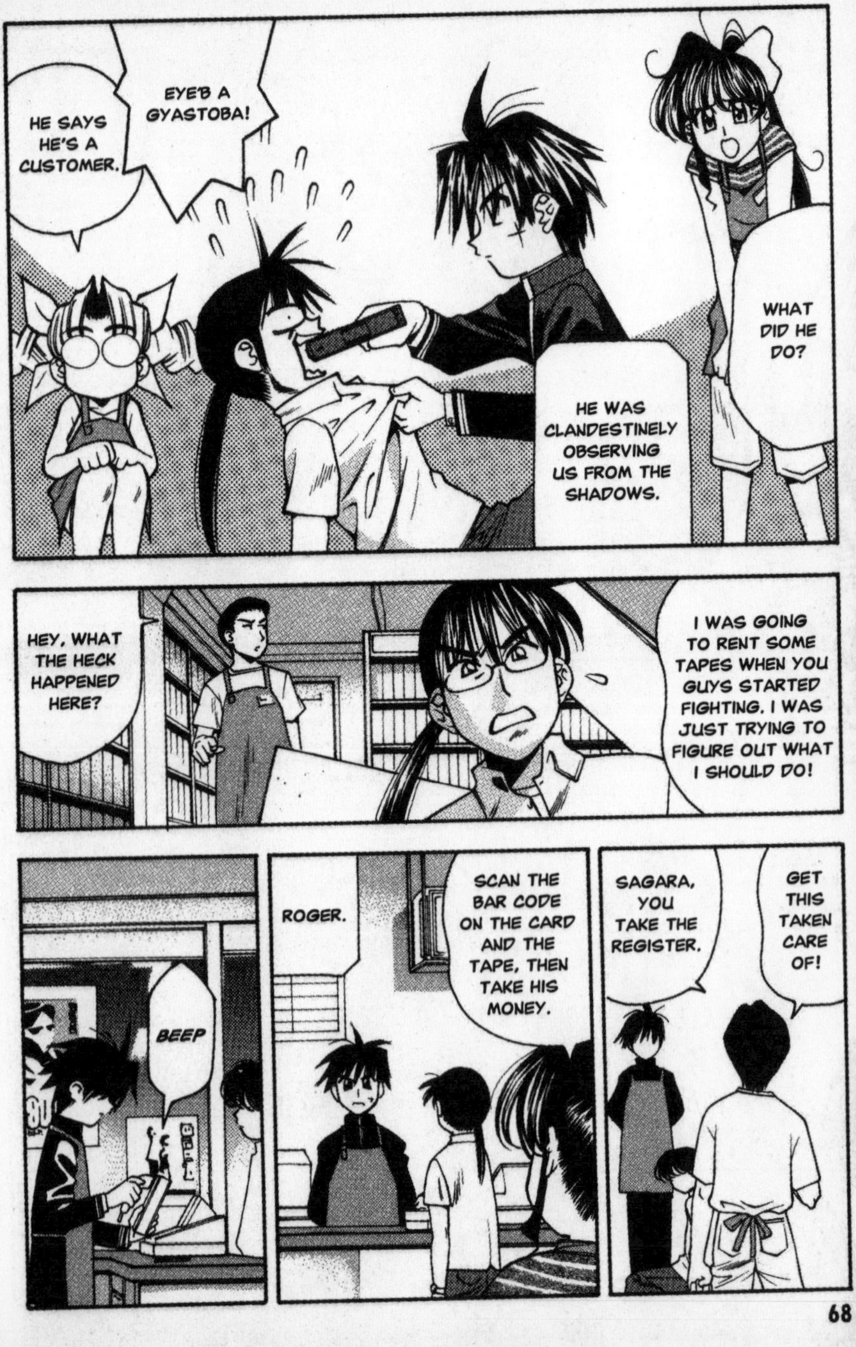

WHAT DID HE DO?
HE WAS CLANDESTINELY OBSERVING US FROM THE SHADOWS.
EYE'B A GYASTOBA!
HE SAYS HE'S A CUSTOMER.
I WAS GOING TO RENT SOME TAPES WHEN YOU GUYS STARTED FIGHTING. I WAS JUST TRYING TO FIGURE OUT WHAT I SHOULD DO!
HEY, WHAT THE HECK HAPPENED HERE?
GET THIS TAKEN CARE OF!
SAGARA, YOU TAKE THE REGISTER.
SCAN THE BAR CODE ON THE CARD AND THE TAPE, THEN TAKE HIS MONEY.
ROGER.
BEEP

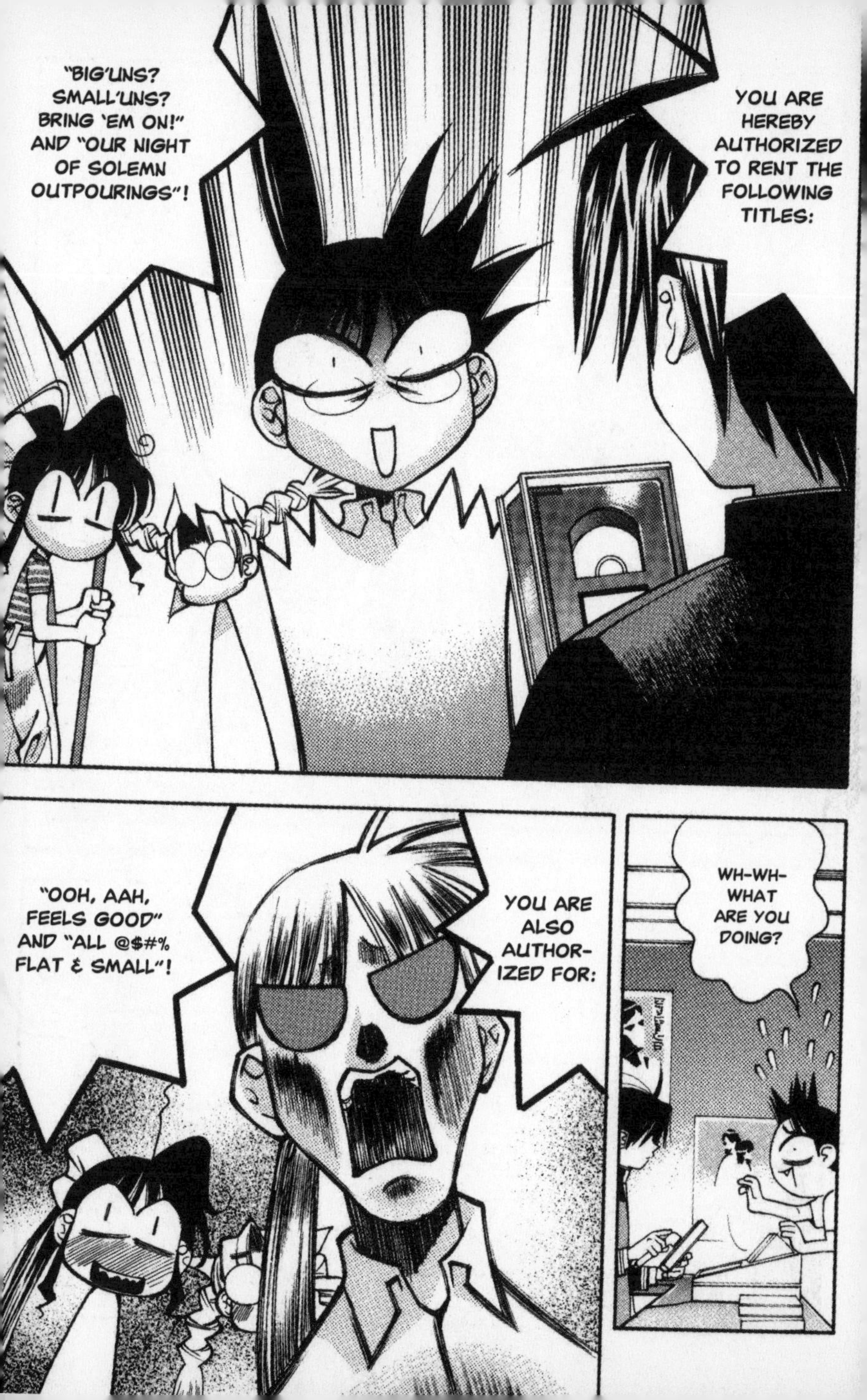
YOU ARE HEREBY AUTHORIZED TO RENT THE FOLLOWING TITLES:
"BIG'UNS? SMALL'UNS? BRING 'EM ON!" AND "OUR NIGHT OF SOLEMN OUTPOURINGS"!
WH-WH-WHAT ARE YOU DOING?
YOU ARE ALSO AUTHOR-IZED FOR:
"OOH, AAH, FEELS GOOD" AND "ALL @$#% FLAT & SMALL"!

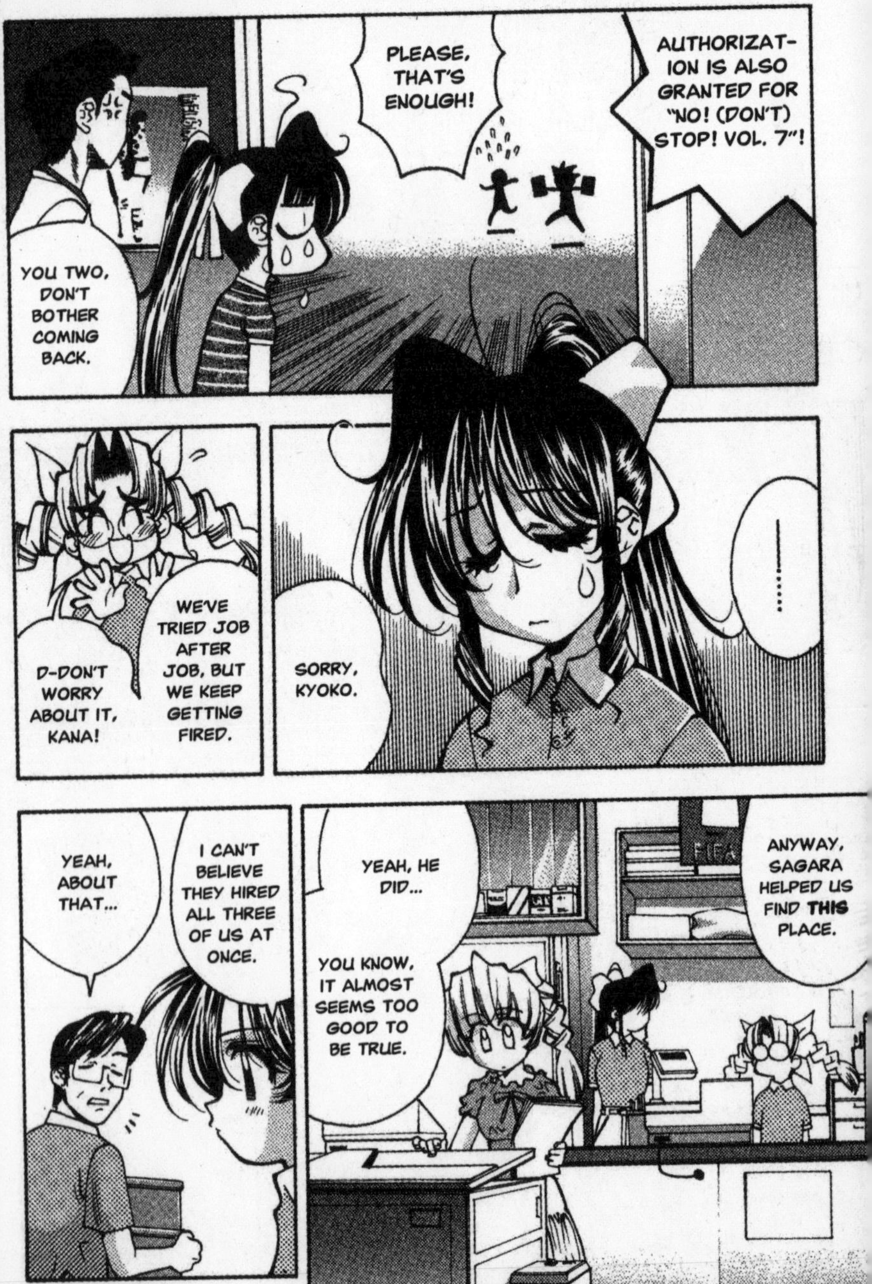
AUTHORIZATION IS ALSO GRANTED FOR "NO! (DON'T) STOP! VOL. 7"!
PLEASE, THAT'S ENOUGH!
YOU TWO, DON'T BOTHER COMING BACK.
......!
SORRY, KYOKO.
WE'VE TRIED JOB AFTER JOB, BUT WE KEEP GETTING FIRED.
D-DON'T WORRY ABOUT IT, KANA!
ANYWAY, SAGARA HELPED US FIND **THIS** PLACE.
YEAH, HE DID...
YOU KNOW, IT ALMOST SEEMS TOO GOOD TO BE TRUE.
I CAN'T BELIEVE THEY HIRED ALL THREE OF US AT ONCE.
YEAH, ABOUT THAT...

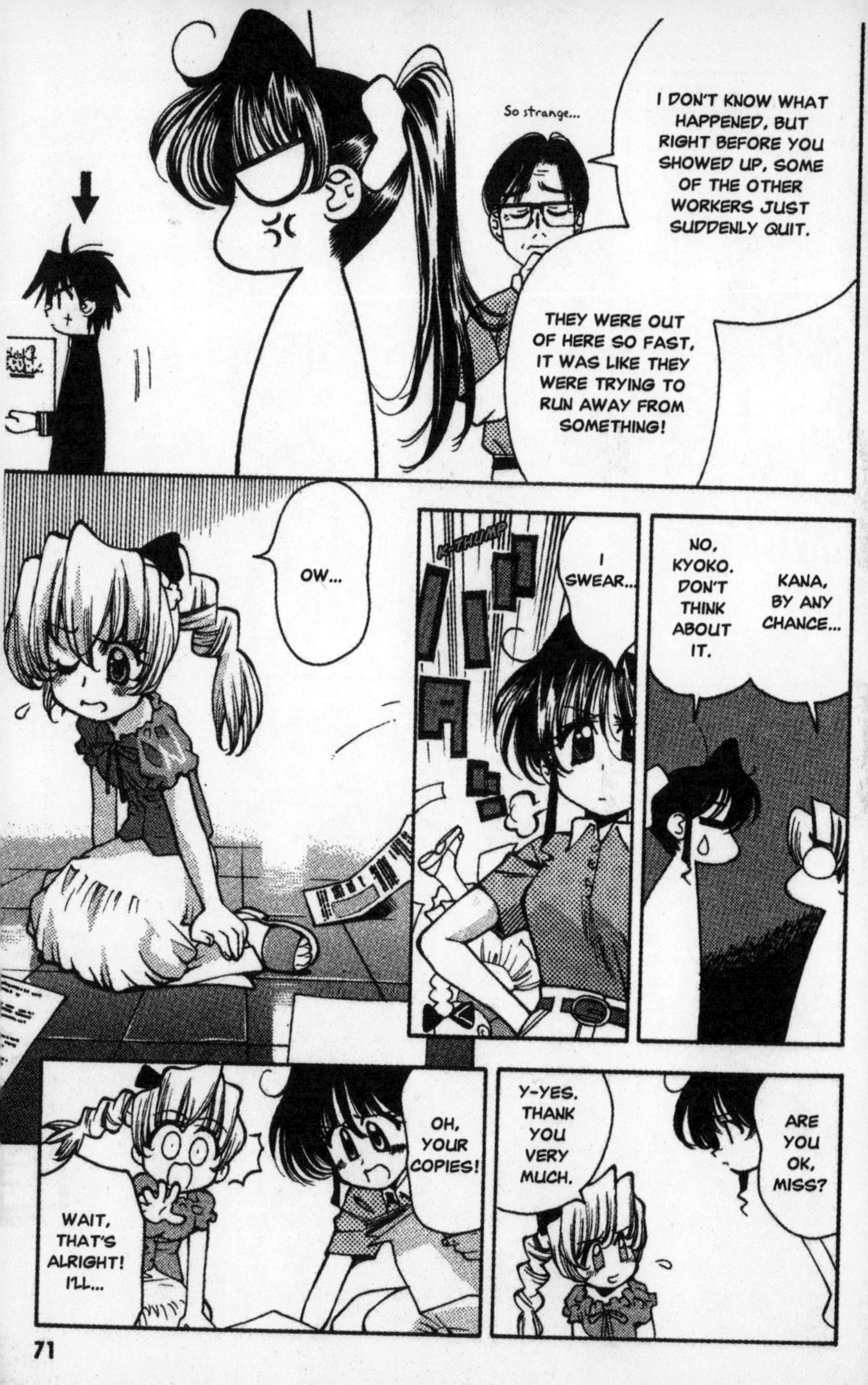
I DON'T KNOW WHAT HAPPENED, BUT RIGHT BEFORE YOU SHOWED UP, SOME OF THE OTHER WORKERS JUST SUDDENLY QUIT.
So strange...
THEY WERE OUT OF HERE SO FAST, IT WAS LIKE THEY WERE TRYING TO RUN AWAY FROM SOMETHING!
KANA, BY ANY CHANCE...
NO, KYOKO. DON'T THINK ABOUT IT.
I SWEAR...
K-THUMP
OW...
ARE YOU OK, MISS?
Y-YES. THANK YOU VERY MUCH.
OH, YOUR COPIES!
WAIT, THAT'S ALRIGHT! I'LL...

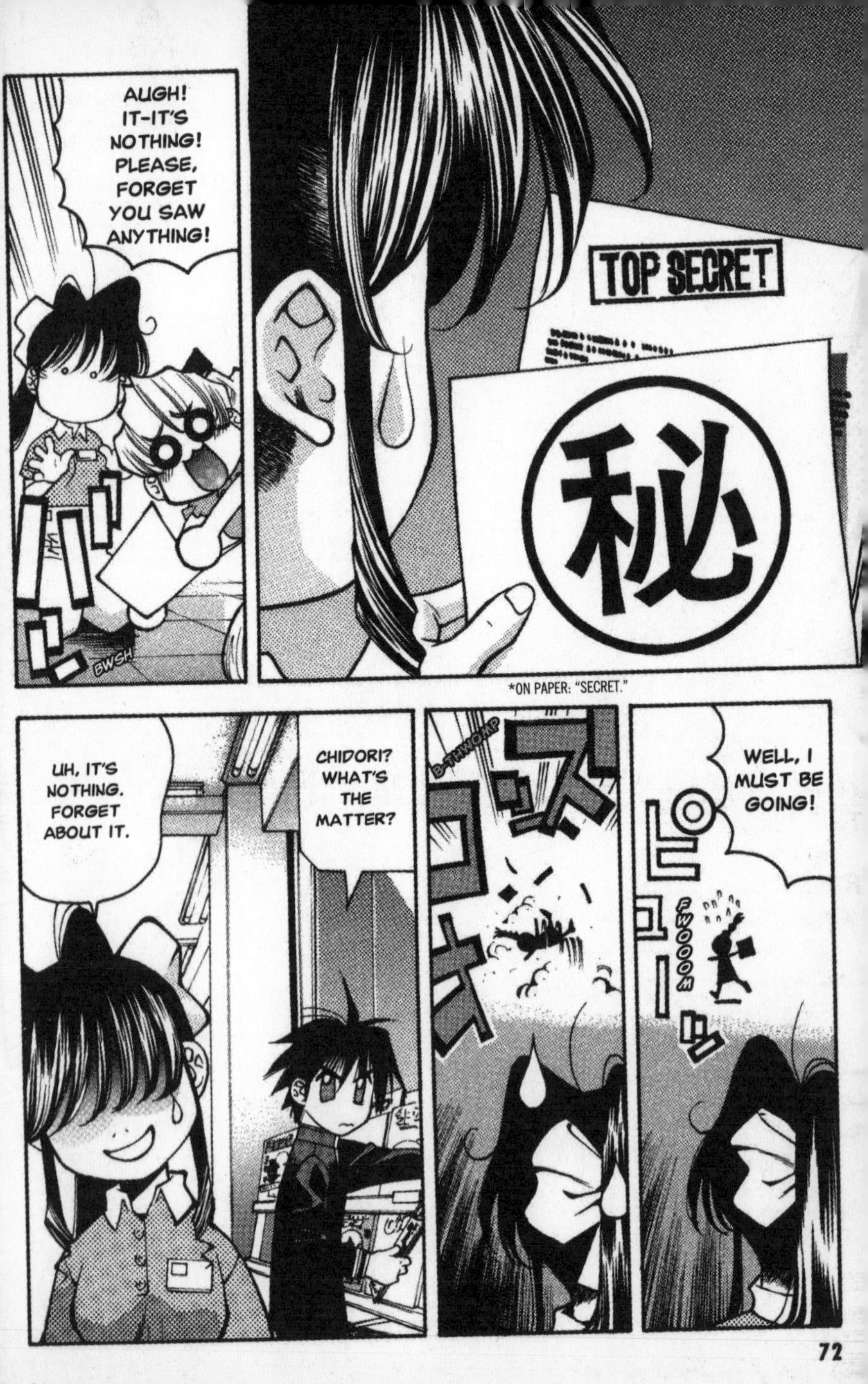
AUGH! IT-IT'S NOTHING! PLEASE, FORGET YOU SAW ANYTHING!
BWSH
TOP SECRET
秘
*ON PAPER: "SECRET."
UH, IT'S NOTHING. FORGET ABOUT IT.
CHIDORI? WHAT'S THE MATTER?
D-THWOMP
WELL, I MUST BE GOING!
FWOOOM

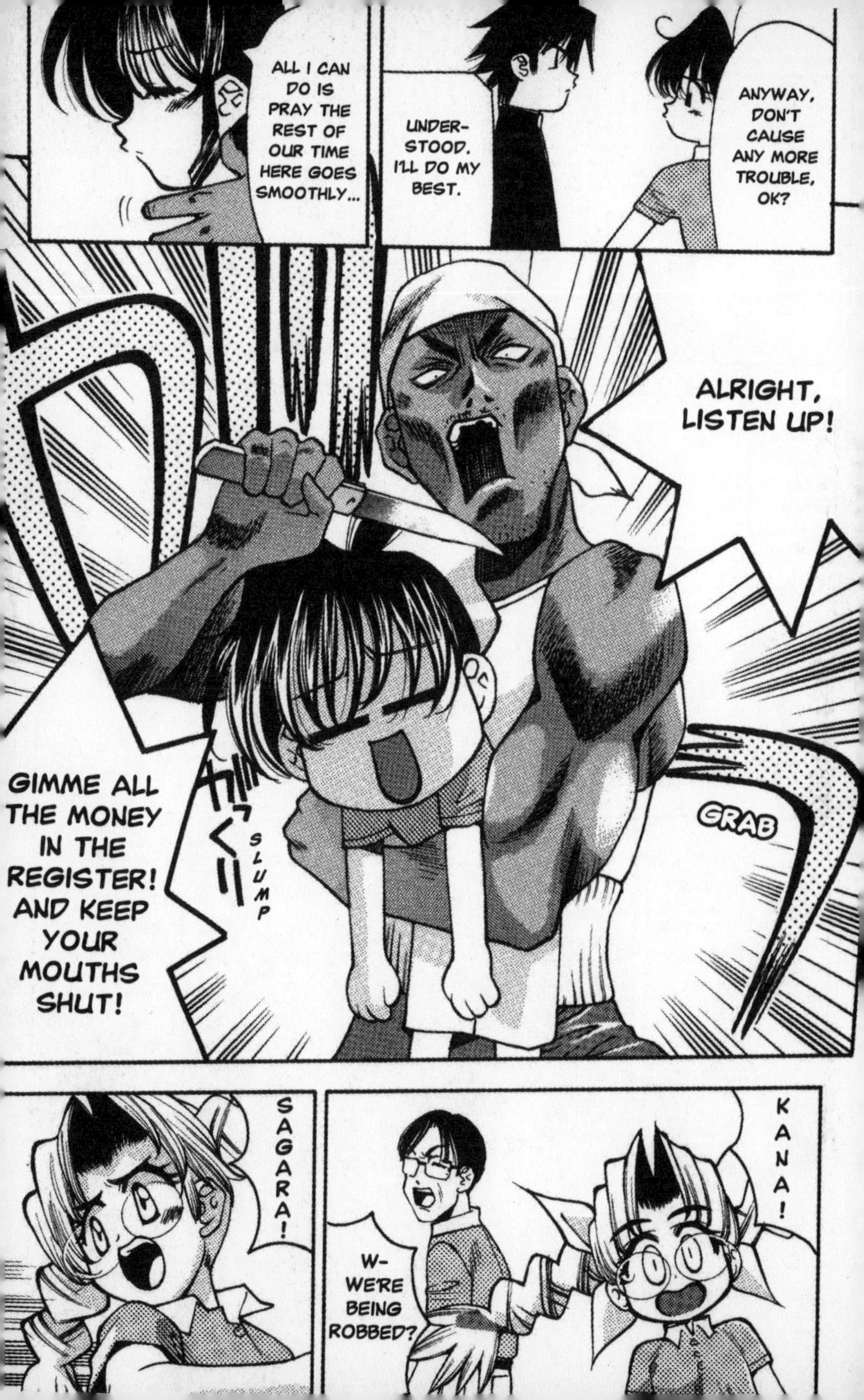
ANYWAY, DON'T CAUSE ANY MORE TROUBLE, OK?
UNDER-STOOD. I'LL DO MY BEST.
ALL I CAN DO IS PRAY THE REST OF OUR TIME HERE GOES SMOOTHLY...
ALRIGHT, LISTEN UP!
GRAB
SLUMP
GIMME ALL THE MONEY IN THE REGISTER! AND KEEP YOUR MOUTHS SHUT!
KANA!
W-WE'RE BEING ROBBED?
SAGARA!

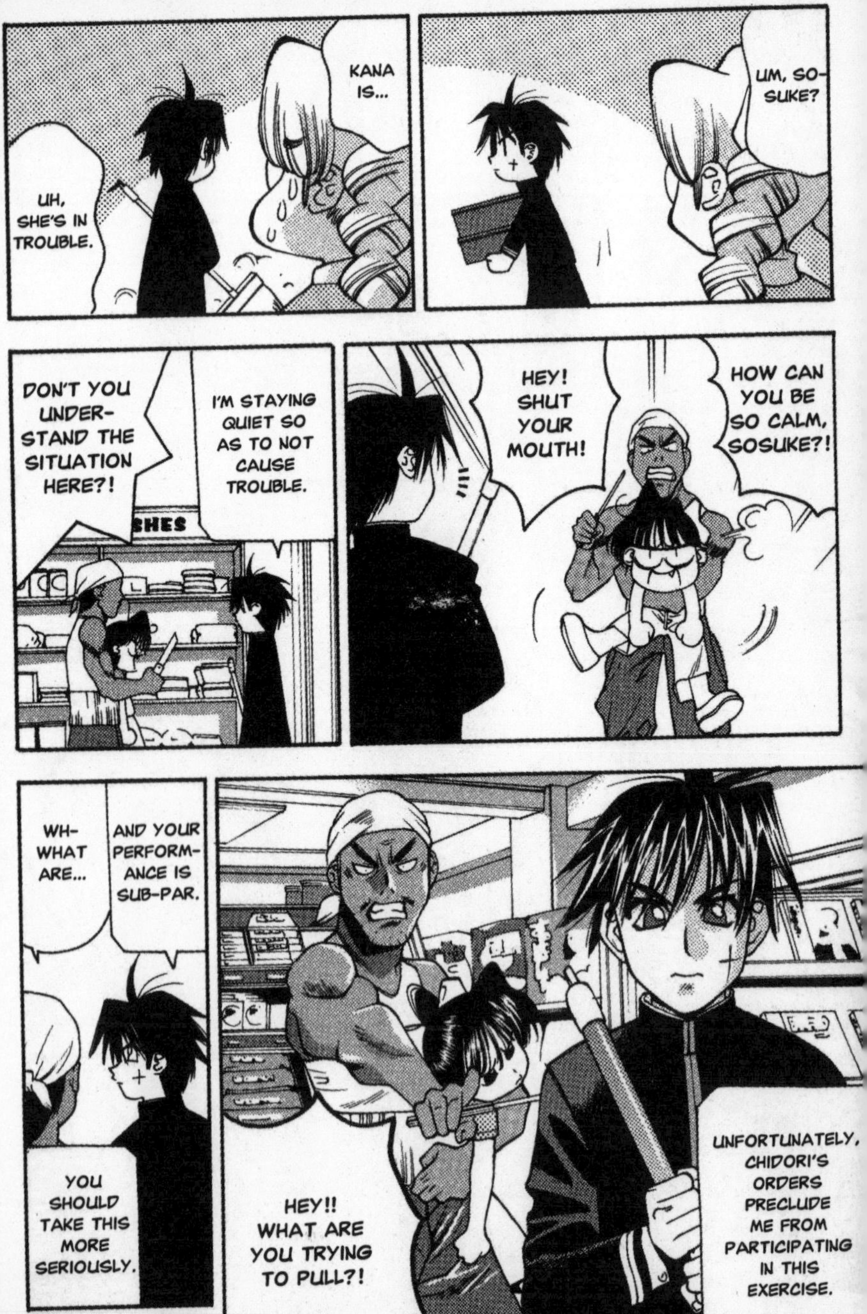
KANA IS...
UH, SHE'S IN TROUBLE.
UM, SO-SUKE?
DON'T YOU UNDER-STAND THE SITUATION HERE?!
I'M STAYING QUIET SO AS TO NOT CAUSE TROUBLE.
HEY! SHUT YOUR MOUTH!
HOW CAN YOU BE SO CALM, SOSUKE?!
WH- WHAT ARE...
AND YOUR PERFORM-ANCE IS SUB-PAR.
YOU SHOULD TAKE THIS MORE SERIOUSLY.
HEY!! WHAT ARE YOU TRYING TO PULL?!
UNFORTUNATELY, CHIDORI'S ORDERS PRECLUDE ME FROM PARTICIPATING IN THIS EXERCISE.

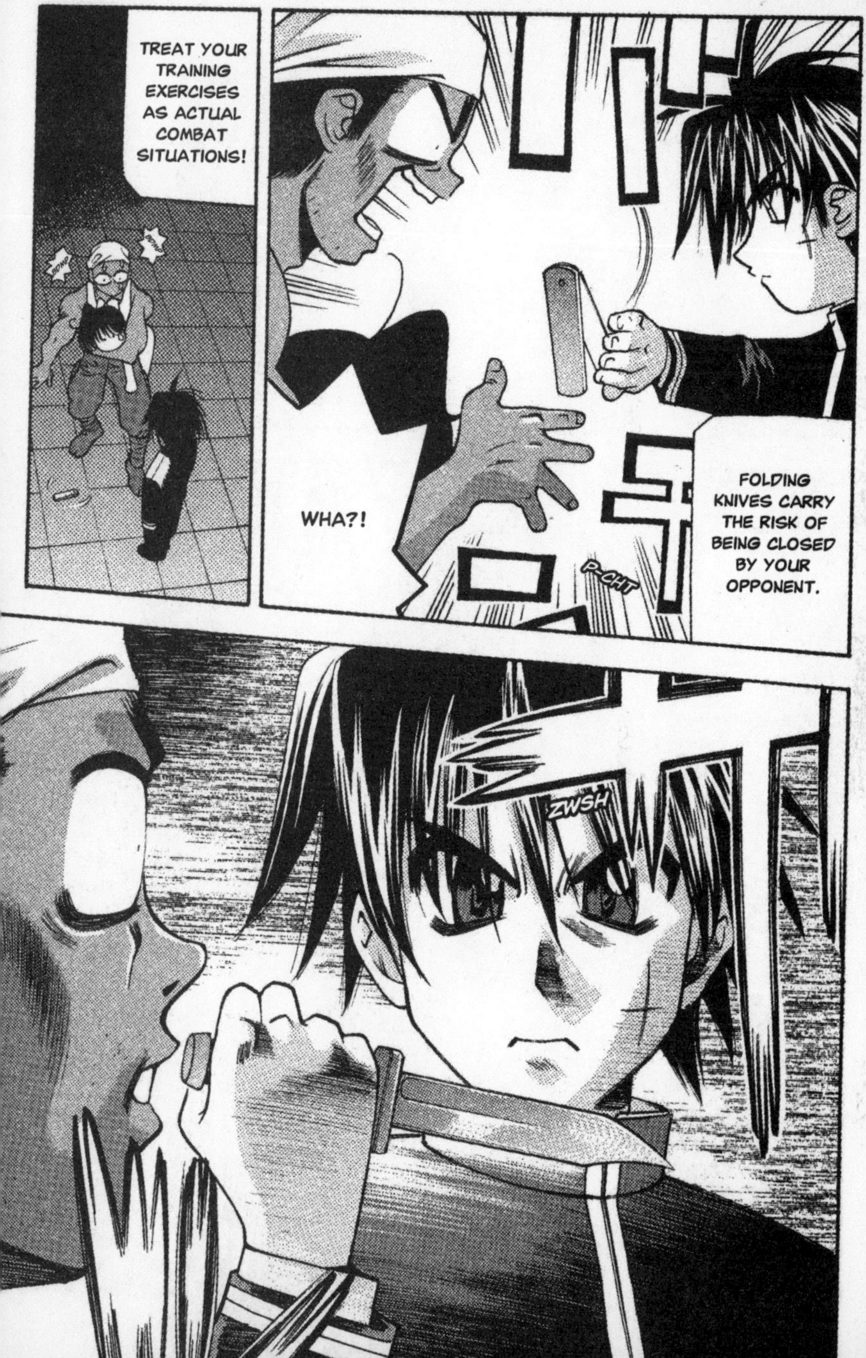
FOLDING KNIVES CARRY THE RISK OF BEING CLOSED BY YOUR OPPONENT.
P-CHT
WHA?!
TREAT YOUR TRAINING EXERCISES AS ACTUAL COMBAT SITUATIONS!
ZWSH

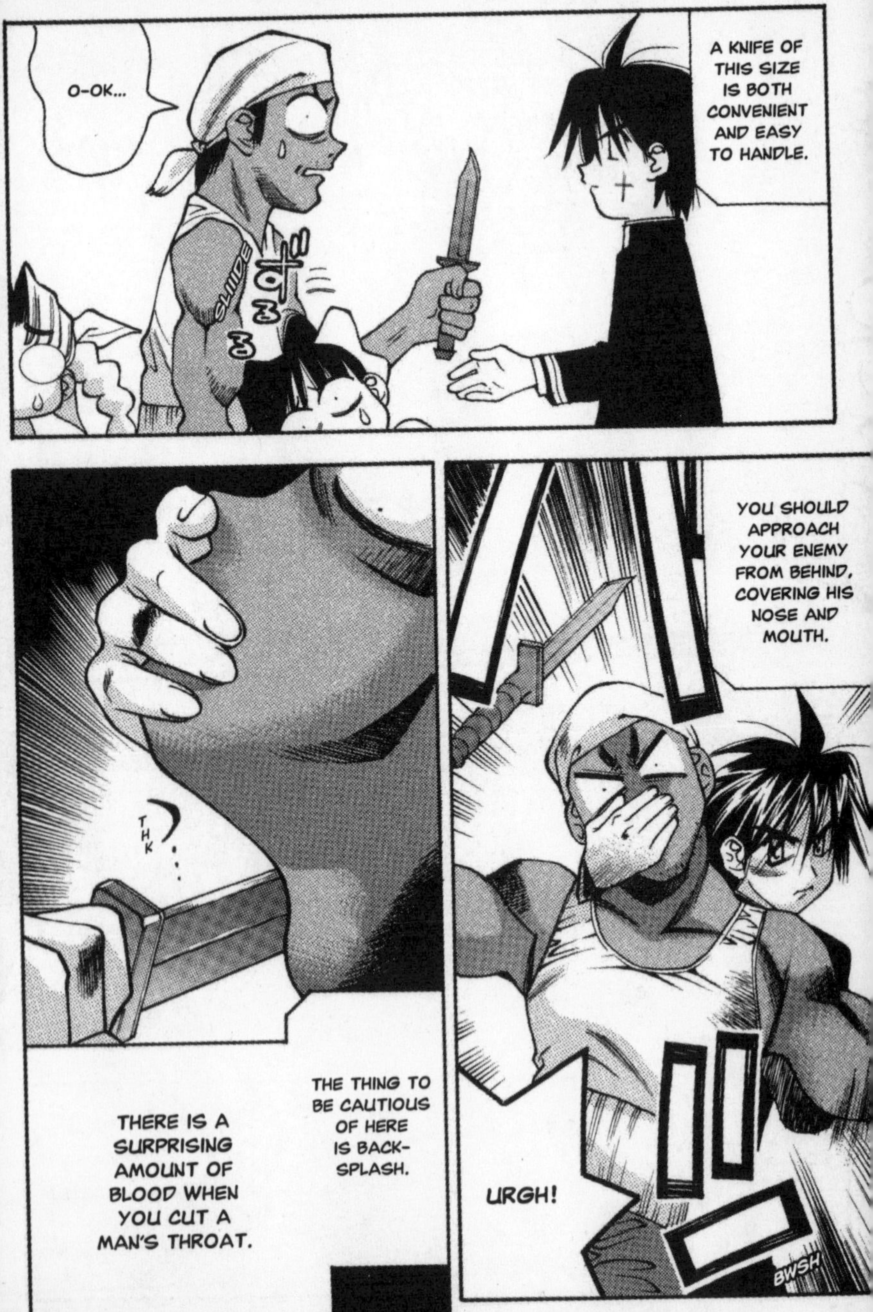
A KNIFE OF THIS SIZE IS BOTH CONVENIENT AND EASY TO HANDLE.
O-OK...
YOU SHOULD APPROACH YOUR ENEMY FROM BEHIND, COVERING HIS NOSE AND MOUTH.
URGH!
BWSH
THK
THE THING TO BE CAUTIOUS OF HERE IS BACK-SPLASH.
THERE IS A SURPRISING AMOUNT OF BLOOD WHEN YOU CUT A MAN'S THROAT.

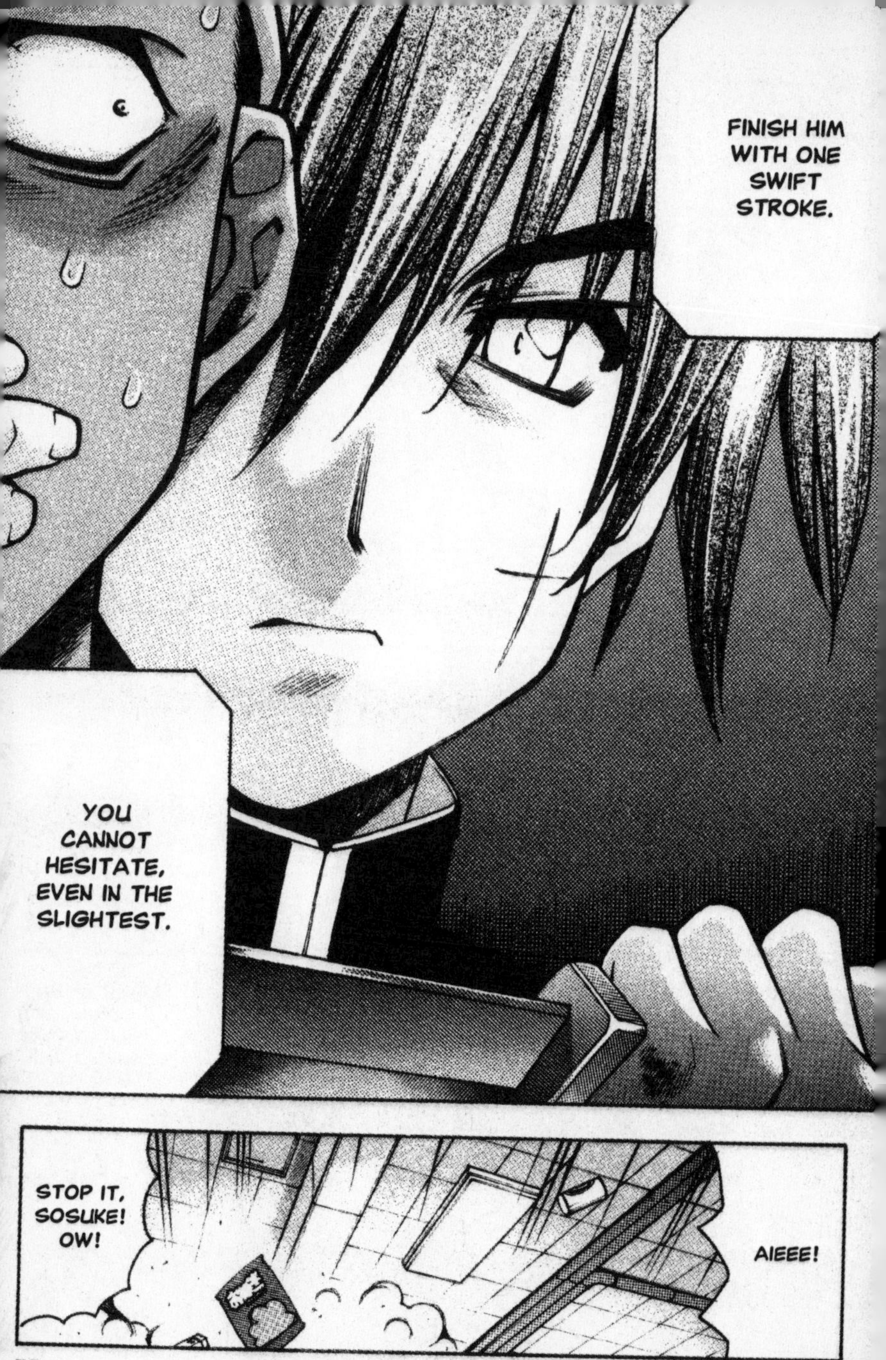
FINISH HIM WITH ONE SWIFT STROKE.
YOU CANNOT HESITATE, EVEN IN THE SLIGHTEST.
AIEEE!
STOP IT, SOSUKE! OW!

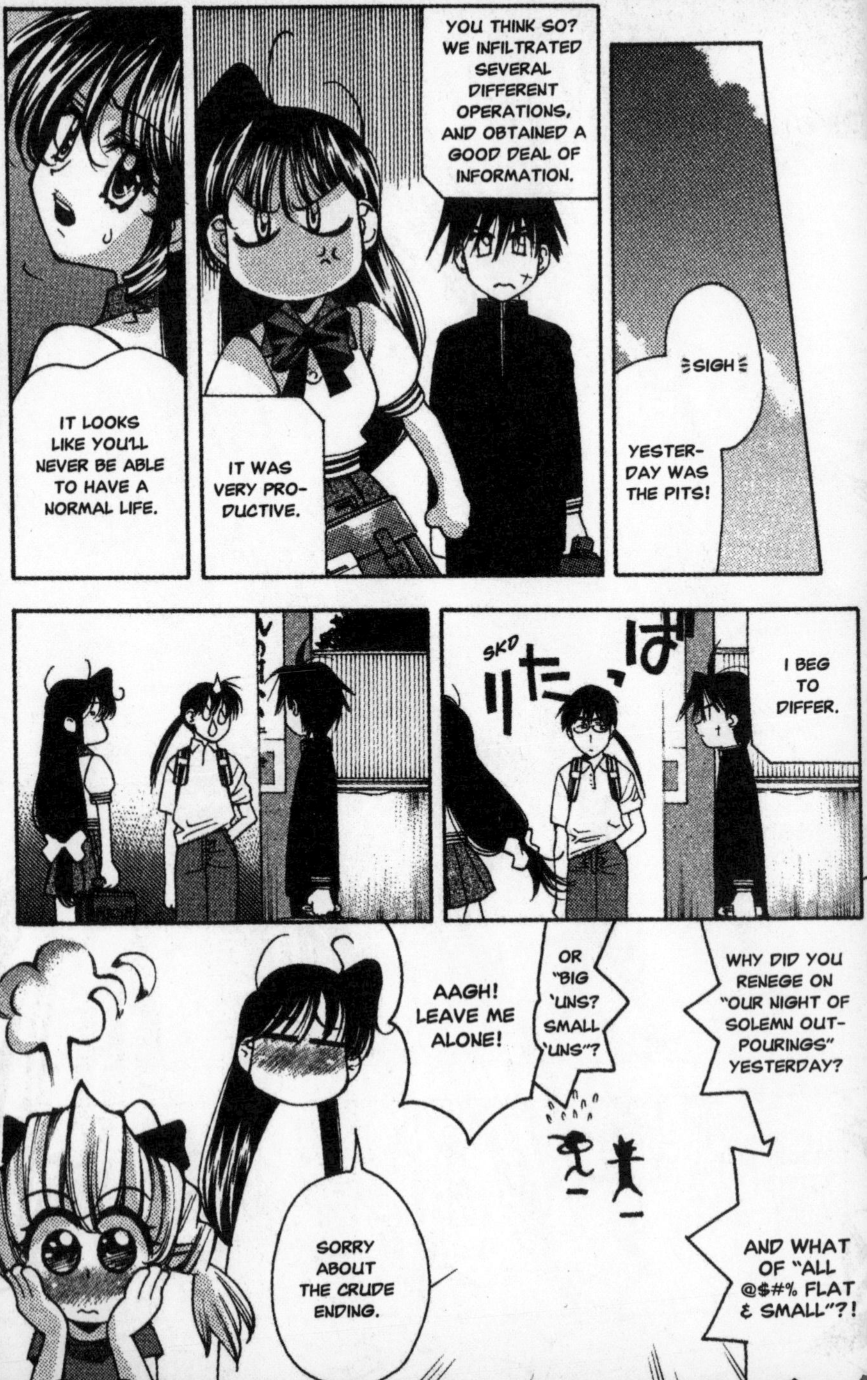

SIGH
YESTER-DAY WAS THE PITS!
YOU THINK SO? WE INFILTRATED SEVERAL DIFFERENT OPERATIONS, AND OBTAINED A GOOD DEAL OF INFORMATION.
IT WAS VERY PRO-DUCTIVE.
IT LOOKS LIKE YOU'LL NEVER BE ABLE TO HAVE A NORMAL LIFE.
I BEG TO DIFFER.
SKD
りた、ば
WHY DID YOU RENEGE ON "OUR NIGHT OF SOLEMN OUT-POURINGS" YESTERDAY?
AND WHAT OF "ALL @$#% FLAT & SMALL"?!
OR "BIG 'UNS? SMALL 'UNS"?
AAGH! LEAVE ME ALONE!
SORRY ABOUT THE CRUDE ENDING.

BOMB 16 FORBIDDEN ELEGY

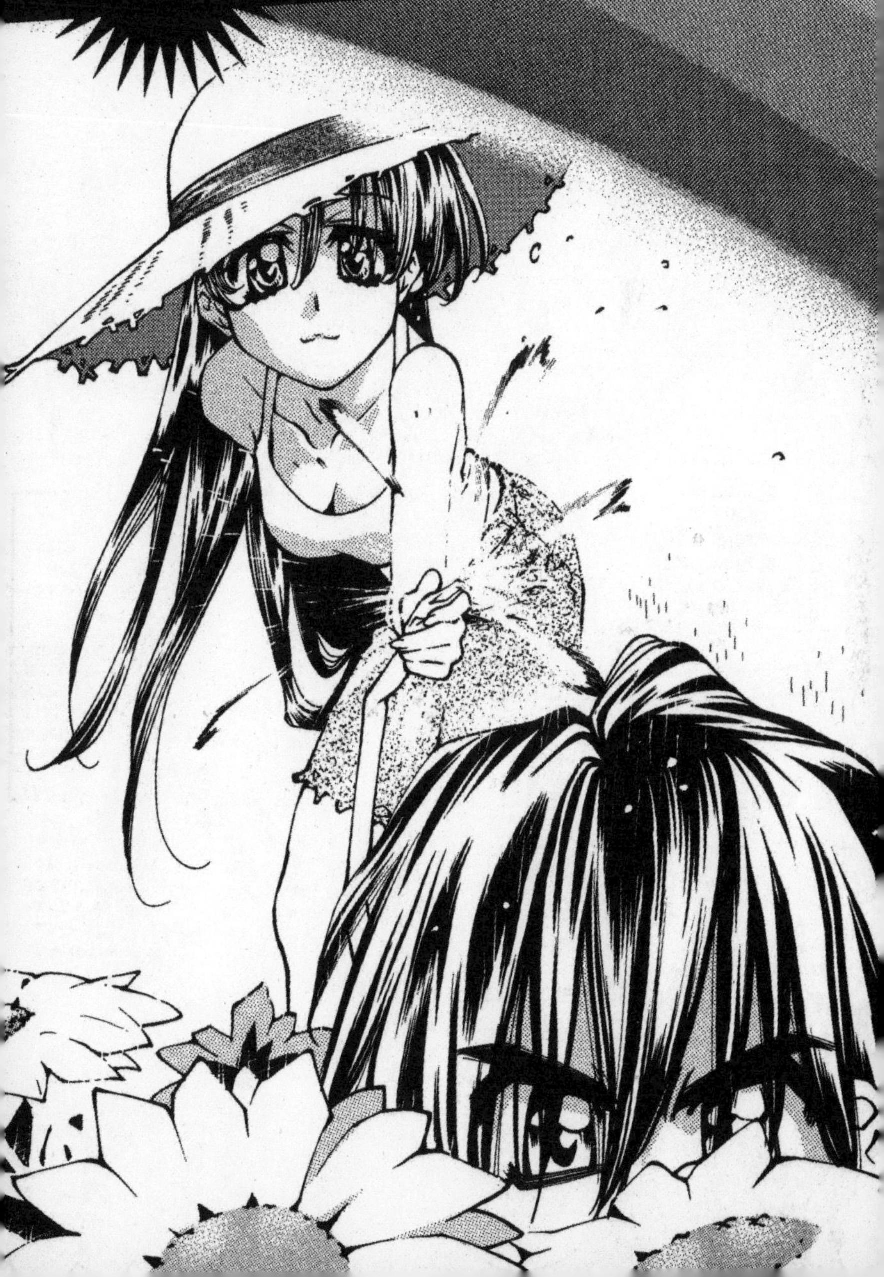

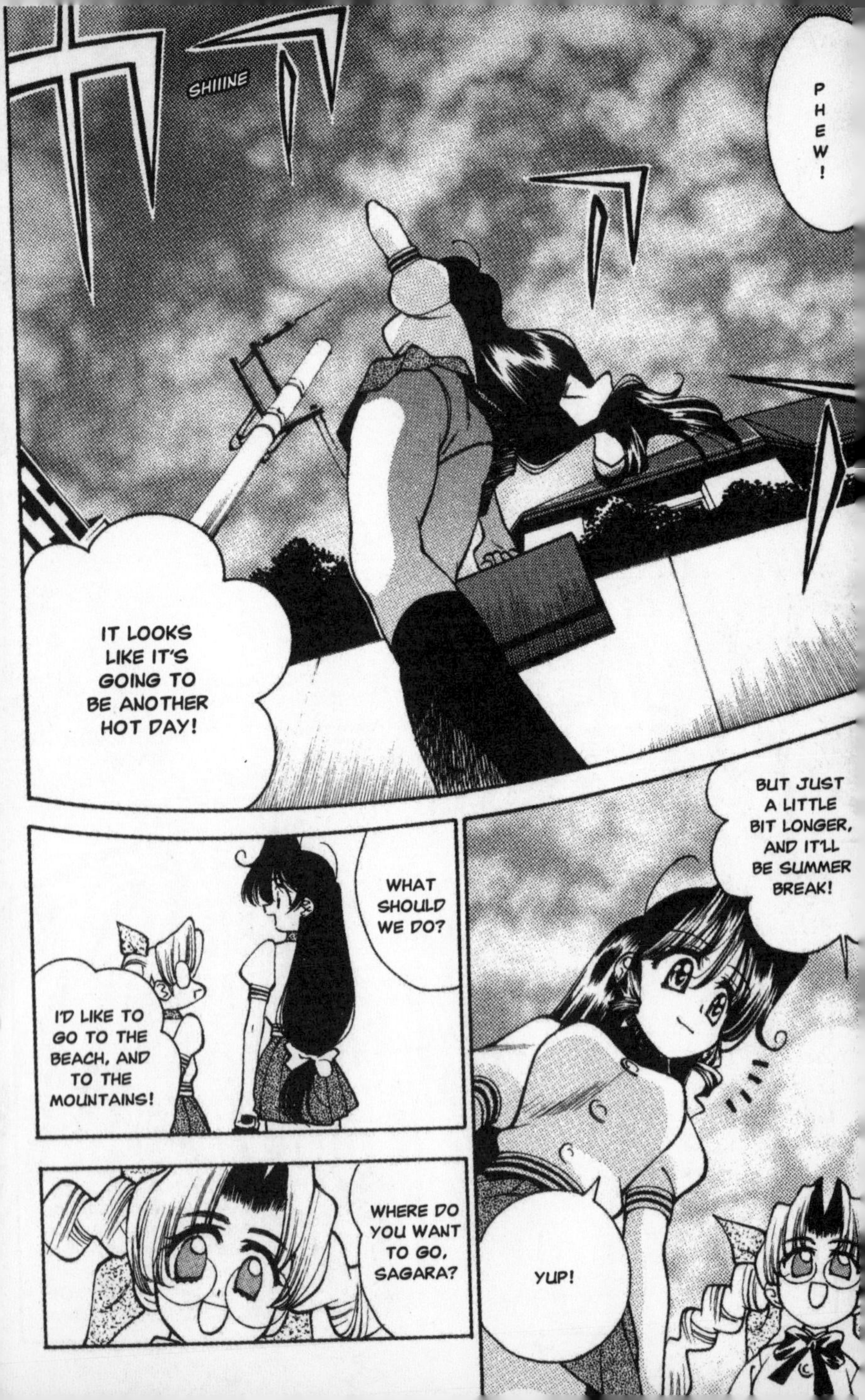
PHEW!
SHIIINE
IT LOOKS LIKE IT'S GOING TO BE ANOTHER HOT DAY!
BUT JUST A LITTLE BIT LONGER, AND IT'LL BE SUMMER BREAK!
YUP!
WHAT SHOULD WE DO?
I'D LIKE TO GO TO THE BEACH, AND TO THE MOUNTAINS!
WHERE DO YOU WANT TO GO, SAGARA?

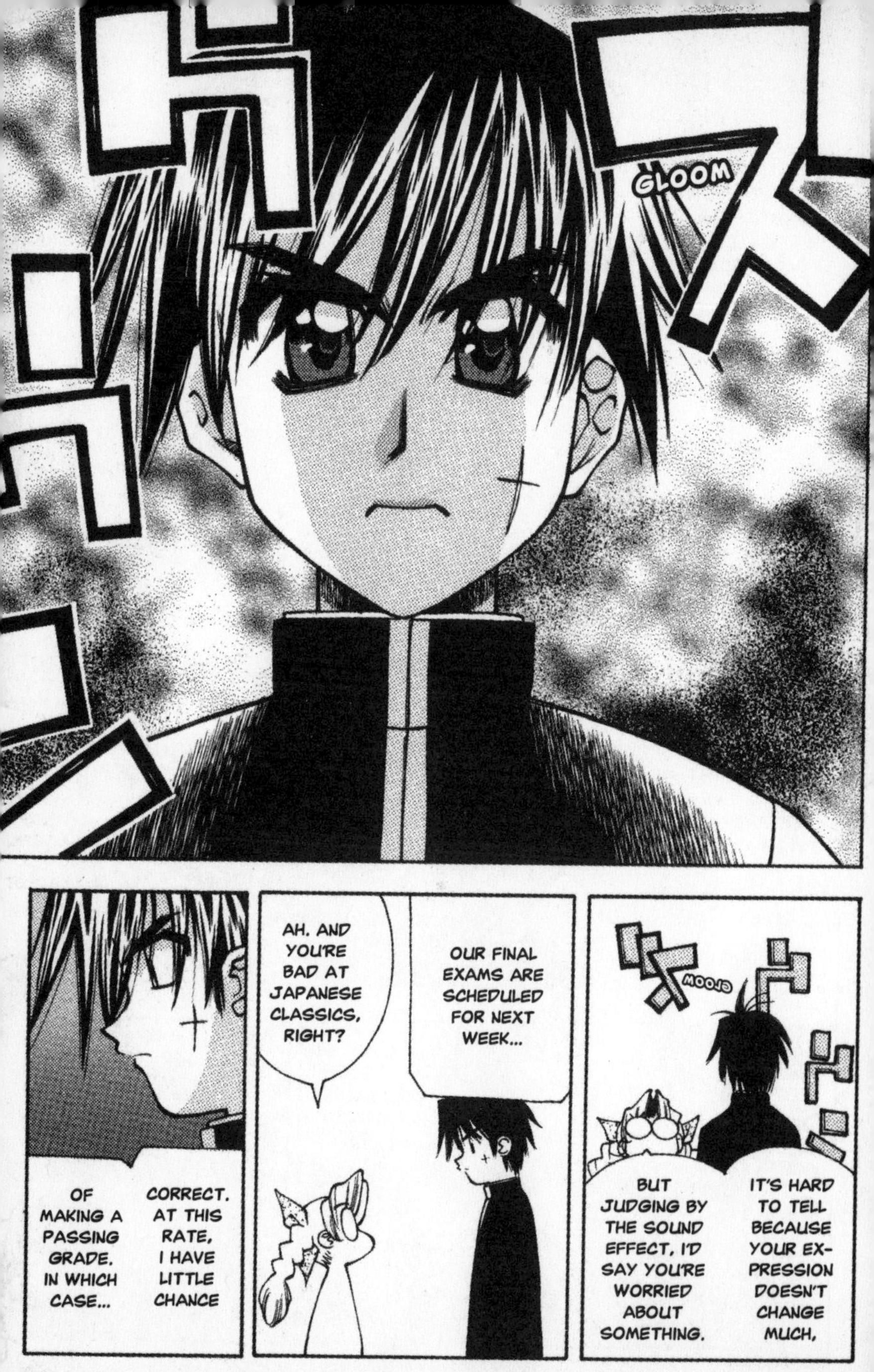
GLOOM
IT'S HARD TO TELL BECAUSE YOUR EXPRESSION DOESN'T CHANGE MUCH,
BUT JUDGING BY THE SOUND EFFECT, I'D SAY YOU'RE WORRIED ABOUT SOMETHING.
OUR FINAL EXAMS ARE SCHEDULED FOR NEXT WEEK...
AH. AND YOU'RE BAD AT JAPANESE CLASSICS, RIGHT?
CORRECT. AT THIS RATE, I HAVE LITTLE CHANCE
OF MAKING A PASSING GRADE. IN WHICH CASE...

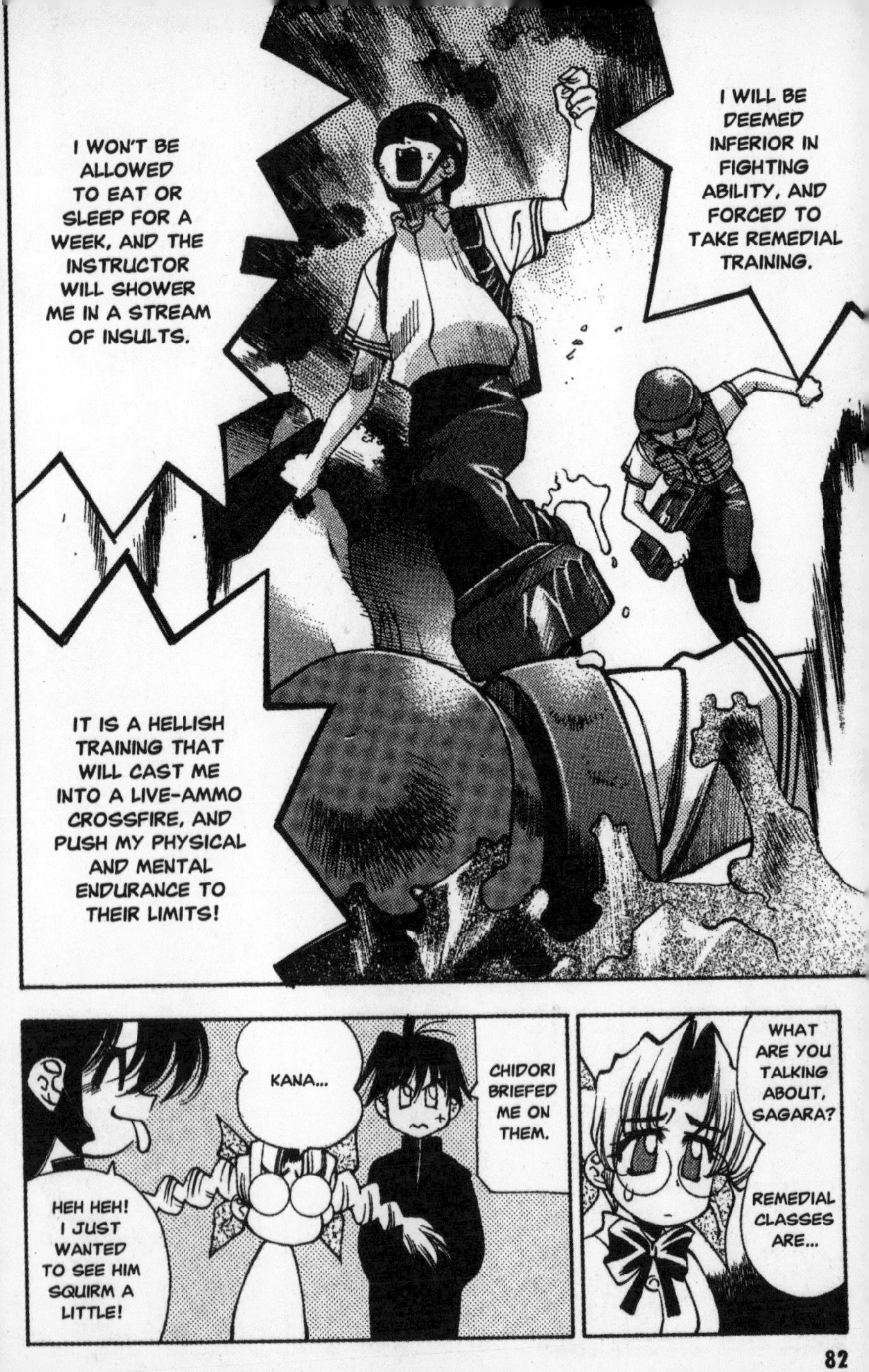
I WILL BE DEEMED INFERIOR IN FIGHTING ABILITY, AND FORCED TO TAKE REMEDIAL TRAINING.
I WON'T BE ALLOWED TO EAT OR SLEEP FOR A WEEK, AND THE INSTRUCTOR WILL SHOWER ME IN A STREAM OF INSULTS.
IT IS A HELLISH TRAINING THAT WILL CAST ME INTO A LIVE-AMMO CROSSFIRE, AND PUSH MY PHYSICAL AND MENTAL ENDURANCE TO THEIR LIMITS!
WHAT ARE YOU TALKING ABOUT, SAGARA?
REMEDIAL CLASSES ARE...
CHIDORI BRIEFED ME ON THEM.
KANA...
HEH HEH! I JUST WANTED TO SEE HIM SQUIRM A LITTLE!

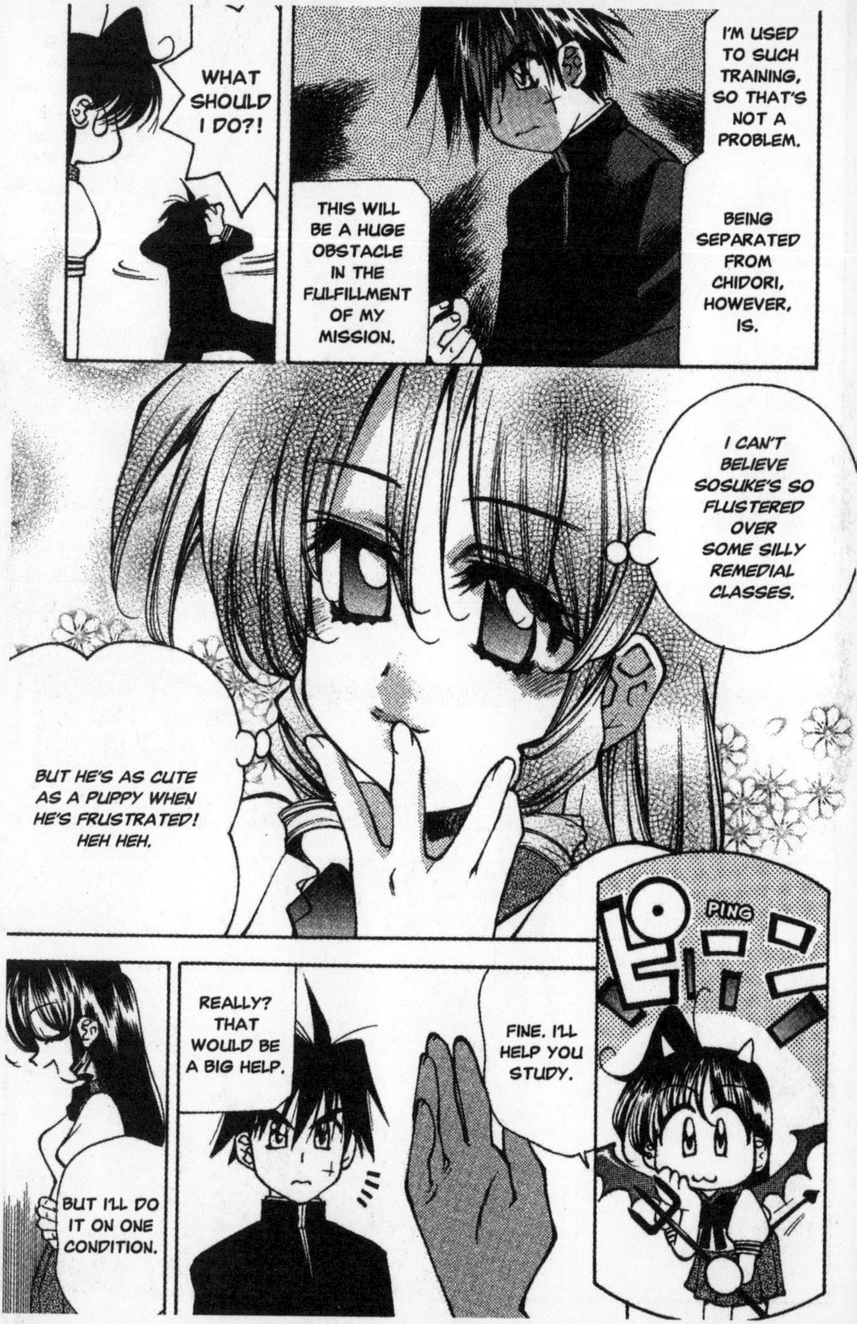
I'M USED TO SUCH TRAINING, SO THAT'S NOT A PROBLEM.
BEING SEPARATED FROM CHIDORI, HOWEVER, IS.
THIS WILL BE A HUGE OBSTACLE IN THE FULFILLMENT OF MY MISSION.
WHAT SHOULD I DO?!
I CAN'T BELIEVE SOSUKE'S SO FLUSTERED OVER SOME SILLY REMEDIAL CLASSES.
BUT HE'S AS CUTE AS A PUPPY WHEN HE'S FRUSTRATED! HEH HEH.
PING
FINE. I'LL HELP YOU STUDY.
REALLY? THAT WOULD BE A BIG HELP.
BUT I'LL DO IT ON ONE CONDITION.

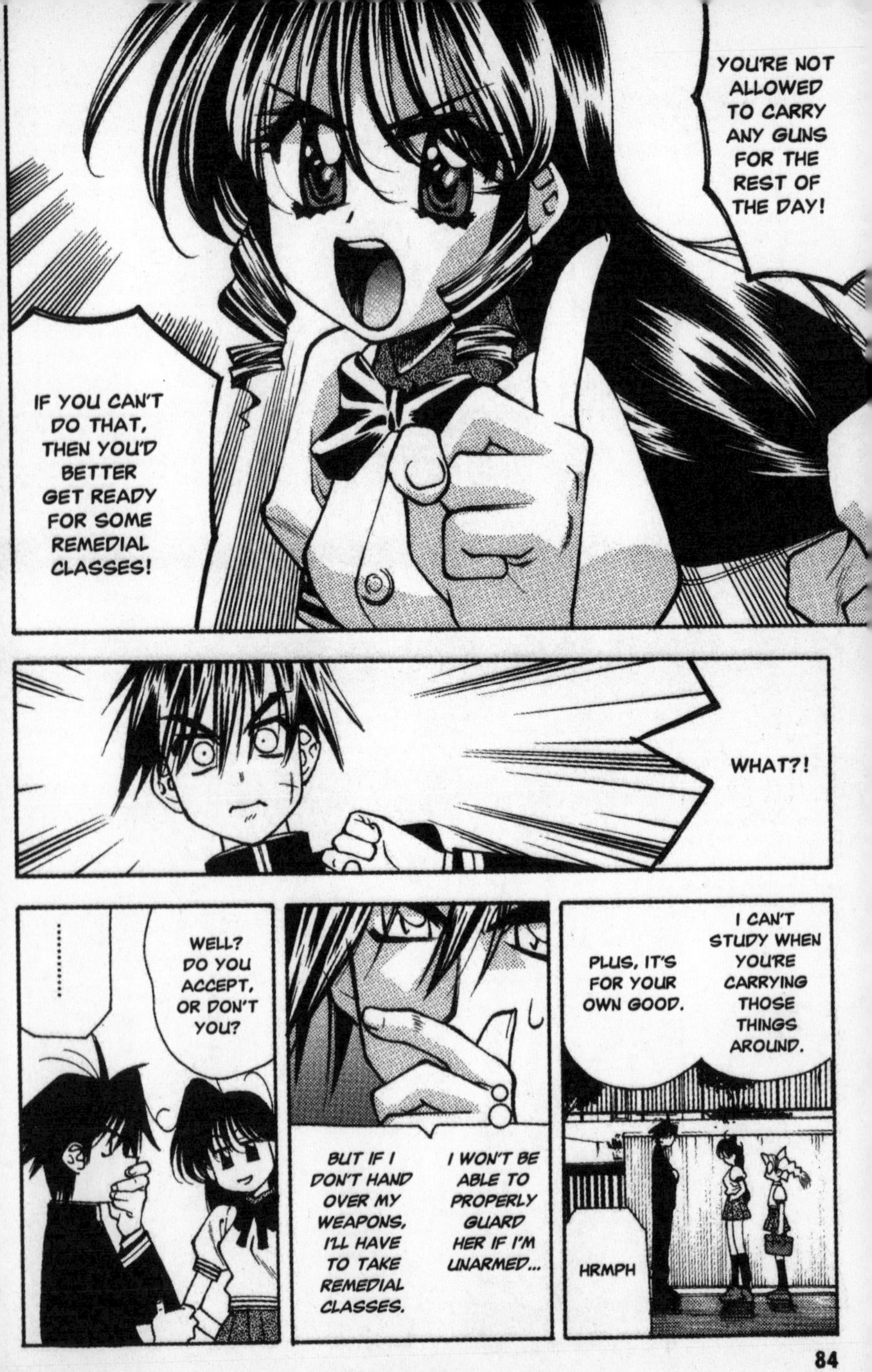

YOU'RE NOT ALLOWED TO CARRY ANY GUNS FOR THE REST OF THE DAY!
IF YOU CAN'T DO THAT, THEN YOU'D BETTER GET READY FOR SOME REMEDIAL CLASSES!
WHAT?!
I CAN'T STUDY WHEN YOU'RE CARRYING THOSE THINGS AROUND.
PLUS, IT'S FOR YOUR OWN GOOD.
HRMPH
I WON'T BE ABLE TO PROPERLY GUARD HER IF I'M UNARMED...
BUT IF I DON'T HAND OVER MY WEAPONS, I'LL HAVE TO TAKE REMEDIAL CLASSES.
WELL? DO YOU ACCEPT, OR DON'T YOU?
....

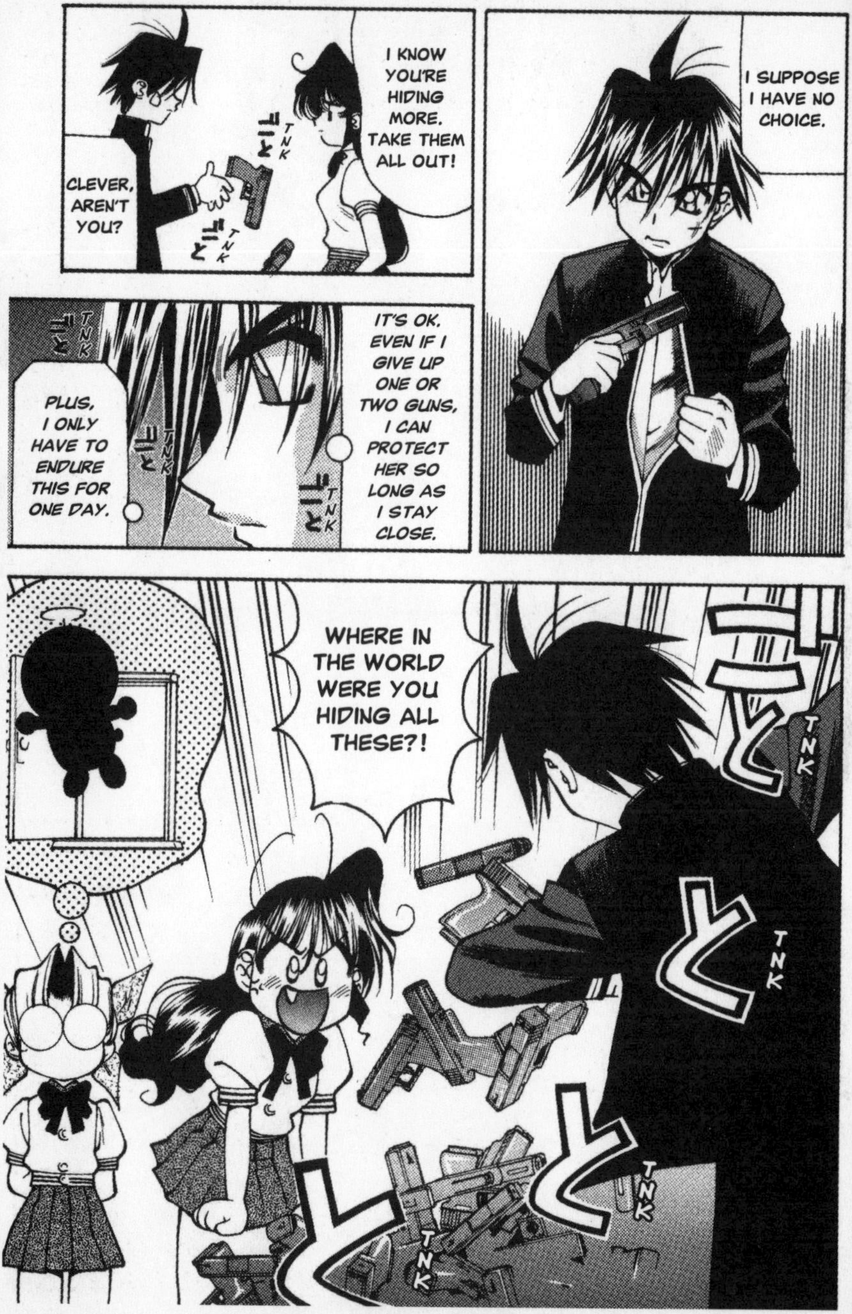
I KNOW YOU'RE HIDING MORE. TAKE THEM ALL OUT!
TNK
CLEVER, AREN'T YOU?
TNK
I SUPPOSE I HAVE NO CHOICE.
TNK
IT'S OK. EVEN IF I GIVE UP ONE OR TWO GUNS, I CAN PROTECT HER SO LONG AS I STAY CLOSE.
PLUS, I ONLY HAVE TO ENDURE THIS FOR ONE DAY.
TNK
TNK
WHERE IN THE WORLD WERE YOU HIDING ALL THESE?!
TNK
TNK
TNK
TNK

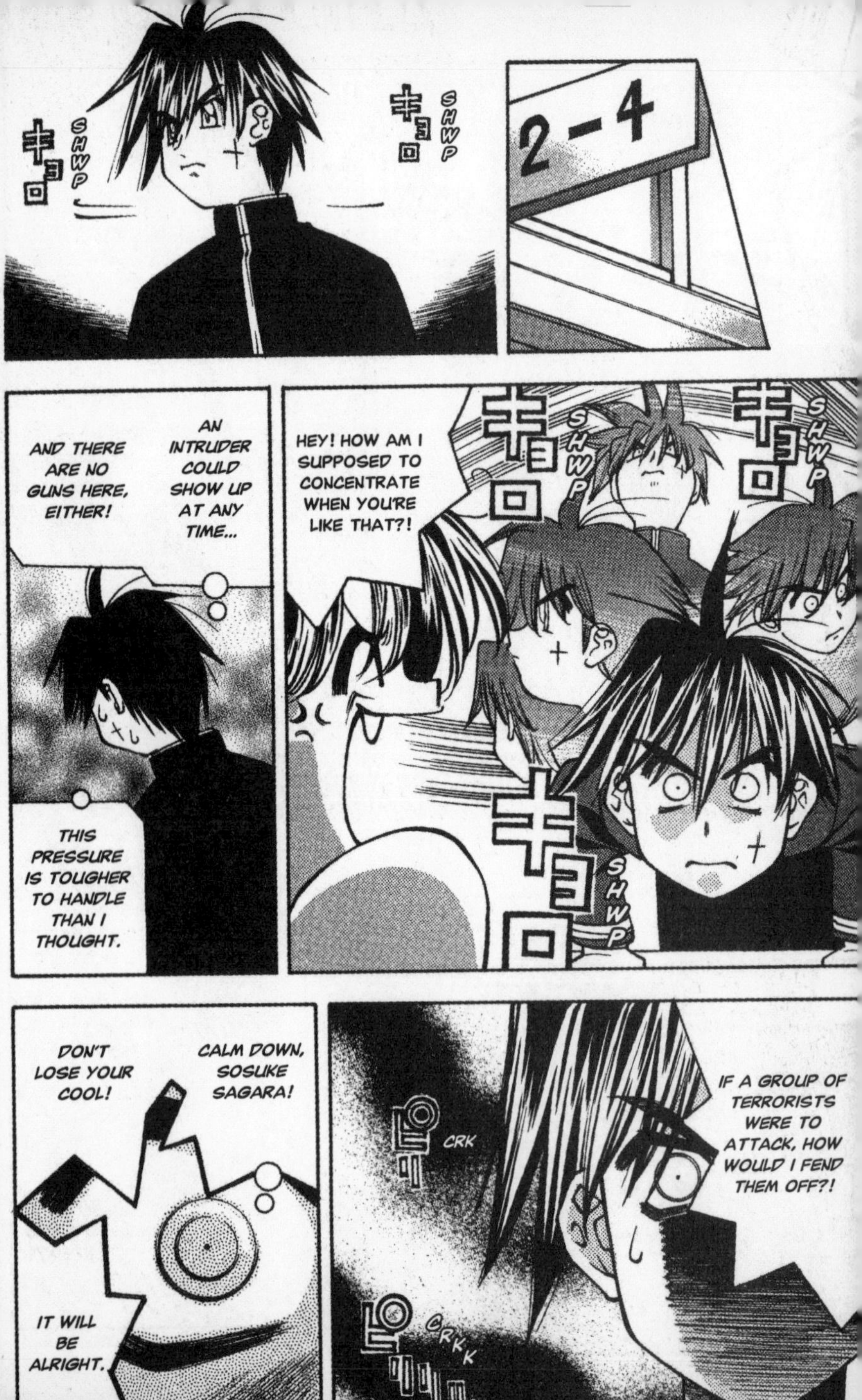
2-4
キョロ
SHWP
キョロ
SHWP
キョロ
SHWP
キョロ
SHWP
HEY! HOW AM I SUPPOSED TO CONCENTRATE WHEN YOU'RE LIKE THAT?!
キョロ
SHWP
AN INTRUDER COULD SHOW UP AT ANY TIME...
AND THERE ARE NO GUNS HERE, EITHER!
THIS PRESSURE IS TOUGHER TO HANDLE THAN I THOUGHT.
IF A GROUP OF TERRORISTS WERE TO ATTACK, HOW WOULD I FEND THEM OFF?!
CRK
CRKK
CALM DOWN, SOSUKE SAGARA!
DON'T LOSE YOUR COOL!
IT WILL BE ALRIGHT.

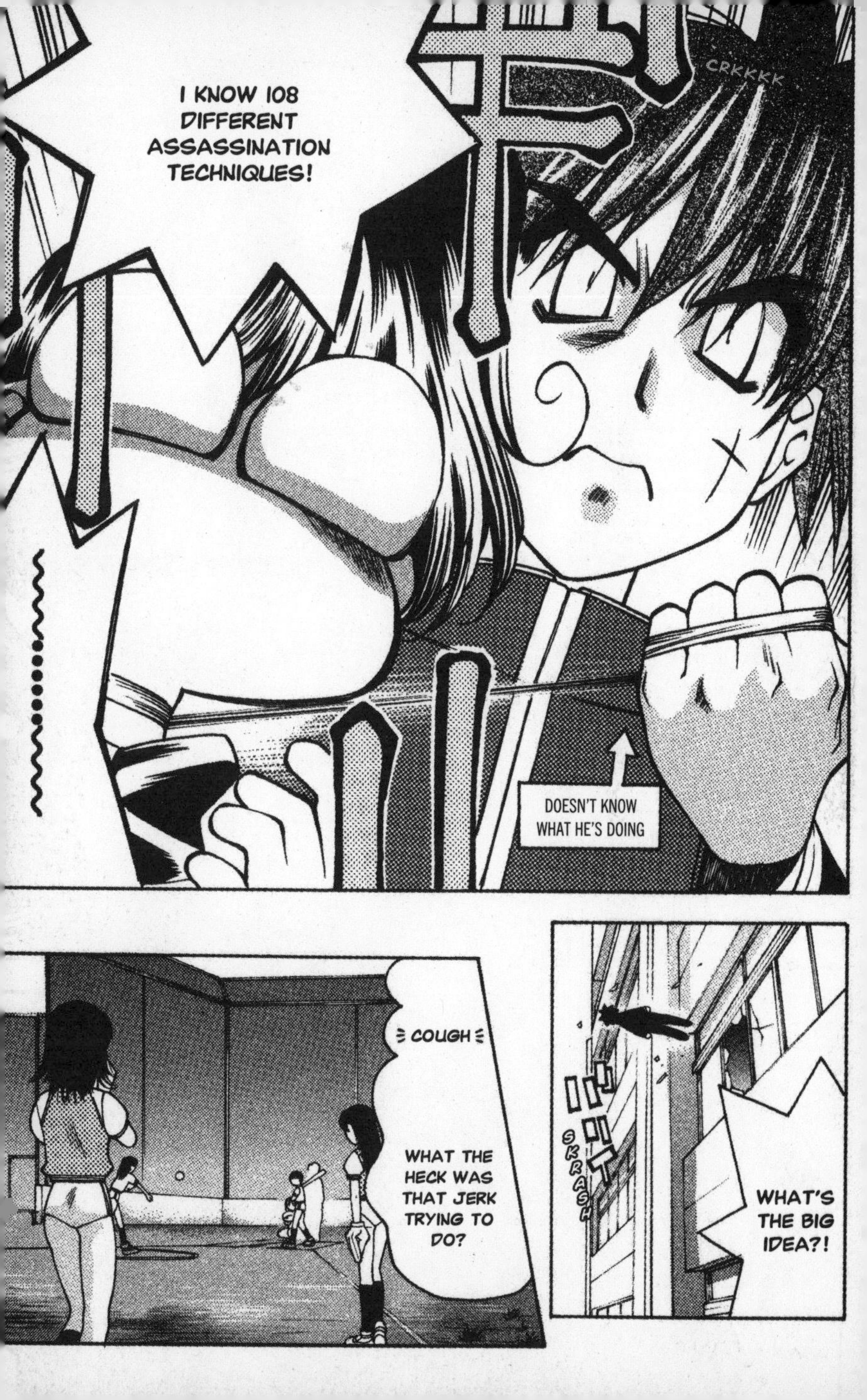
I KNOW 108 DIFFERENT ASSASSINATION TECHNIQUES!
CRKKKK
DOESN'T KNOW WHAT HE'S DOING
WHAT'S THE BIG IDEA?!
SKRASH
COUGH
WHAT THE HECK WAS THAT JERK TRYING TO DO?

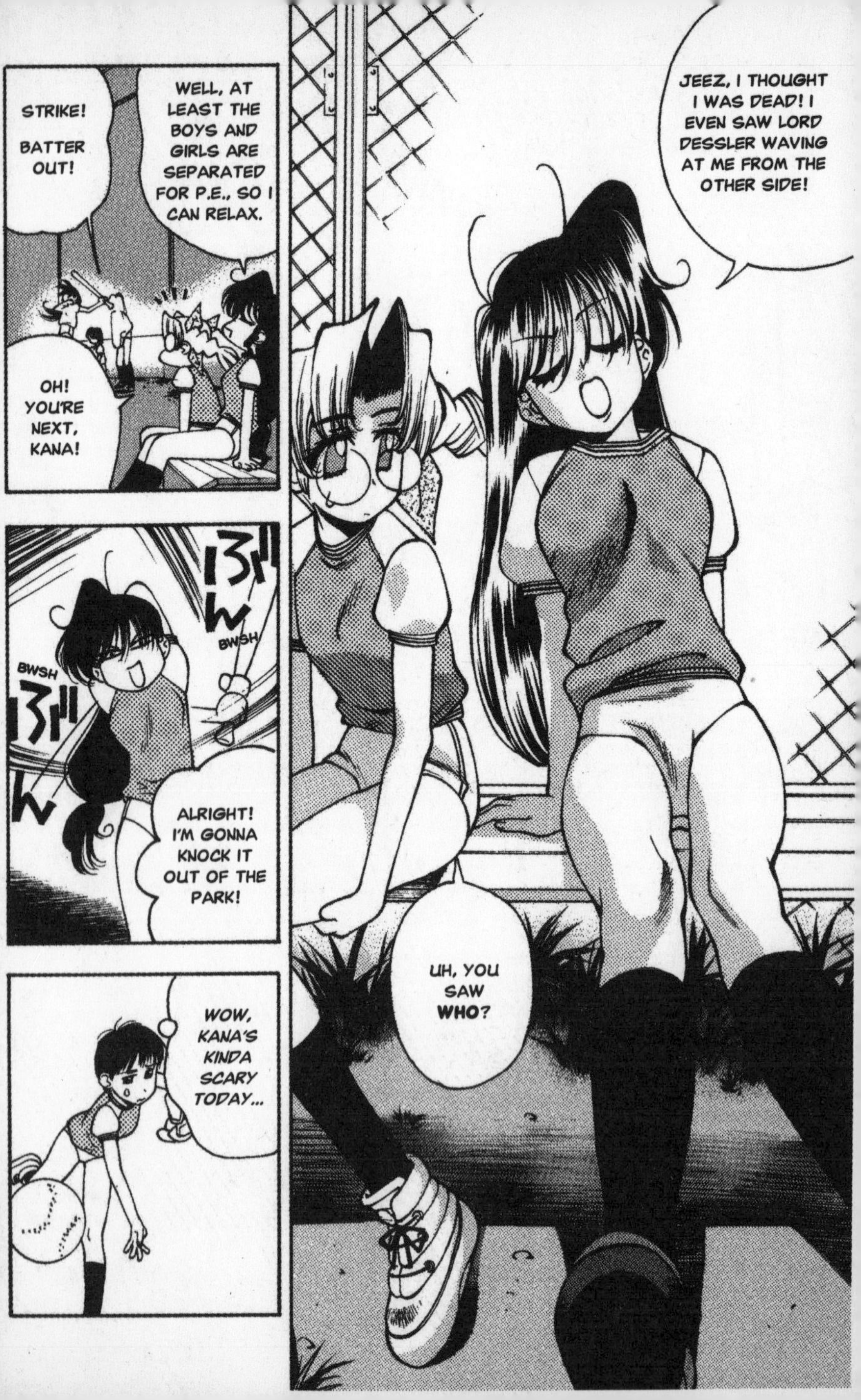
JEEZ, I THOUGHT I WAS DEAD! I EVEN SAW LORD DESSLER WAVING AT ME FROM THE OTHER SIDE!
UH, YOU SAW **WHO**?
STRIKE!
BATTER OUT!
WELL, AT LEAST THE BOYS AND GIRLS ARE SEPARATED FOR P.E., SO I CAN RELAX.
OH! YOU'RE NEXT, KANA!
BWSH
BWSH
ALRIGHT! I'M GONNA KNOCK IT OUT OF THE PARK!
WOW, KANA'S KINDA SCARY TODAY...

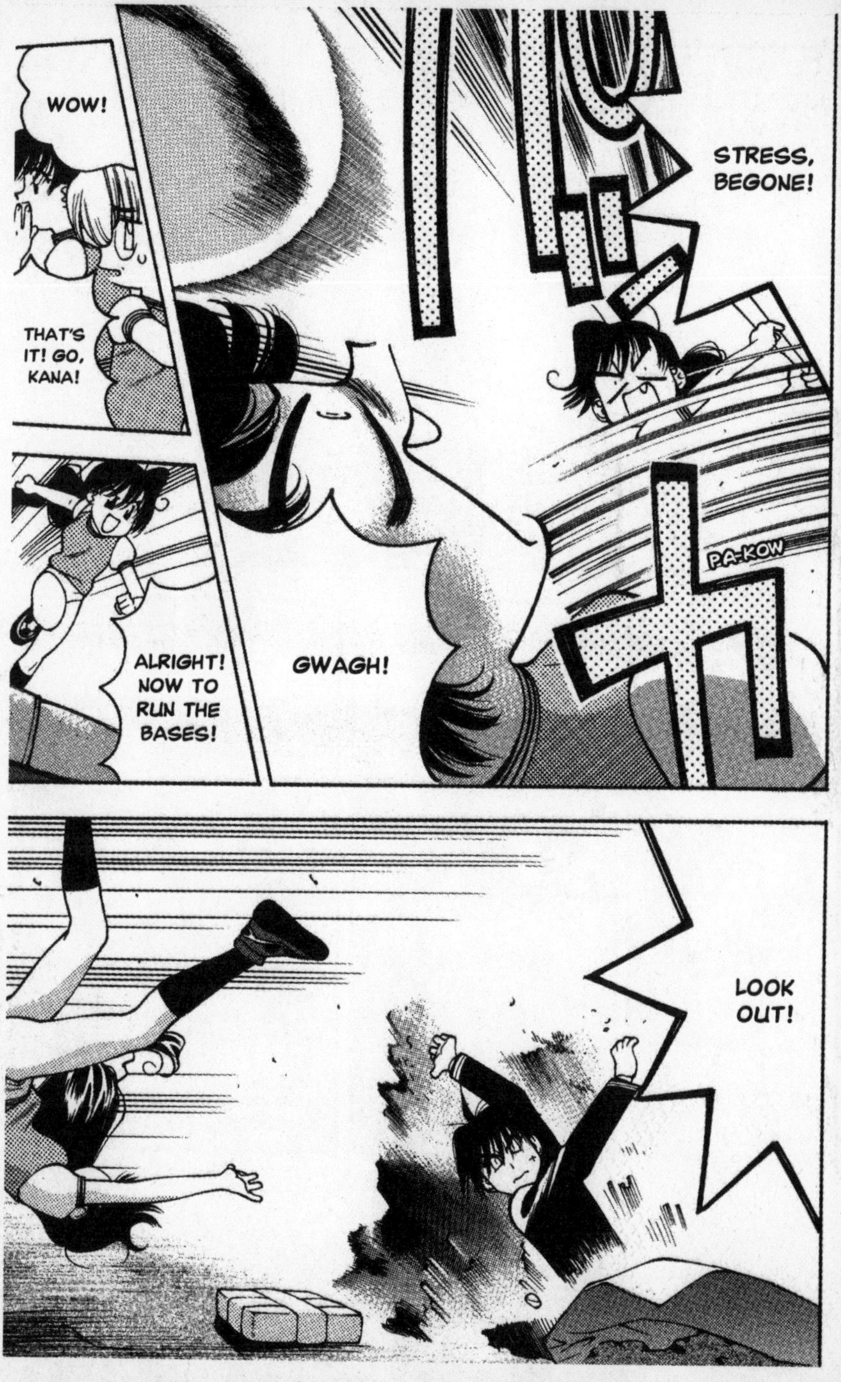

STRESS, BEGONE!
WOW!
THAT'S IT! GO, KANA!
PA-KOW
GWAGH!
ALRIGHT! NOW TO RUN THE BASES!
LOOK OUT!

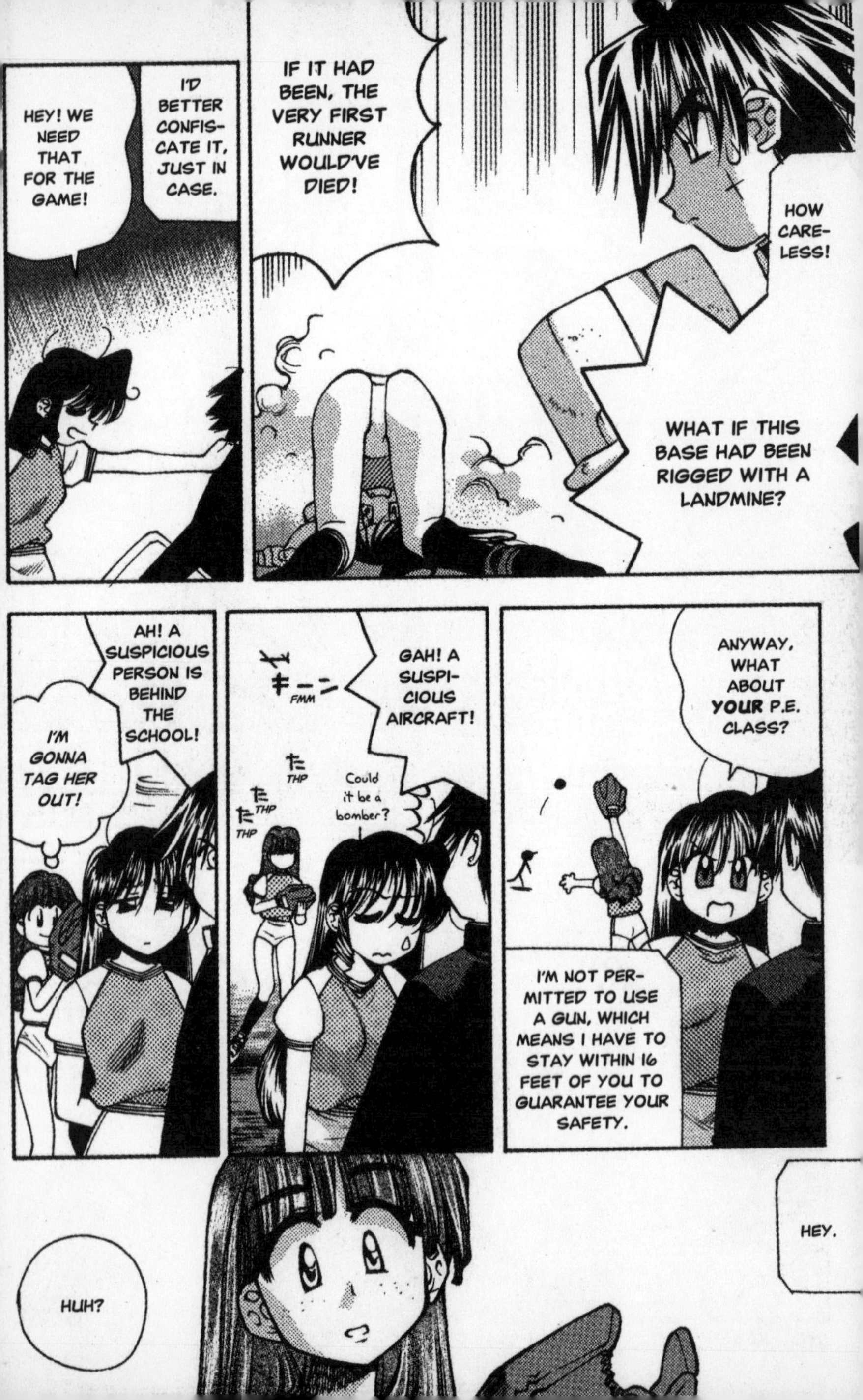
HOW CARE-LESS!
WHAT IF THIS BASE HAD BEEN RIGGED WITH A LANDMINE?
IF IT HAD BEEN, THE VERY FIRST RUNNER WOULD'VE DIED!
I'D BETTER CONFISCATE IT, JUST IN CASE.
HEY! WE NEED THAT FOR THE GAME!
ANYWAY, WHAT ABOUT YOUR P.E. CLASS?
I'M NOT PERMITTED TO USE A GUN, WHICH MEANS I HAVE TO STAY WITHIN 16 FEET OF YOU TO GUARANTEE YOUR SAFETY.
GAH! A SUSPICIOUS AIRCRAFT!
キーン FMM
Could it be a bomber?
た THP
た THP
た THP
AH! A SUSPICIOUS PERSON IS BEHIND THE SCHOOL!
I'M GONNA TAG HER OUT!
HEY.
HUH?

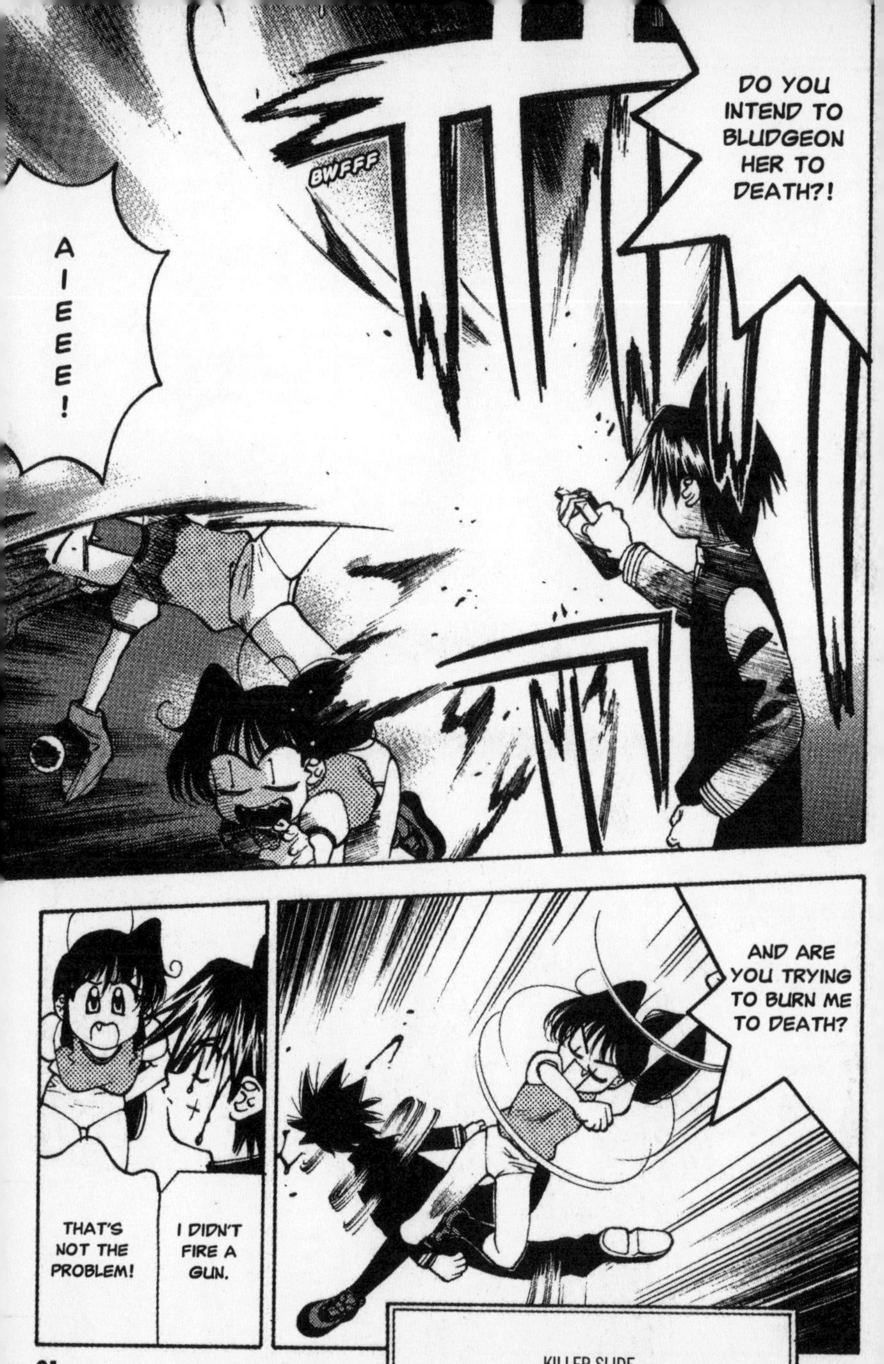
DO YOU INTEND TO BLUDGEON HER TO DEATH?!
BWFFF
AIEEE!
AND ARE YOU TRYING TO BURN ME TO DEATH?
I DIDN'T FIRE A GUN.
THAT'S NOT THE PROBLEM!

KILLER SLIDE

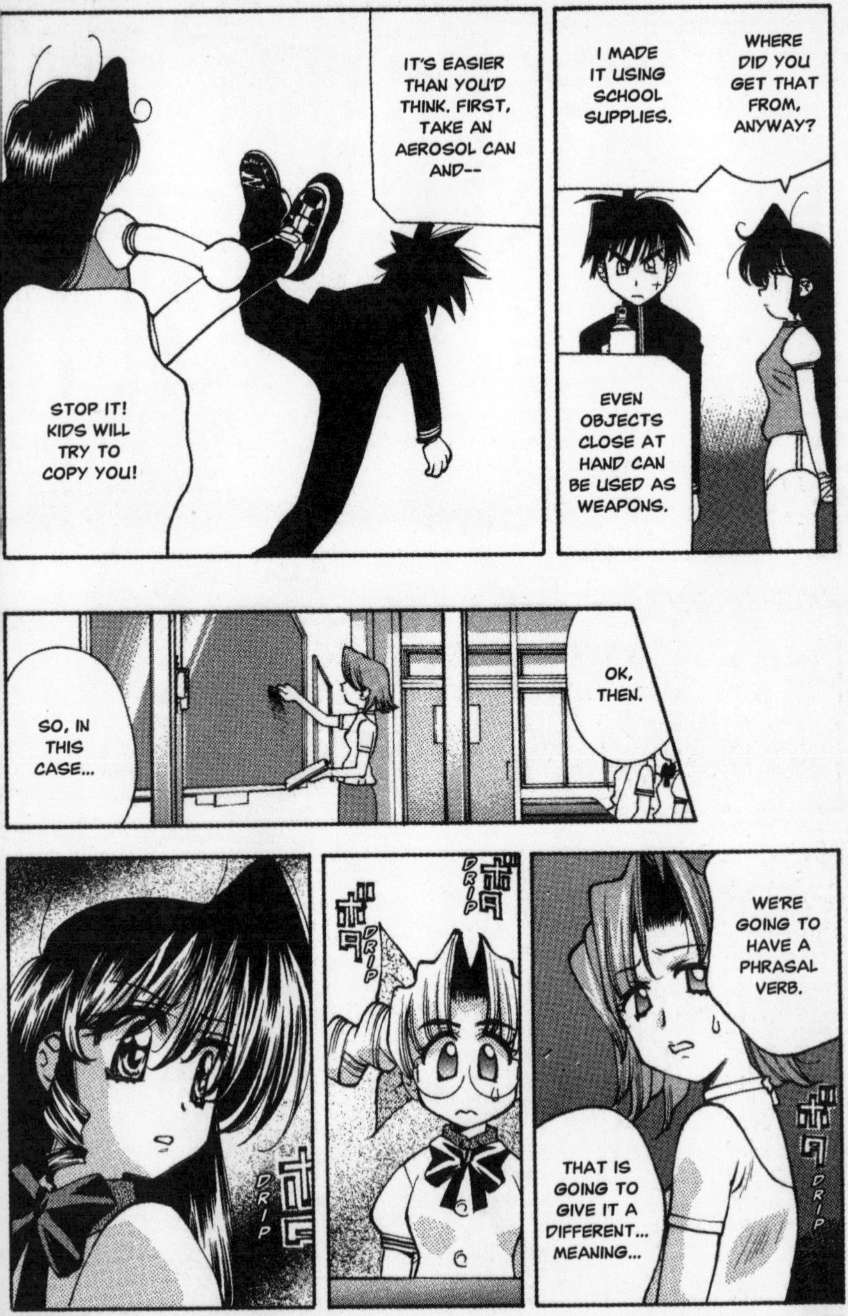
WHERE DID YOU GET THAT FROM, ANYWAY?
I MADE IT USING SCHOOL SUPPLIES.
EVEN OBJECTS CLOSE AT HAND CAN BE USED AS WEAPONS.
IT'S EASIER THAN YOU'D THINK. FIRST, TAKE AN AEROSOL CAN AND--
STOP IT! KIDS WILL TRY TO COPY YOU!
OK, THEN.
SO, IN THIS CASE...
WE'RE GOING TO HAVE A PHRASAL VERB.
DRIP
THAT IS GOING TO GIVE IT A DIFFERENT... MEANING...
DRIP
DRIP
DRIP

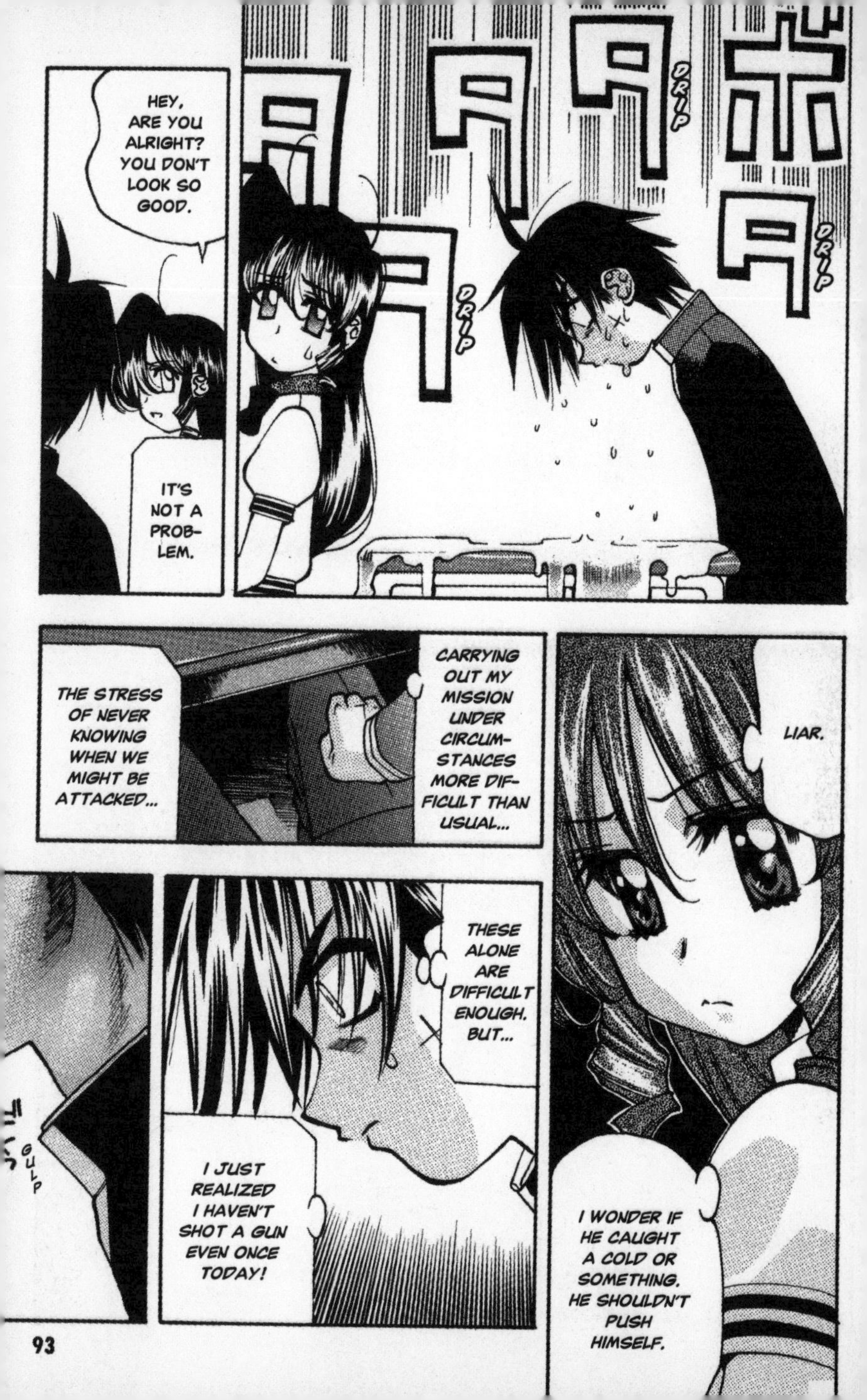

ボタタタ
DRIP
DRIP
DRIP
HEY, ARE YOU ALRIGHT? YOU DON'T LOOK SO GOOD.
IT'S NOT A PROB-LEM.
LIAR.
CARRYING OUT MY MISSION UNDER CIRCUM-STANCES MORE DIF-FICULT THAN USUAL...
THE STRESS OF NEVER KNOWING WHEN WE MIGHT BE ATTACKED...
THESE ALONE ARE DIFFICULT ENOUGH. BUT...
I JUST REALIZED I HAVEN'T SHOT A GUN EVEN ONCE TODAY!
GULP
I WONDER IF HE CAUGHT A COLD OR SOMETHING. HE SHOULDN'T PUSH HIMSELF.

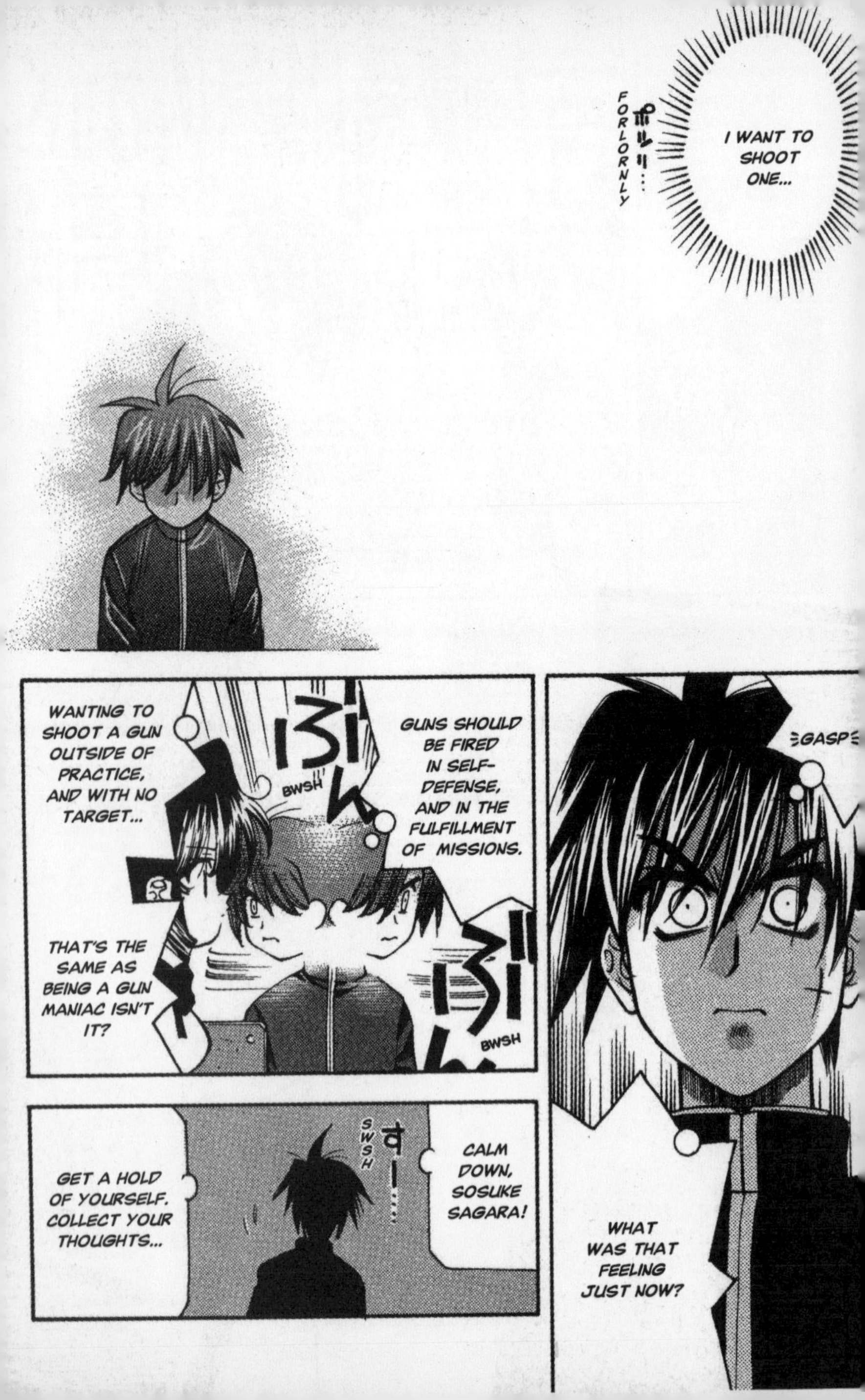
I WANT TO SHOOT ONE...
ポツリ…
FORLORNLY
GASP
WHAT WAS THAT FEELING JUST NOW?
GUNS SHOULD BE FIRED IN SELF-DEFENSE, AND IN THE FULFILLMENT OF MISSIONS.
ぶん
BWSH
WANTING TO SHOOT A GUN OUTSIDE OF PRACTICE, AND WITH NO TARGET...
ぶん
BWSH
THAT'S THE SAME AS BEING A GUN MANIAC ISN'T IT?
CALM DOWN, SOSUKE SAGARA!
すー…
SWSH
GET A HOLD OF YOURSELF. COLLECT YOUR THOUGHTS...

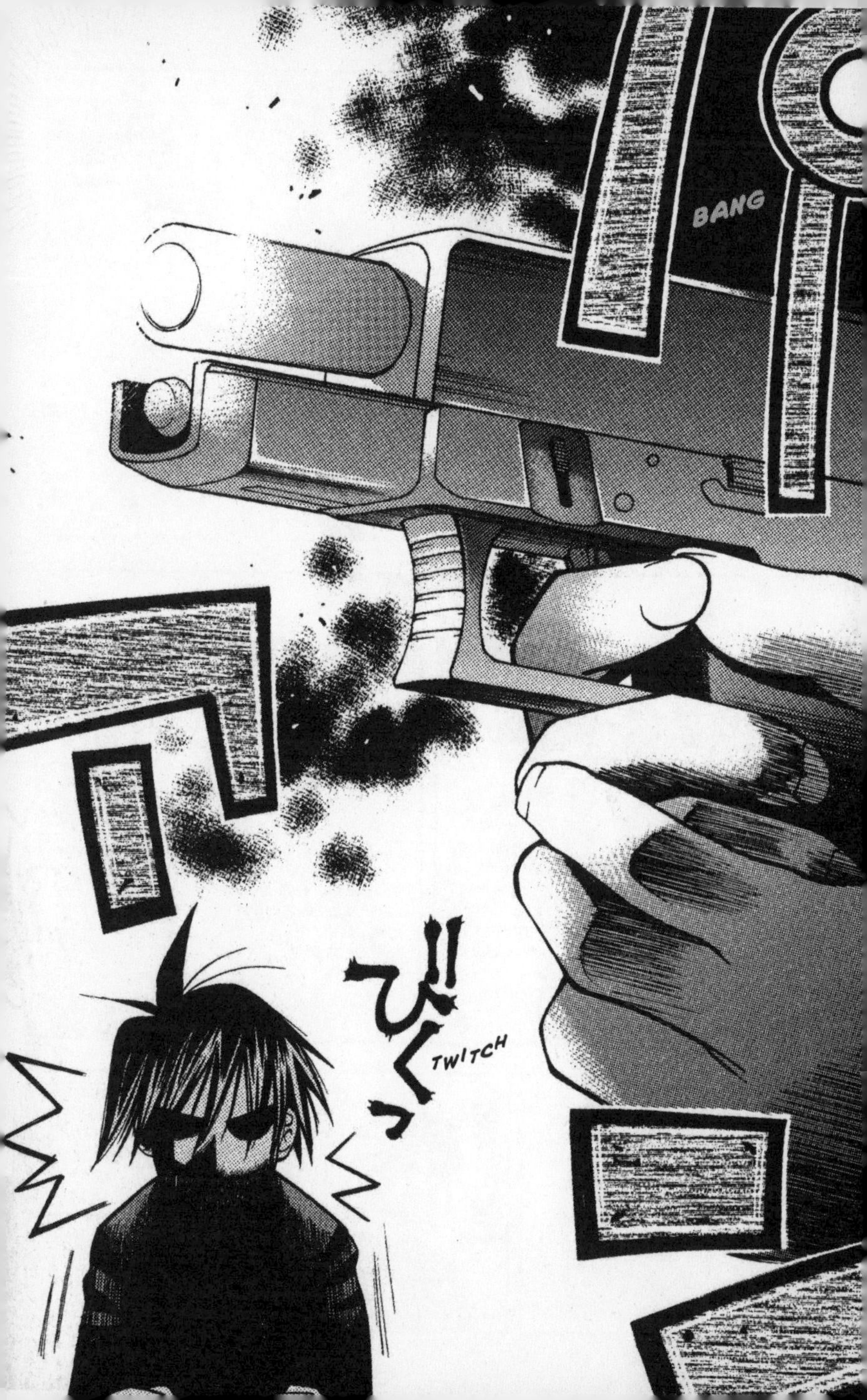
BANG
ビクッ!!
TWITCH

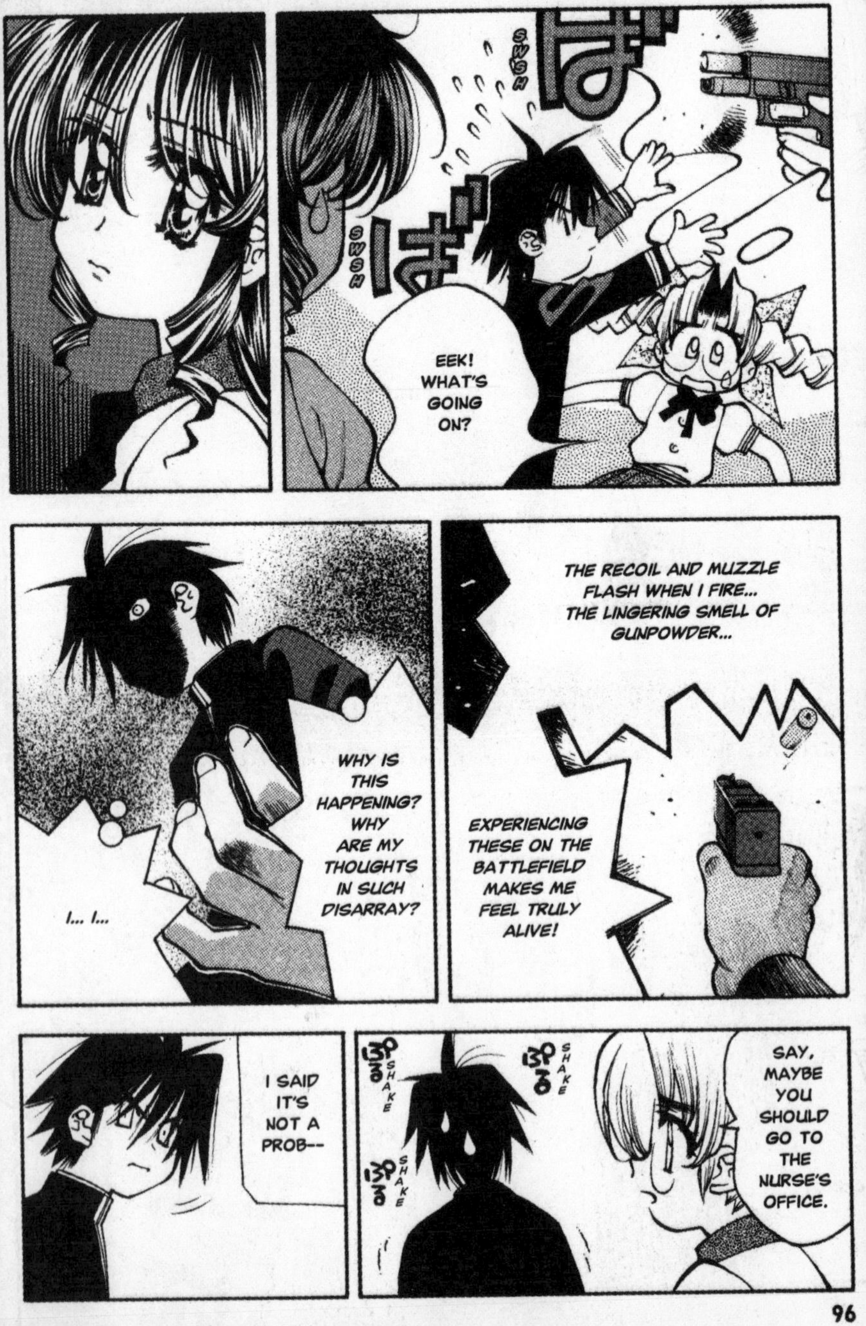
SWSH
SWSH
EEK! WHAT'S GOING ON?
THE RECOIL AND MUZZLE FLASH WHEN I FIRE... THE LINGERING SMELL OF GUNPOWDER...
EXPERIENCING THESE ON THE BATTLEFIELD MAKES ME FEEL TRULY ALIVE!
WHY IS THIS HAPPENING? WHY ARE MY THOUGHTS IN SUCH DISARRAY?
I... I...
SAY, MAYBE YOU SHOULD GO TO THE NURSE'S OFFICE.
SHAKE
SHAKE
SHAKE
I SAID IT'S NOT A PROB--

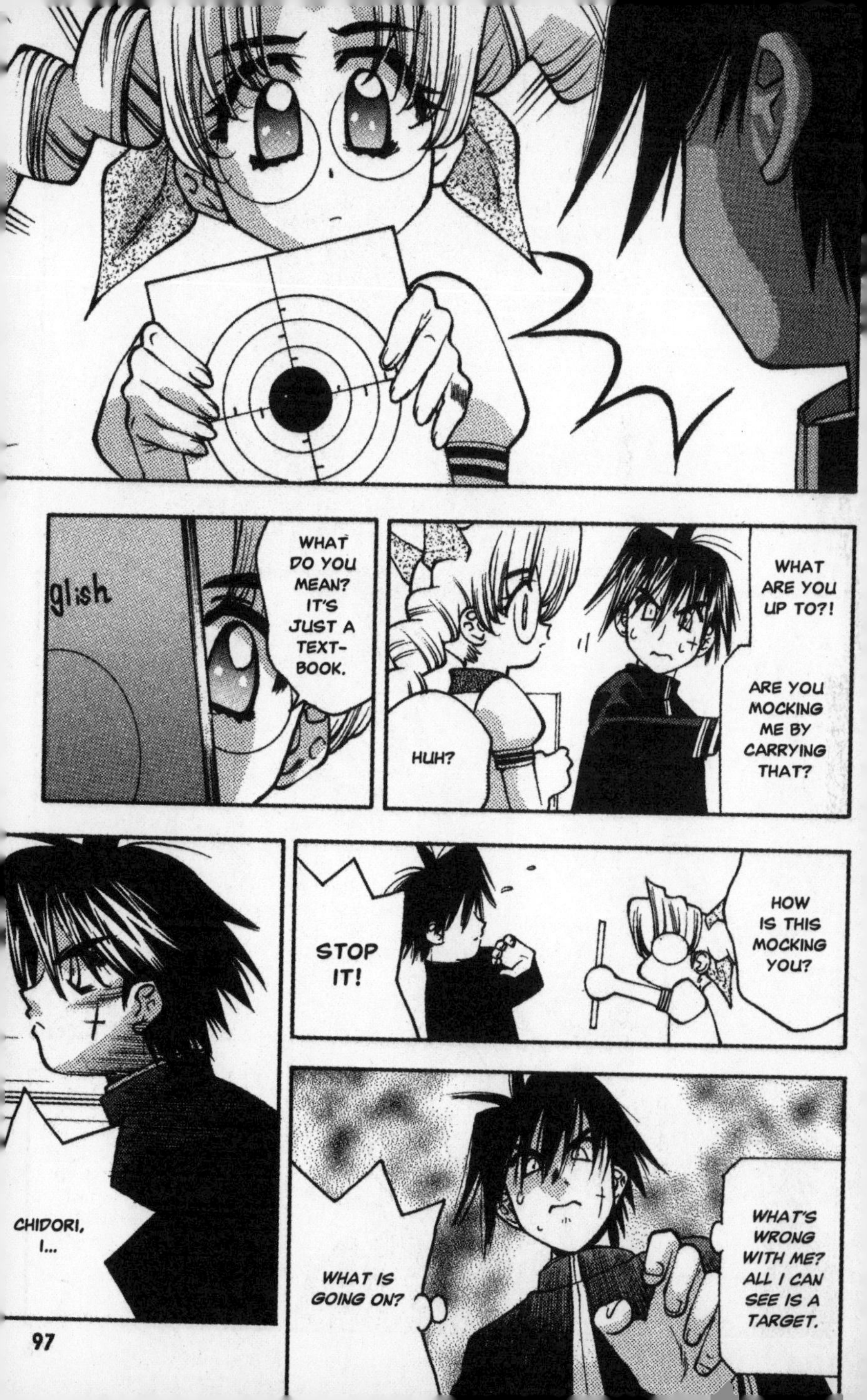

WHAT ARE YOU UP TO?!
ARE YOU MOCKING ME BY CARRYING THAT?
HUH?
glish
WHAT DO YOU MEAN? IT'S JUST A TEXT-BOOK.
HOW IS THIS MOCKING YOU?
STOP IT!
WHAT'S WRONG WITH ME? ALL I CAN SEE IS A TARGET.
WHAT IS GOING ON?
CHIDORI, I...

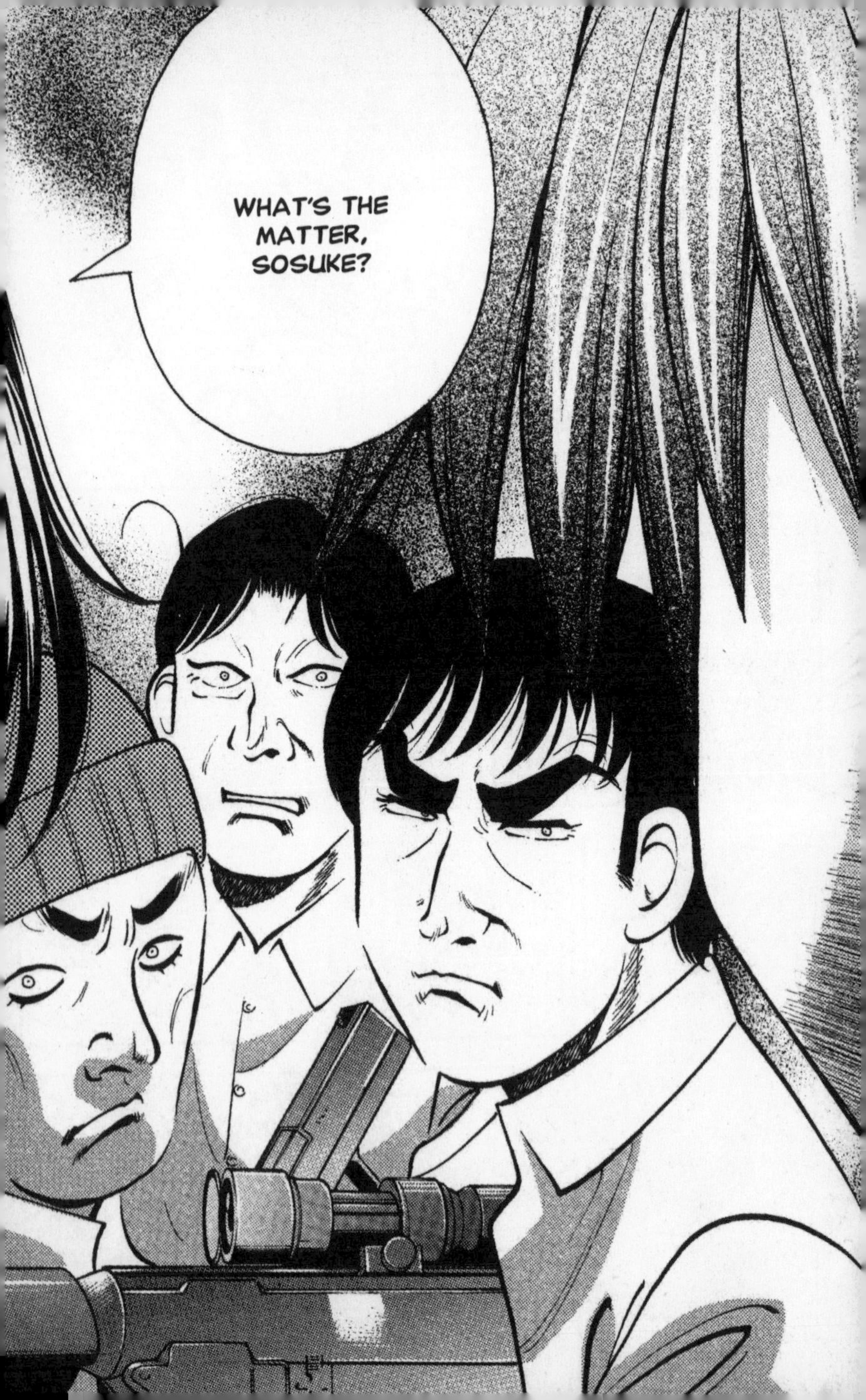
WHAT'S THE MATTER, SOSUKE?

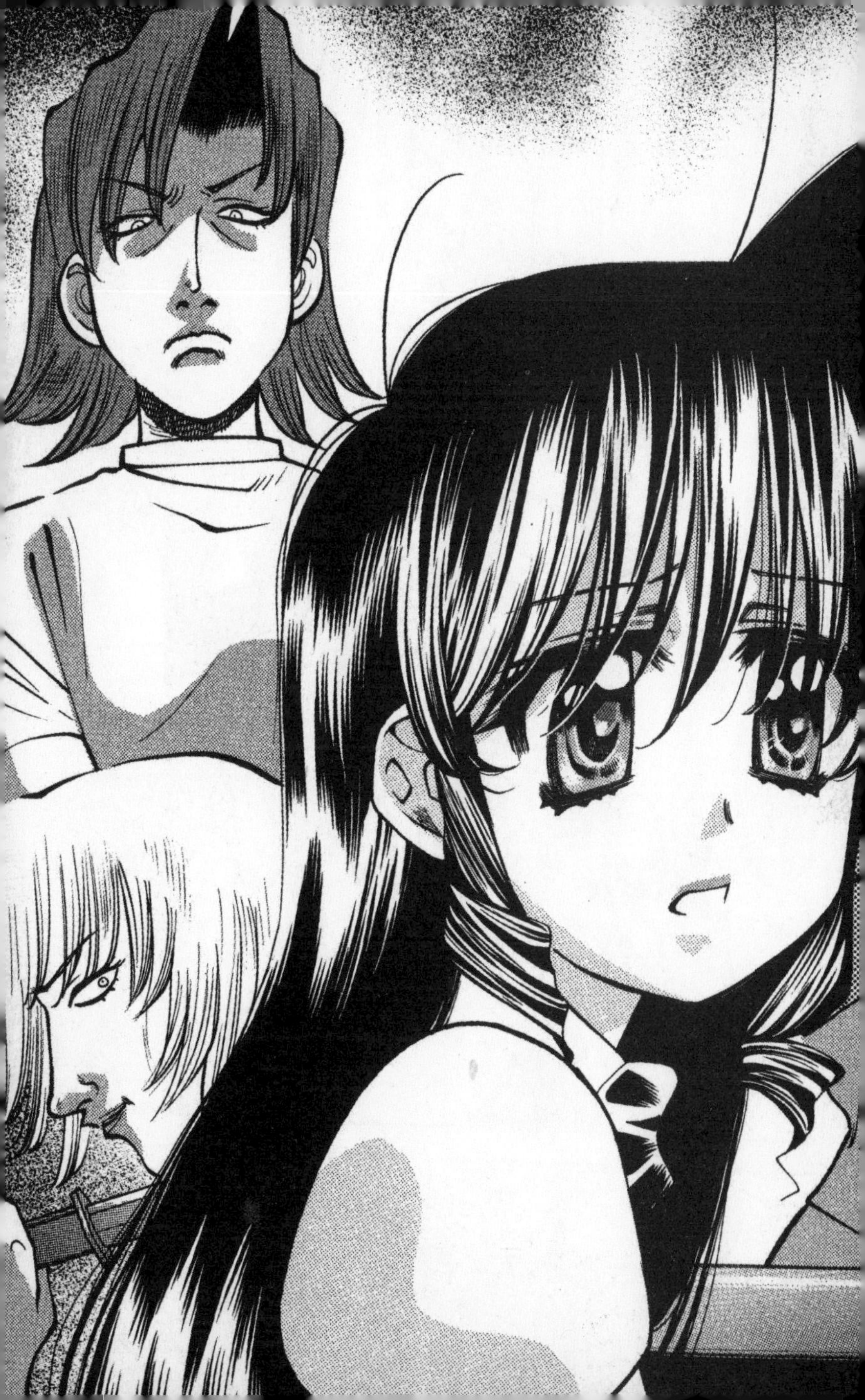

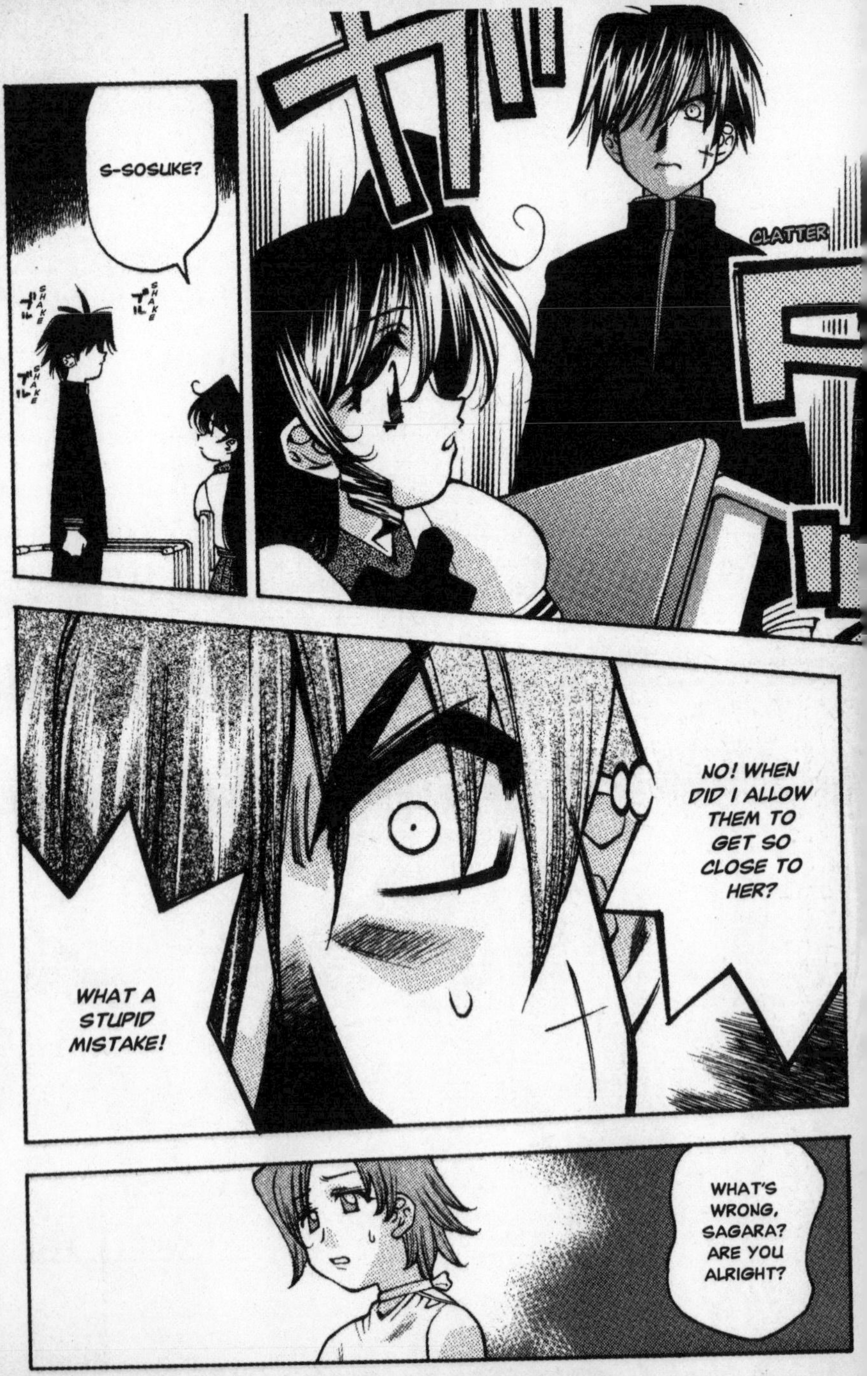
CLATTER
S-SOSUKE?
SHAKE
SHAKE
SHAKE
NO! WHEN DID I ALLOW THEM TO GET SO CLOSE TO HER?
WHAT A STUPID MISTAKE!
WHAT'S WRONG, SAGARA? ARE YOU ALRIGHT?

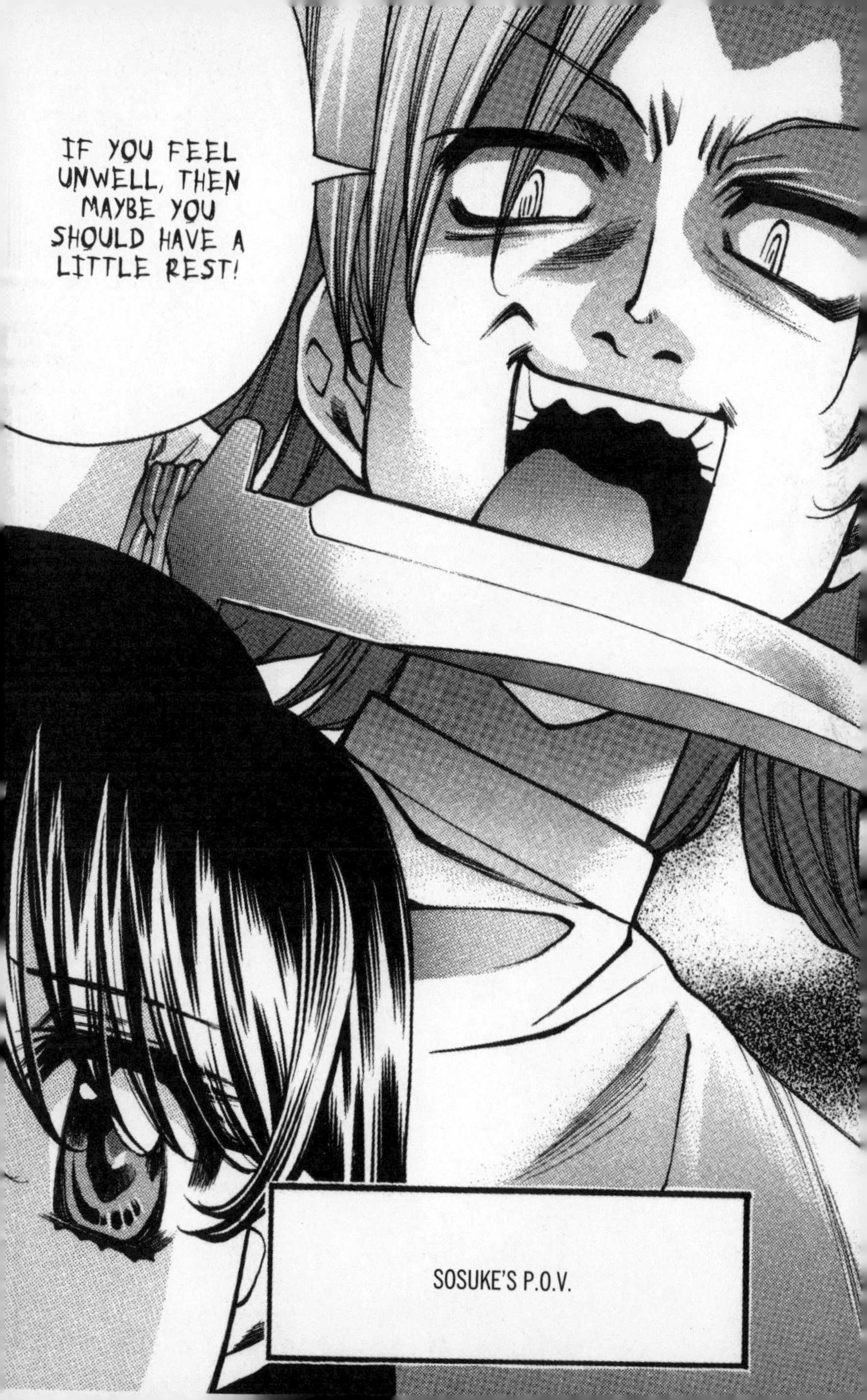
IF YOU FEEL UNWELL, THEN MAYBE YOU SHOULD HAVE A LITTLE REST!
SOSUKE'S P.O.V.

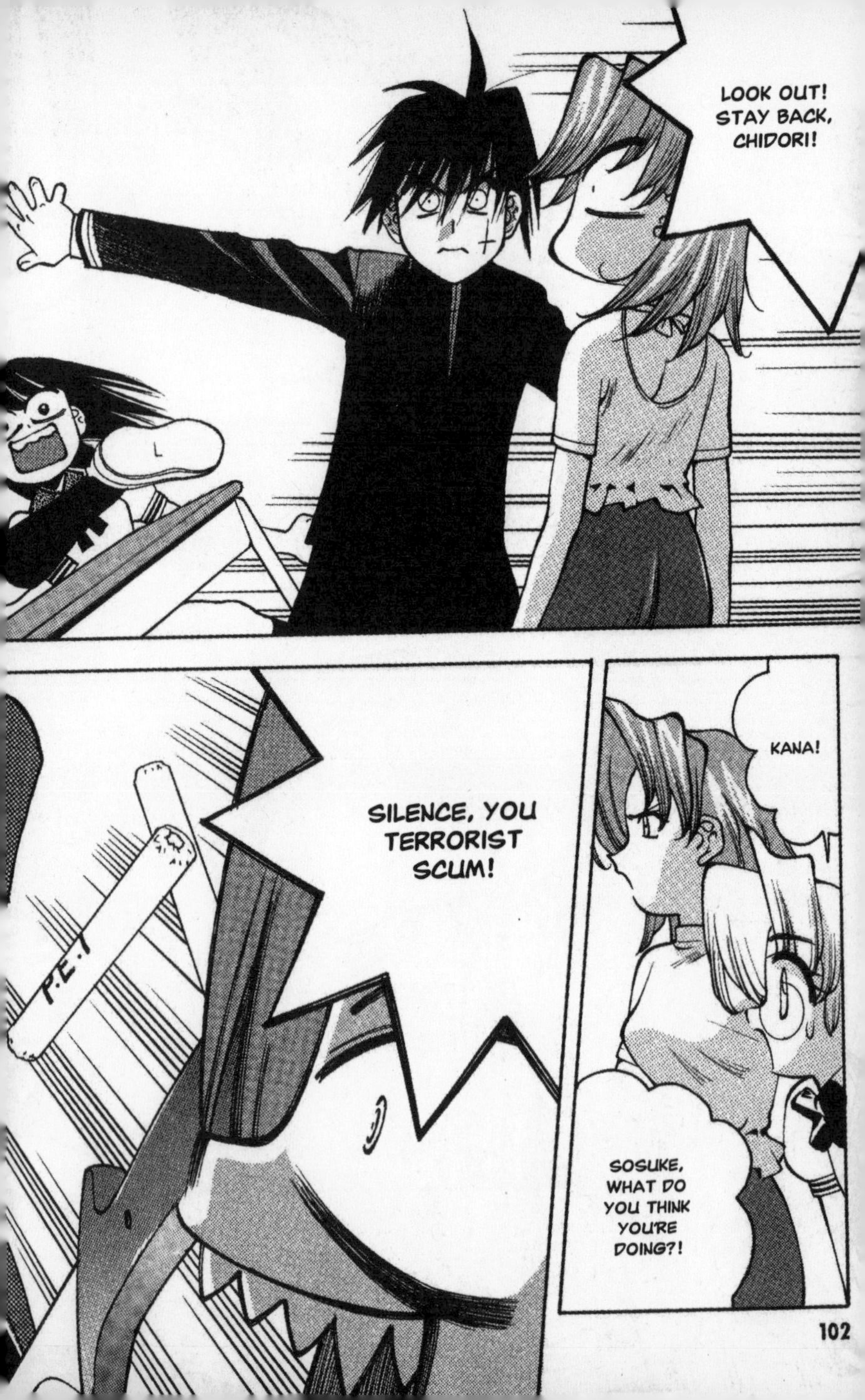
LOOK OUT! STAY BACK, CHIDORI!
KANA!
SOSUKE, WHAT DO YOU THINK YOU'RE DOING?!
SILENCE, YOU TERRORIST SCUM!
P.E. 1

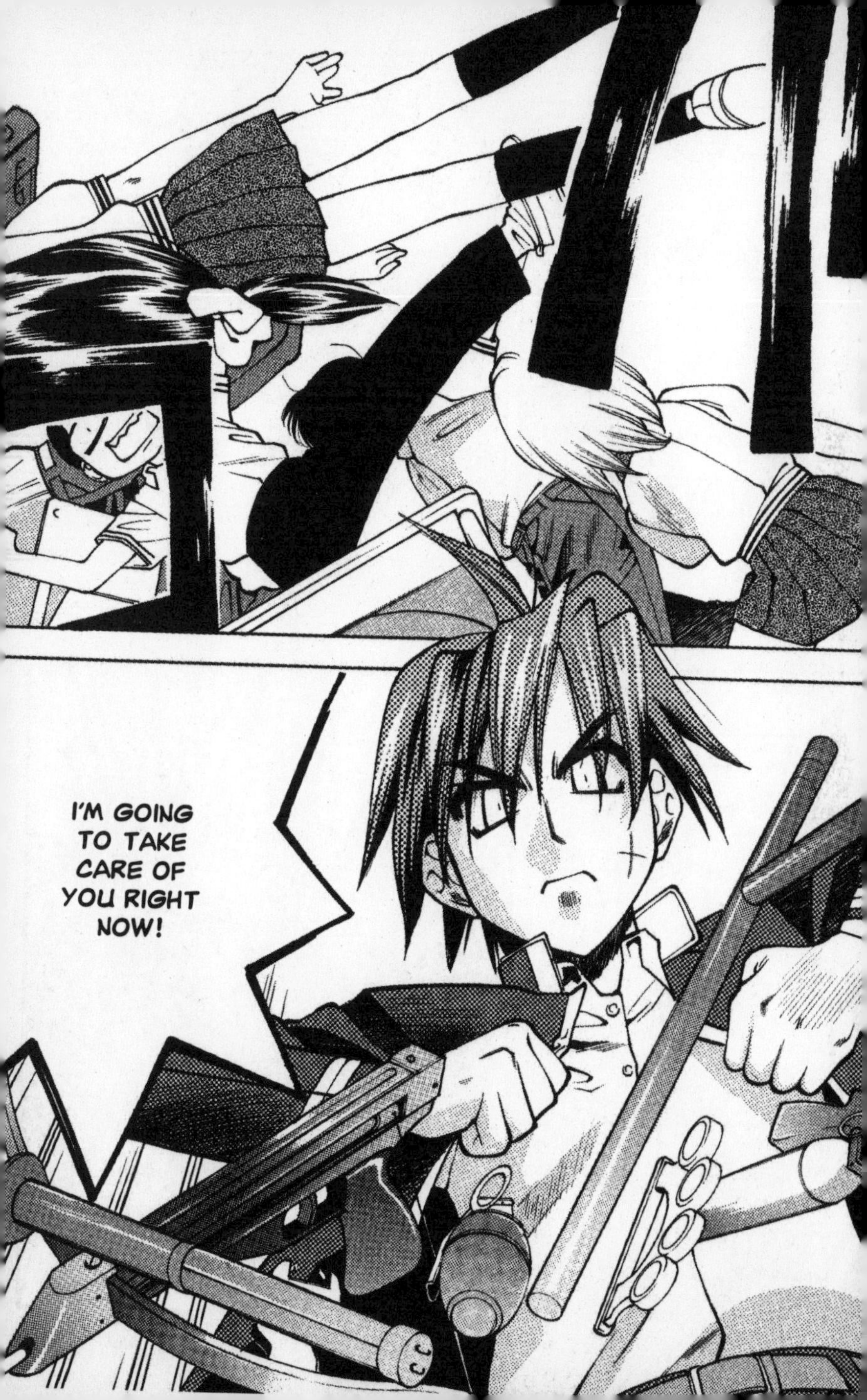
I'M GOING TO TAKE CARE OF YOU RIGHT NOW!

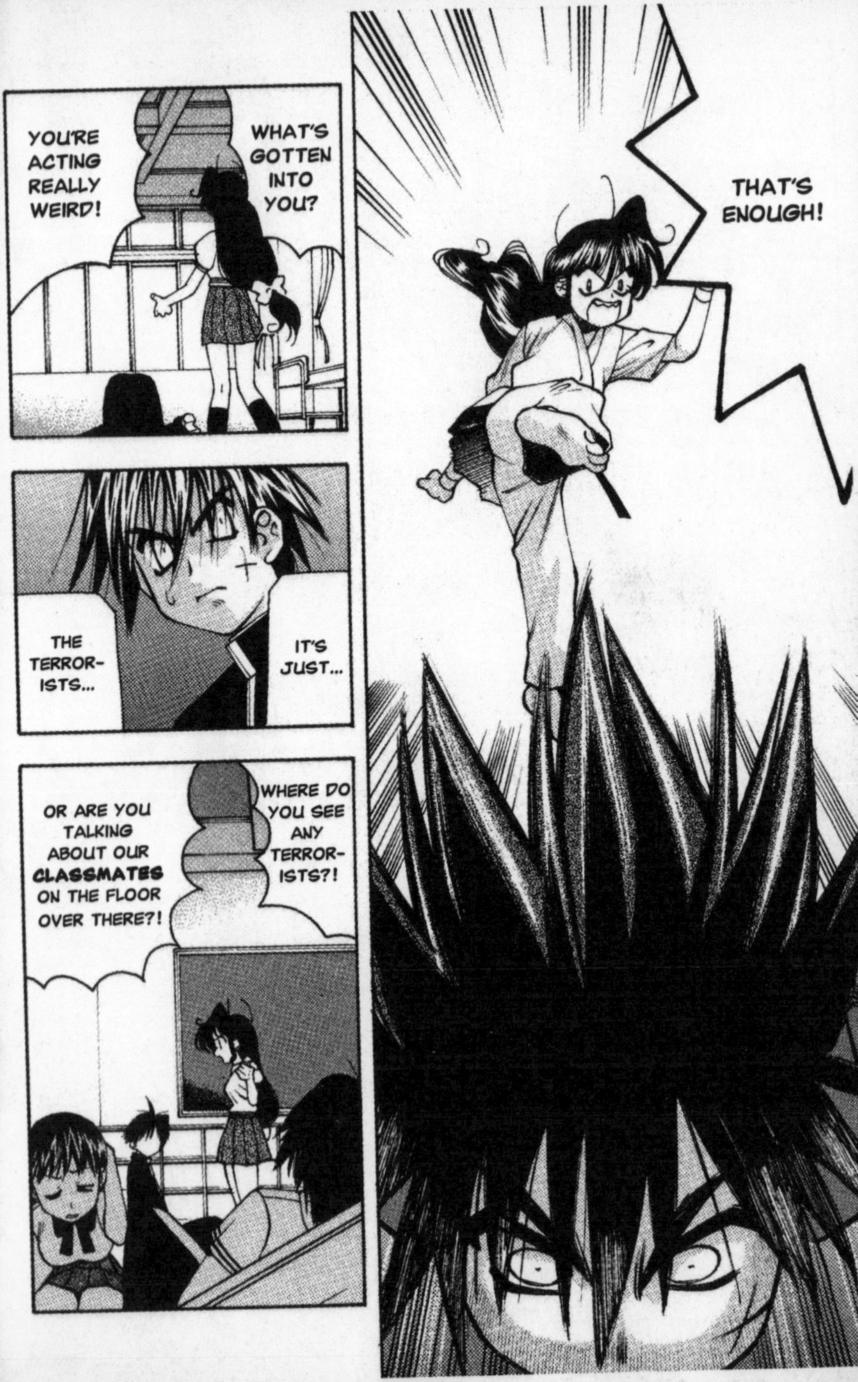
WHAT'S GOTTEN INTO YOU?
YOU'RE ACTING REALLY WEIRD!
IT'S JUST...
THE TERROR-ISTS...
WHERE DO YOU SEE ANY TERROR-ISTS?!
OR ARE YOU TALKING ABOUT OUR **CLASSMATES** ON THE FLOOR OVER THERE?!
THAT'S ENOUGH!

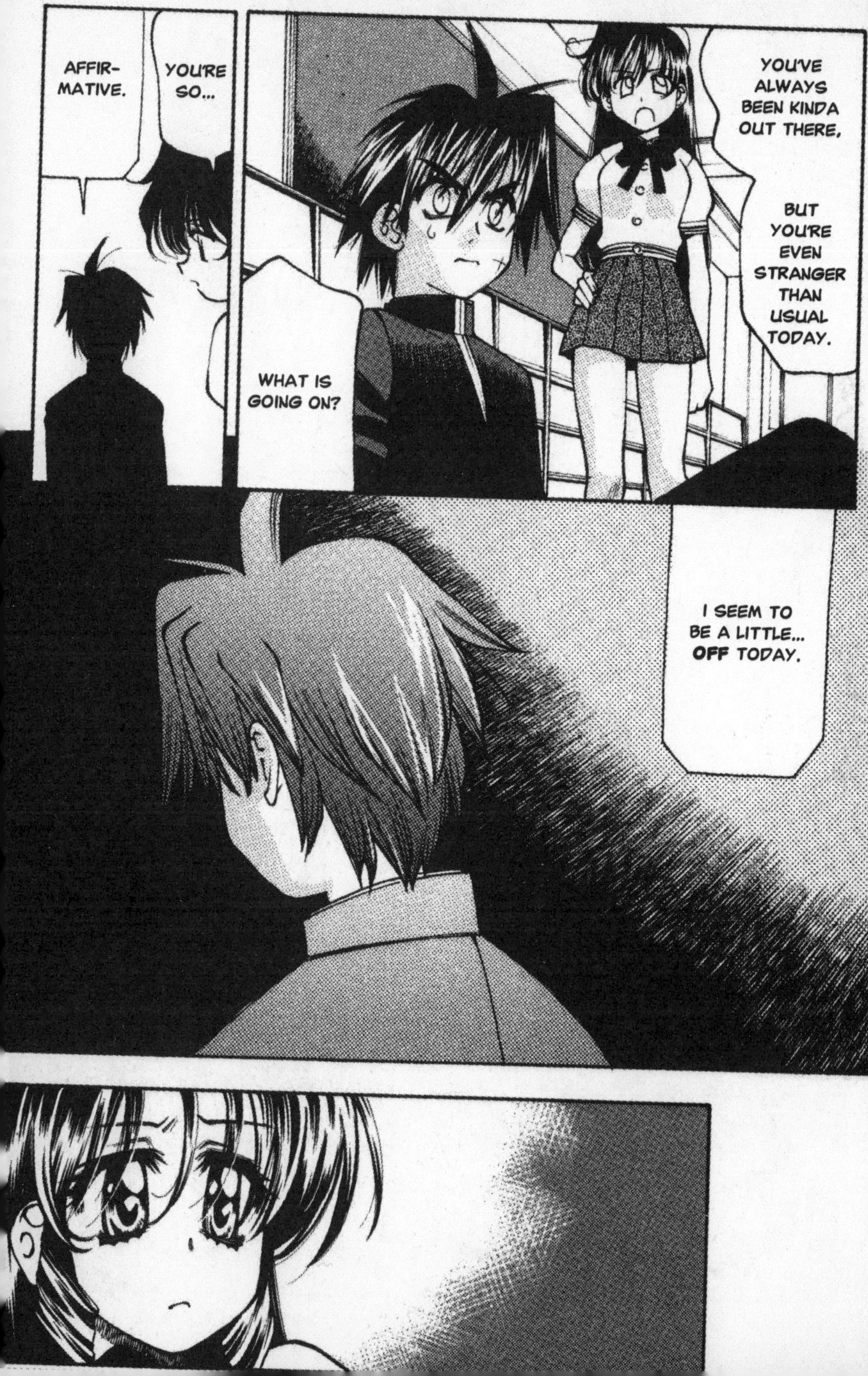
YOU'VE ALWAYS BEEN KINDA OUT THERE,
BUT YOU'RE EVEN STRANGER THAN USUAL TODAY.
WHAT IS GOING ON?
YOU'RE SO...
AFFIRMATIVE.
I SEEM TO BE A LITTLE... **OFF** TODAY.

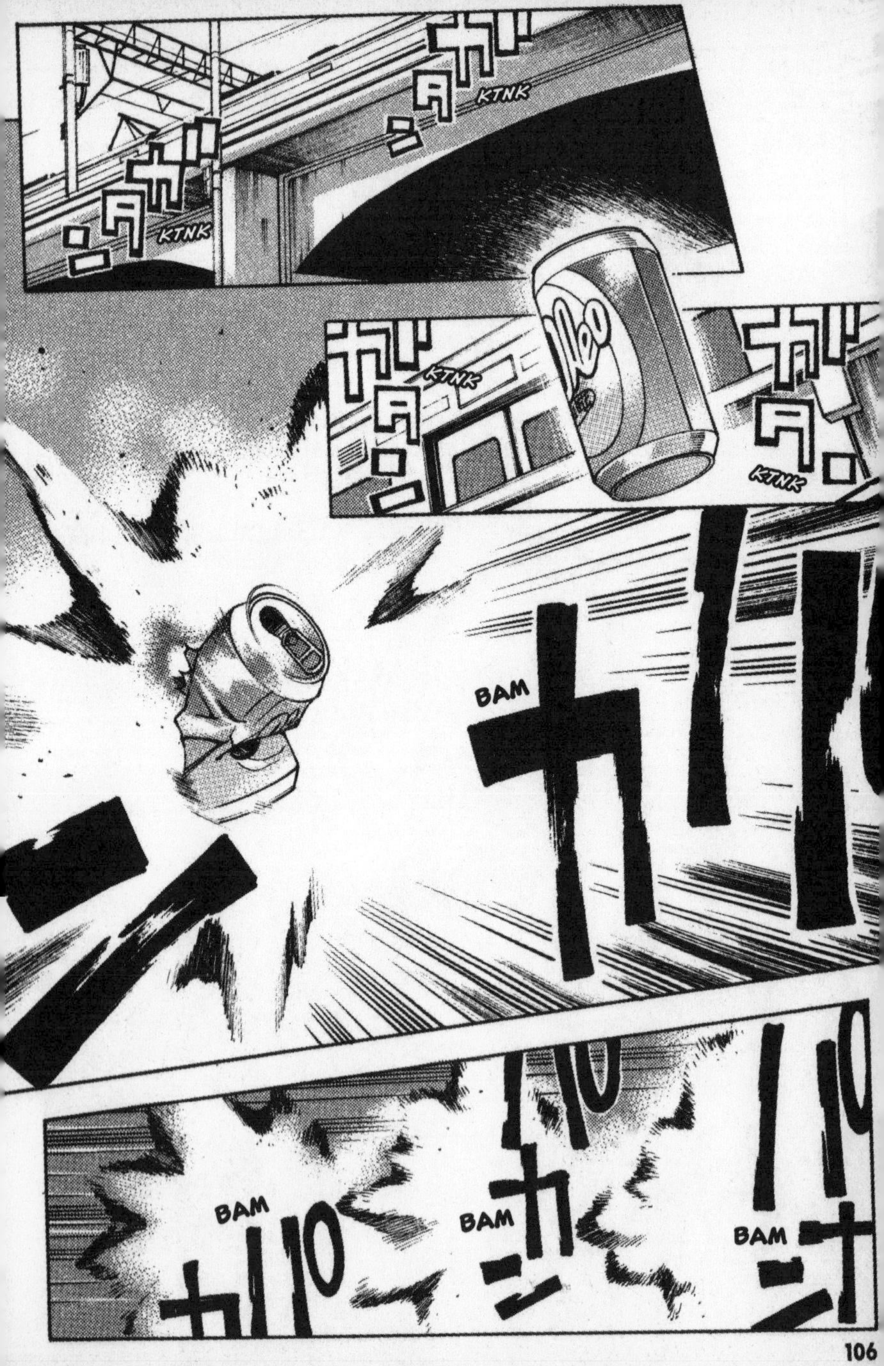
KTNK
KTNK
KTNK
KTNK
BAM
BAM
BAM
BAM

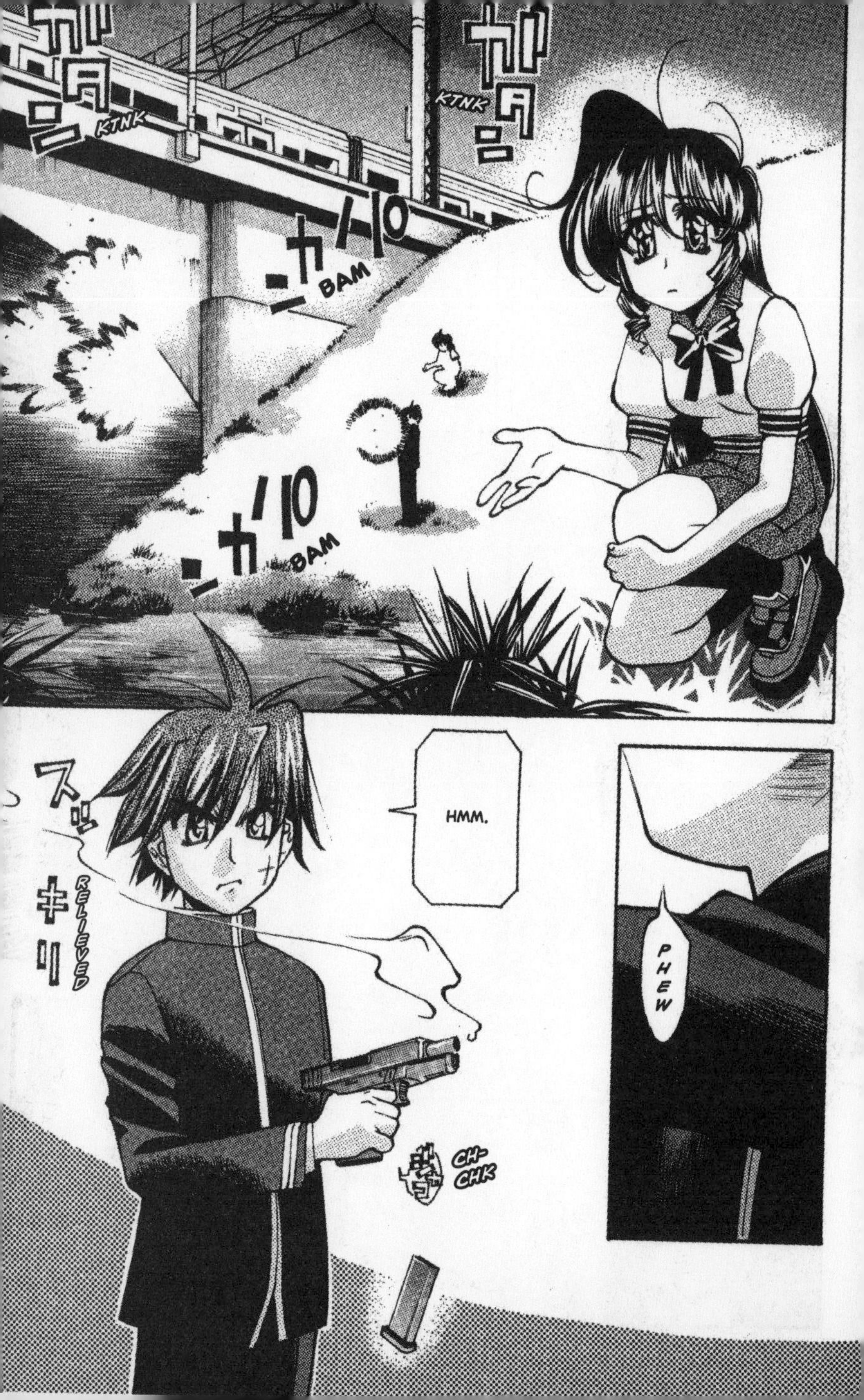
KTNK
KTNK
BAM
BAM
PHEW
HMM.
RELIEVED
CH-CHK

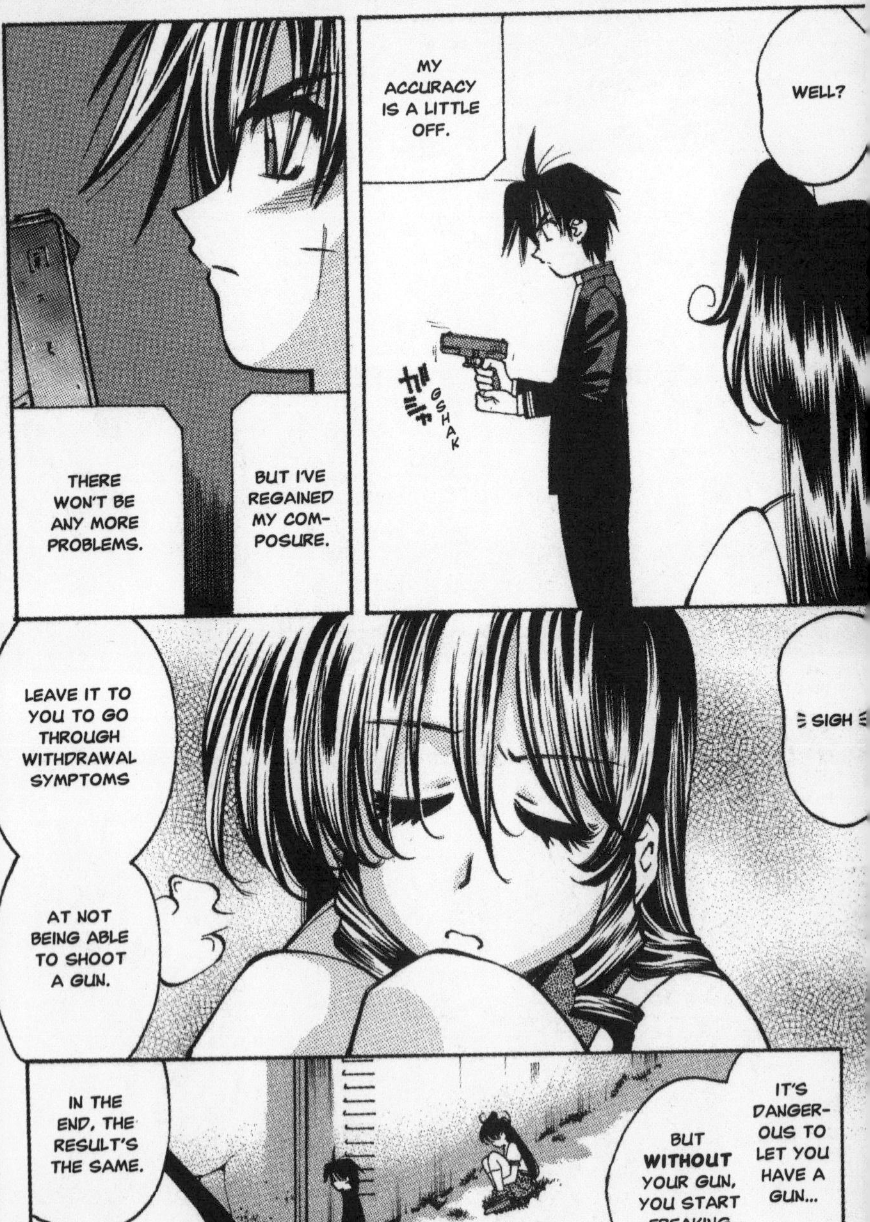
WELL?
MY ACCURACY IS A LITTLE OFF.
GSHAK
BUT I'VE REGAINED MY COMPOSURE.
THERE WON'T BE ANY MORE PROBLEMS.
SIGH
LEAVE IT TO YOU TO GO THROUGH WITHDRAWAL SYMPTOMS
AT NOT BEING ABLE TO SHOOT A GUN.
IT'S DANGEROUS TO LET YOU HAVE A GUN...
BUT **WITHOUT** YOUR GUN, YOU START FREAKING OUT.
IN THE END, THE RESULT'S THE SAME.

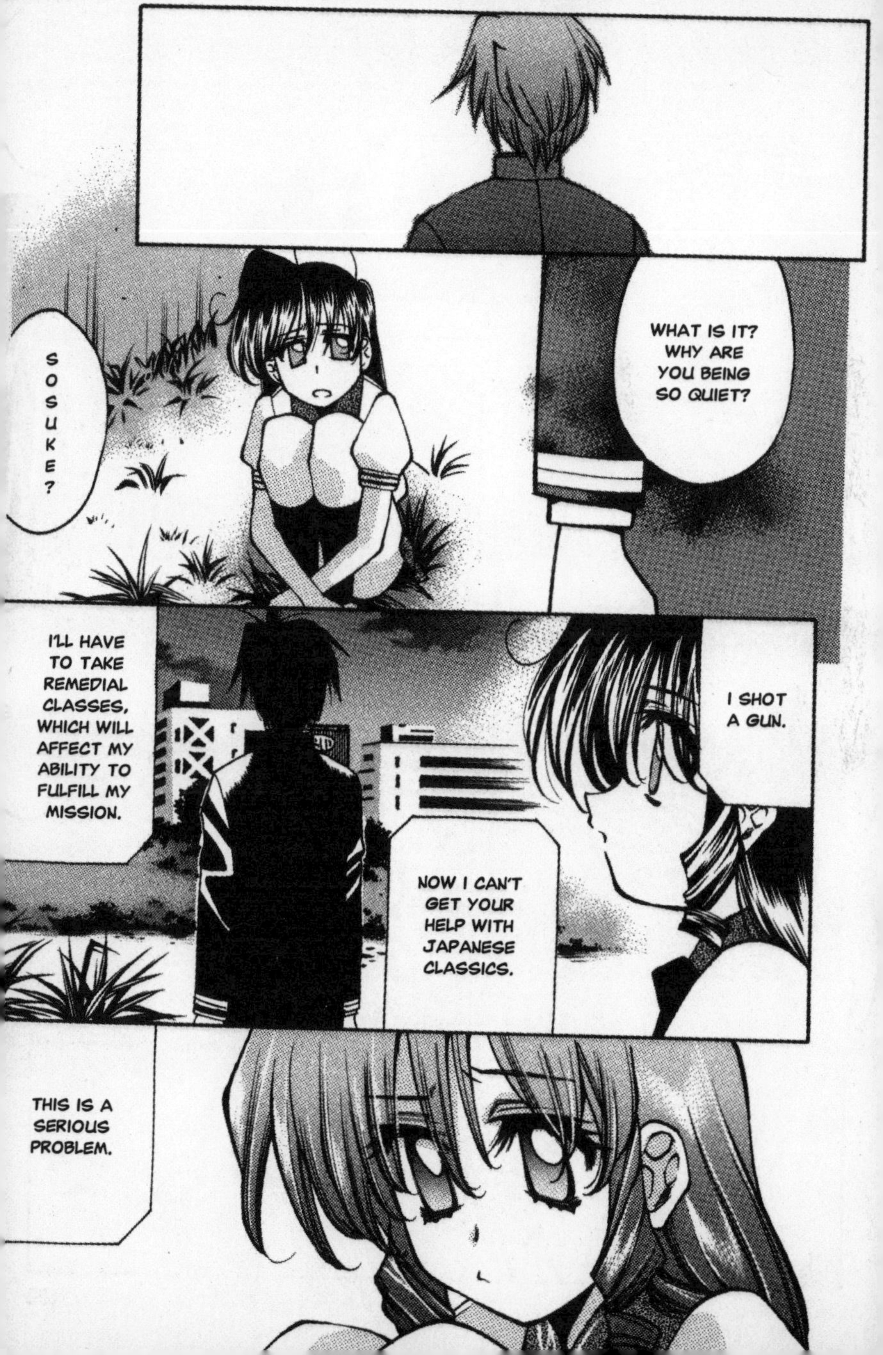
WHAT IS IT? WHY ARE YOU BEING SO QUIET?
SOSUKE?
I SHOT A GUN.
NOW I CAN'T GET YOUR HELP WITH JAPANESE CLASSICS.
I'LL HAVE TO TAKE REMEDIAL CLASSES, WHICH WILL AFFECT MY ABILITY TO FULFILL MY MISSION.
THIS IS A SERIOUS PROBLEM.

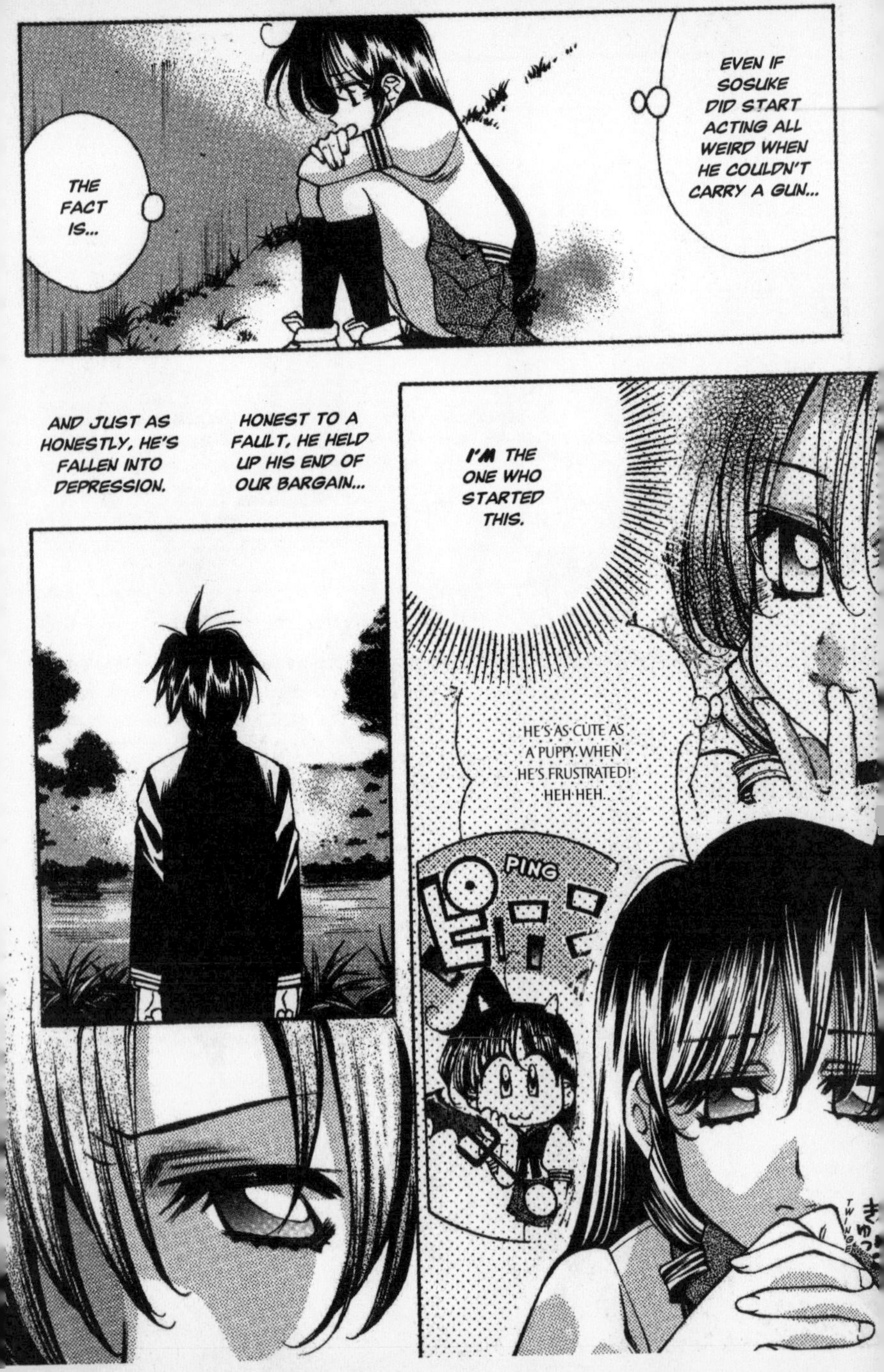
EVEN IF SOSUKE DID START ACTING ALL WEIRD WHEN HE COULDN'T CARRY A GUN...
THE FACT IS...
I'M THE ONE WHO STARTED THIS.
HONEST TO A FAULT, HE HELD UP HIS END OF OUR BARGAIN...
AND JUST AS HONESTLY, HE'S FALLEN INTO DEPRESSION.
HE'S AS CUTE AS A PUPPY WHEN HE'S FRUSTRATED! HEH HEH..
PING
TWINGE

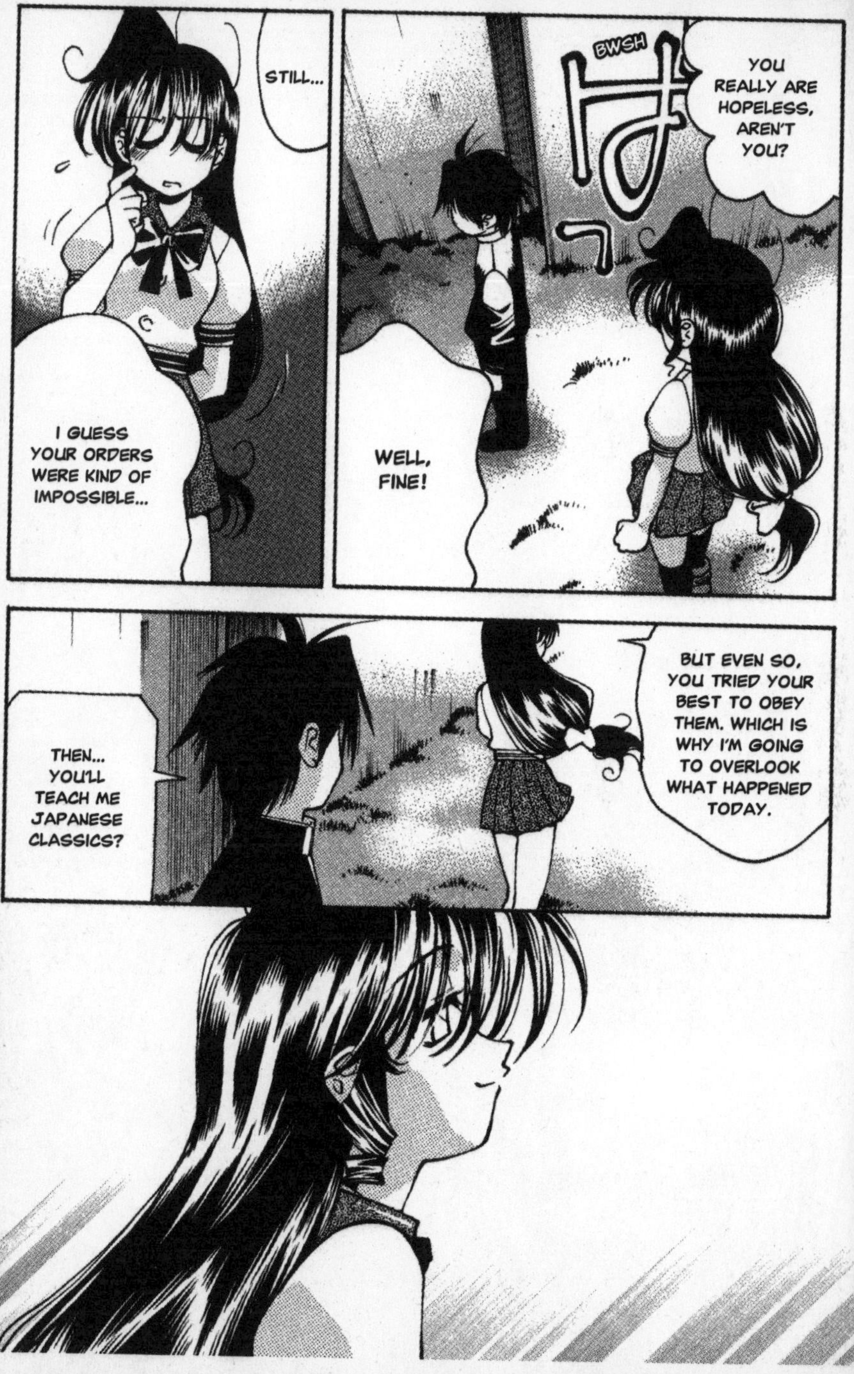
BWSH
はっ
YOU REALLY ARE HOPELESS, AREN'T YOU?
WELL, FINE!
STILL...
I GUESS YOUR ORDERS WERE KIND OF IMPOSSIBLE...
BUT EVEN SO, YOU TRIED YOUR BEST TO OBEY THEM. WHICH IS WHY I'M GOING TO OVERLOOK WHAT HAPPENED TODAY.
THEN... YOU'LL TEACH ME JAPANESE CLASSICS?

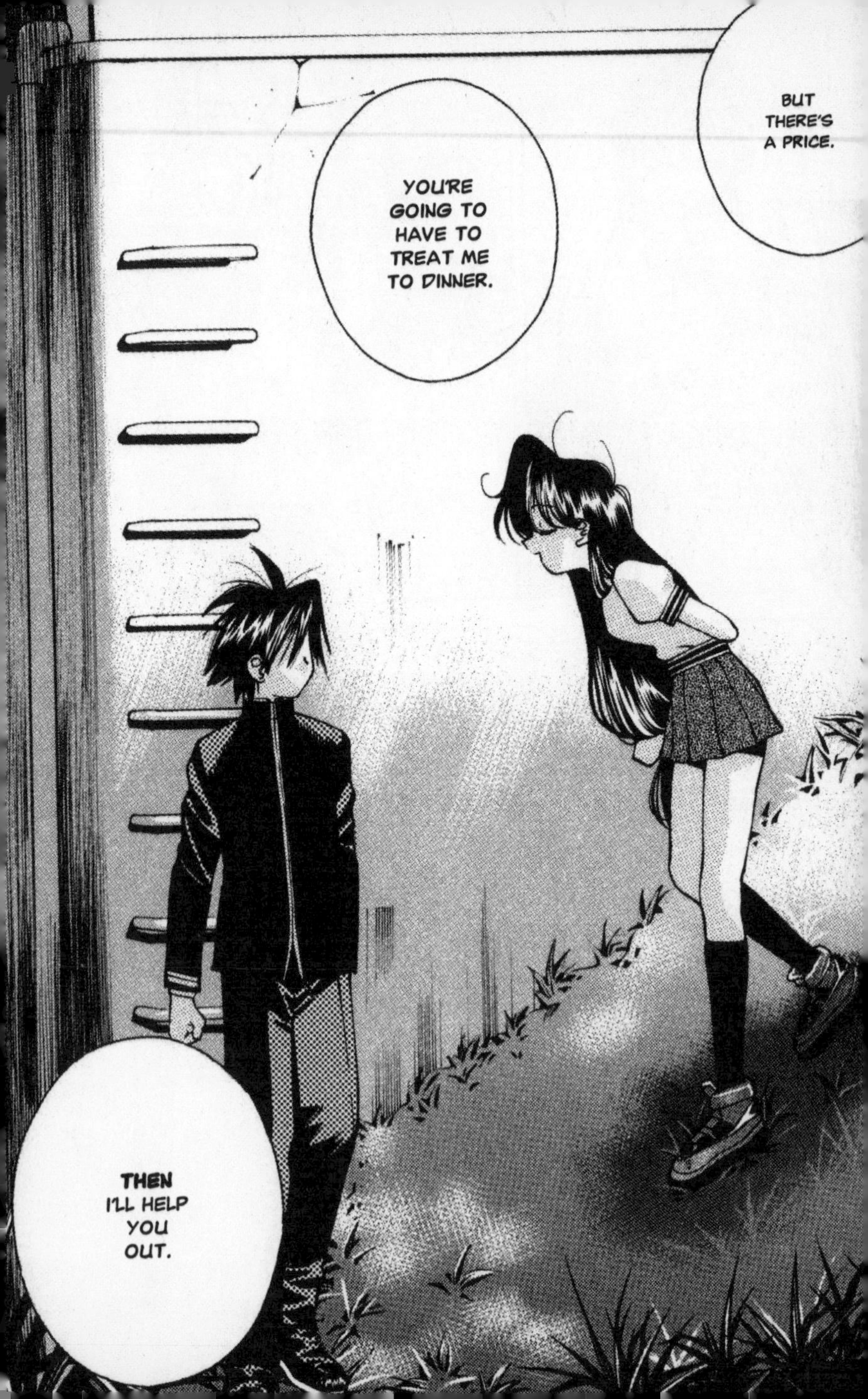
BUT THERE'S A PRICE.
YOU'RE GOING TO HAVE TO TREAT ME TO DINNER.
THEN I'LL HELP YOU OUT.

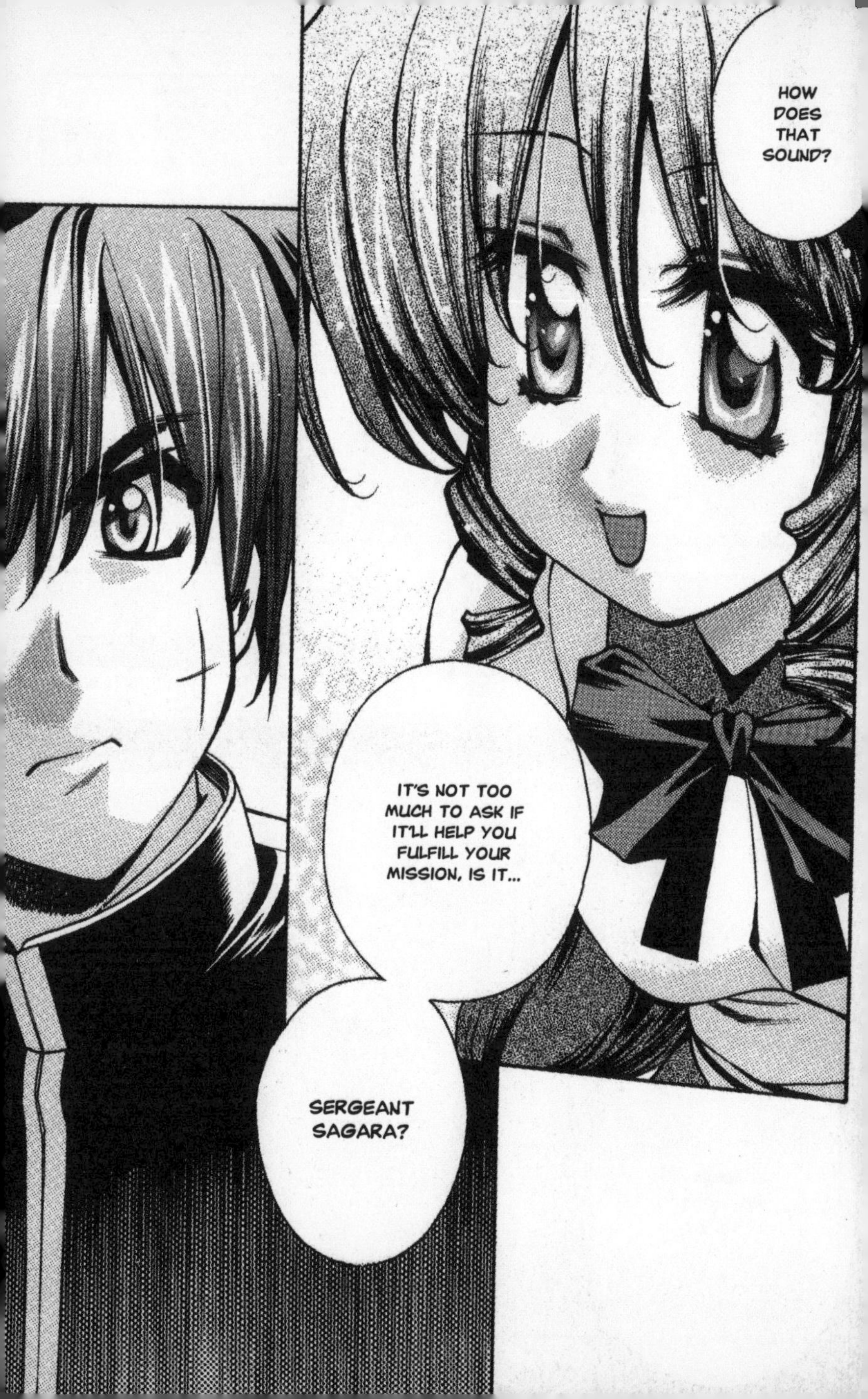
HOW DOES THAT SOUND?
IT'S NOT TOO MUCH TO ASK IF IT'LL HELP YOU FULFILL YOUR MISSION, IS IT...
SERGEANT SAGARA?

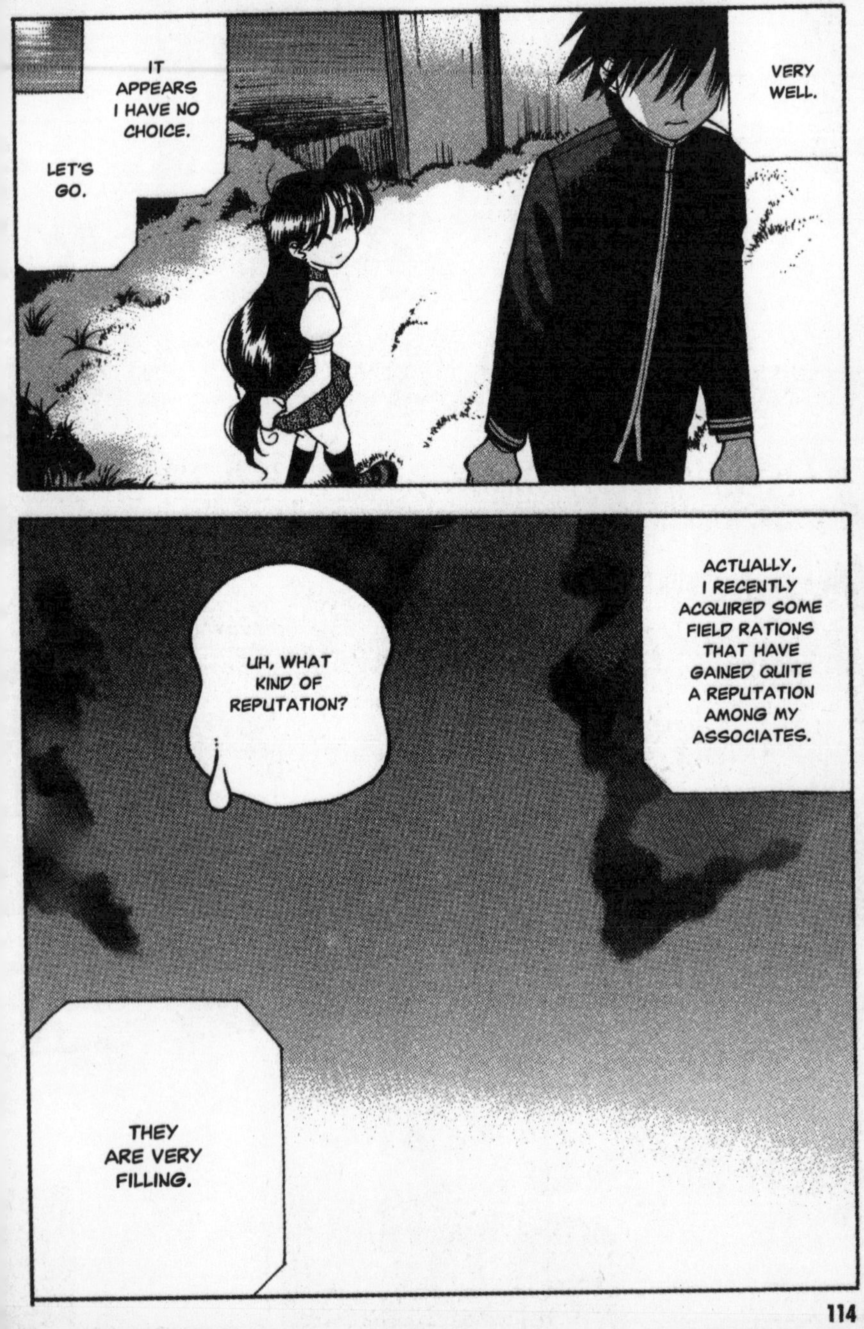
IT APPEARS I HAVE NO CHOICE.
LET'S GO.
VERY WELL.
ACTUALLY, I RECENTLY ACQUIRED SOME FIELD RATIONS THAT HAVE GAINED QUITE A REPUTATION AMONG MY ASSOCIATES.
UH, WHAT KIND OF REPUTATION?
THEY ARE VERY FILLING.

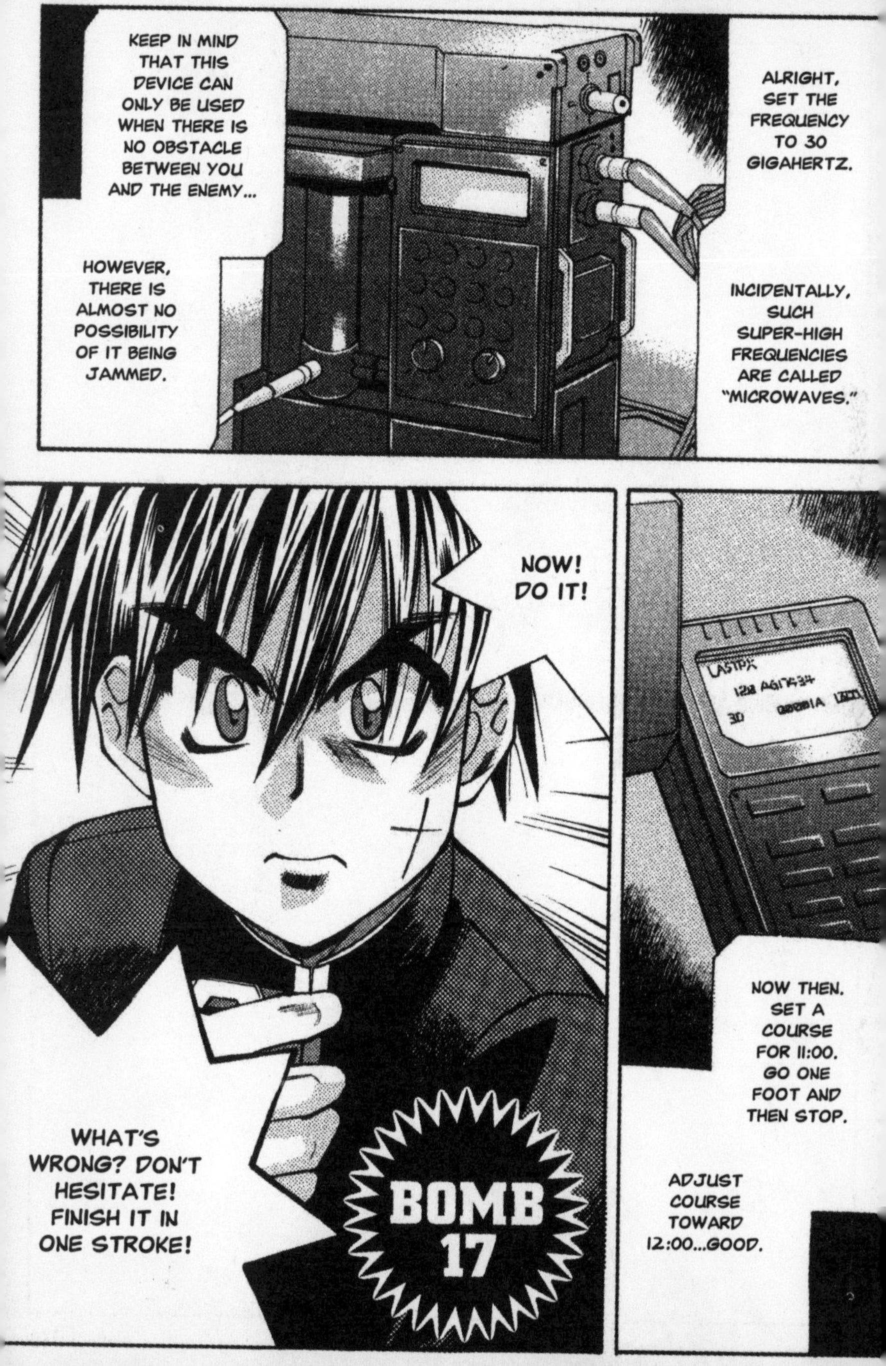
ALRIGHT, SET THE FREQUENCY TO 30 GIGAHERTZ.
INCIDENTALLY, SUCH SUPER-HIGH FREQUENCIES ARE CALLED "MICROWAVES."
KEEP IN MIND THAT THIS DEVICE CAN ONLY BE USED WHEN THERE IS NO OBSTACLE BETWEEN YOU AND THE ENEMY...
HOWEVER, THERE IS ALMOST NO POSSIBILITY OF IT BEING JAMMED.
NOW THEN. SET A COURSE FOR 11:00. GO ONE FOOT AND THEN STOP.
ADJUST COURSE TOWARD 12:00...GOOD.
NOW! DO IT!
WHAT'S WRONG? DON'T HESITATE! FINISH IT IN ONE STROKE!
BOMB 17

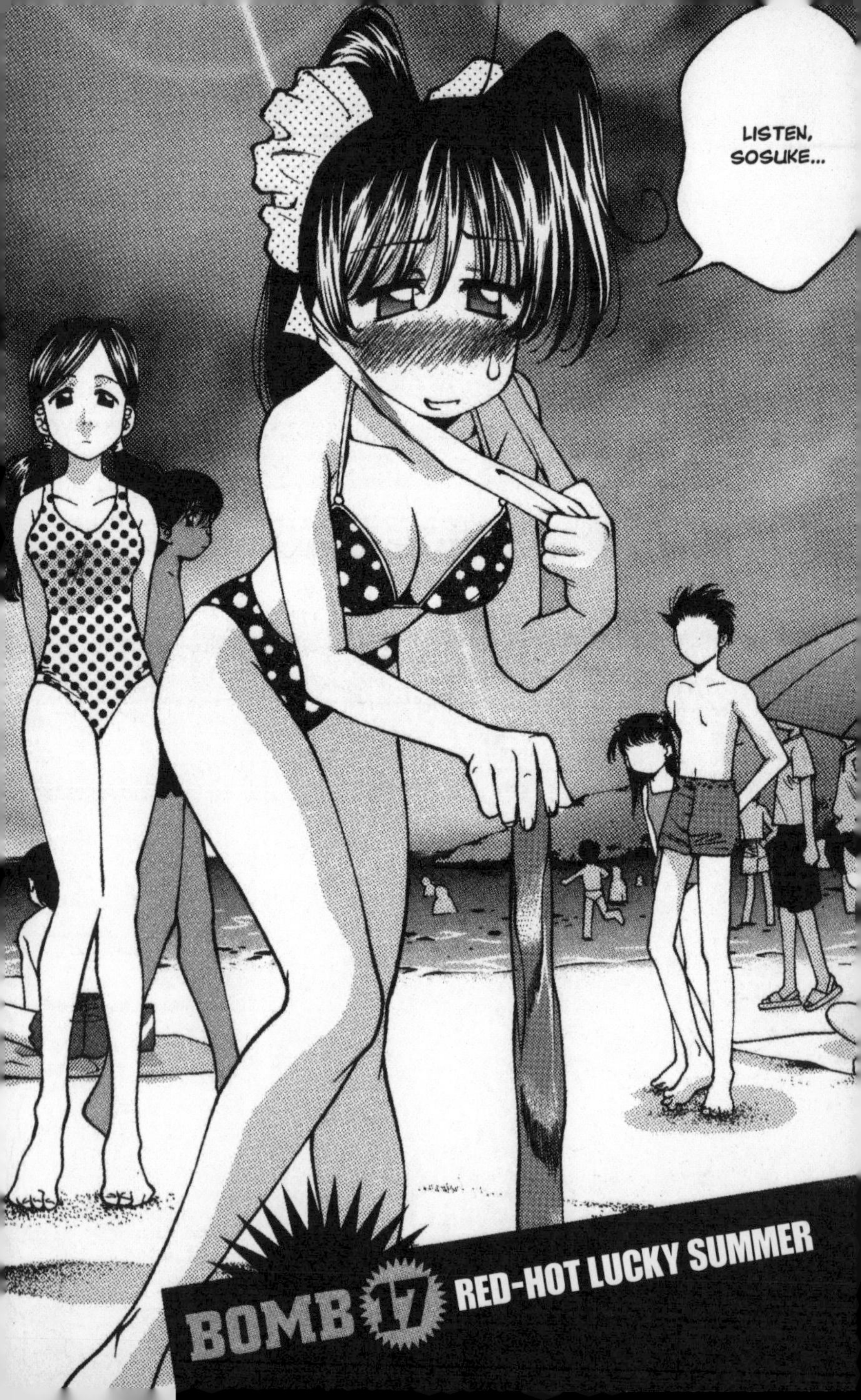
LISTEN, SOSUKE...
BOMB 17
RED-HOT LUCKY SUMMER

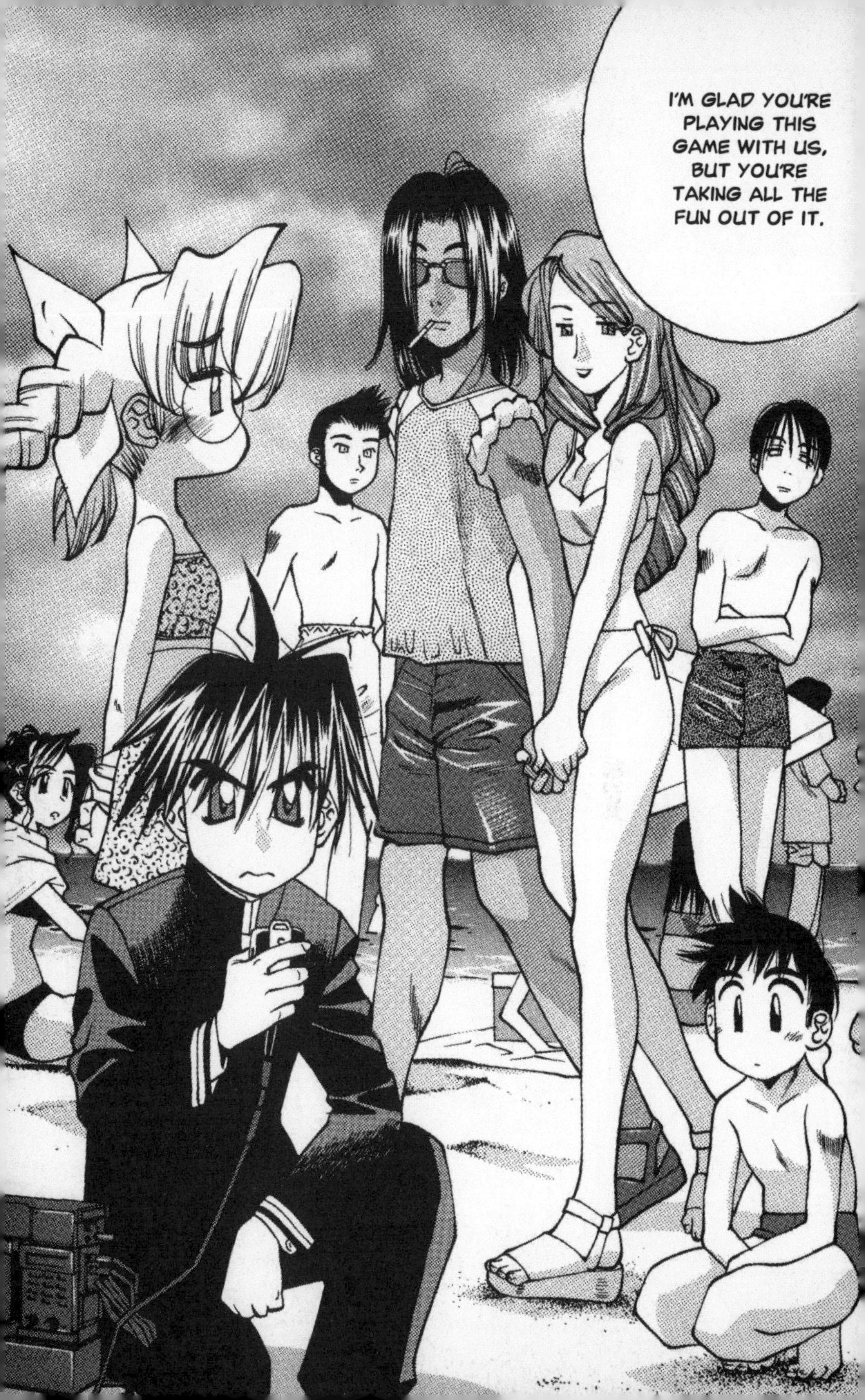
I'M GLAD YOU'RE PLAYING THIS GAME WITH US, BUT YOU'RE TAKING ALL THE FUN OUT OF IT.

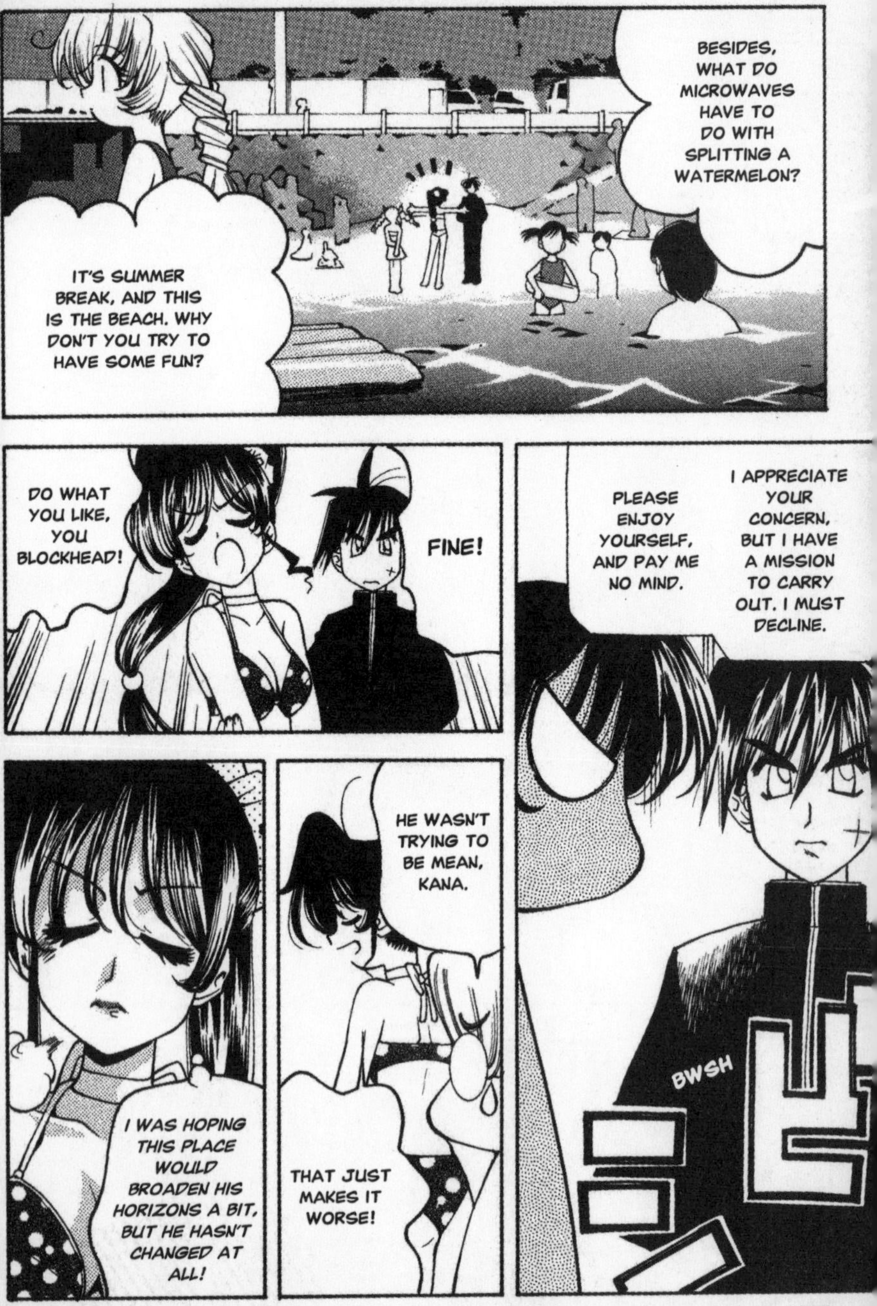
BESIDES, WHAT DO MICROWAVES HAVE TO DO WITH SPLITTING A WATERMELON?
IT'S SUMMER BREAK, AND THIS IS THE BEACH. WHY DON'T YOU TRY TO HAVE SOME FUN?
I APPRECIATE YOUR CONCERN, BUT I HAVE A MISSION TO CARRY OUT. I MUST DECLINE.
PLEASE ENJOY YOURSELF, AND PAY ME NO MIND.
FINE!
DO WHAT YOU LIKE, YOU BLOCKHEAD!
BWSH
HE WASN'T TRYING TO BE MEAN, KANA.
THAT JUST MAKES IT WORSE!
I WAS HOPING THIS PLACE WOULD BROADEN HIS HORIZONS A BIT, BUT HE HASN'T CHANGED AT ALL!

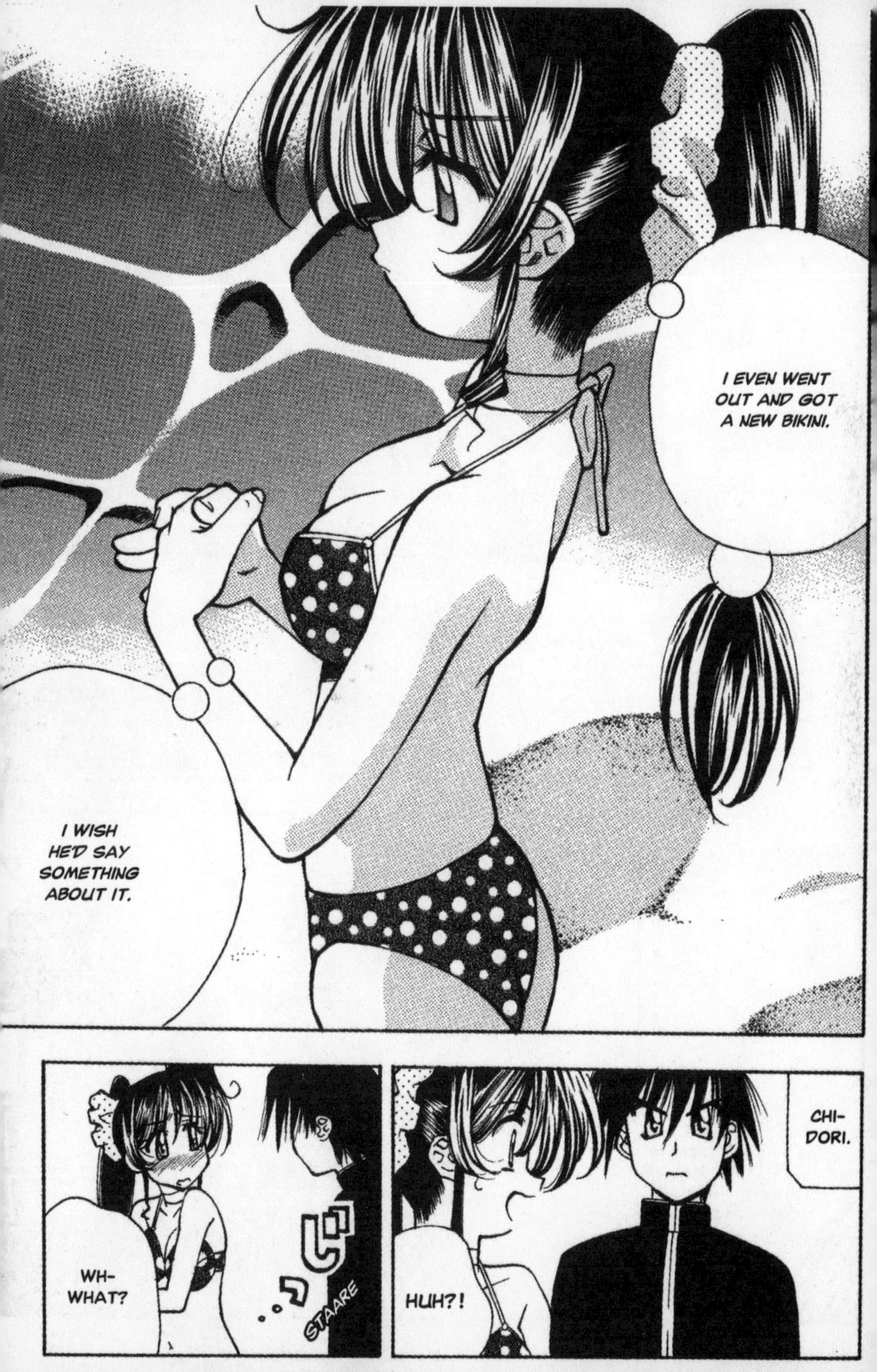
I EVEN WENT OUT AND GOT A NEW BIKINI.
I WISH HE'D SAY SOMETHING ABOUT IT.
CHI-DORI.
HUH?!
STAARE
WH-WHAT?

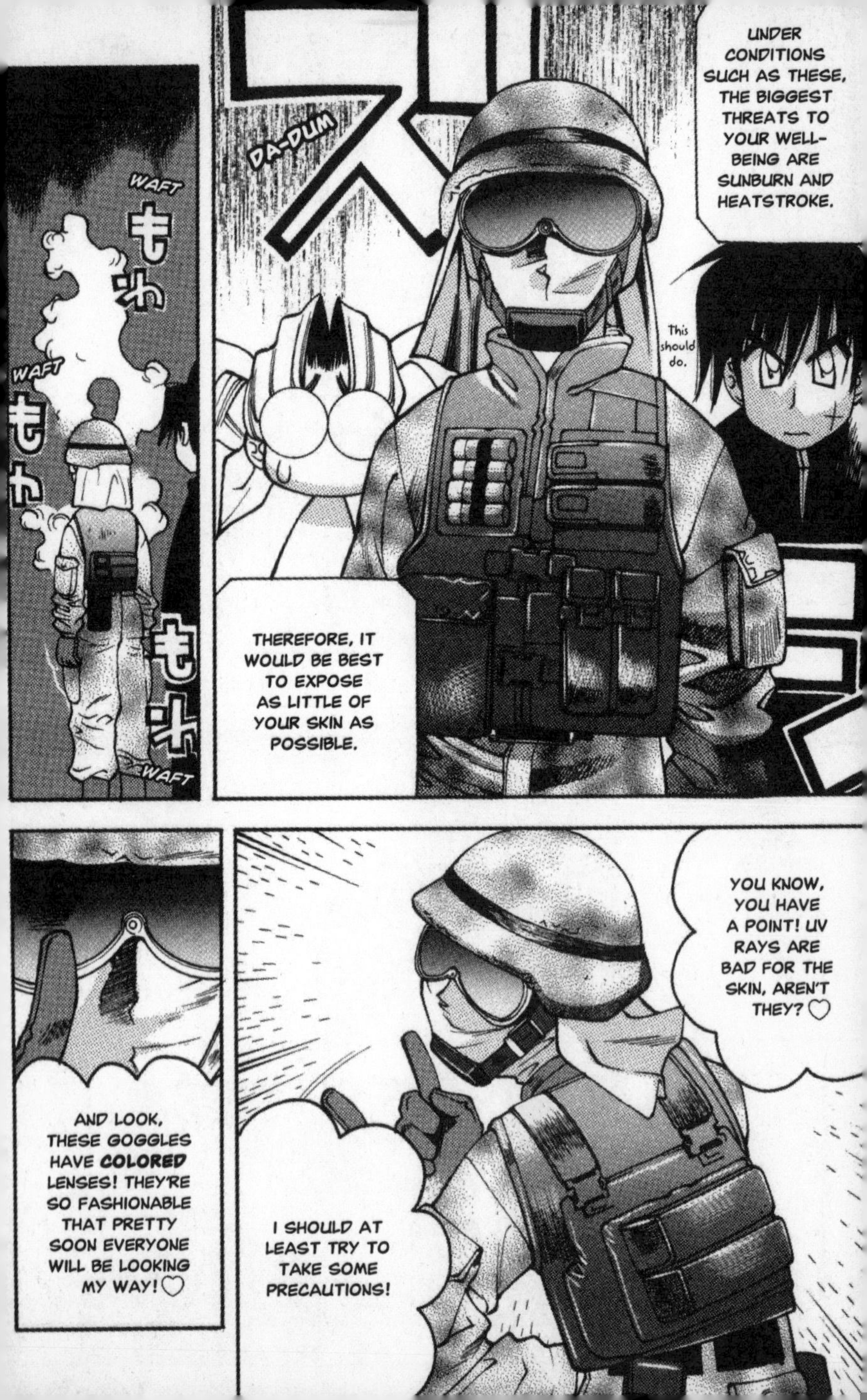

UNDER CONDITIONS SUCH AS THESE, THE BIGGEST THREATS TO YOUR WELL-BEING ARE SUNBURN AND HEATSTROKE.
DA-DUM
This should do.
THEREFORE, IT WOULD BE BEST TO EXPOSE AS LITTLE OF YOUR SKIN AS POSSIBLE.
WAFT
もわ
WAFT
もわ
もわ
WAFT
YOU KNOW, YOU HAVE A POINT! UV RAYS ARE BAD FOR THE SKIN, AREN'T THEY? ♡
I SHOULD AT LEAST TRY TO TAKE SOME PRECAUTIONS!
AND LOOK, THESE GOGGLES HAVE **COLORED** LENSES! THEY'RE SO FASHIONABLE THAT PRETTY SOON EVERYONE WILL BE LOOKING MY WAY! ♡

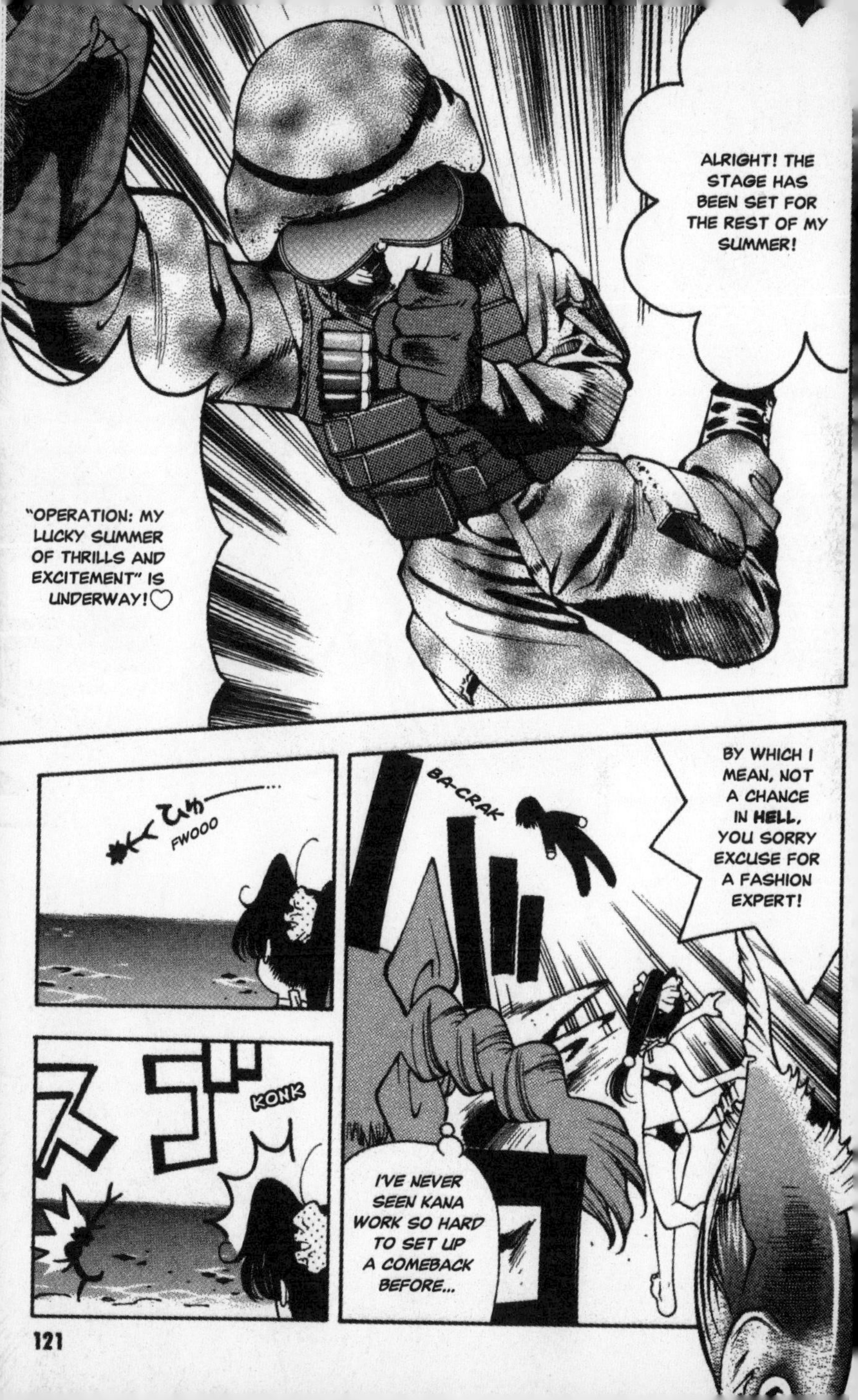
ALRIGHT! THE STAGE HAS BEEN SET FOR THE REST OF MY SUMMER!
"OPERATION: MY LUCKY SUMMER OF THRILLS AND EXCITEMENT" IS UNDERWAY! ♡
BY WHICH I MEAN, NOT A CHANCE IN HELL, YOU SORRY EXCUSE FOR A FASHION EXPERT!
BA-CRAK
I'VE NEVER SEEN KANA WORK SO HARD TO SET UP A COMEBACK BEFORE...
FWOOO
KONK

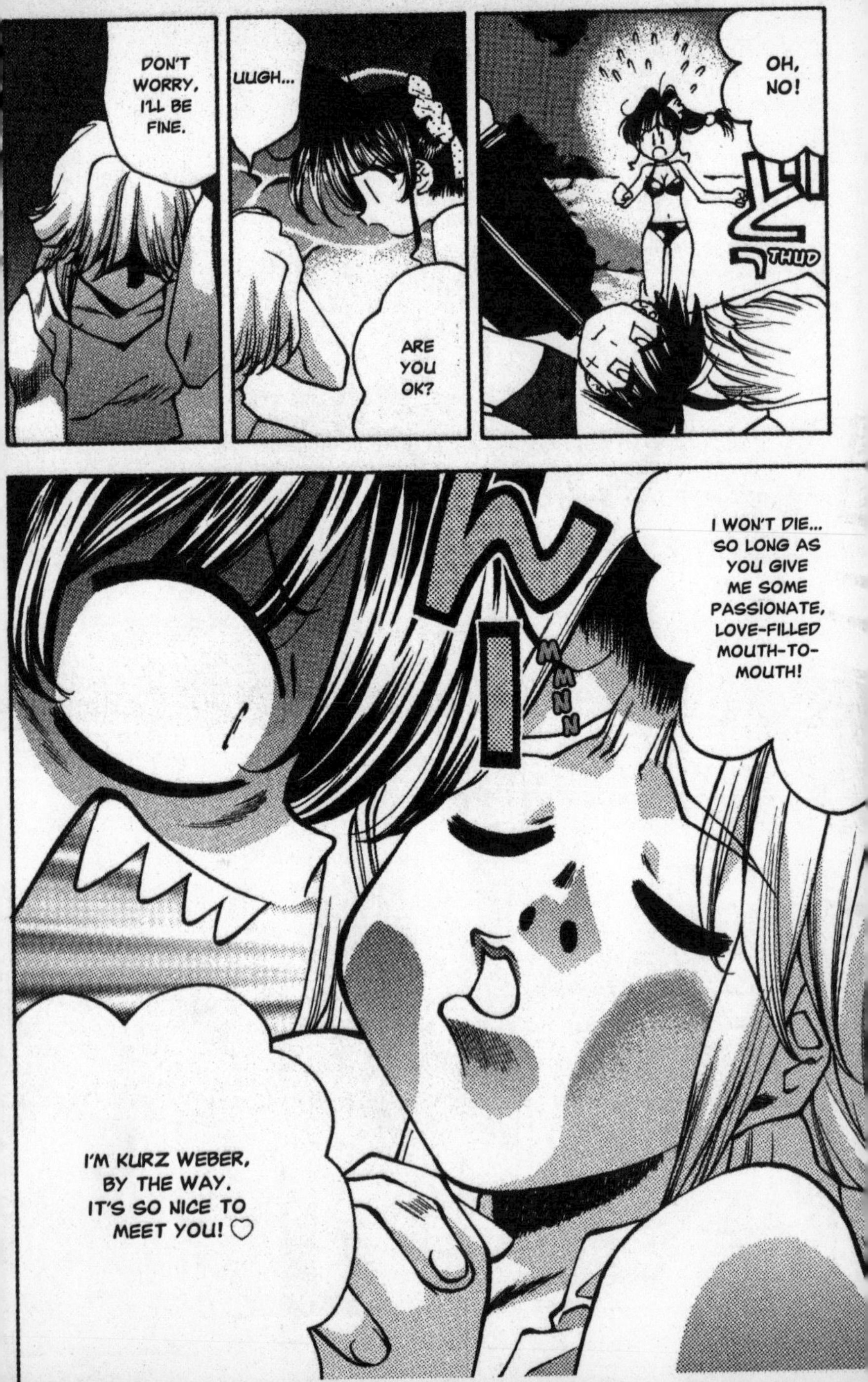
OH, NO!
THUD
UUGH...
ARE YOU OK?
DON'T WORRY, I'LL BE FINE.
I WON'T DIE... SO LONG AS YOU GIVE ME SOME PASSIONATE, LOVE-FILLED MOUTH-TO-MOUTH!
MMNN
I'M KURZ WEBER, BY THE WAY. IT'S SO NICE TO MEET YOU! ♡

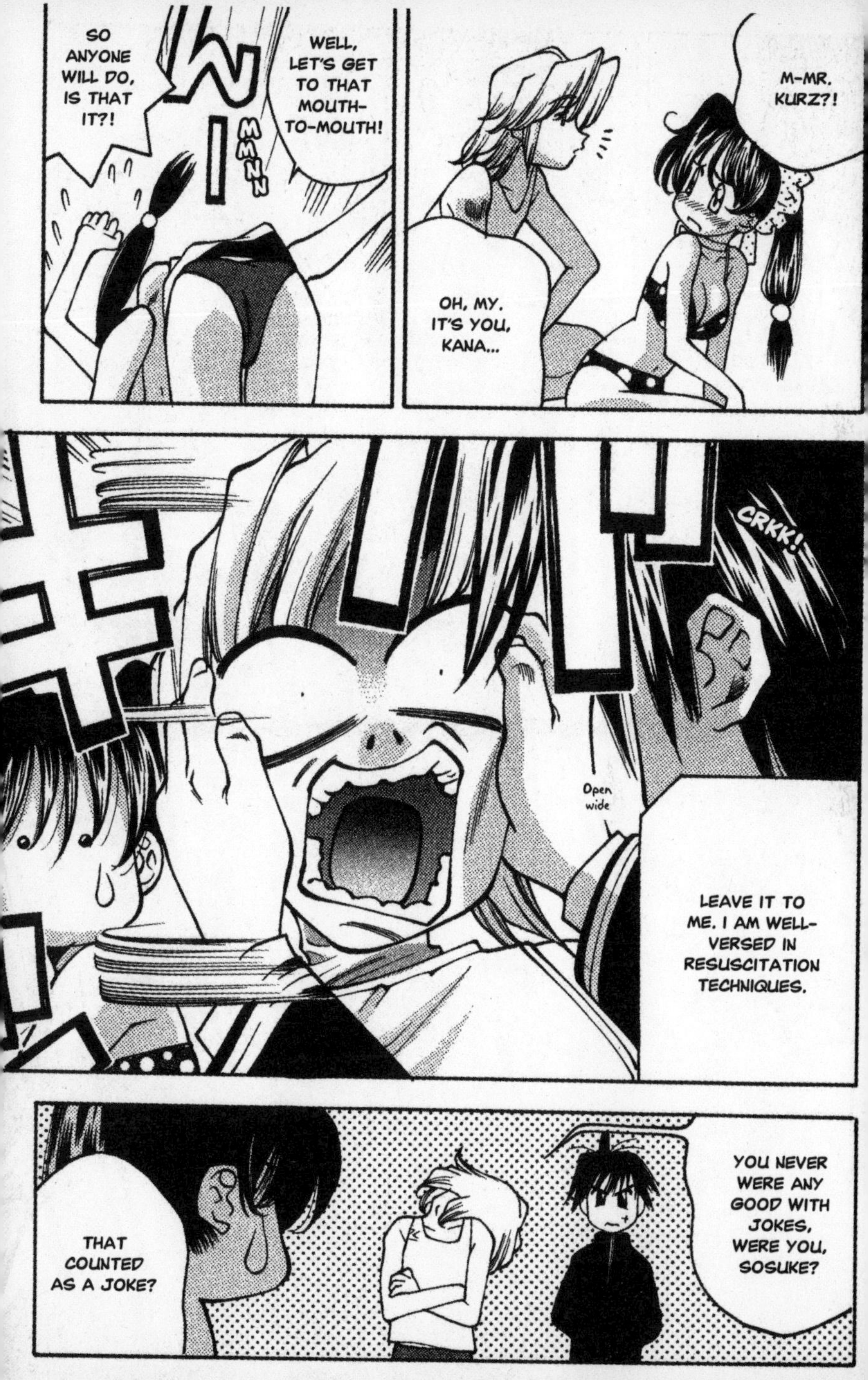
M-MR. KURZ?!
OH, MY. IT'S YOU, KANA...
WELL, LET'S GET TO THAT MOUTH-TO-MOUTH!
MMNN
SO ANYONE WILL DO, IS THAT IT?!
CRKK!
LEAVE IT TO ME. I AM WELL-VERSED IN RESUSCITATION TECHNIQUES.
Open wide
YOU NEVER WERE ANY GOOD WITH JOKES, WERE YOU, SOSUKE?
THAT COUNTED AS A JOKE?

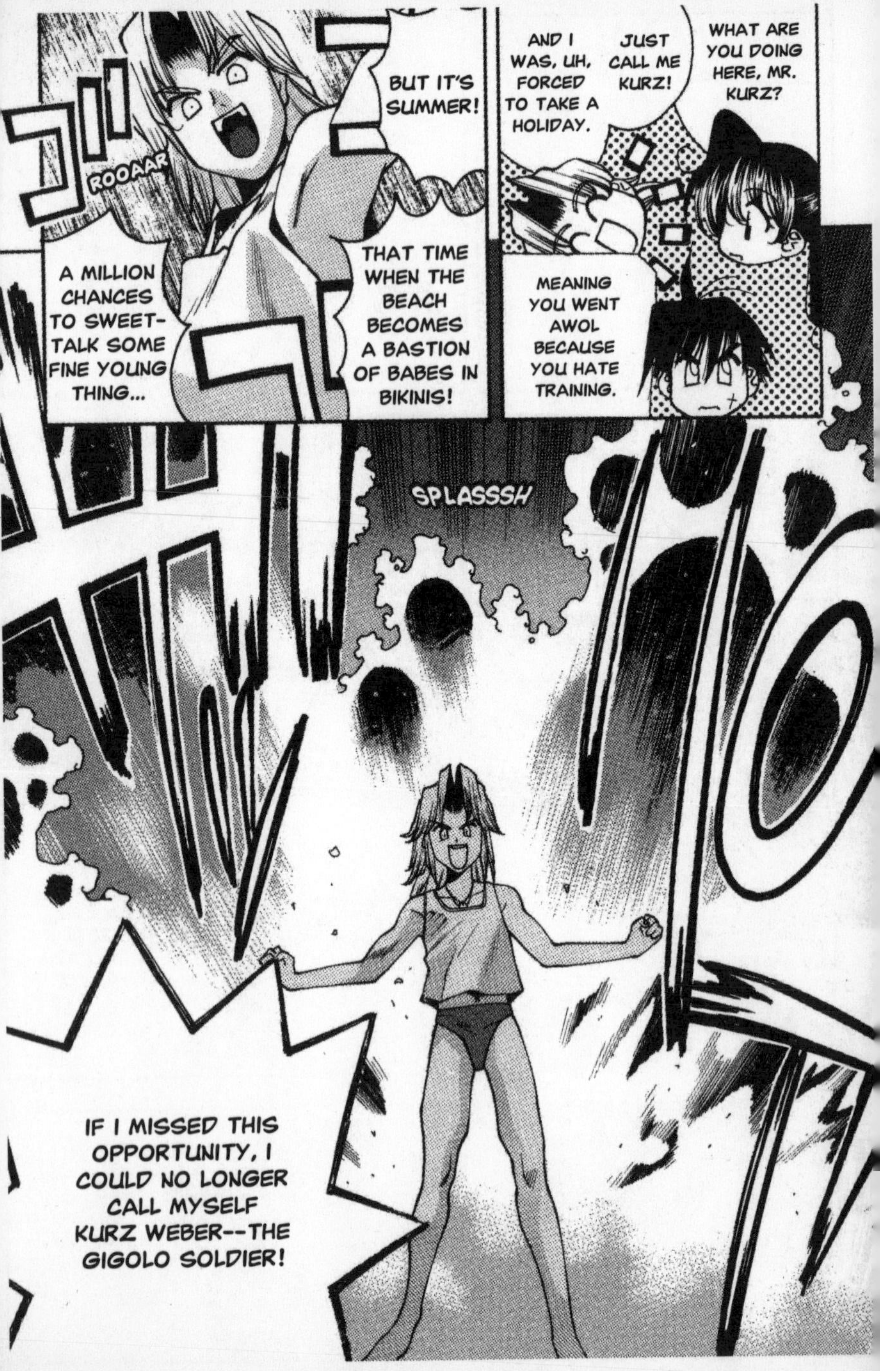
WHAT ARE YOU DOING HERE, MR. KURZ?
JUST CALL ME KURZ!
AND I WAS, UH, FORCED TO TAKE A HOLIDAY.
MEANING YOU WENT AWOL BECAUSE YOU HATE TRAINING.
BUT IT'S SUMMER!
ROOAAR
THAT TIME WHEN THE BEACH BECOMES A BASTION OF BABES IN BIKINIS!
A MILLION CHANCES TO SWEET-TALK SOME FINE YOUNG THING...
SPLASSSH
IF I MISSED THIS OPPORTUNITY, I COULD NO LONGER CALL MYSELF KURZ WEBER--THE GIGOLO SOLDIER!

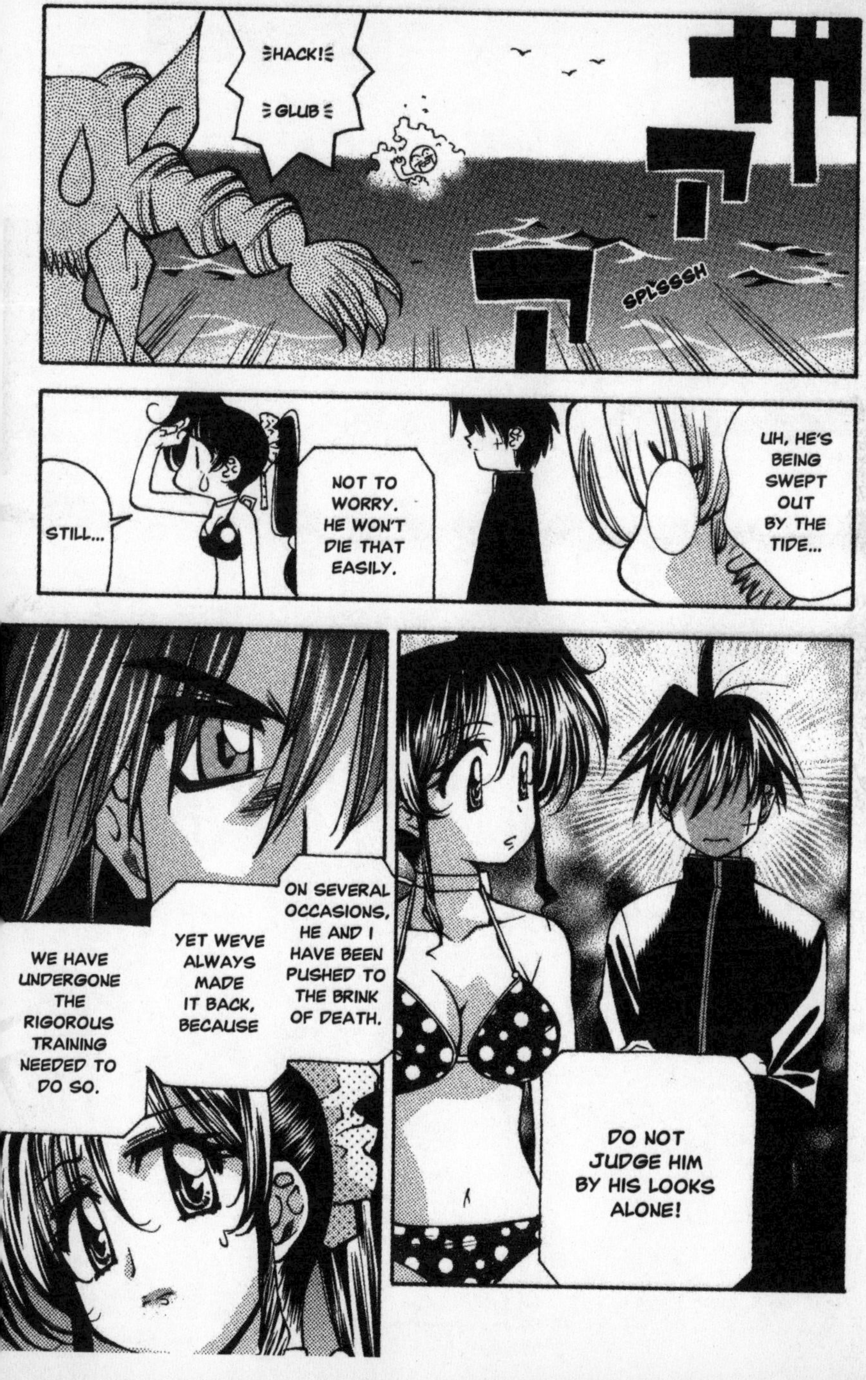
SPLSSSH
HACK!
GLUB
UH, HE'S BEING SWEPT OUT BY THE TIDE...
NOT TO WORRY. HE WON'T DIE THAT EASILY.
STILL...
DO NOT JUDGE HIM BY HIS LOOKS ALONE!
ON SEVERAL OCCASIONS, HE AND I HAVE BEEN PUSHED TO THE BRINK OF DEATH.
YET WE'VE ALWAYS MADE IT BACK, BECAUSE
WE HAVE UNDERGONE THE RIGOROUS TRAINING NEEDED TO DO SO.

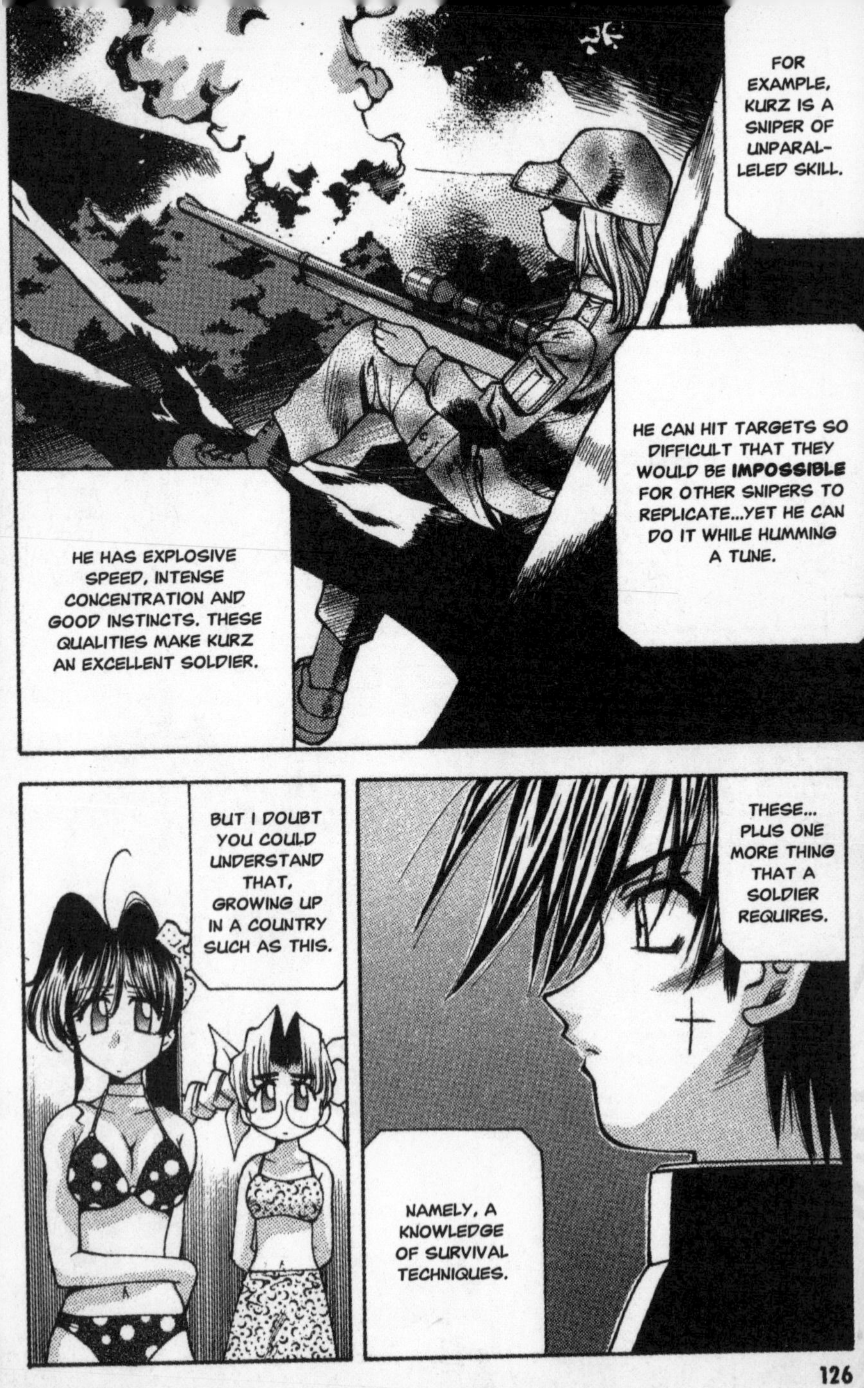
FOR EXAMPLE, KURZ IS A SNIPER OF UNPARAL-LELED SKILL.
HE CAN HIT TARGETS SO DIFFICULT THAT THEY WOULD BE **IMPOSSIBLE** FOR OTHER SNIPERS TO REPLICATE...YET HE CAN DO IT WHILE HUMMING A TUNE.
HE HAS EXPLOSIVE SPEED, INTENSE CONCENTRATION AND GOOD INSTINCTS. THESE QUALITIES MAKE KURZ AN EXCELLENT SOLDIER.
THESE... PLUS ONE MORE THING THAT A SOLDIER REQUIRES.
NAMELY, A KNOWLEDGE OF SURVIVAL TECHNIQUES.
BUT I DOUBT YOU COULD UNDERSTAND THAT, GROWING UP IN A COUNTRY SUCH AS THIS.

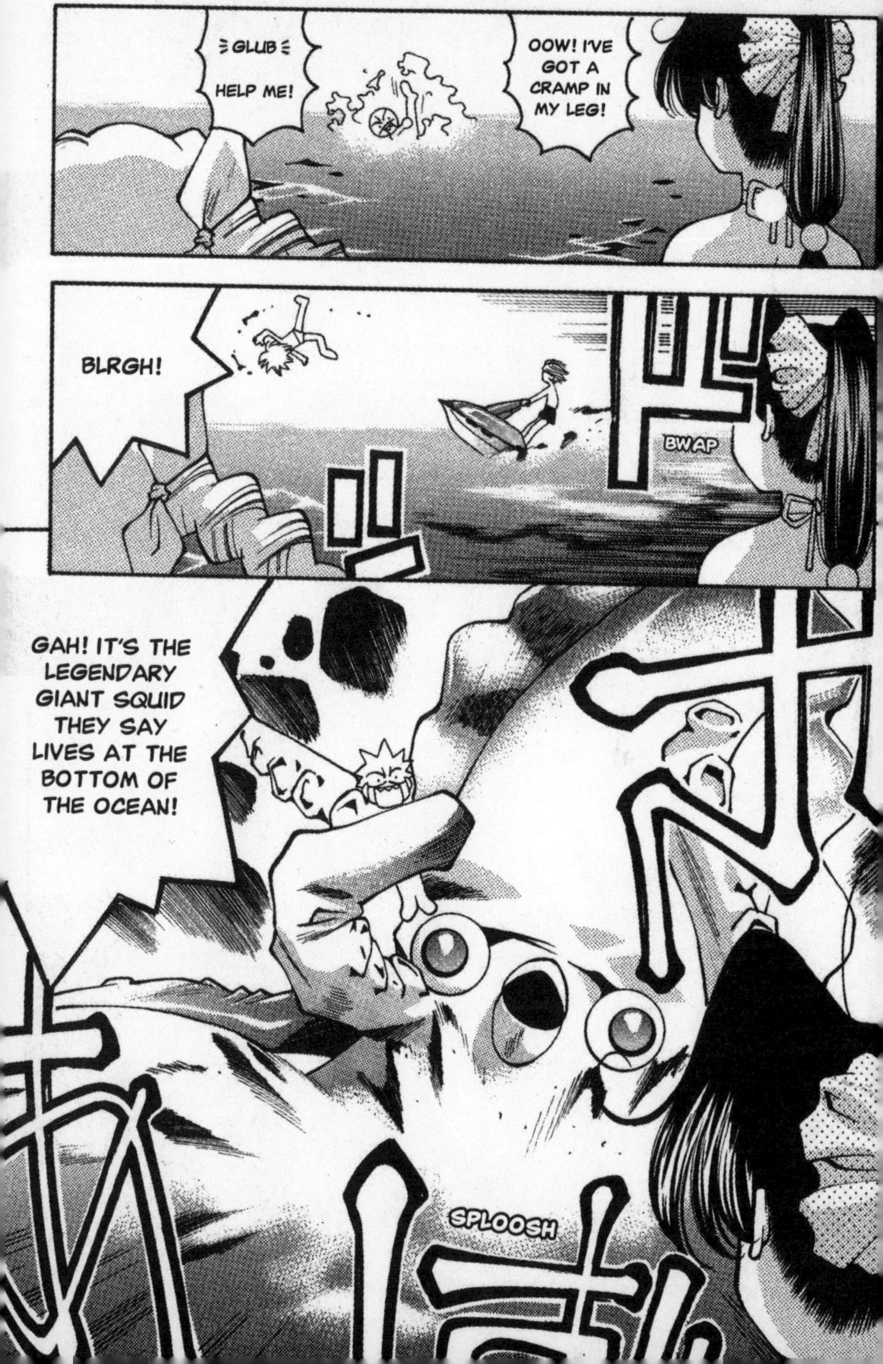
OOW! I'VE GOT A CRAMP IN MY LEG!
GLUB
HELP ME!
BWAP
BLRGH!
GAH! IT'S THE LEGENDARY GIANT SQUID THEY SAY LIVES AT THE BOTTOM OF THE OCEAN!
SPLOOSH

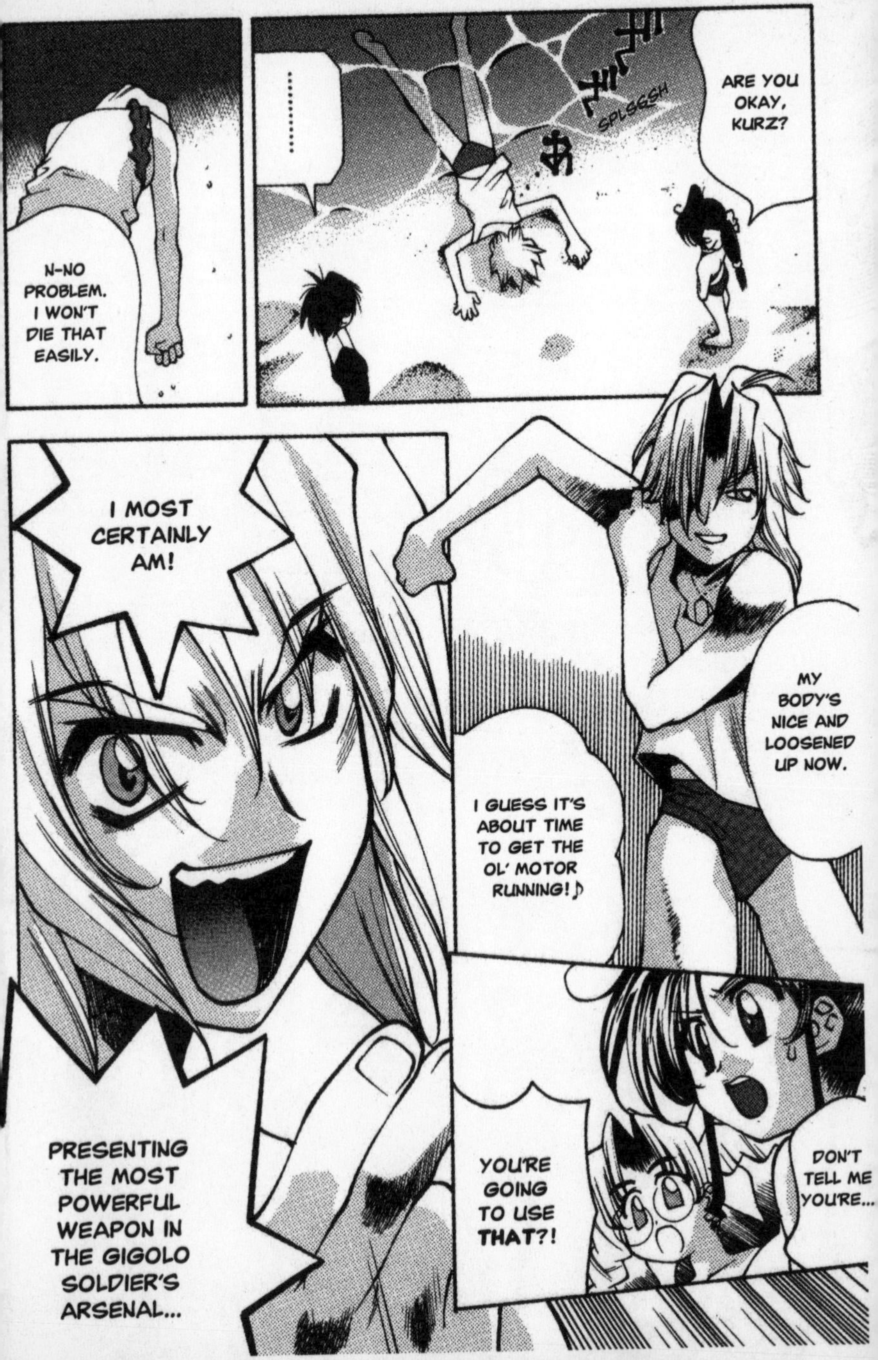
ARE YOU OKAY, KURZ?
......
SPLSSSH
N-NO PROBLEM. I WON'T DIE THAT EASILY.
MY BODY'S NICE AND LOOSENED UP NOW.
I GUESS IT'S ABOUT TIME TO GET THE OL' MOTOR RUNNING!♪
DON'T TELL ME YOU'RE...
YOU'RE GOING TO USE **THAT**?!
I MOST CERTAINLY AM!
PRESENTING THE MOST POWERFUL WEAPON IN THE GIGOLO SOLDIER'S ARSENAL...

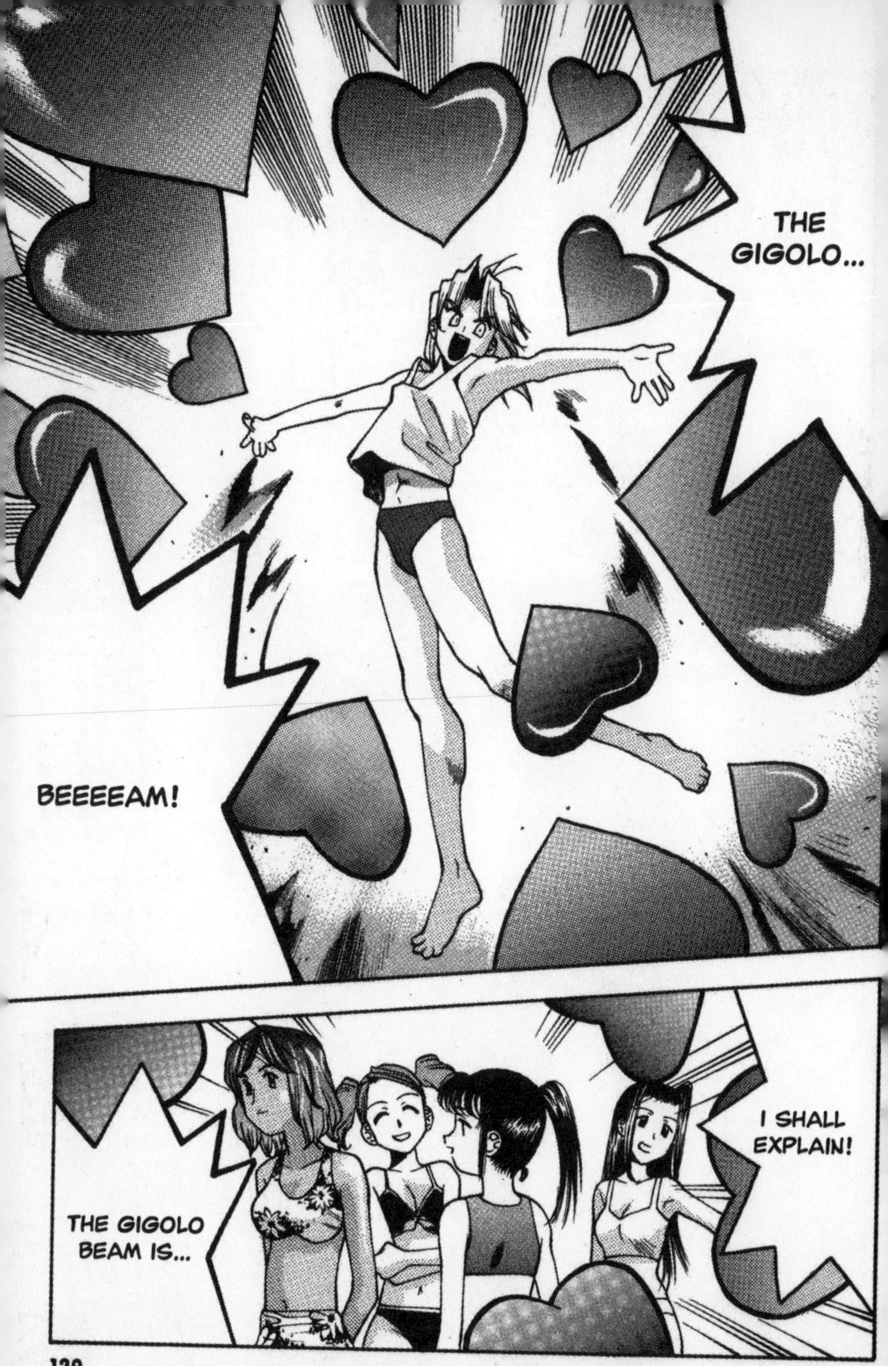
THE GIGOLO...
BEEEEAM!
I SHALL EXPLAIN!
THE GIGOLO BEAM IS...

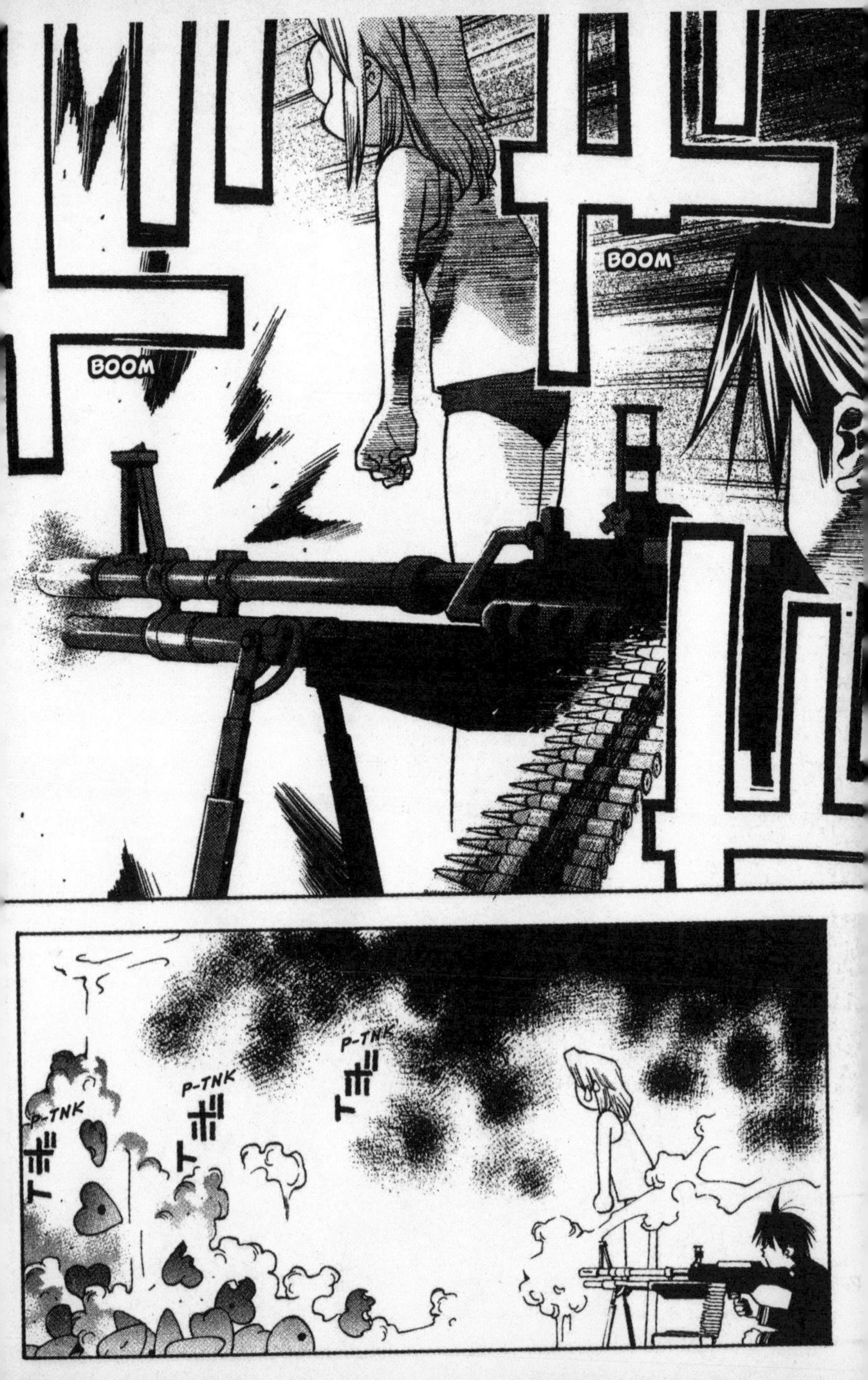
BOOM
BOOM
P-TNK
P-TNK
P-TNK

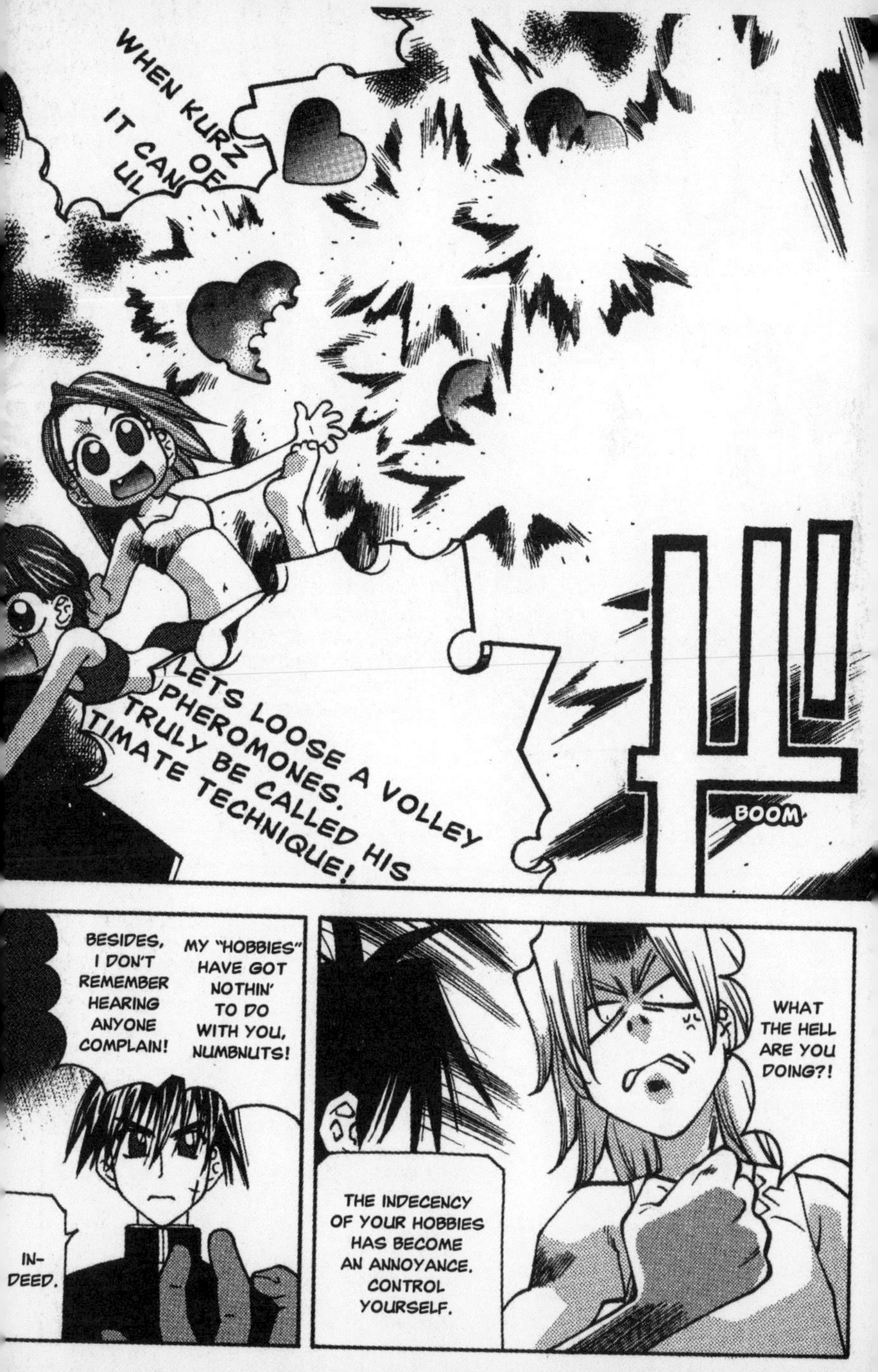
WHEN KURZ LETS LOOSE A VOLLEY OF PHEROMONES. IT CAN TRULY BE CALLED HIS ULTIMATE TECHNIQUE!
BOOM
WHAT THE HELL ARE YOU DOING?!
THE INDECENCY OF YOUR HOBBIES HAS BECOME AN ANNOYANCE. CONTROL YOURSELF.
MY "HOBBIES" HAVE GOT NOTHIN' TO DO WITH YOU, NUMBNUTS!
BESIDES, I DON'T REMEMBER HEARING ANYONE COMPLAIN!
IN-DEED.

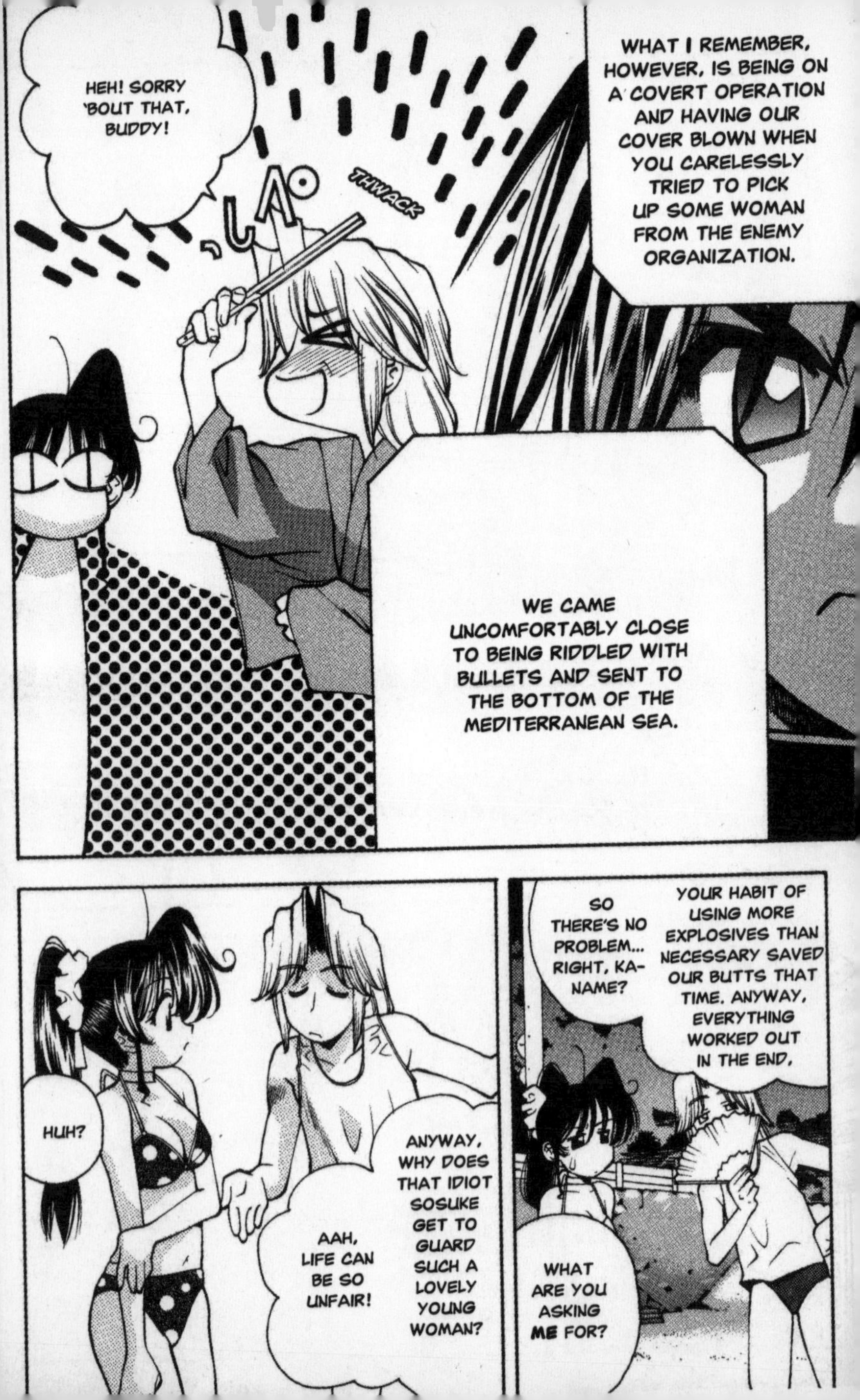
WHAT I REMEMBER, HOWEVER, IS BEING ON A COVERT OPERATION AND HAVING OUR COVER BLOWN WHEN YOU CARELESSLY TRIED TO PICK UP SOME WOMAN FROM THE ENEMY ORGANIZATION.
WE CAME UNCOMFORTABLY CLOSE TO BEING RIDDLED WITH BULLETS AND SENT TO THE BOTTOM OF THE MEDITERRANEAN SEA.
THWACK
HEH! SORRY 'BOUT THAT, BUDDY!
YOUR HABIT OF USING MORE EXPLOSIVES THAN NECESSARY SAVED OUR BUTTS THAT TIME. ANYWAY, EVERYTHING WORKED OUT IN THE END,
SO THERE'S NO PROBLEM... RIGHT, KANAME?
WHAT ARE YOU ASKING **ME** FOR?
ANYWAY, WHY DOES THAT IDIOT SOSUKE GET TO GUARD SUCH A LOVELY YOUNG WOMAN?
AAH, LIFE CAN BE SO UNFAIR!
HUH?

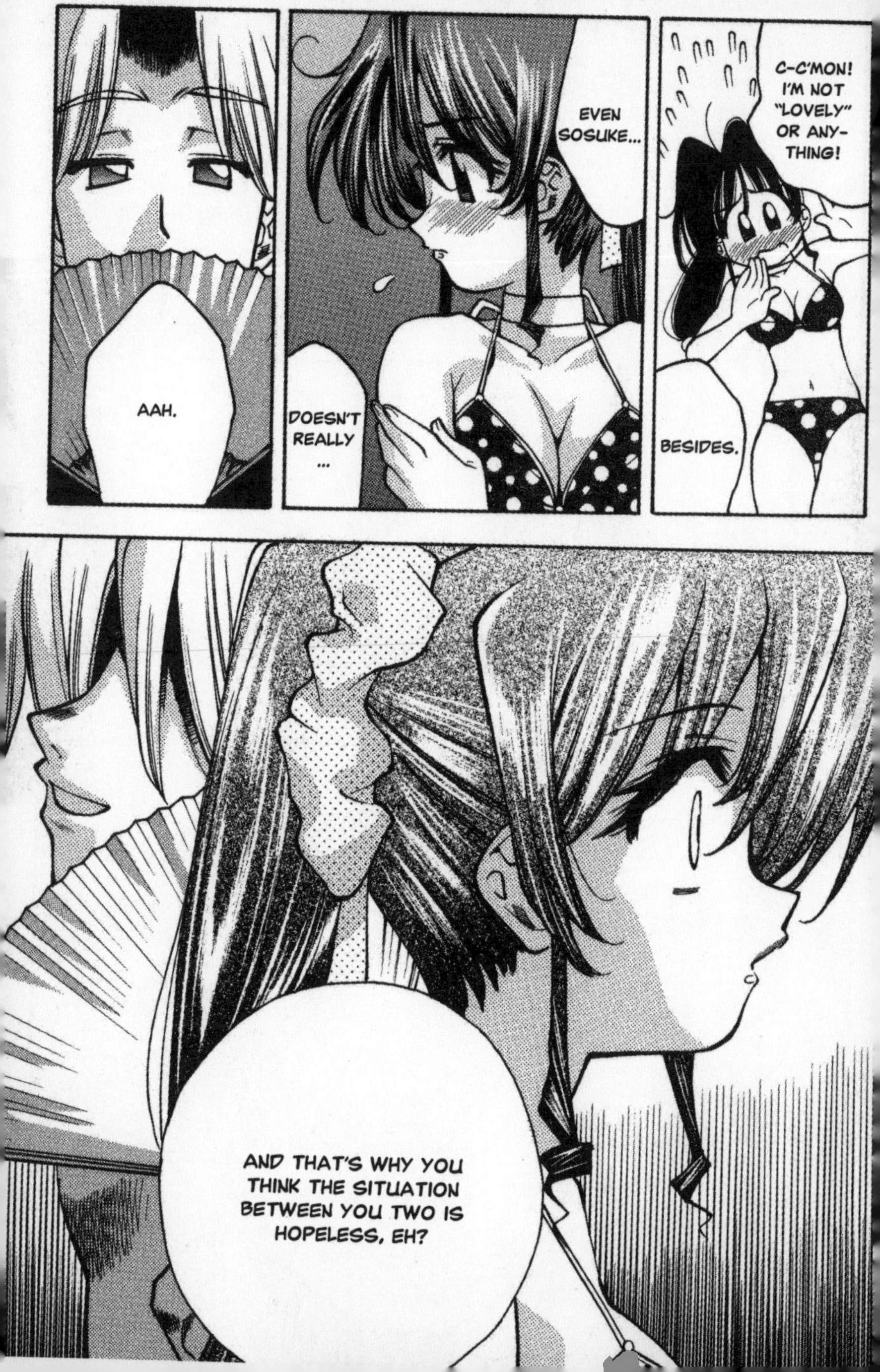
C-C'MON! I'M NOT "LOVELY" OR ANY-THING!
BESIDES.
EVEN SOSUKE...
DOESN'T REALLY ...
AAH.
AND THAT'S WHY YOU THINK THE SITUATION BETWEEN YOU TWO IS HOPELESS, EH?

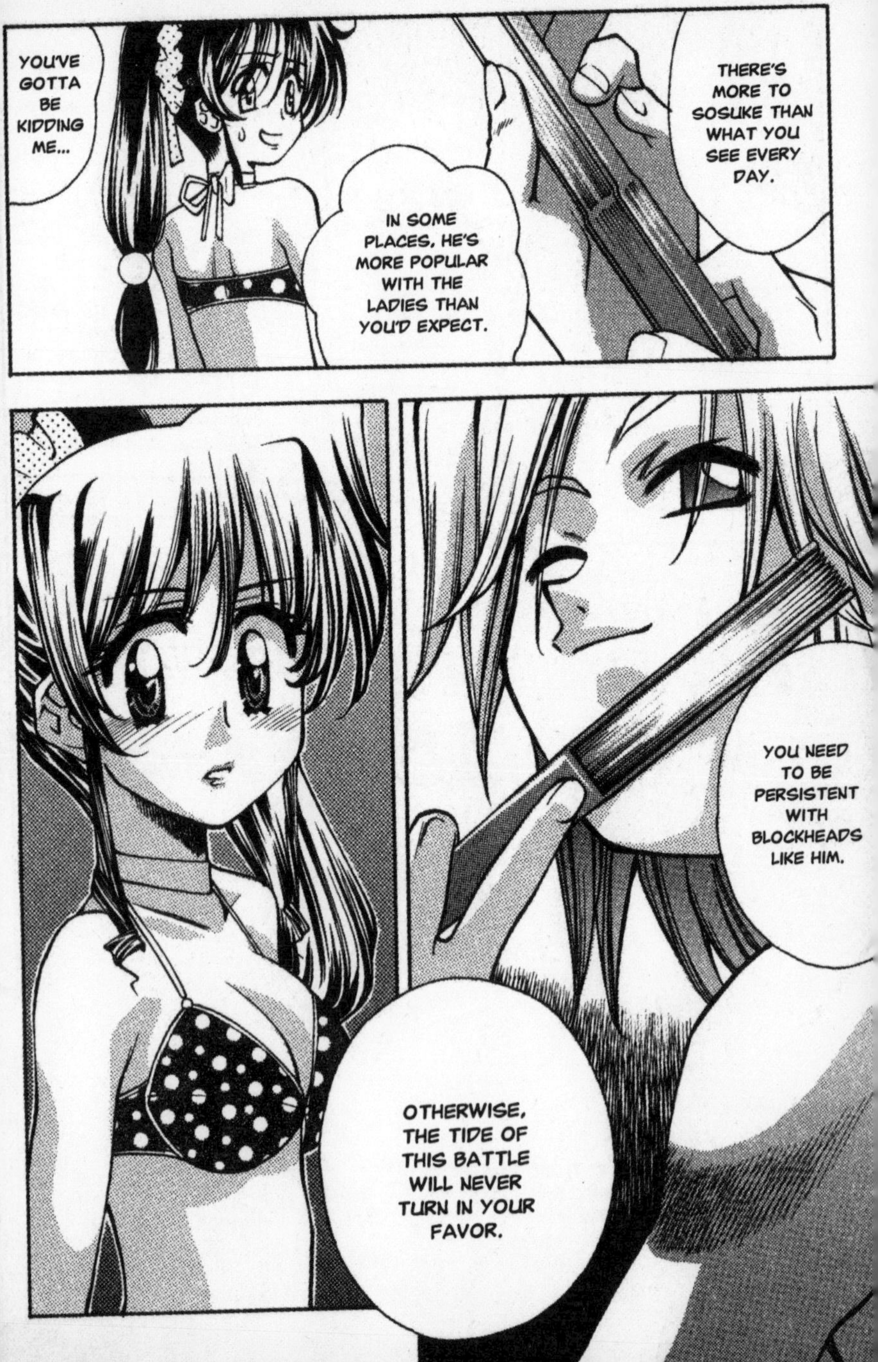
THERE'S MORE TO SOSUKE THAN WHAT YOU SEE EVERY DAY.
IN SOME PLACES, HE'S MORE POPULAR WITH THE LADIES THAN YOU'D EXPECT.
YOU'VE GOTTA BE KIDDING ME...
YOU NEED TO BE PERSISTENT WITH BLOCKHEADS LIKE HIM.
OTHERWISE, THE TIDE OF THIS BATTLE WILL NEVER TURN IN YOUR FAVOR.

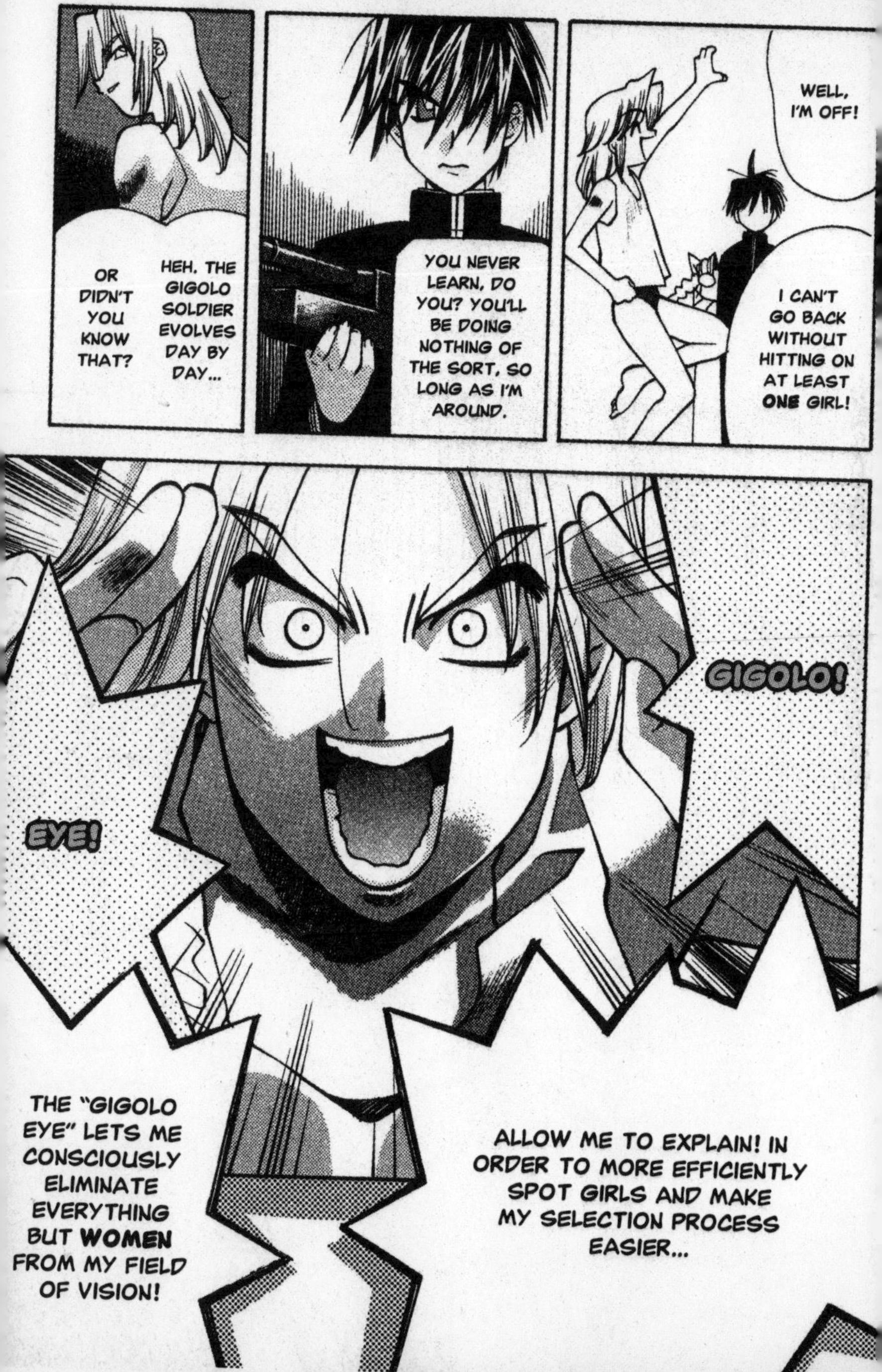
WELL, I'M OFF!
I CAN'T GO BACK WITHOUT HITTING ON AT LEAST **ONE** GIRL!
YOU NEVER LEARN, DO YOU? YOU'LL BE DOING NOTHING OF THE SORT, SO LONG AS I'M AROUND.
HEH, THE GIGOLO SOLDIER EVOLVES DAY BY DAY...
OR DIDN'T YOU KNOW THAT?
GIGOLO!
EYE!
ALLOW ME TO EXPLAIN! IN ORDER TO MORE EFFICIENTLY SPOT GIRLS AND MAKE MY SELECTION PROCESS EASIER...
THE "GIGOLO EYE" LETS ME CONSCIOUSLY ELIMINATE EVERYTHING BUT **WOMEN** FROM MY FIELD OF VISION!

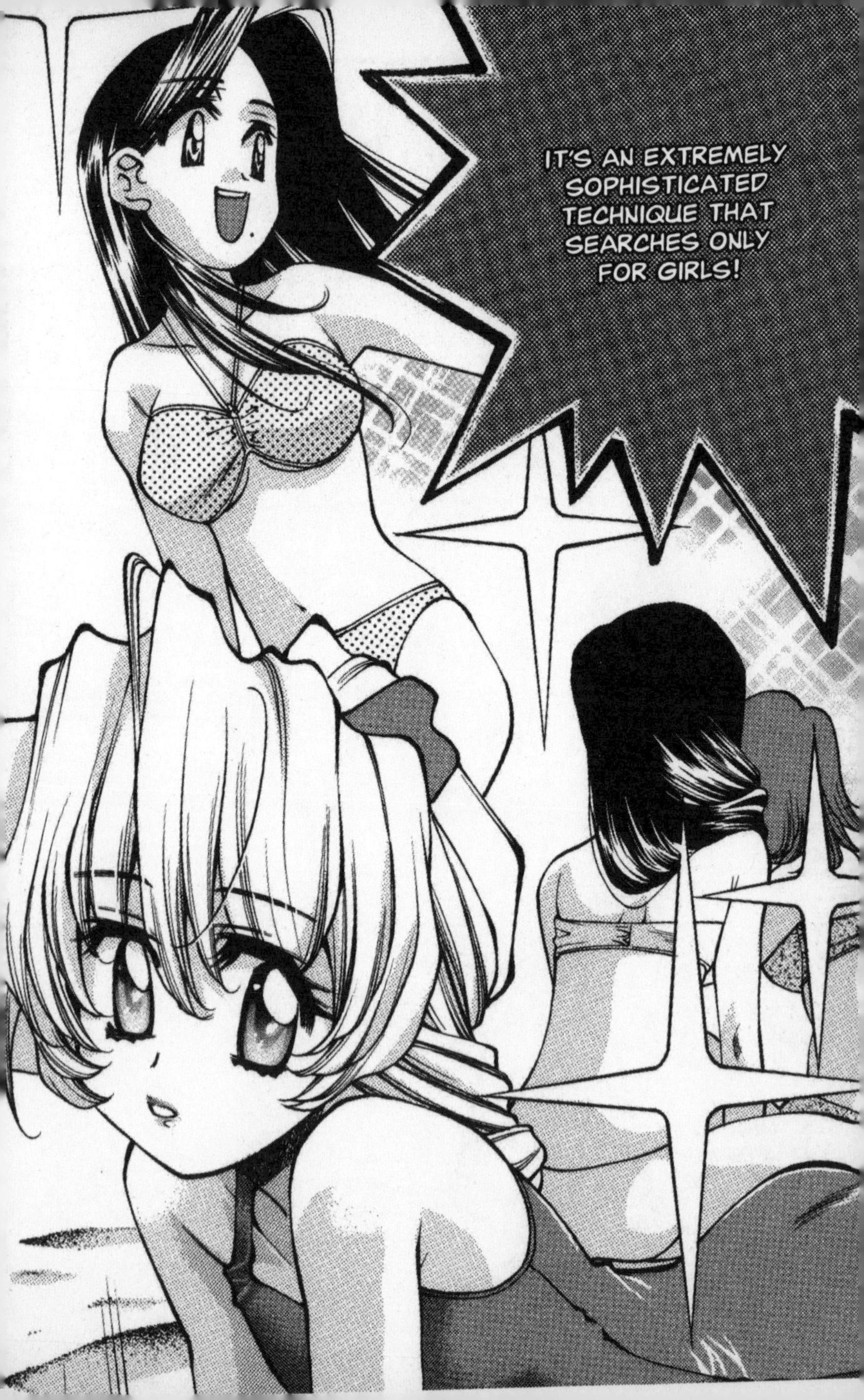
IT'S AN EXTREMELY SOPHISTICATED TECHNIQUE THAT SEARCHES ONLY FOR GIRLS!

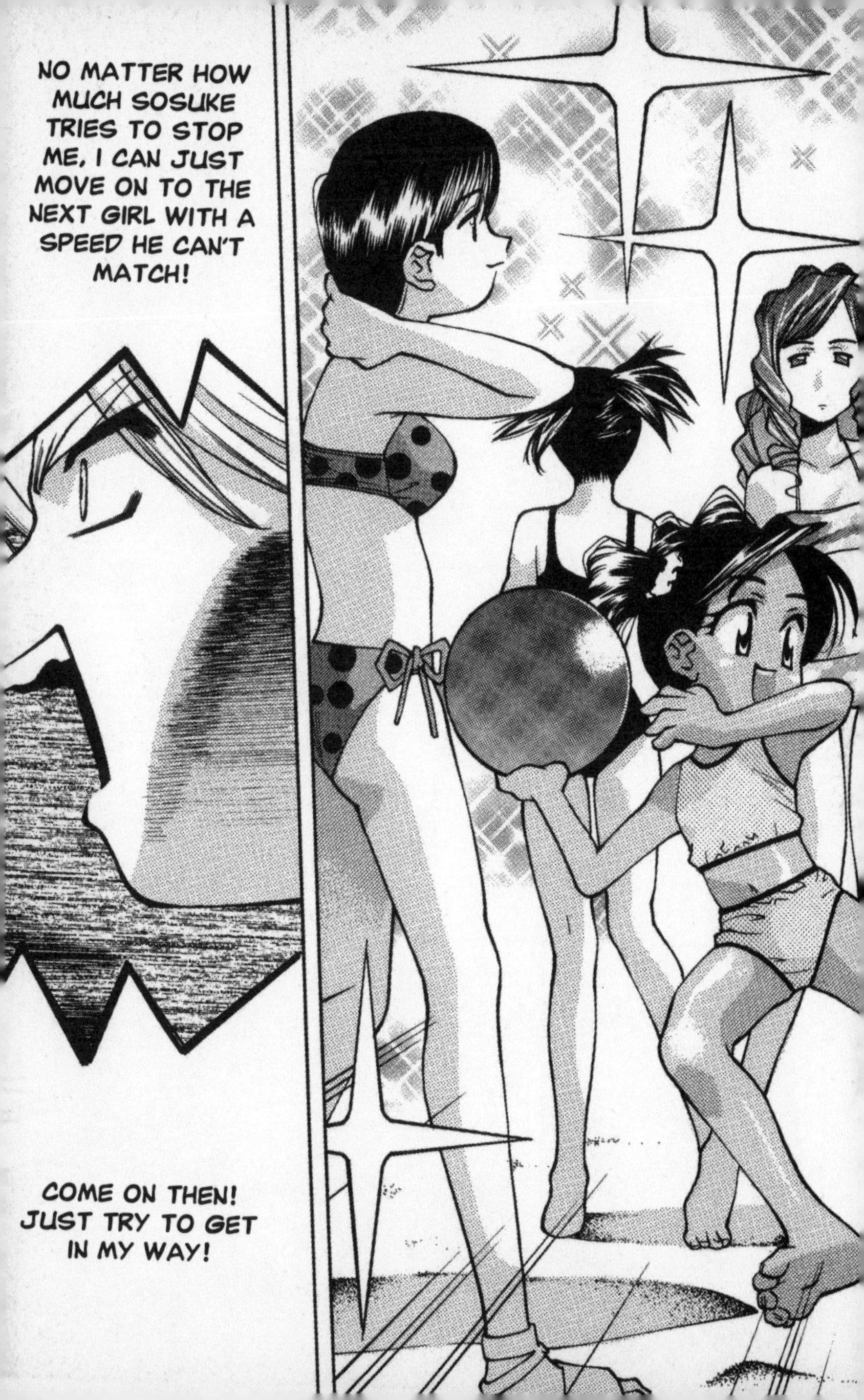
NO MATTER HOW MUCH SOSUKE TRIES TO STOP ME, I CAN JUST MOVE ON TO THE NEXT GIRL WITH A SPEED HE CAN'T MATCH!
COME ON THEN! JUST TRY TO GET IN MY WAY!

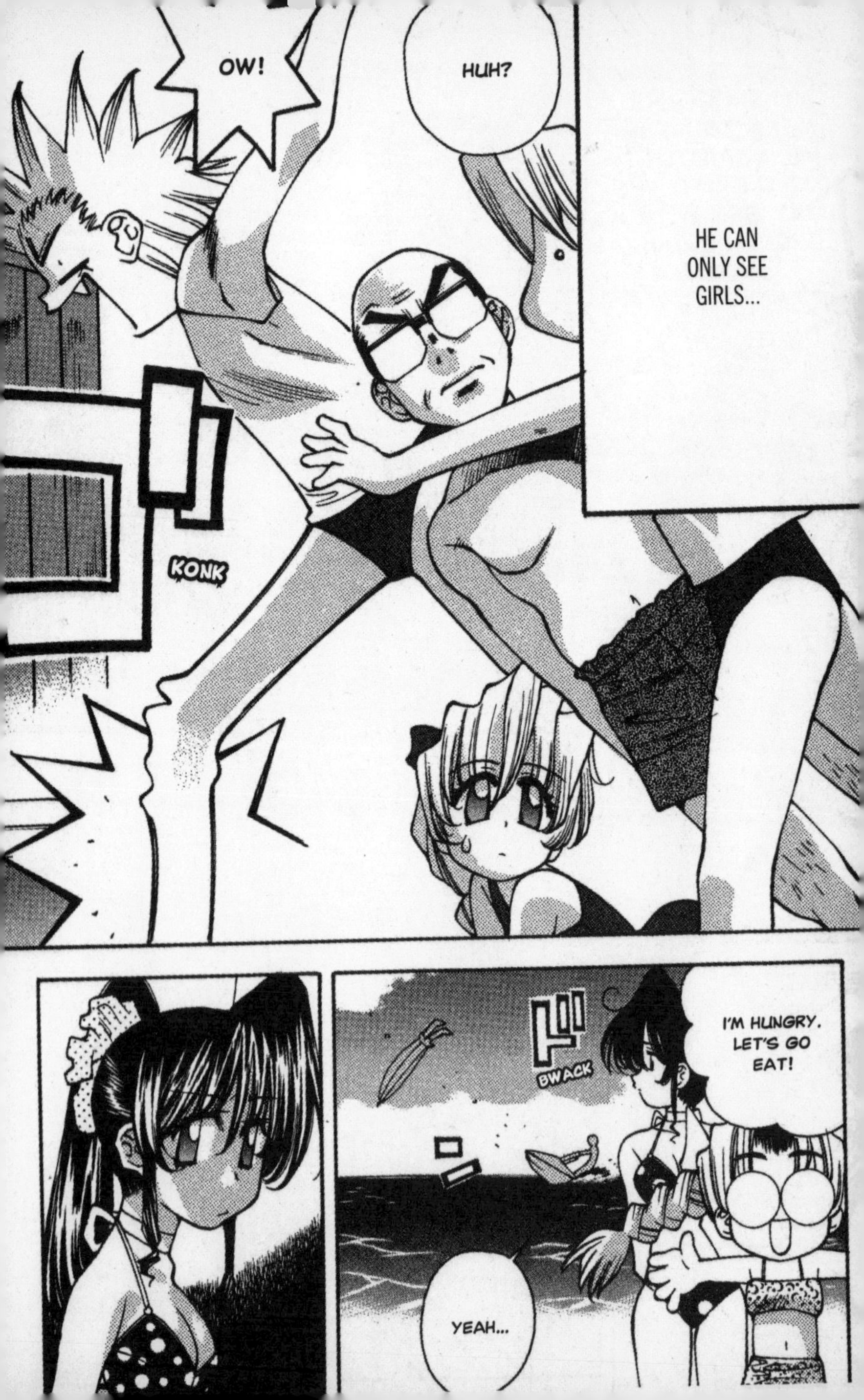
HUH?
OW!
HE CAN ONLY SEE GIRLS...
KONK
I'M HUNGRY. LET'S GO EAT!
BWACK
YEAH...

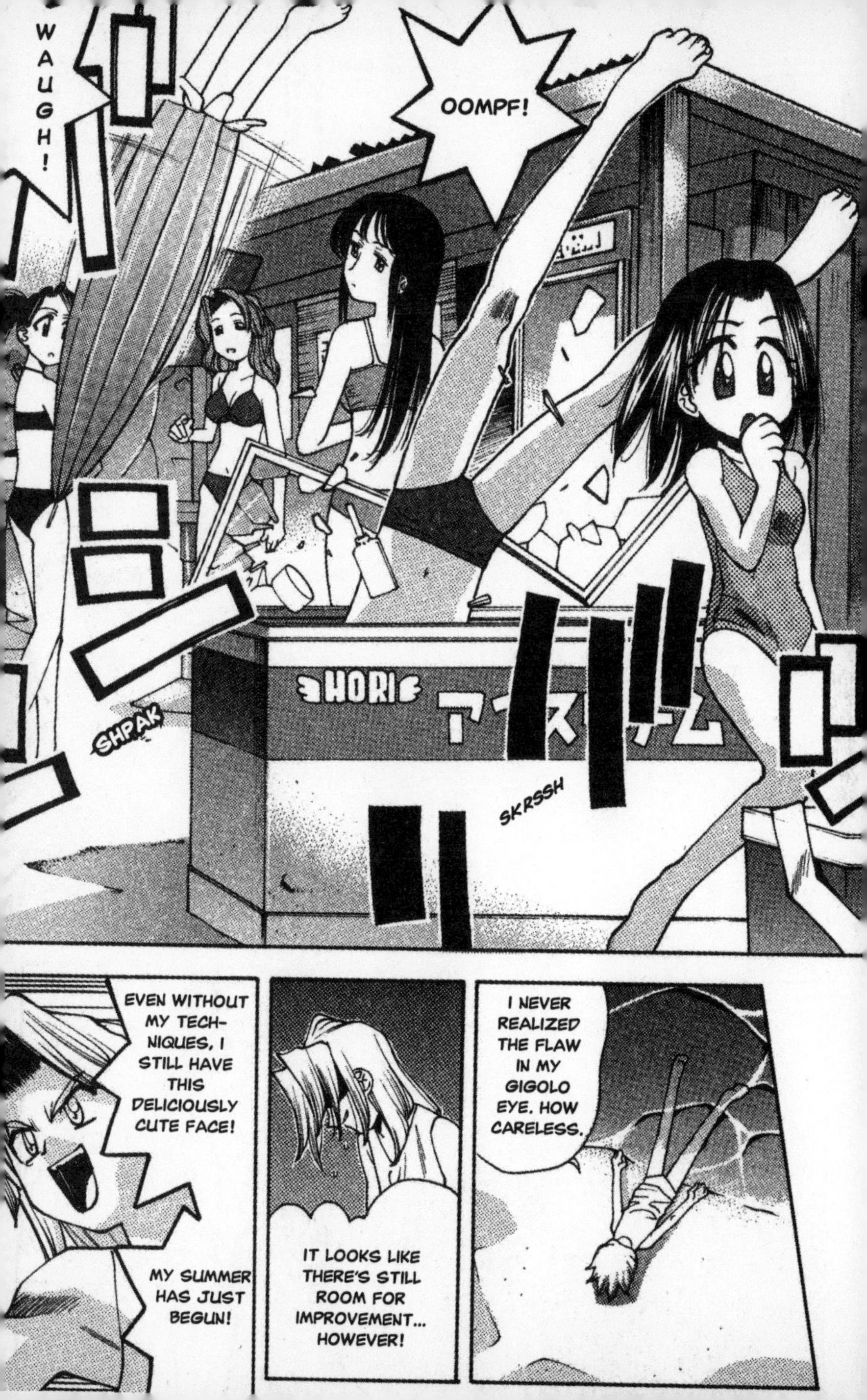
OOMPF!
WAUGH!
HORI
SKRSSH
SHPAK
I NEVER REALIZED THE FLAW IN MY GIGOLO EYE. HOW CARELESS.
IT LOOKS LIKE THERE'S STILL ROOM FOR IMPROVEMENT... HOWEVER!
EVEN WITHOUT MY TECH-NIQUES, I STILL HAVE THIS DELICIOUSLY CUTE FACE!
MY SUMMER HAS JUST BEGUN!

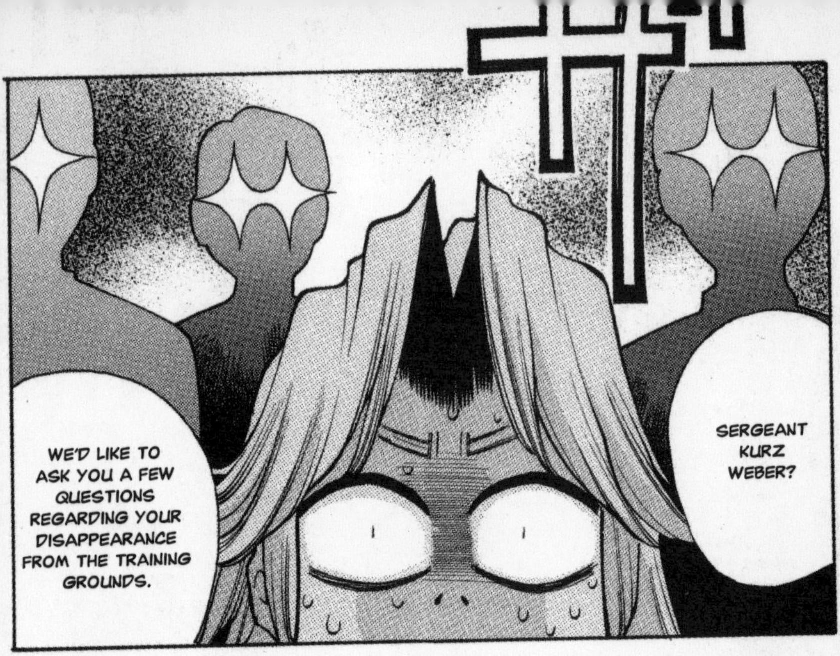
SERGEANT KURZ WEBER?
WE'D LIKE TO ASK YOU A FEW QUESTIONS REGARDING YOUR DISAPPEARANCE FROM THE TRAINING GROUNDS.

MY SUMMER YEAR.

THE END.

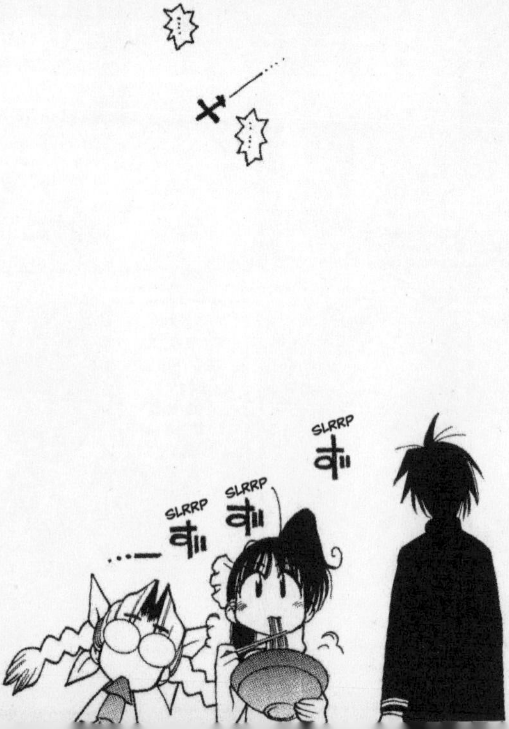
SLRRP
SLRRP
SLRRP

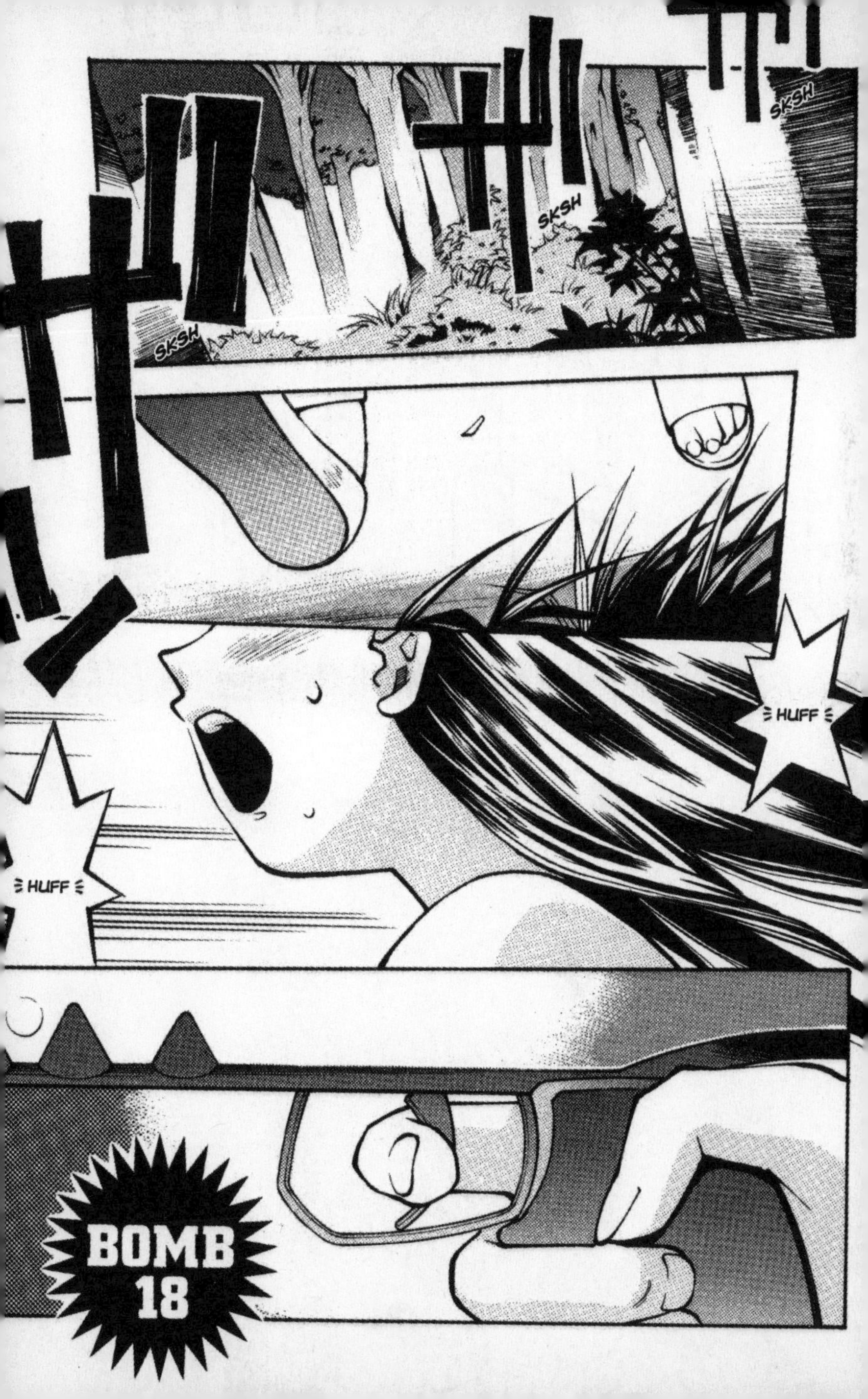

SKSH
SKSH
SKSH
HUFF
HUFF
BOMB 18

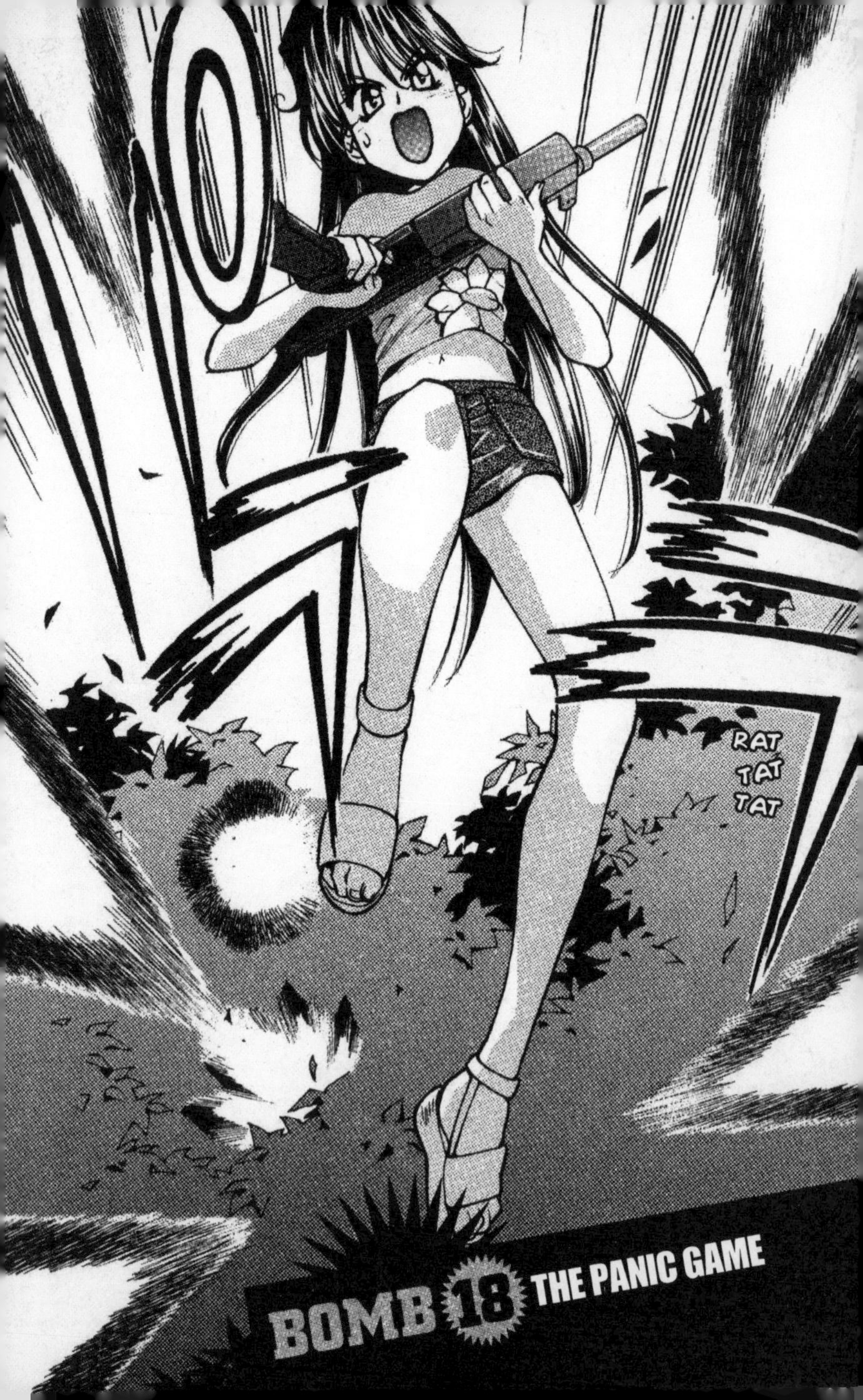
RAT
TAT
TAT
BOMB 18 THE PANIC GAME

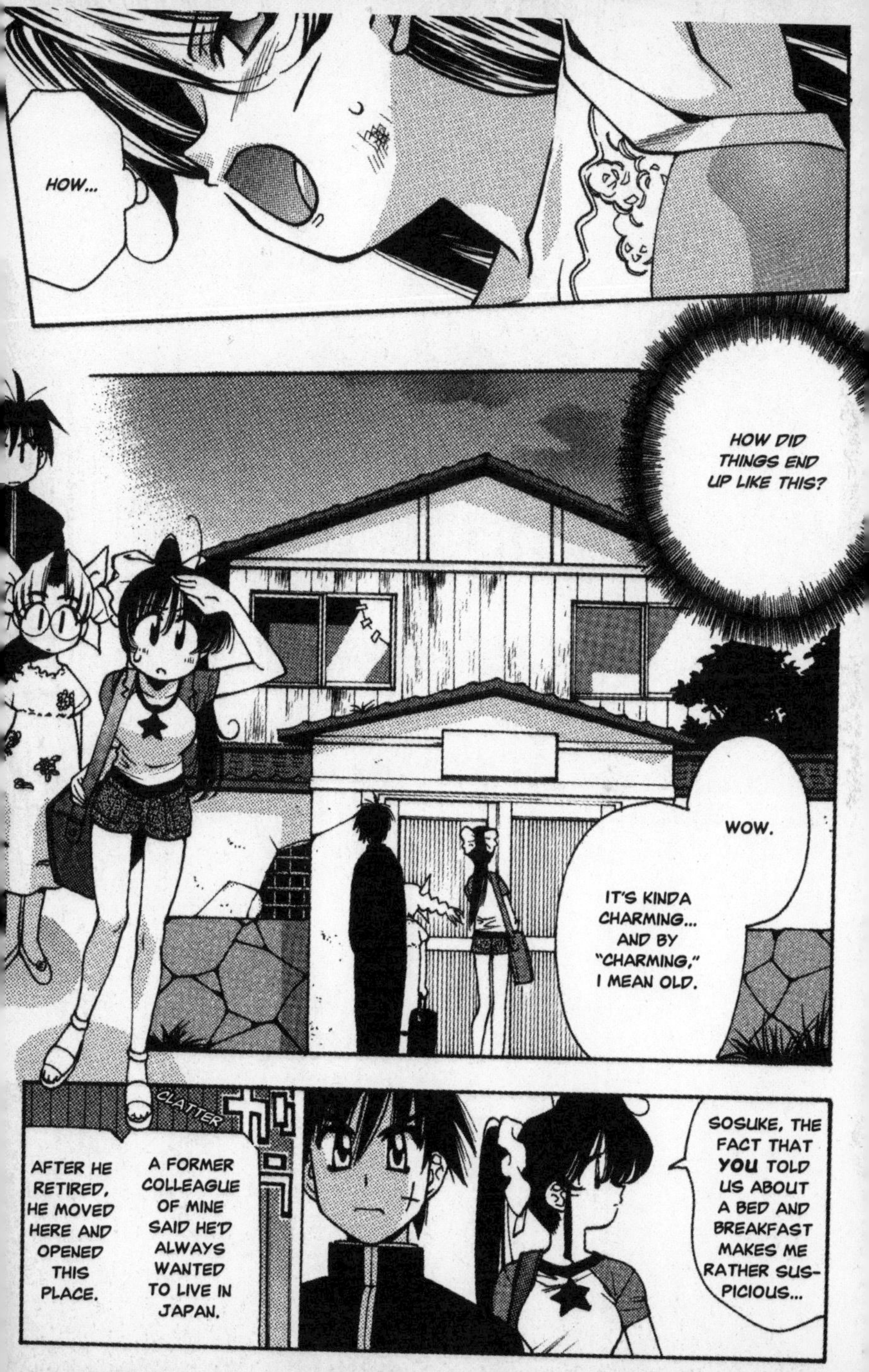
HOW...
HOW DID THINGS END UP LIKE THIS?
WOW.
IT'S KINDA CHARMING... AND BY "CHARMING," I MEAN OLD.
CLATTER
SOSUKE, THE FACT THAT YOU TOLD US ABOUT A BED AND BREAKFAST MAKES ME RATHER SUS-PICIOUS...
A FORMER COLLEAGUE OF MINE SAID HE'D ALWAYS WANTED TO LIVE IN JAPAN.
AFTER HE RETIRED, HE MOVED HERE AND OPENED THIS PLACE.

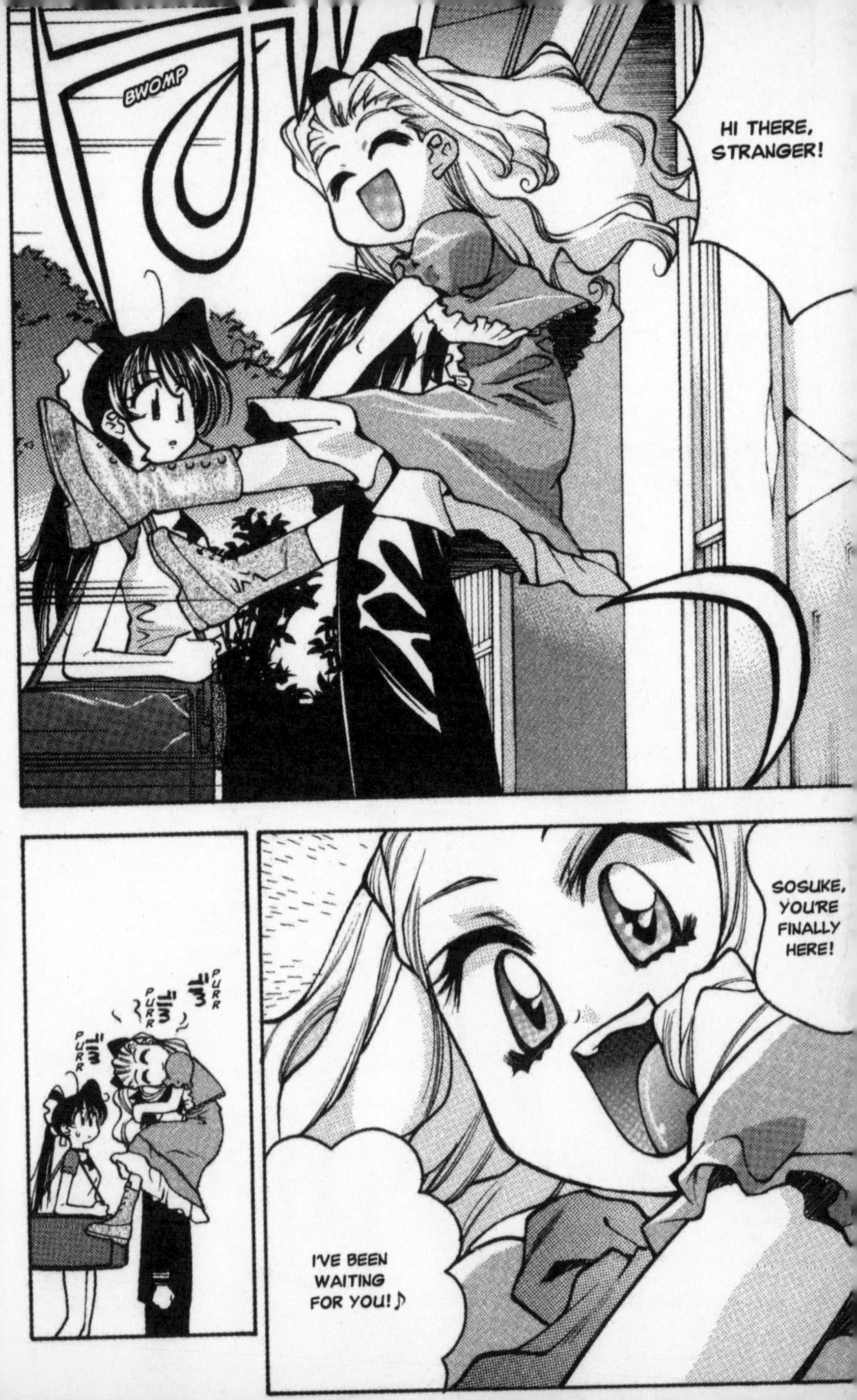
BWOMP
HI THERE, STRANGER!
SOSUKE, YOU'RE FINALLY HERE!
I'VE BEEN WAITING FOR YOU!♪
PURR
PURR
PURR

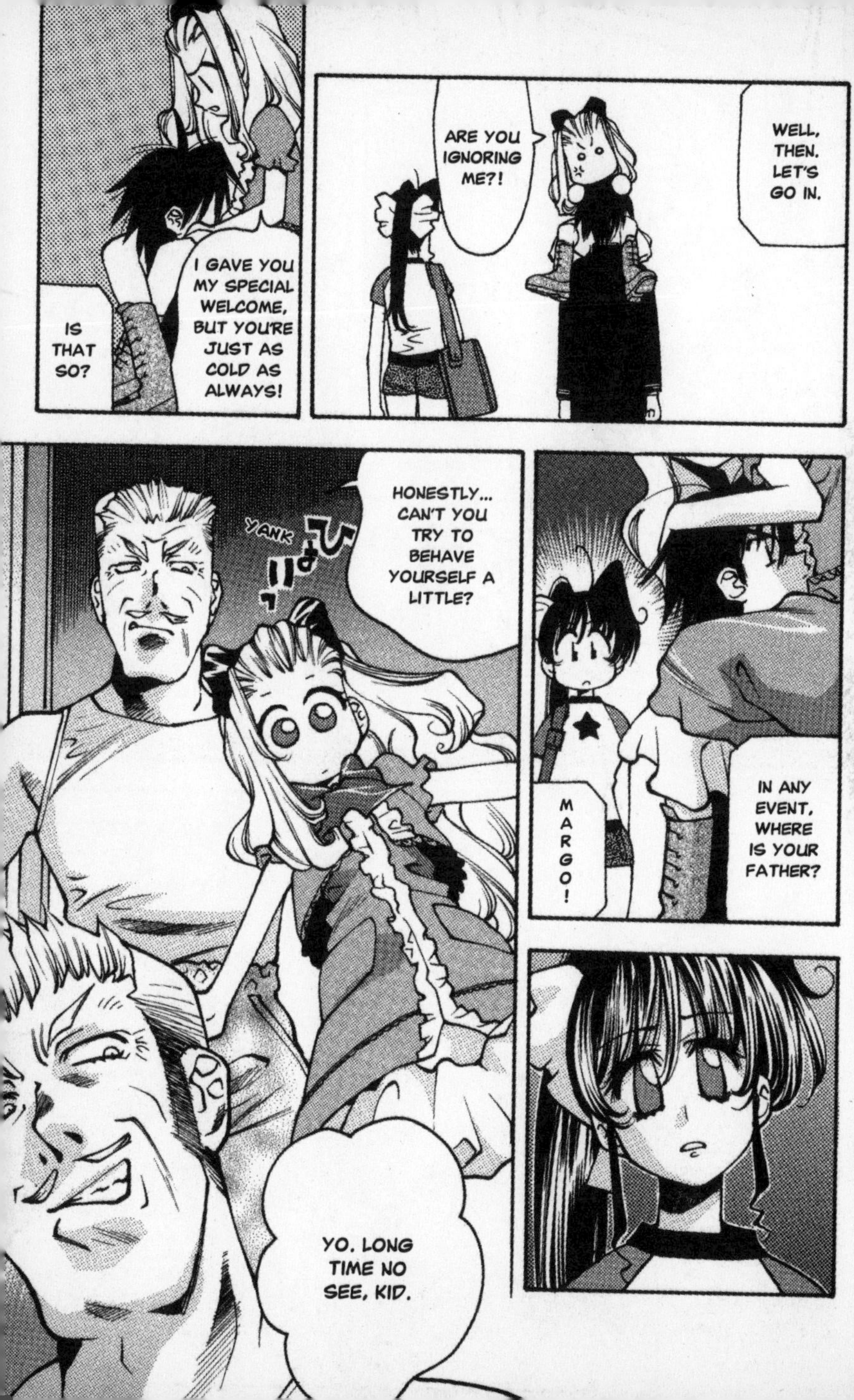

WELL, THEN. LET'S GO IN.
ARE YOU IGNORING ME?!
I GAVE YOU MY SPECIAL WELCOME, BUT YOU'RE JUST AS COLD AS ALWAYS!
IS THAT SO?
IN ANY EVENT, WHERE IS YOUR FATHER?
MARGO!
HONESTLY... CAN'T YOU TRY TO BEHAVE YOURSELF A LITTLE?
YANK
YO. LONG TIME NO SEE, KID.

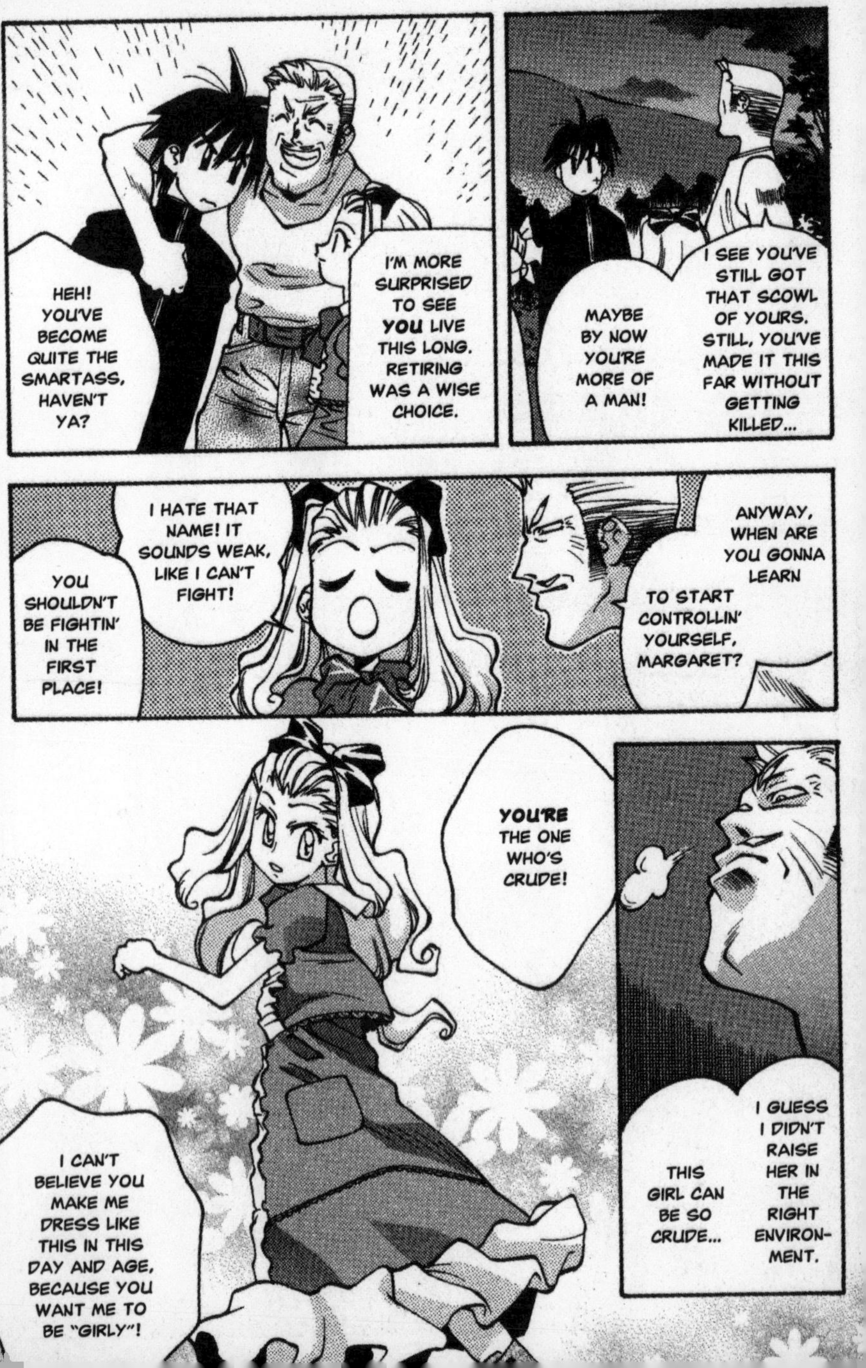

I SEE YOU'VE STILL GOT THAT SCOWL OF YOURS. STILL, YOU'VE MADE IT THIS FAR WITHOUT GETTING KILLED...
MAYBE BY NOW YOU'RE MORE OF A MAN!
I'M MORE SURPRISED TO SEE **YOU** LIVE THIS LONG. RETIRING WAS A WISE CHOICE.
HEH! YOU'VE BECOME QUITE THE SMARTASS, HAVEN'T YA?
ANYWAY, WHEN ARE YOU GONNA LEARN
TO START CONTROLLIN' YOURSELF, MARGARET?
I HATE THAT NAME! IT SOUNDS WEAK, LIKE I CAN'T FIGHT!
YOU SHOULDN'T BE FIGHTIN' IN THE FIRST PLACE!
I GUESS I DIDN'T RAISE HER IN THE RIGHT ENVIRON-MENT.
THIS GIRL CAN BE SO CRUDE...
YOU'RE THE ONE WHO'S CRUDE!
I CAN'T BELIEVE YOU MAKE ME DRESS LIKE THIS IN THIS DAY AND AGE, BECAUSE YOU WANT ME TO BE "GIRLY"!

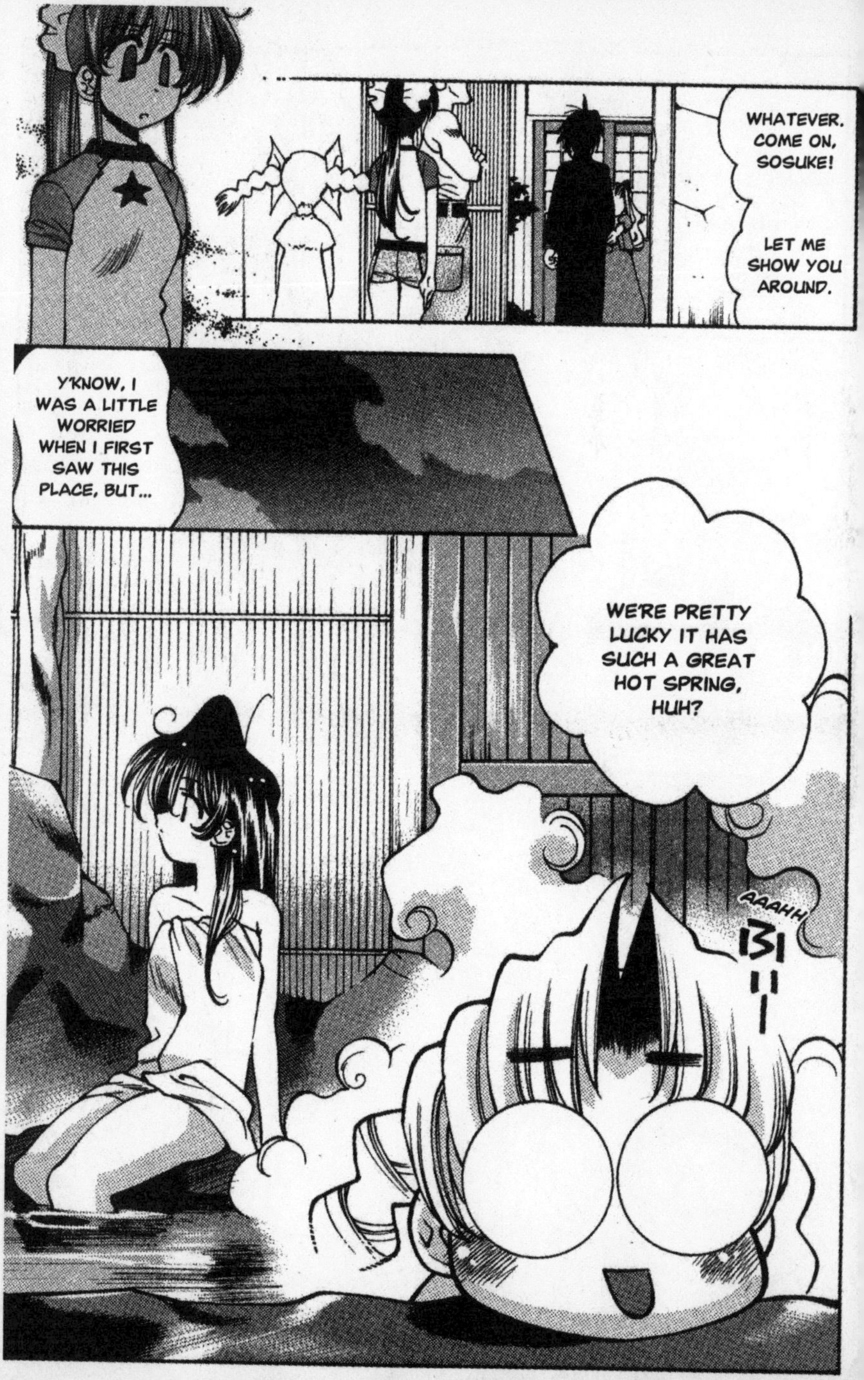
WHATEVER. COME ON, SOSUKE!
LET ME SHOW YOU AROUND.
Y'KNOW, I WAS A LITTLE WORRIED WHEN I FIRST SAW THIS PLACE, BUT...
WE'RE PRETTY LUCKY IT HAS SUCH A GREAT HOT SPRING, HUH?
AAAHH

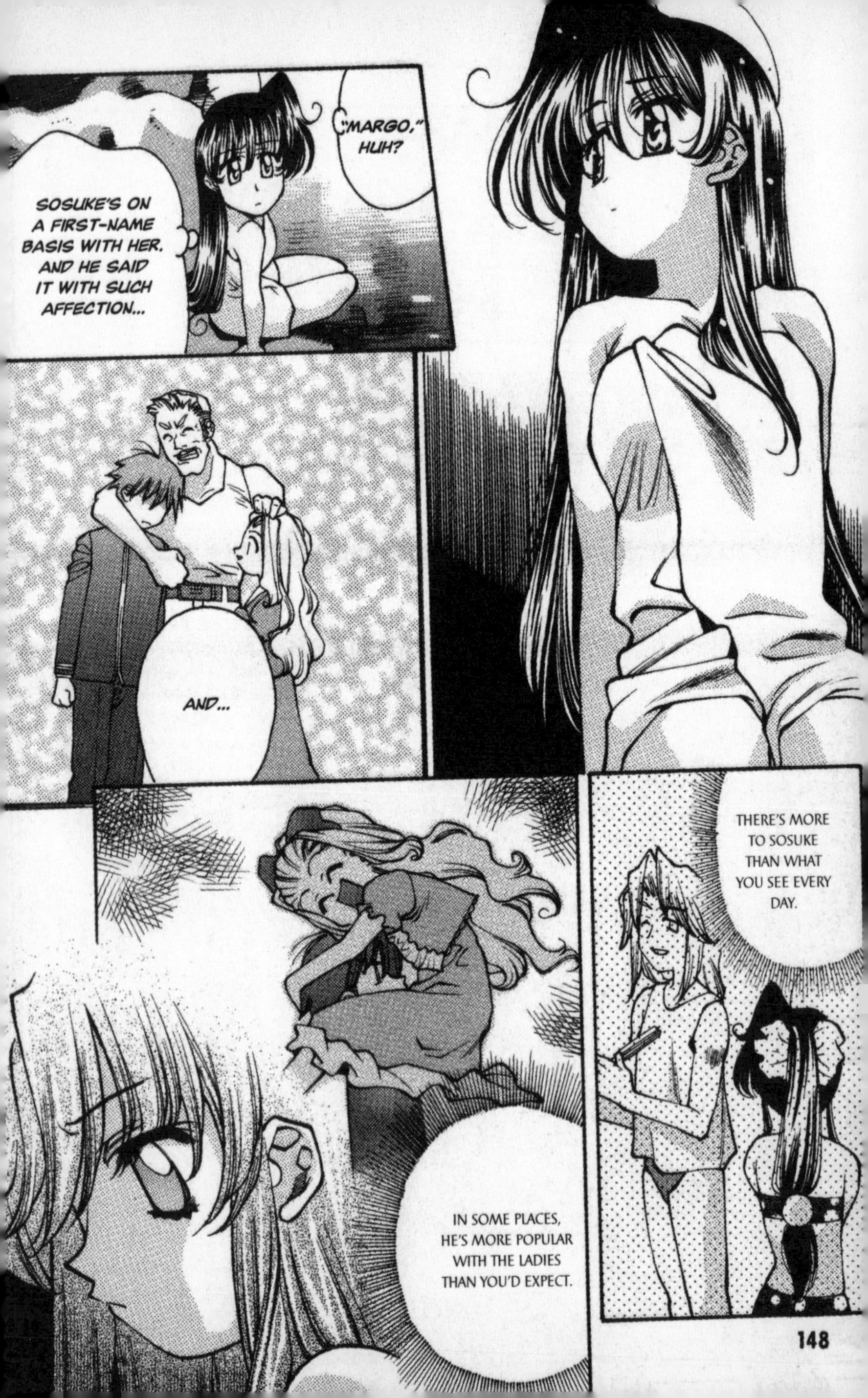

"MARGO," HUH?
SOSUKE'S ON A FIRST-NAME BASIS WITH HER. AND HE SAID IT WITH SUCH AFFECTION...
AND...
THERE'S MORE TO SOSUKE THAN WHAT YOU SEE EVERY DAY.
IN SOME PLACES, HE'S MORE POPULAR WITH THE LADIES THAN YOU'D EXPECT.

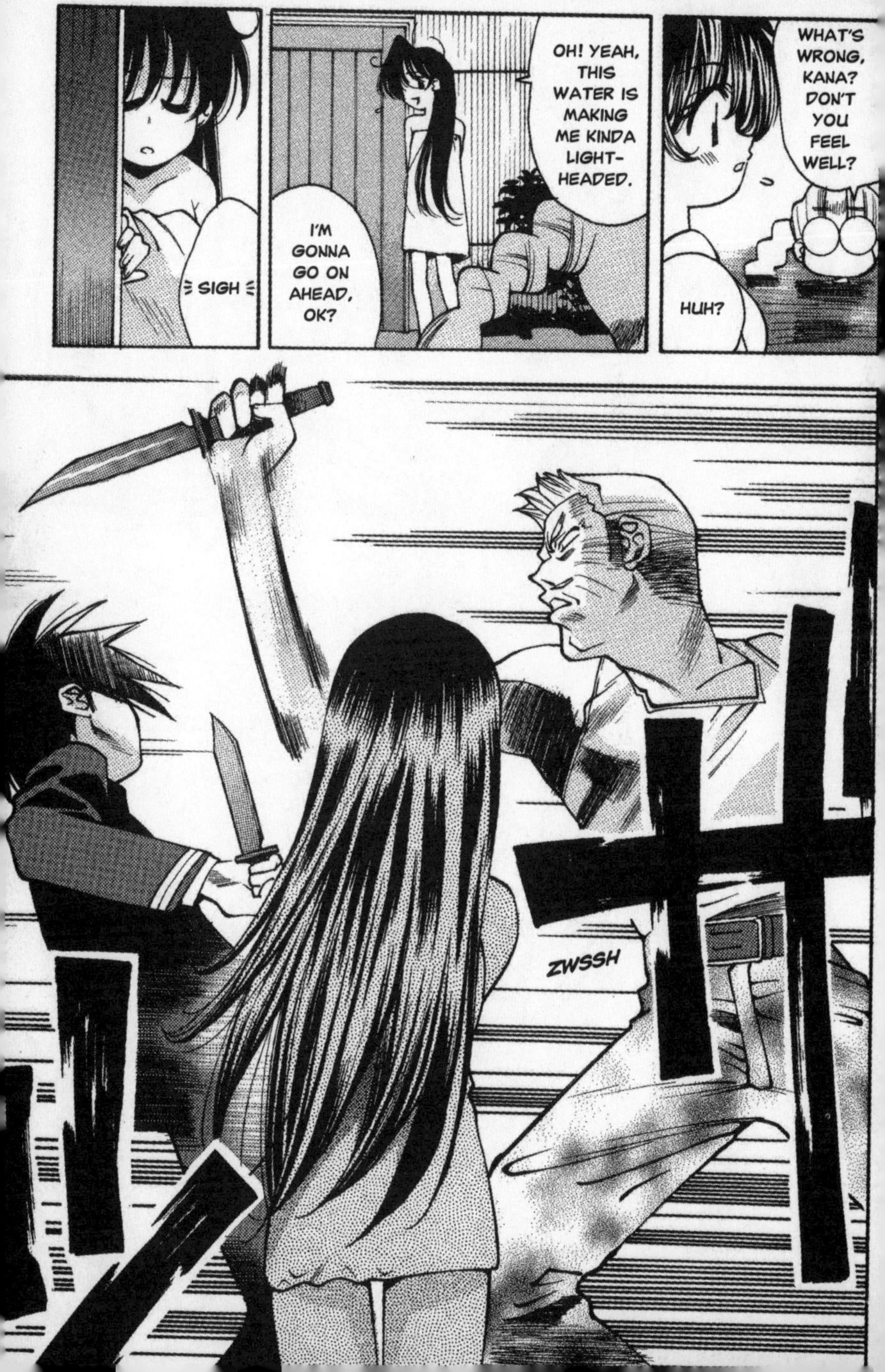
WHAT'S WRONG, KANA? DON'T YOU FEEL WELL?
HUH?
OH! YEAH, THIS WATER IS MAKING ME KINDA LIGHT-HEADED.
I'M GONNA GO ON AHEAD, OK?
SIGH
ZWSSH

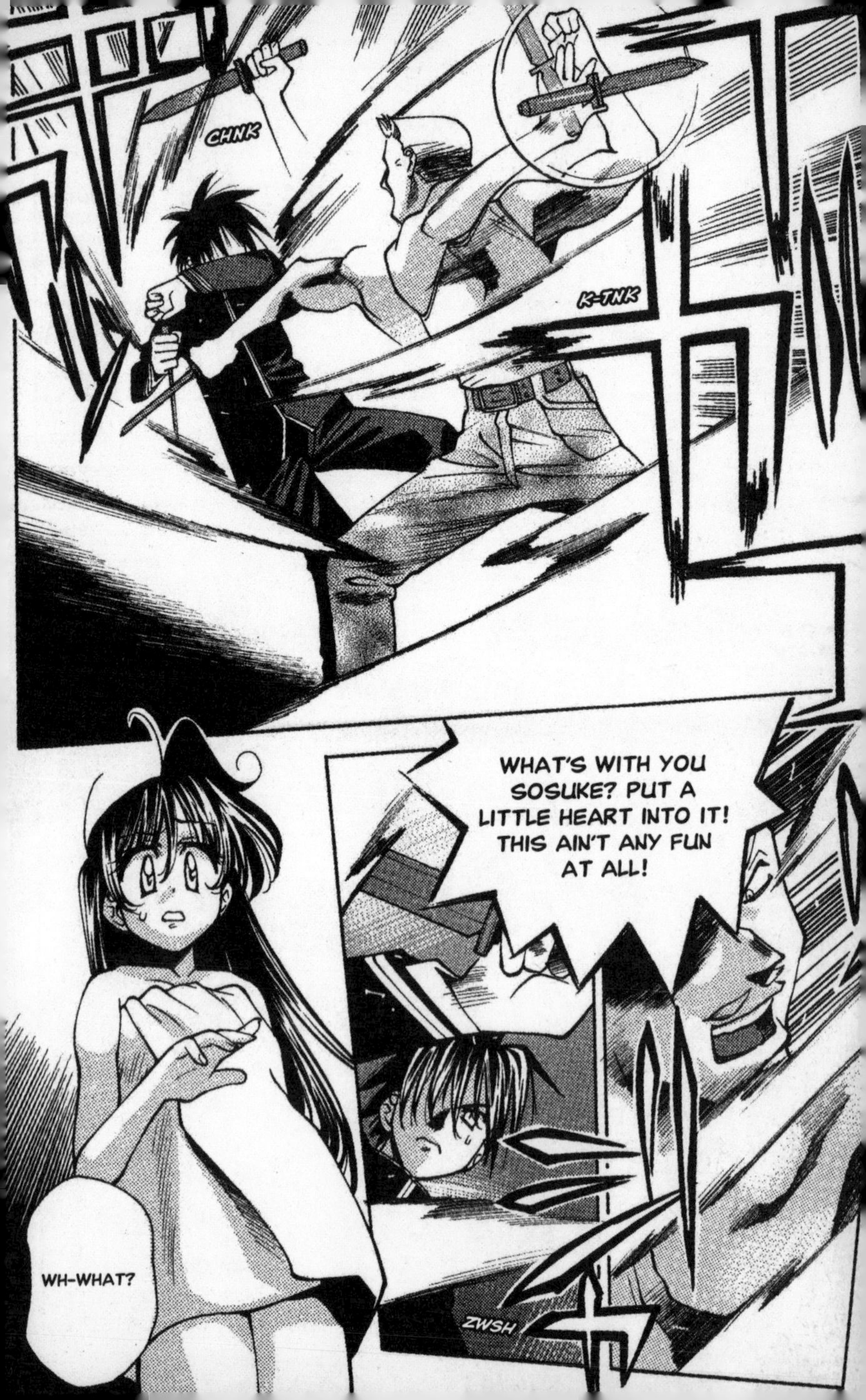
CHNK
K-TNK
WHAT'S WITH YOU SOSUKE? PUT A LITTLE HEART INTO IT! THIS AIN'T ANY FUN AT ALL!
ZWSH
WH-WHAT?

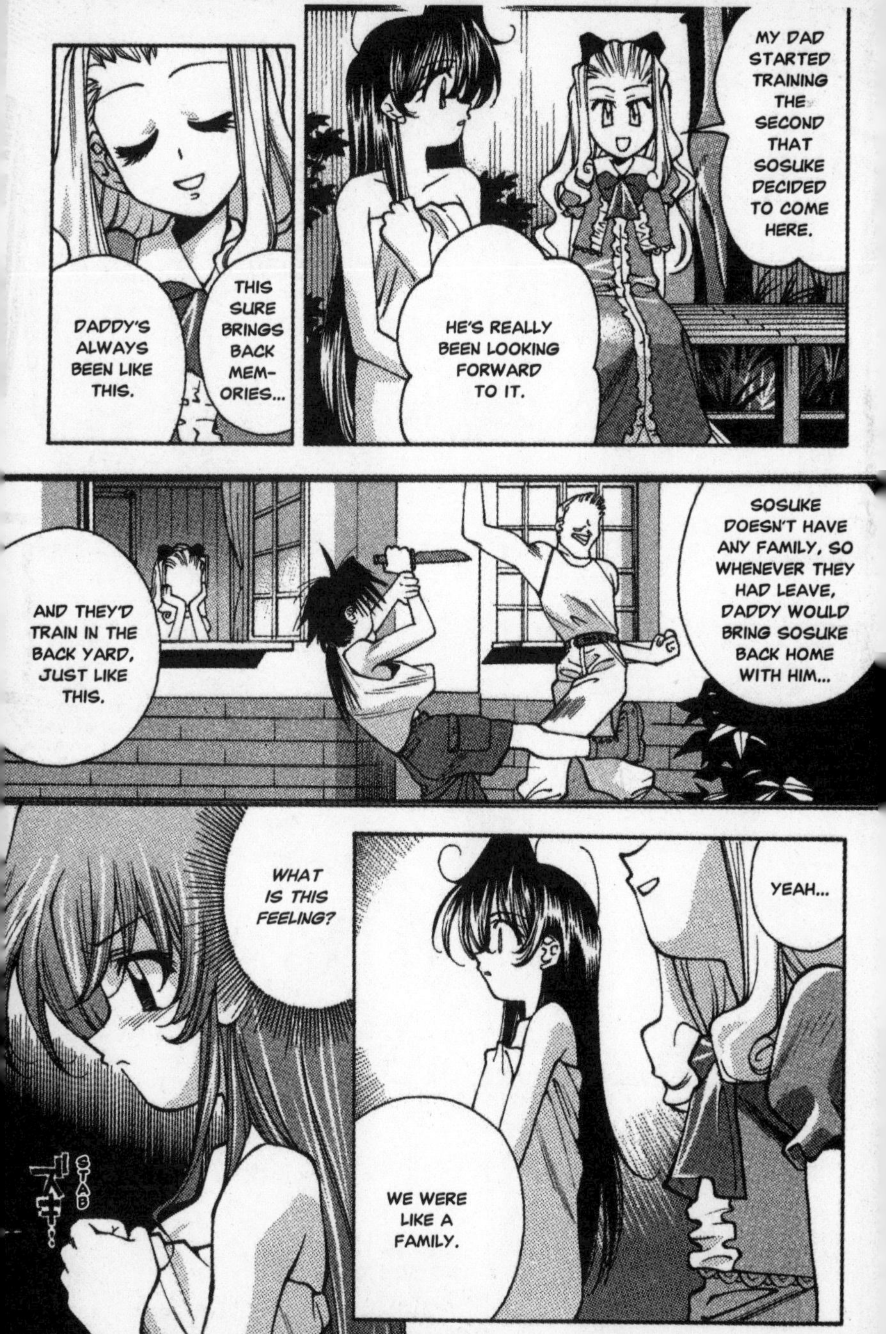
MY DAD STARTED TRAINING THE SECOND THAT SOSUKE DECIDED TO COME HERE.
HE'S REALLY BEEN LOOKING FORWARD TO IT.
THIS SURE BRINGS BACK MEM-ORIES...
DADDY'S ALWAYS BEEN LIKE THIS.
SOSUKE DOESN'T HAVE ANY FAMILY, SO WHENEVER THEY HAD LEAVE, DADDY WOULD BRING SOSUKE BACK HOME WITH HIM...
AND THEY'D TRAIN IN THE BACK YARD, JUST LIKE THIS.
YEAH...
WE WERE LIKE A FAMILY.
WHAT IS THIS FEELING?
STAB

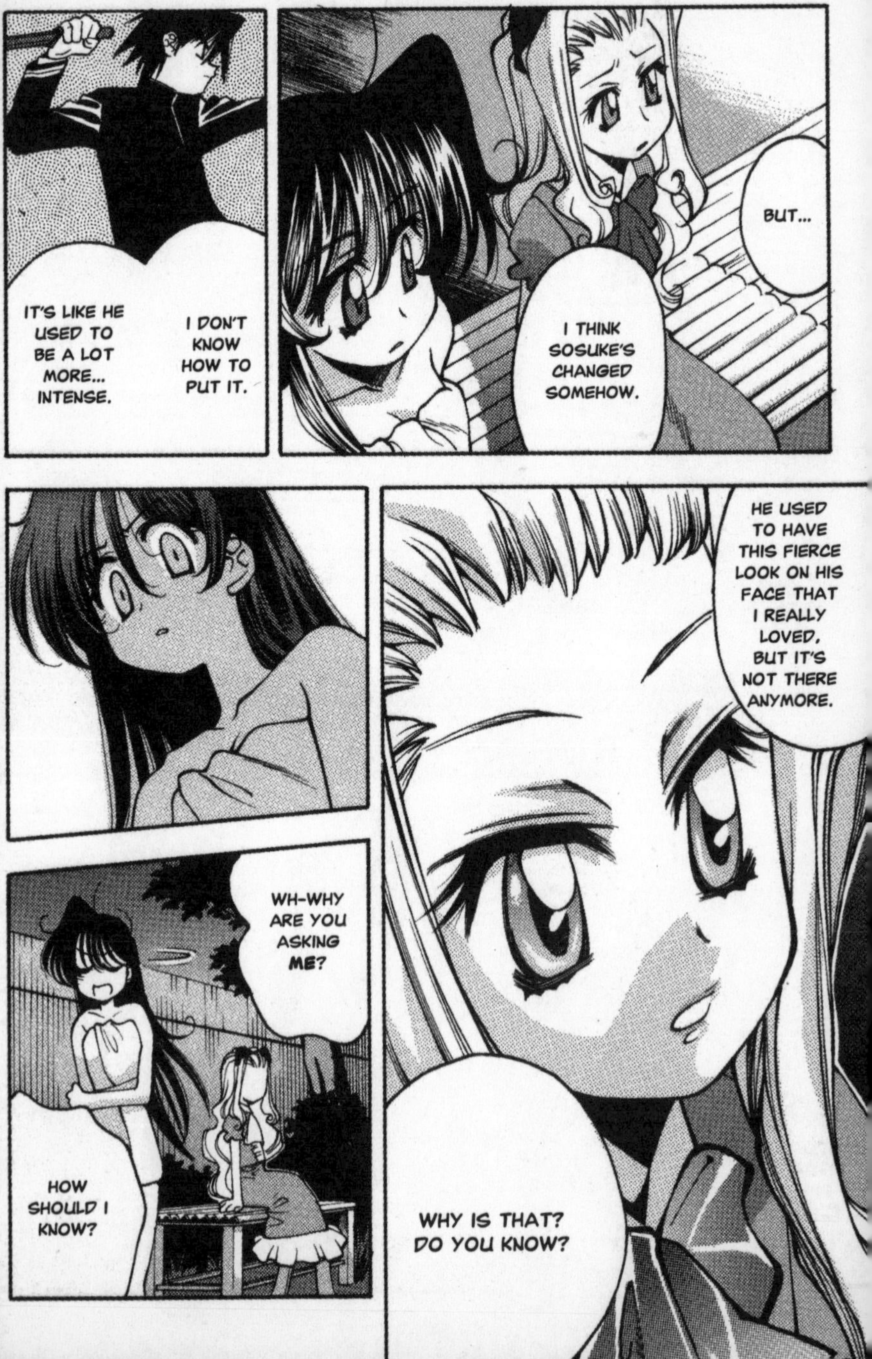
BUT...
I THINK SOSUKE'S CHANGED SOMEHOW.
I DON'T KNOW HOW TO PUT IT.
IT'S LIKE HE USED TO BE A LOT MORE... INTENSE.
HE USED TO HAVE THIS FIERCE LOOK ON HIS FACE THAT I REALLY LOVED, BUT IT'S NOT THERE ANYMORE.
WHY IS THAT? DO YOU KNOW?
WH-WHY ARE YOU ASKING ME?
HOW SHOULD I KNOW?

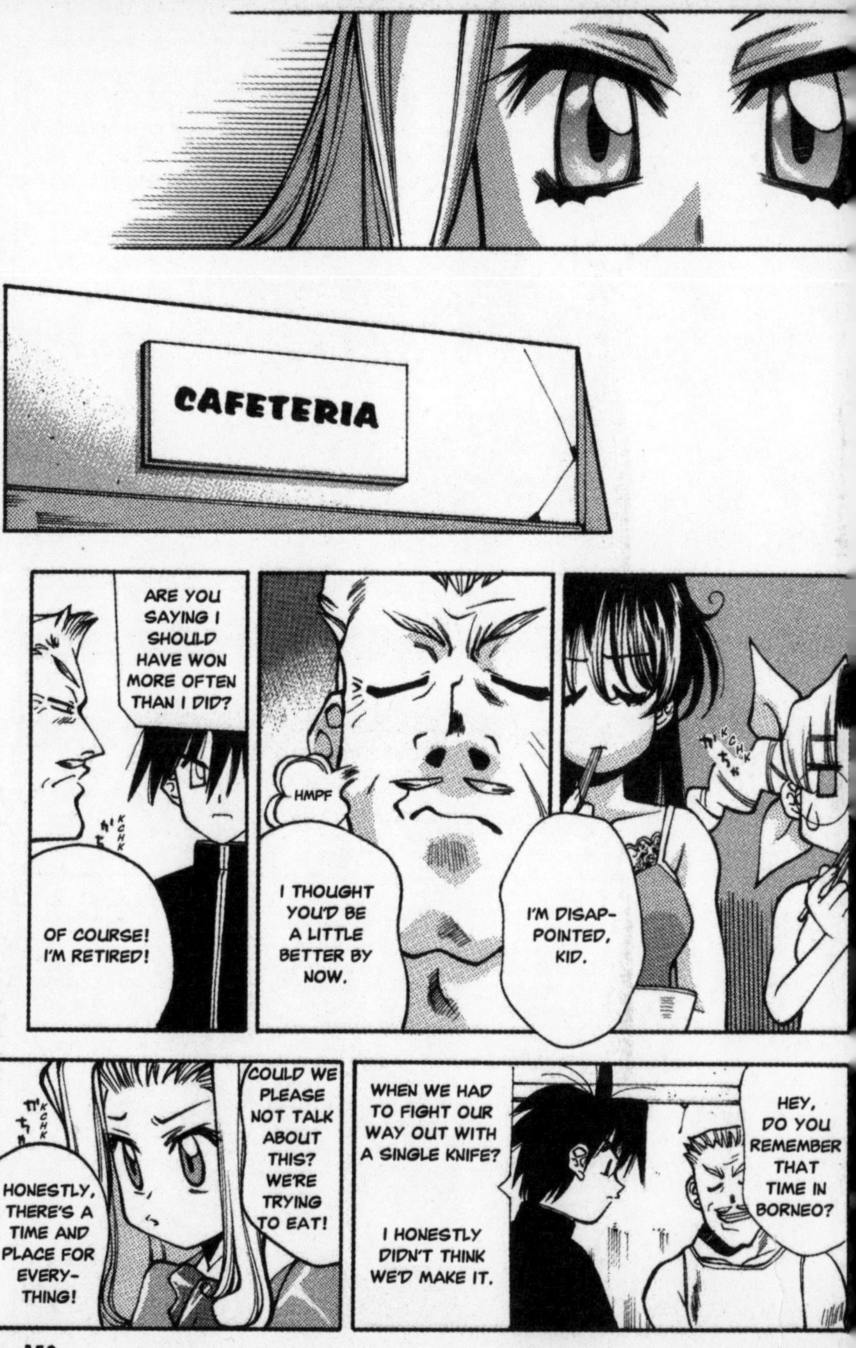
CAFETERIA
KCHK
I'M DISAPPOINTED, KID.
HMPF
I THOUGHT YOU'D BE A LITTLE BETTER BY NOW.
ARE YOU SAYING I SHOULD HAVE WON MORE OFTEN THAN I DID?
KCHK
OF COURSE! I'M RETIRED!
HEY, DO YOU REMEMBER THAT TIME IN BORNEO?
WHEN WE HAD TO FIGHT OUR WAY OUT WITH A SINGLE KNIFE?
I HONESTLY DIDN'T THINK WE'D MAKE IT.
COULD WE PLEASE NOT TALK ABOUT THIS? WE'RE TRYING TO EAT!
KCHK
HONESTLY, THERE'S A TIME AND PLACE FOR EVERY-THING!

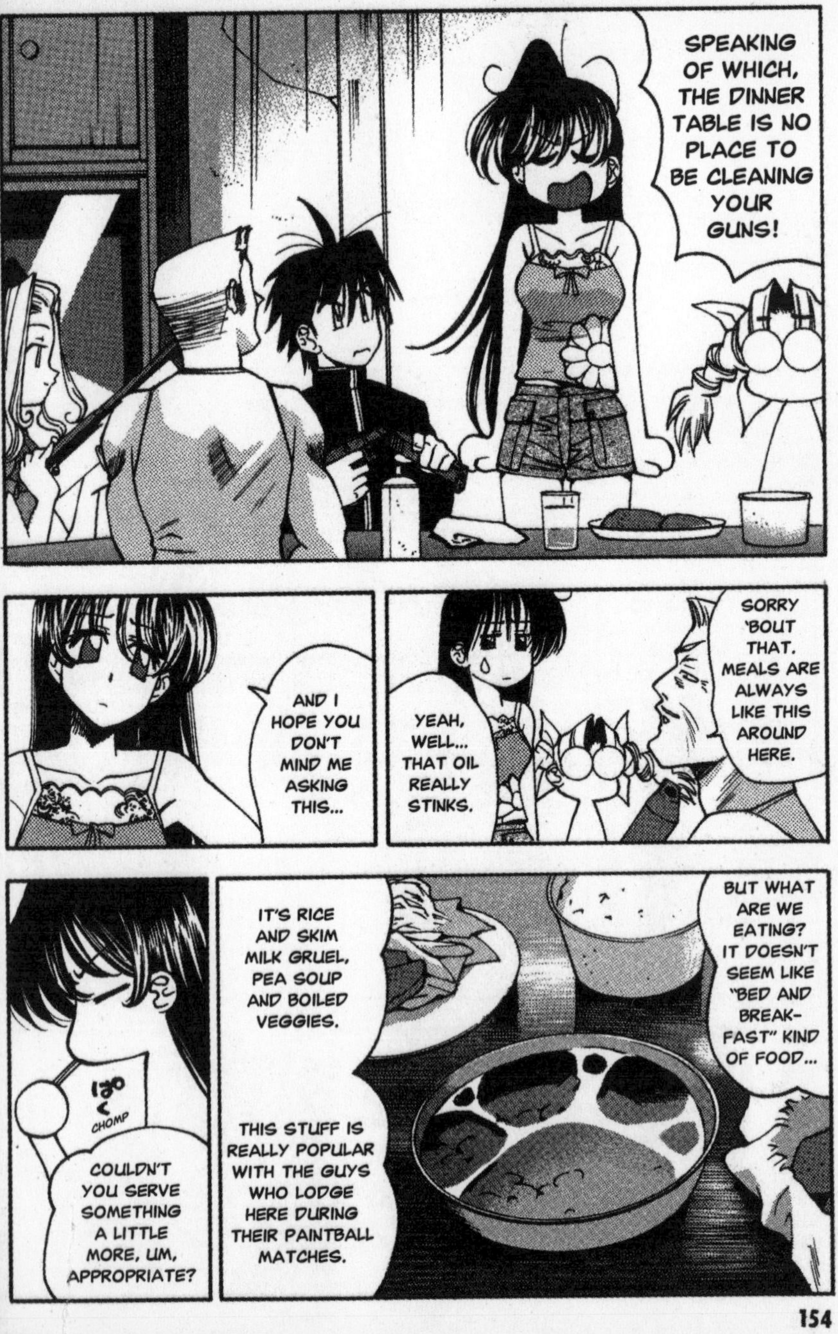
SPEAKING OF WHICH, THE DINNER TABLE IS NO PLACE TO BE CLEANING YOUR GUNS!
SORRY 'BOUT THAT. MEALS ARE ALWAYS LIKE THIS AROUND HERE.
YEAH, WELL... THAT OIL REALLY STINKS.
AND I HOPE YOU DON'T MIND ME ASKING THIS...
BUT WHAT ARE WE EATING? IT DOESN'T SEEM LIKE "BED AND BREAK-FAST" KIND OF FOOD...
IT'S RICE AND SKIM MILK GRUEL, PEA SOUP AND BOILED VEGGIES.
THIS STUFF IS REALLY POPULAR WITH THE GUYS WHO LODGE HERE DURING THEIR PAINTBALL MATCHES.
ぱく
CHOMP
COULDN'T YOU SERVE SOMETHING A LITTLE MORE, UM, APPROPRIATE?

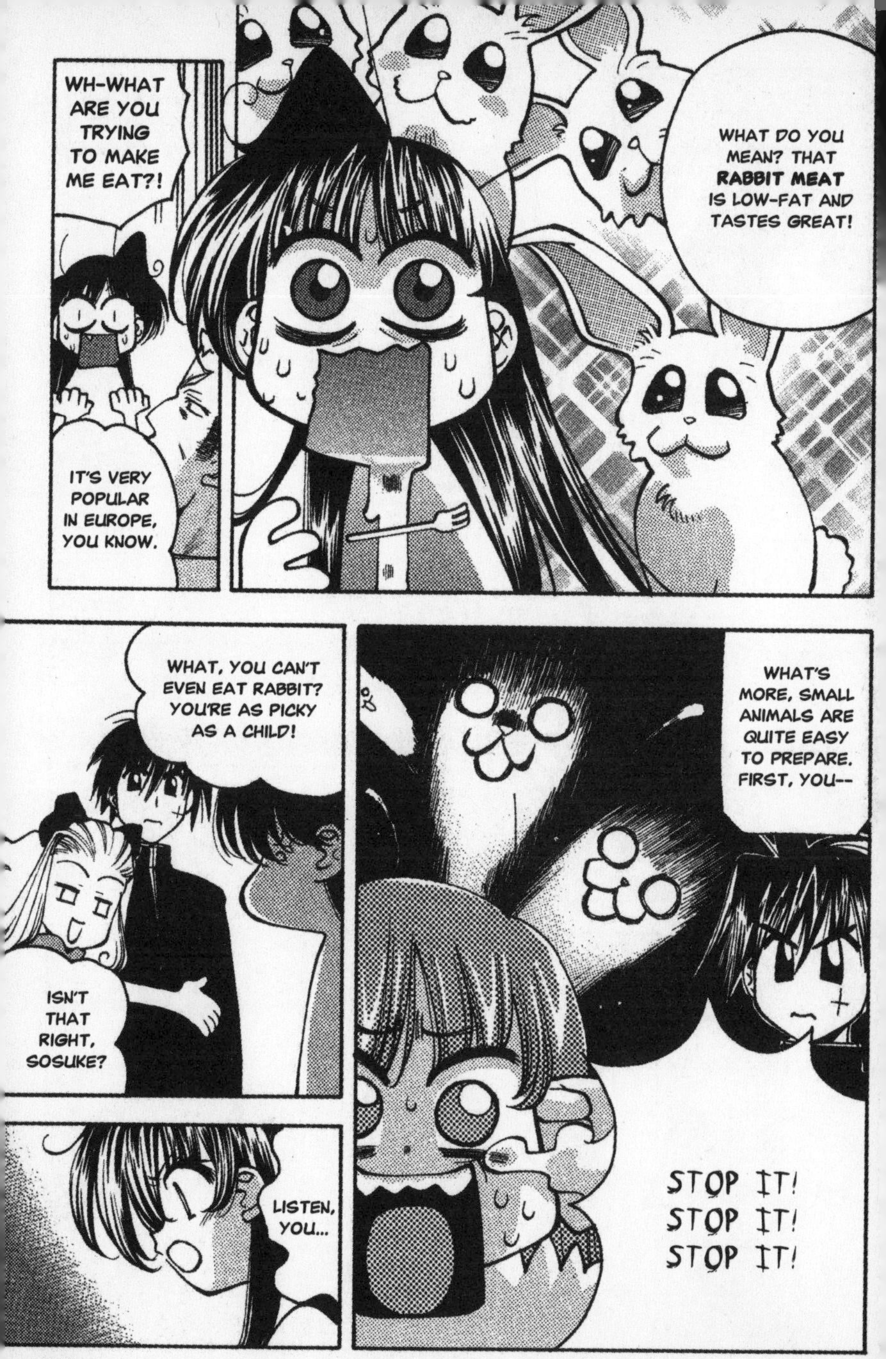
WH-WHAT ARE YOU TRYING TO MAKE ME EAT?!
WHAT DO YOU MEAN? THAT **RABBIT MEAT** IS LOW-FAT AND TASTES GREAT!
IT'S VERY POPULAR IN EUROPE, YOU KNOW.
WHAT'S MORE, SMALL ANIMALS ARE QUITE EASY TO PREPARE. FIRST, YOU--
WHAT, YOU CAN'T EVEN EAT RABBIT? YOU'RE AS PICKY AS A CHILD!
ISN'T THAT RIGHT, SOSUKE?
LISTEN, YOU...
STOP IT! STOP IT! STOP IT!

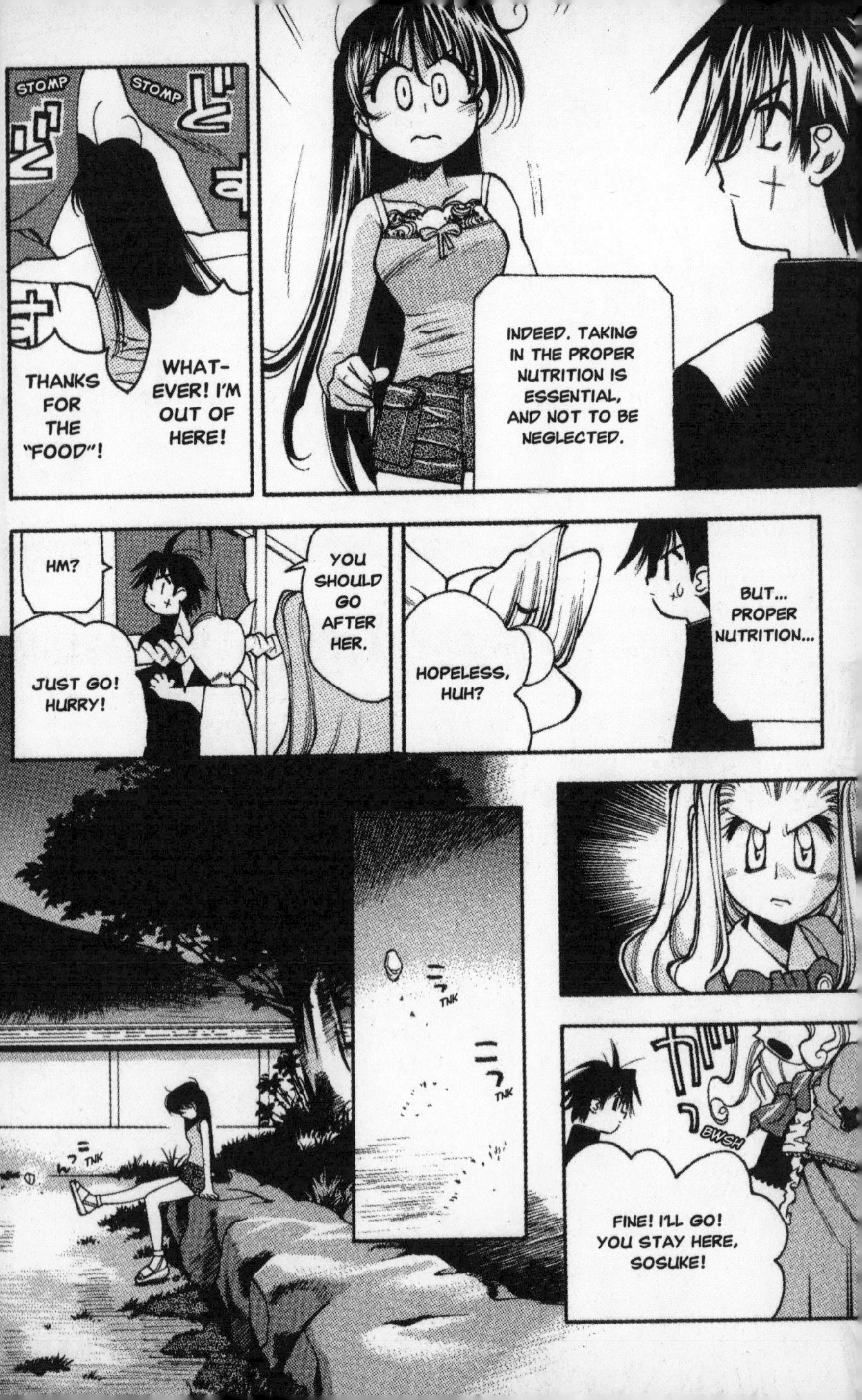
INDEED. TAKING IN THE PROPER NUTRITION IS ESSENTIAL, AND NOT TO BE NEGLECTED.
STOMP
STOMP
WHAT-EVER! I'M OUT OF HERE!
THANKS FOR THE "FOOD"!
BUT... PROPER NUTRITION...
HOPELESS, HUH?
YOU SHOULD GO AFTER HER.
HM?
JUST GO! HURRY!
BWSH
FINE! I'LL GO! YOU STAY HERE, SOSUKE!
TNK
TNK
TNK

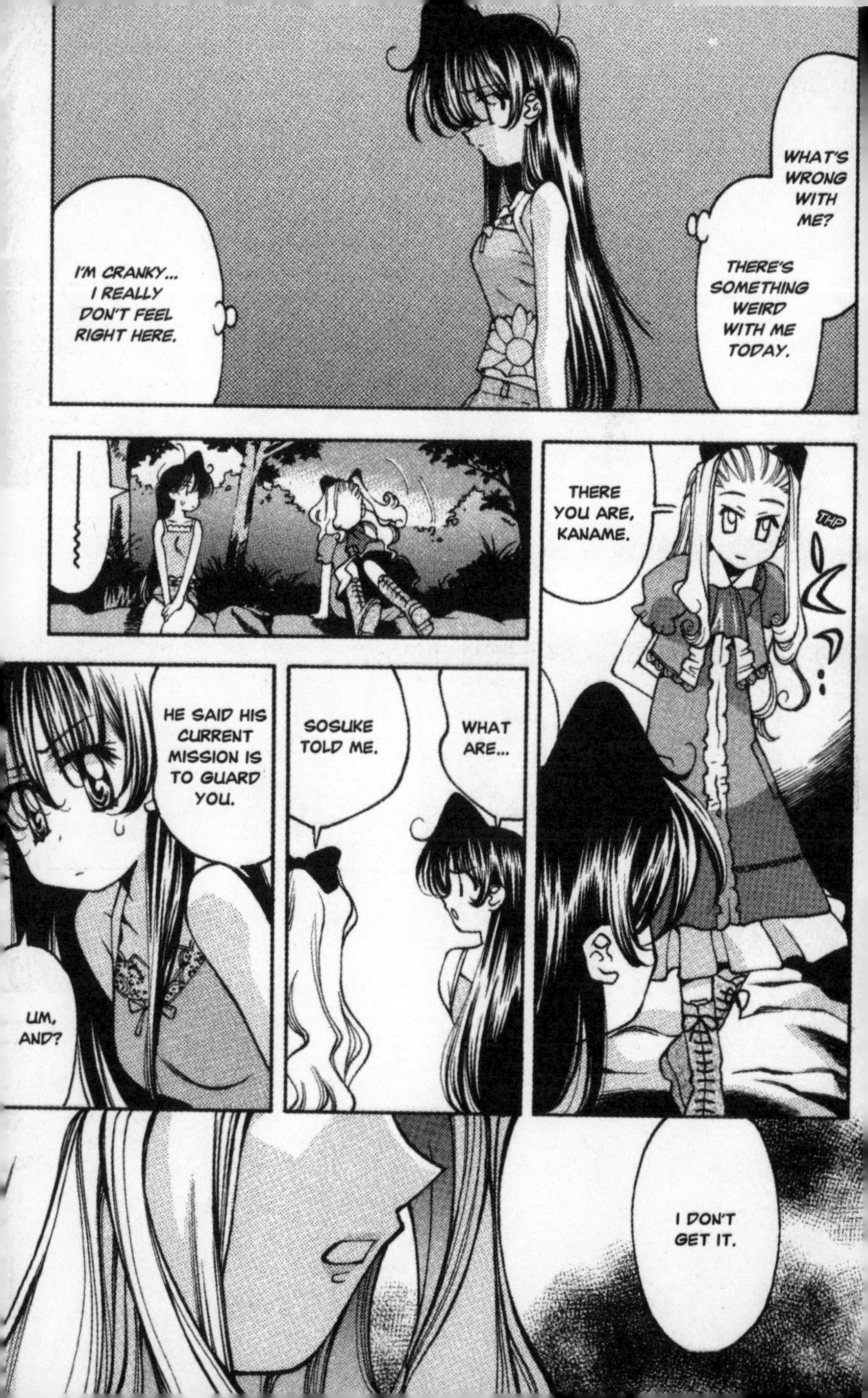
WHAT'S WRONG WITH ME?
THERE'S SOMETHING WEIRD WITH ME TODAY.
I'M CRANKY... I REALLY DON'T FEEL RIGHT HERE.
THP
THERE YOU ARE, KANAME.
WHAT ARE...
SOSUKE TOLD ME.
HE SAID HIS CURRENT MISSION IS TO GUARD YOU.
UM, AND?
I DON'T GET IT.

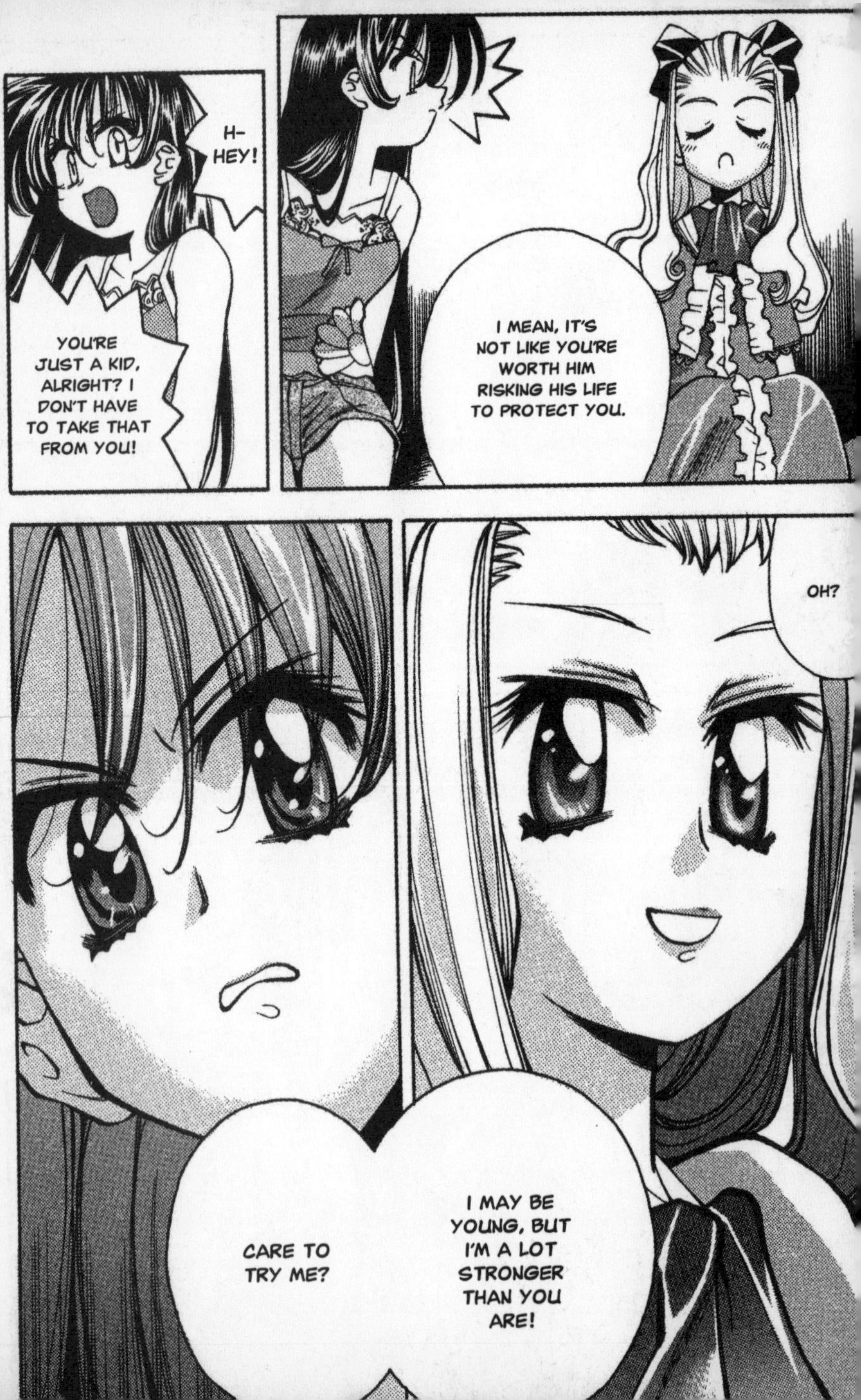
I MEAN, IT'S NOT LIKE YOU'RE WORTH HIM RISKING HIS LIFE TO PROTECT YOU.
H- HEY!
YOU'RE JUST A KID, ALRIGHT? I DON'T HAVE TO TAKE THAT FROM YOU!
OH?
I MAY BE YOUNG, BUT I'M A LOT STRONGER THAN YOU ARE!
CARE TO TRY ME?

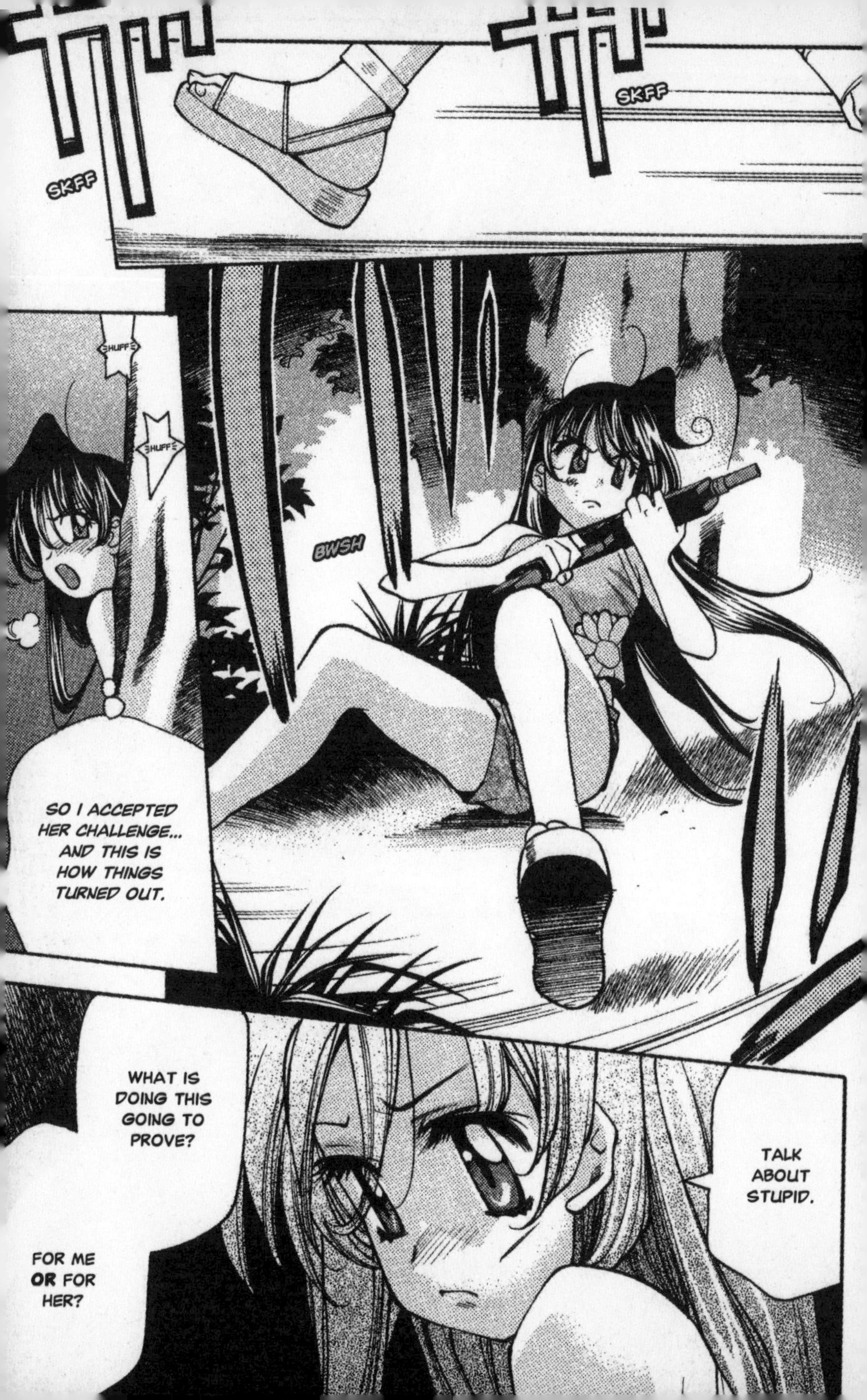
SKFF
SKFF
HUFF
HUFF
BWSH
SO I ACCEPTED HER CHALLENGE... AND THIS IS HOW THINGS TURNED OUT.
TALK ABOUT STUPID.
WHAT IS DOING THIS GOING TO PROVE?
FOR ME OR FOR HER?

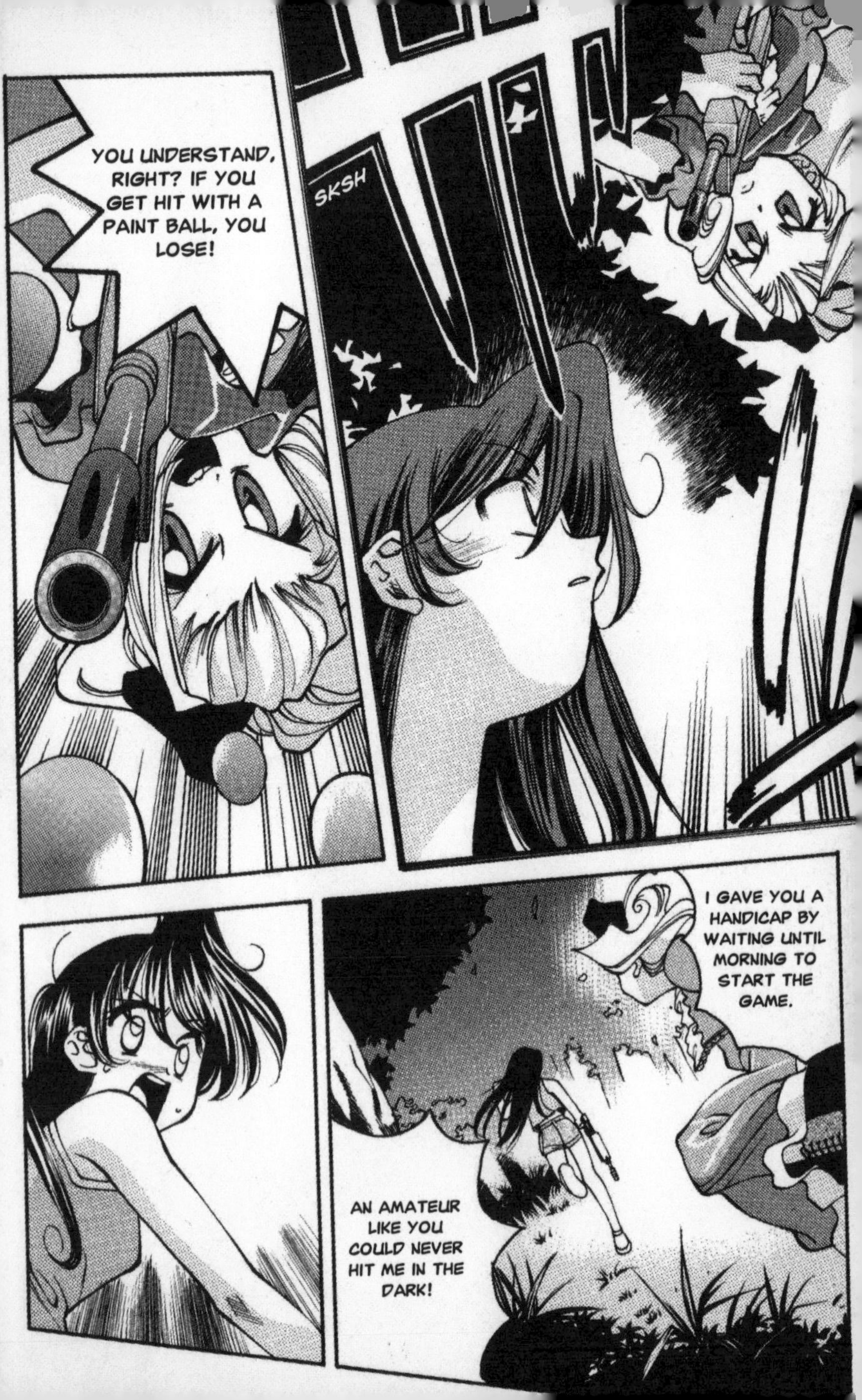
SKSH
YOU UNDERSTAND, RIGHT? IF YOU GET HIT WITH A PAINT BALL, YOU LOSE!
I GAVE YOU A HANDICAP BY WAITING UNTIL MORNING TO START THE GAME.
AN AMATEUR LIKE YOU COULD NEVER HIT ME IN THE DARK!

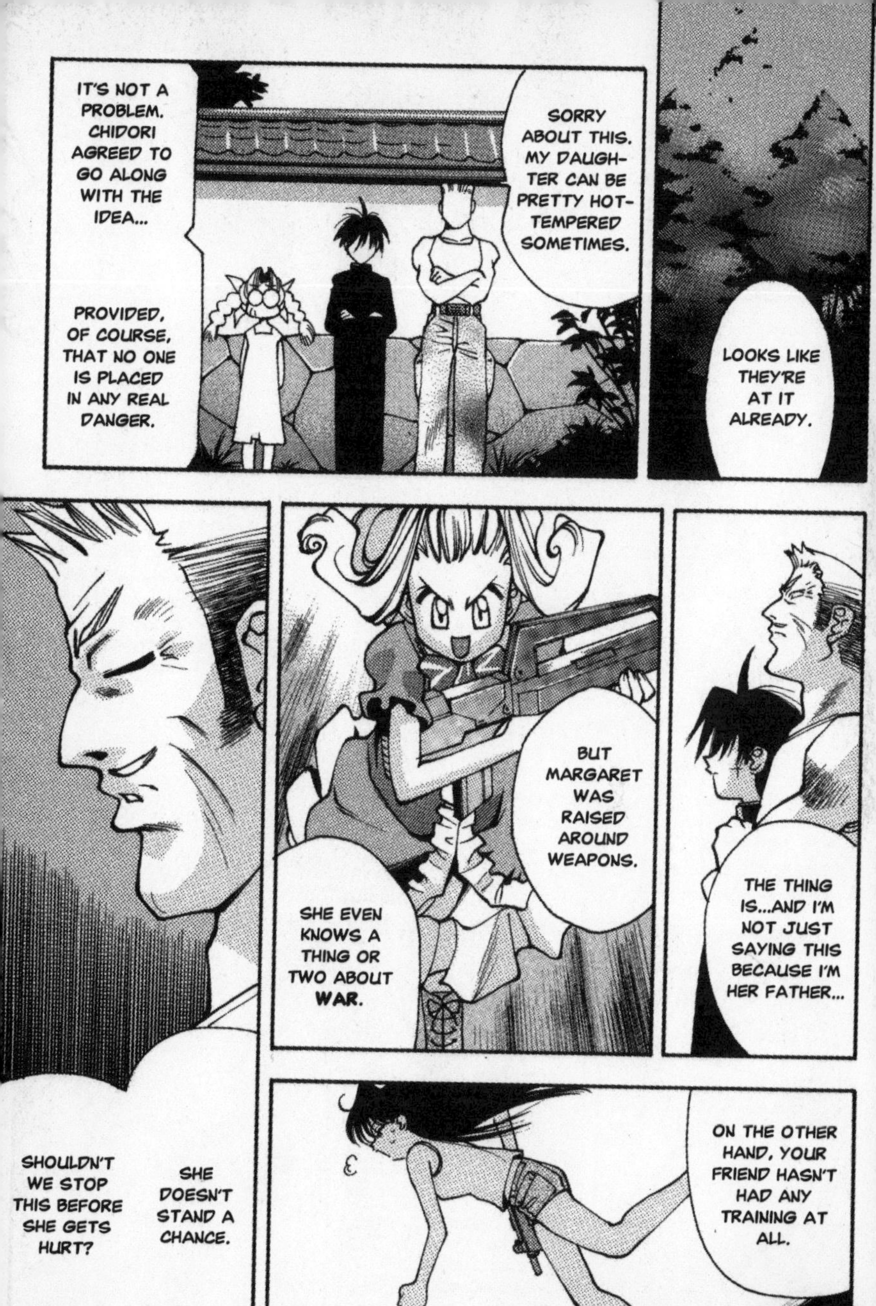
LOOKS LIKE THEY'RE AT IT ALREADY.
SORRY ABOUT THIS. MY DAUGHTER CAN BE PRETTY HOT-TEMPERED SOMETIMES.
IT'S NOT A PROBLEM. CHIDORI AGREED TO GO ALONG WITH THE IDEA...
PROVIDED, OF COURSE, THAT NO ONE IS PLACED IN ANY REAL DANGER.
THE THING IS...AND I'M NOT JUST SAYING THIS BECAUSE I'M HER FATHER...
BUT MARGARET WAS RAISED AROUND WEAPONS.
SHE EVEN KNOWS A THING OR TWO ABOUT WAR.
ON THE OTHER HAND, YOUR FRIEND HASN'T HAD ANY TRAINING AT ALL.
SHE DOESN'T STAND A CHANCE.
SHOULDN'T WE STOP THIS BEFORE SHE GETS HURT?

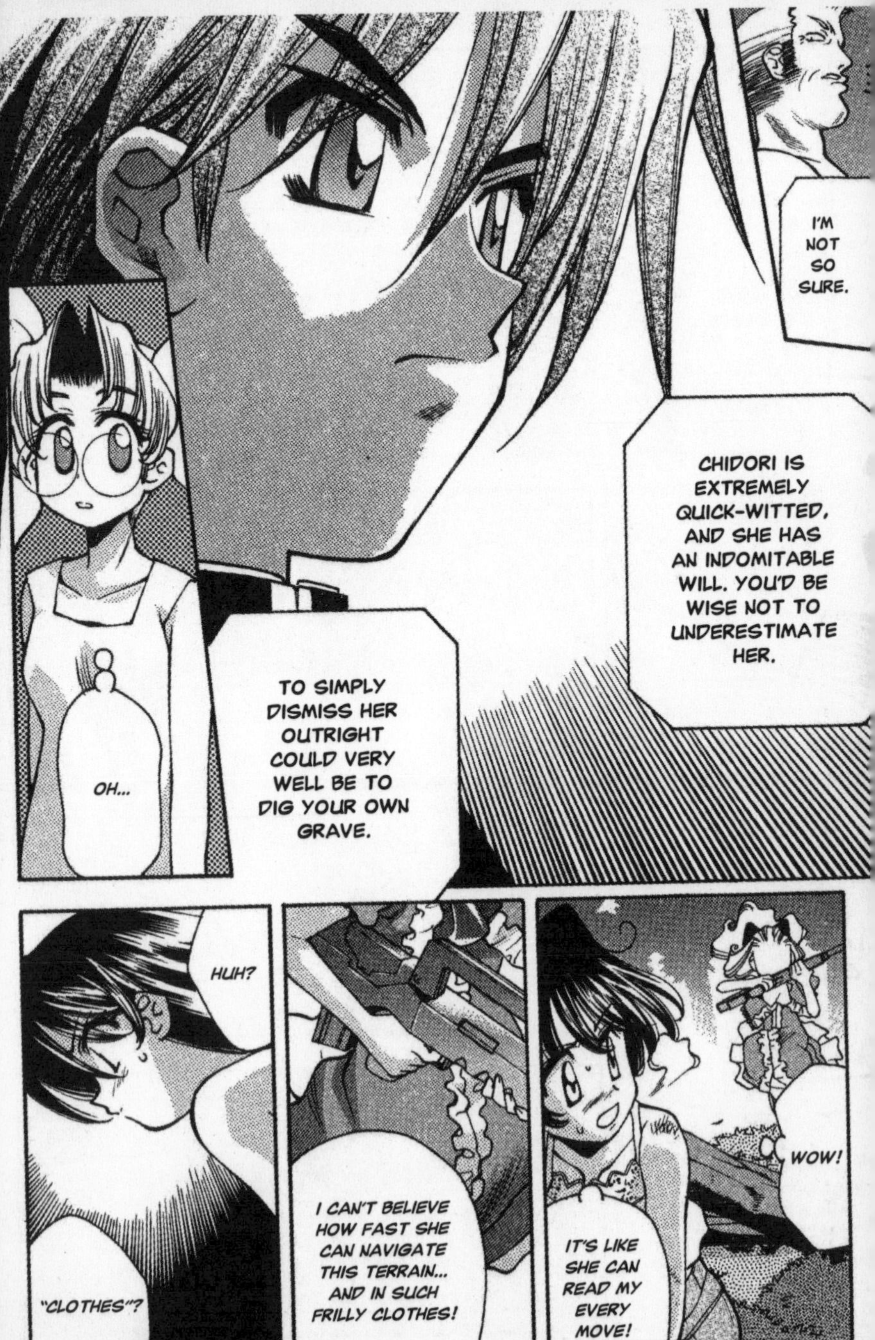
I'M NOT SO SURE.
CHIDORI IS EXTREMELY QUICK-WITTED, AND SHE HAS AN INDOMITABLE WILL. YOU'D BE WISE NOT TO UNDERESTIMATE HER.
TO SIMPLY DISMISS HER OUTRIGHT COULD VERY WELL BE TO DIG YOUR OWN GRAVE.
OH...
WOW!
IT'S LIKE SHE CAN READ MY EVERY MOVE!
I CAN'T BELIEVE HOW FAST SHE CAN NAVIGATE THIS TERRAIN... AND IN SUCH FRILLY CLOTHES!
HUH?
"CLOTHES"?

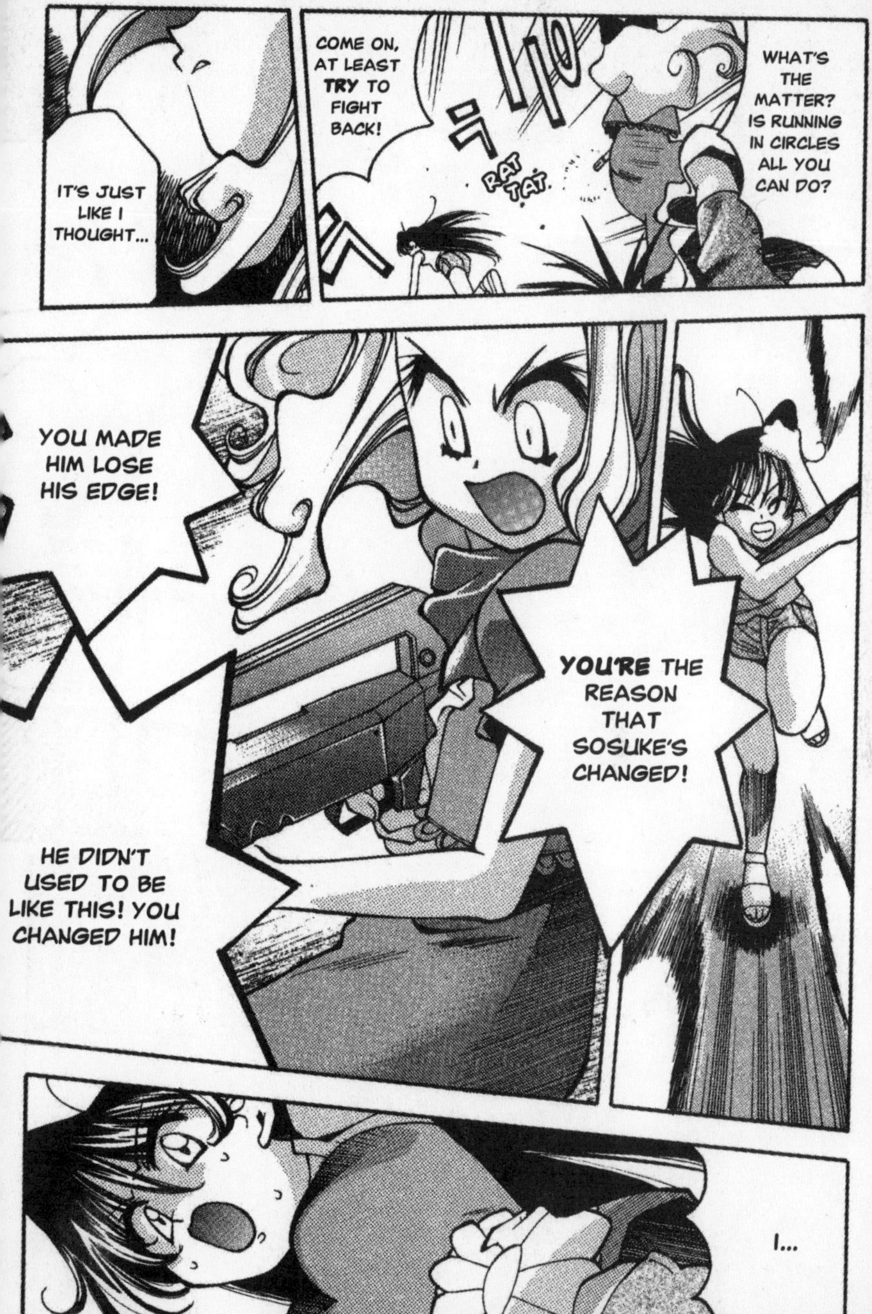
WHAT'S THE MATTER? IS RUNNING IN CIRCLES ALL YOU CAN DO?
COME ON, AT LEAST TRY TO FIGHT BACK!
RAT TAT
IT'S JUST LIKE I THOUGHT...
YOU'RE THE REASON THAT SOSUKE'S CHANGED!
YOU MADE HIM LOSE HIS EDGE!
HE DIDN'T USED TO BE LIKE THIS! YOU CHANGED HIM!
I...

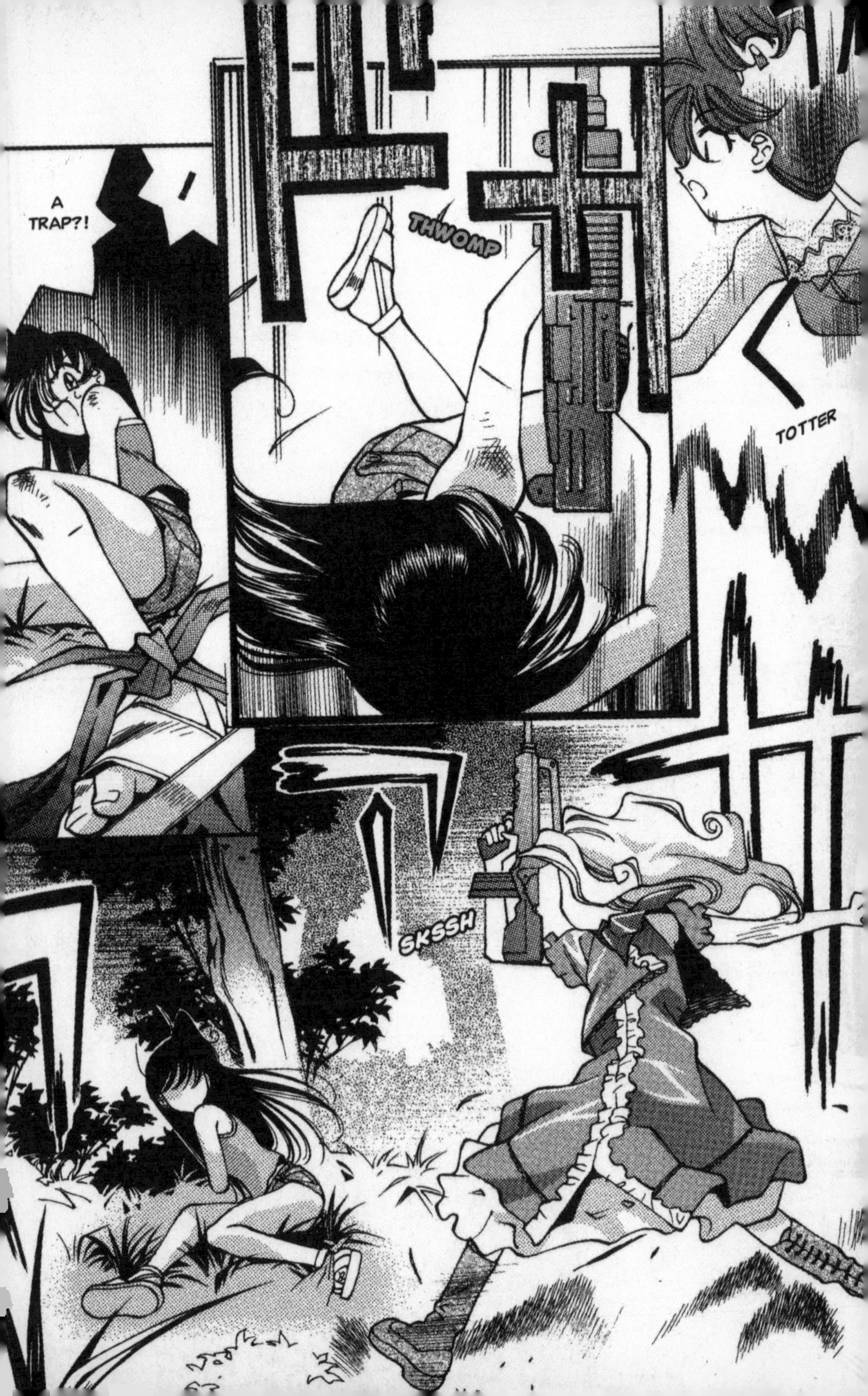
TOTTER
THWOMP
A TRAP?!
SKSSH

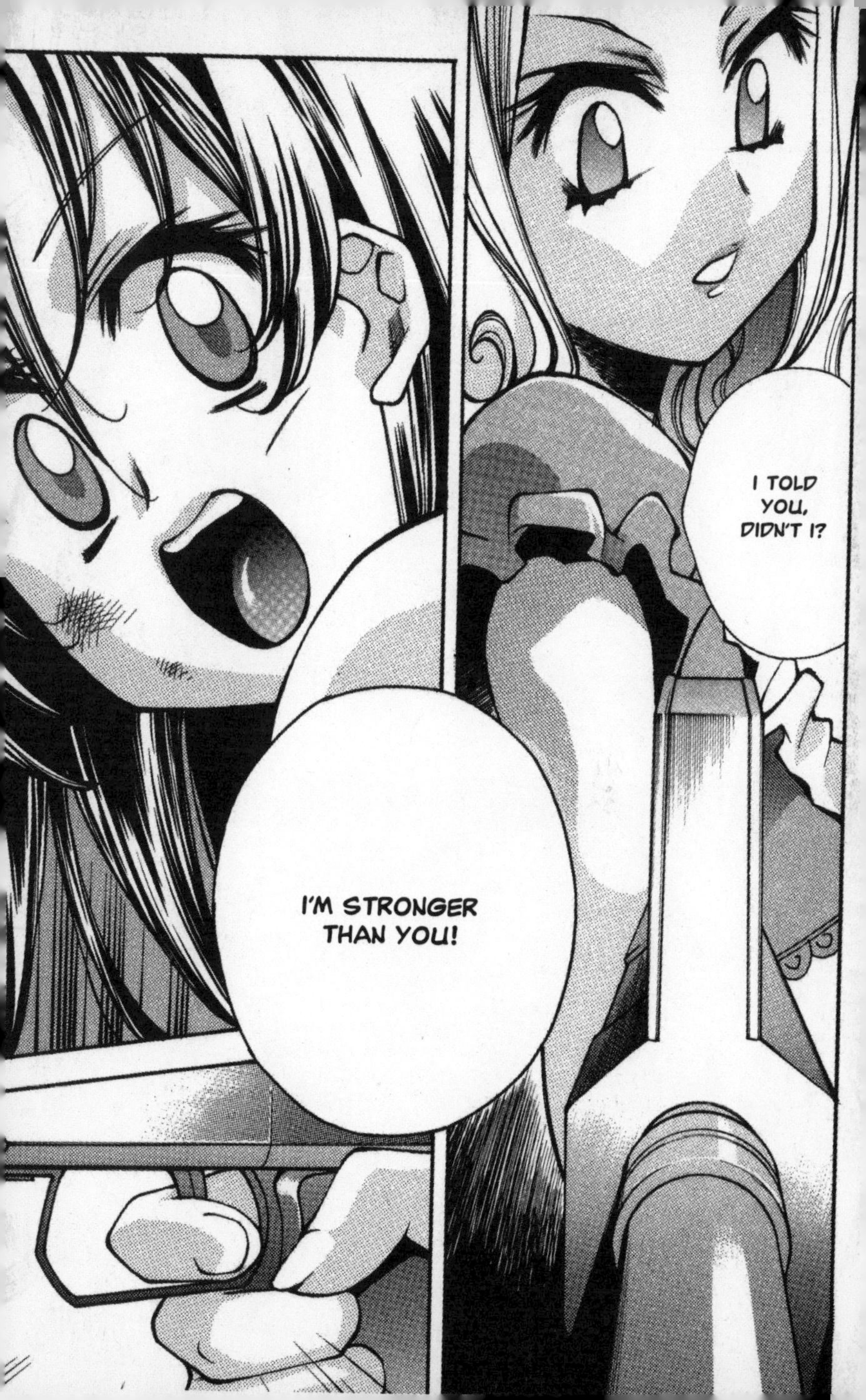
I TOLD YOU, DIDN'T I?
I'M STRONGER THAN YOU!

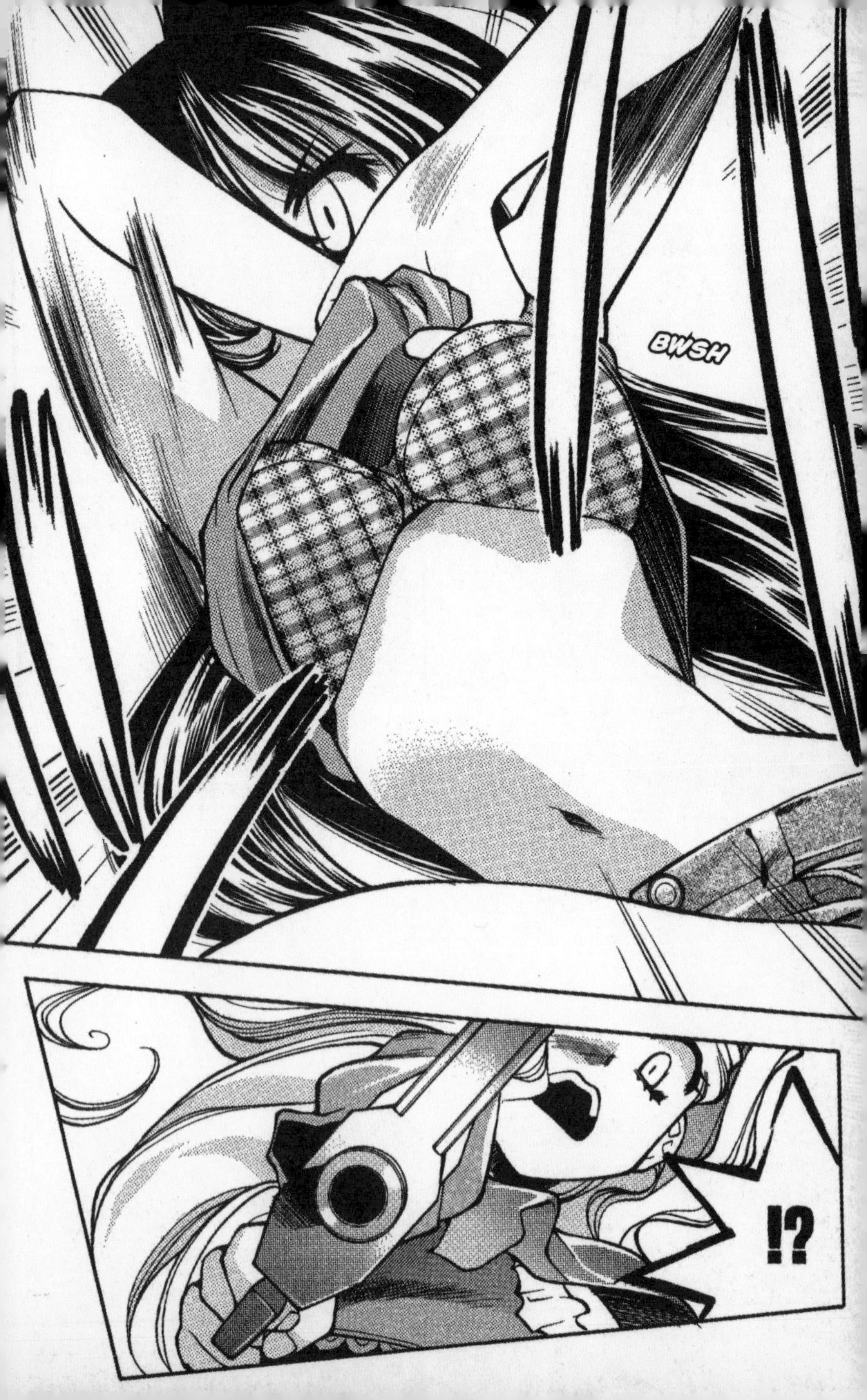
BWSH
!?

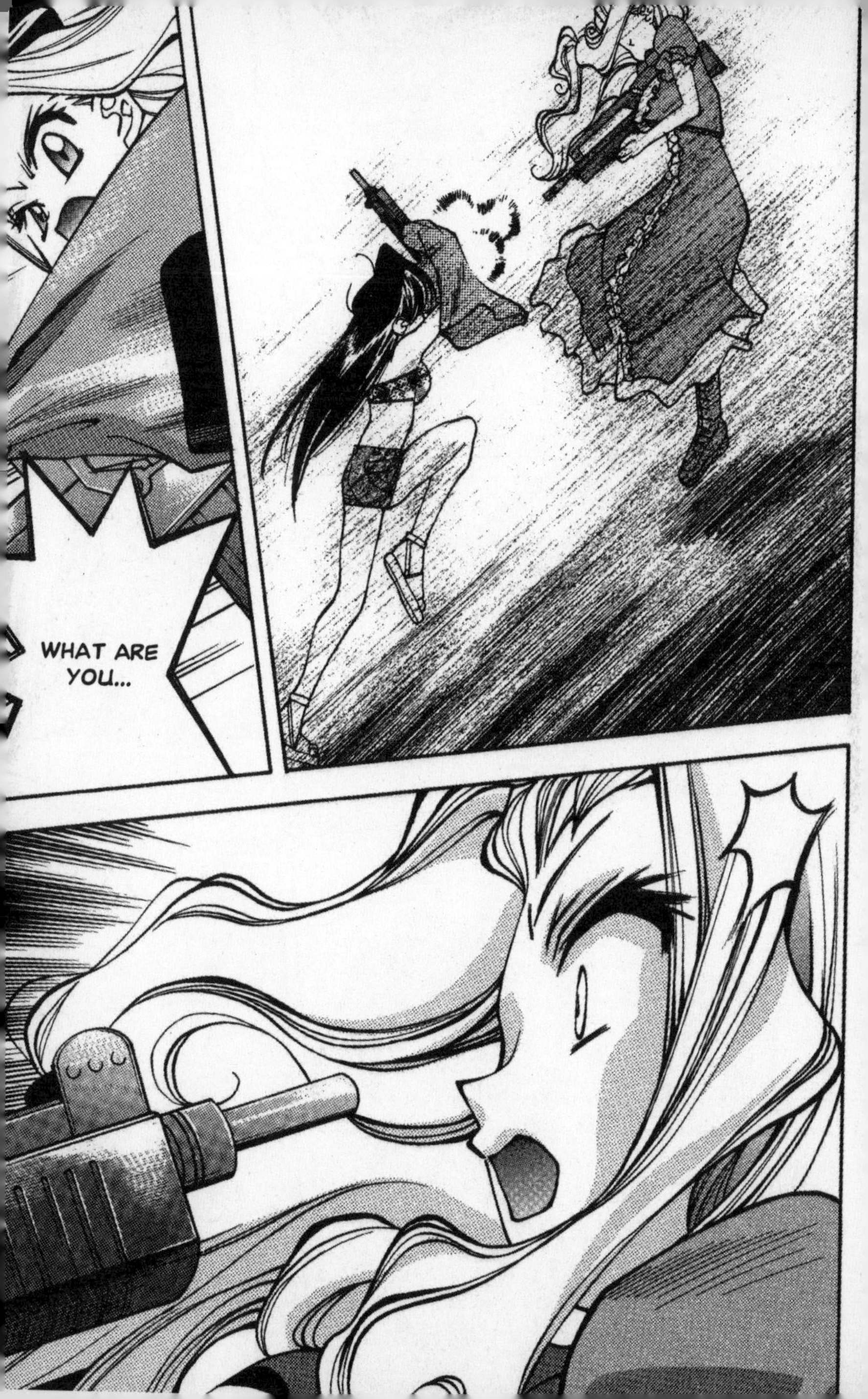
WHAT ARE YOU...

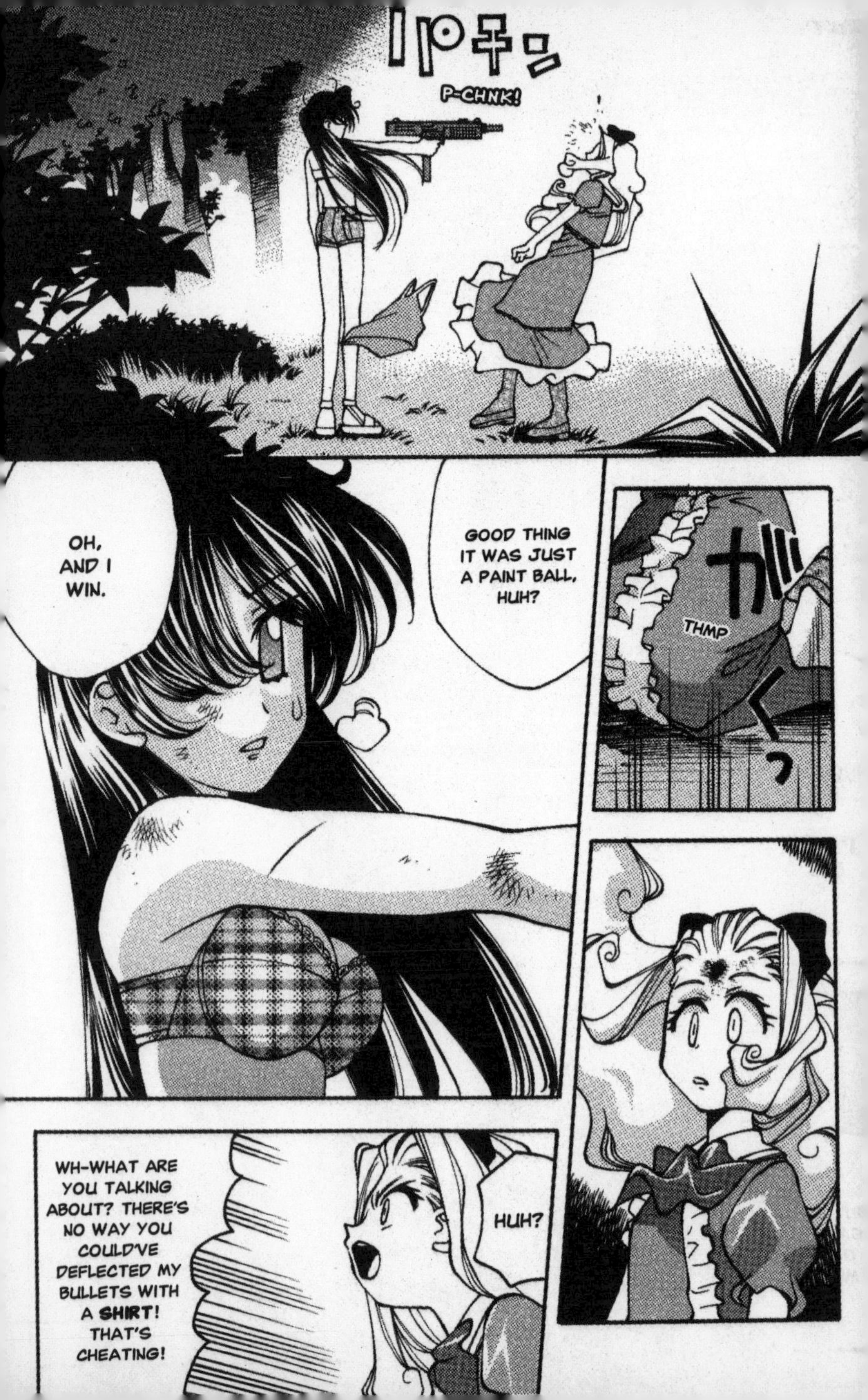
P-CHNK!
THMP
GOOD THING IT WAS JUST A PAINT BALL, HUH?
OH, AND I WIN.
HUH?
WH-WHAT ARE YOU TALKING ABOUT? THERE'S NO WAY YOU COULD'VE DEFLECTED MY BULLETS WITH A **SHIRT**! THAT'S CHEATING!

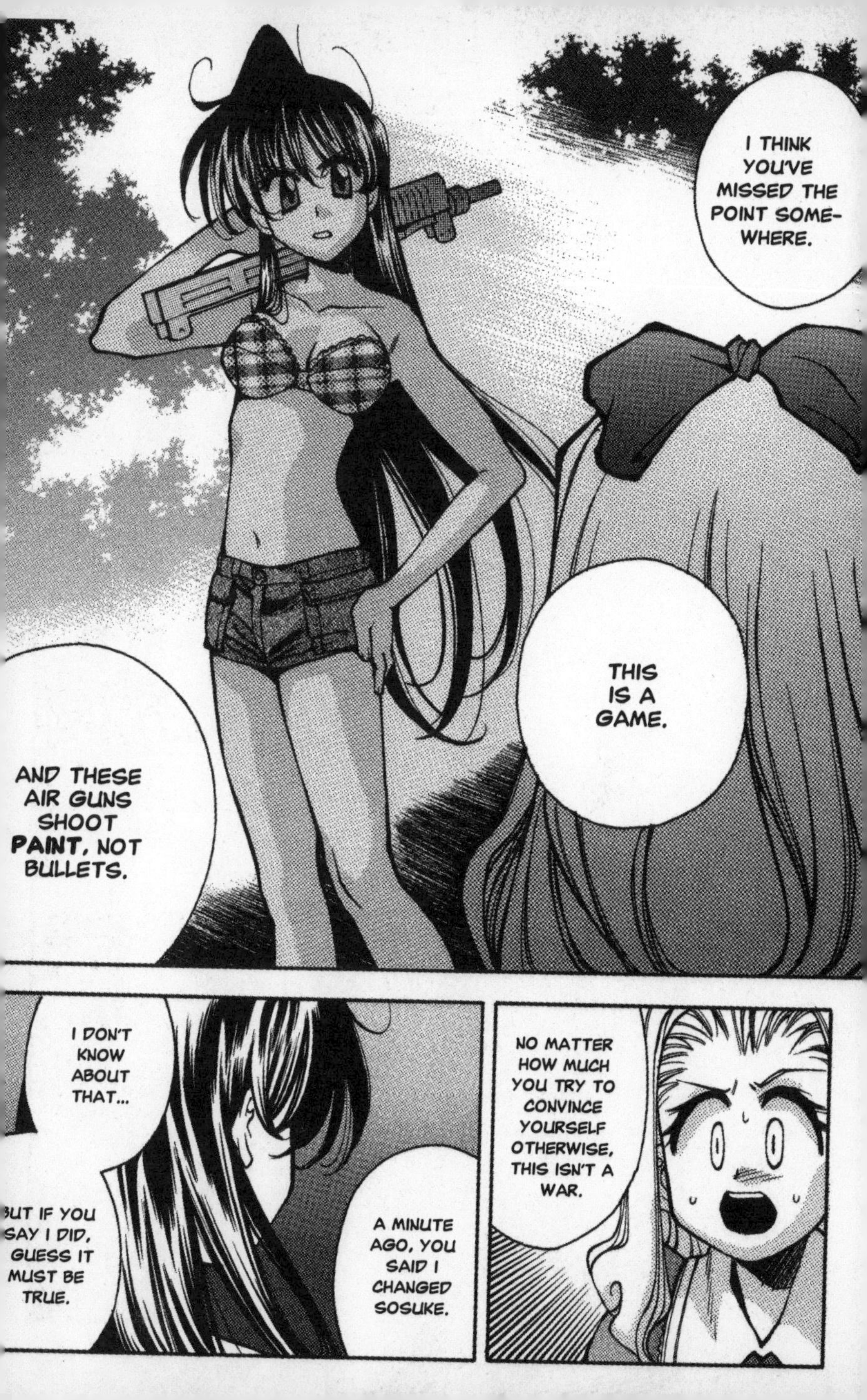

I THINK YOU'VE MISSED THE POINT SOME-WHERE.
THIS IS A GAME.
AND THESE AIR GUNS SHOOT **PAINT**, NOT BULLETS.
NO MATTER HOW MUCH YOU TRY TO CONVINCE YOURSELF OTHERWISE, THIS ISN'T A WAR.
A MINUTE AGO, YOU SAID I CHANGED SOSUKE.
I DON'T KNOW ABOUT THAT...
UT IF YOU SAY I DID, GUESS IT MUST BE TRUE.

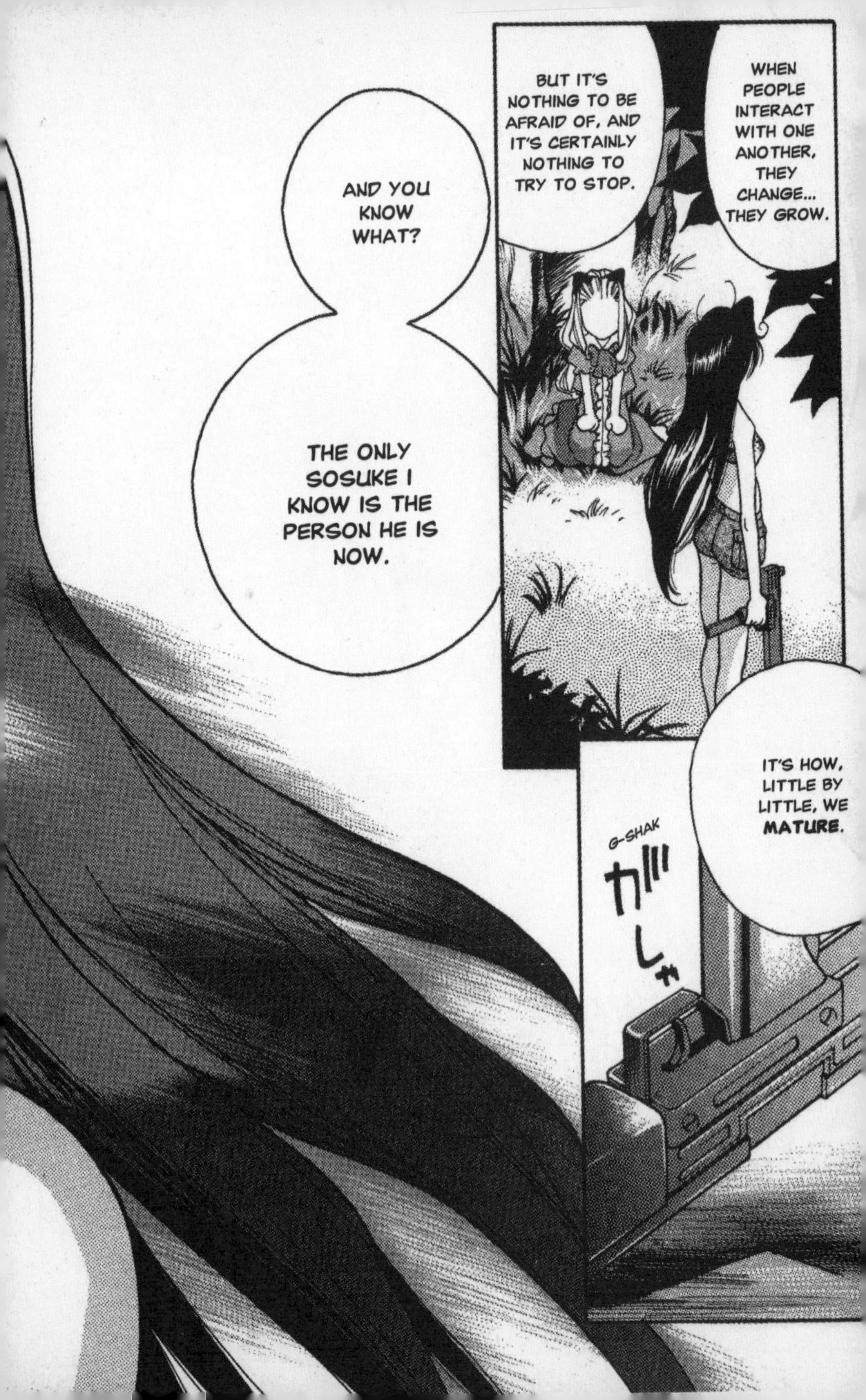

WHEN PEOPLE INTERACT WITH ONE ANOTHER, THEY CHANGE... THEY GROW.
BUT IT'S NOTHING TO BE AFRAID OF, AND IT'S CERTAINLY NOTHING TO TRY TO STOP.
IT'S HOW, LITTLE BY LITTLE, WE **MATURE**.
G-SHAK
ガしゃ
AND YOU KNOW WHAT?
THE ONLY SOSUKE I KNOW IS THE PERSON HE IS NOW.

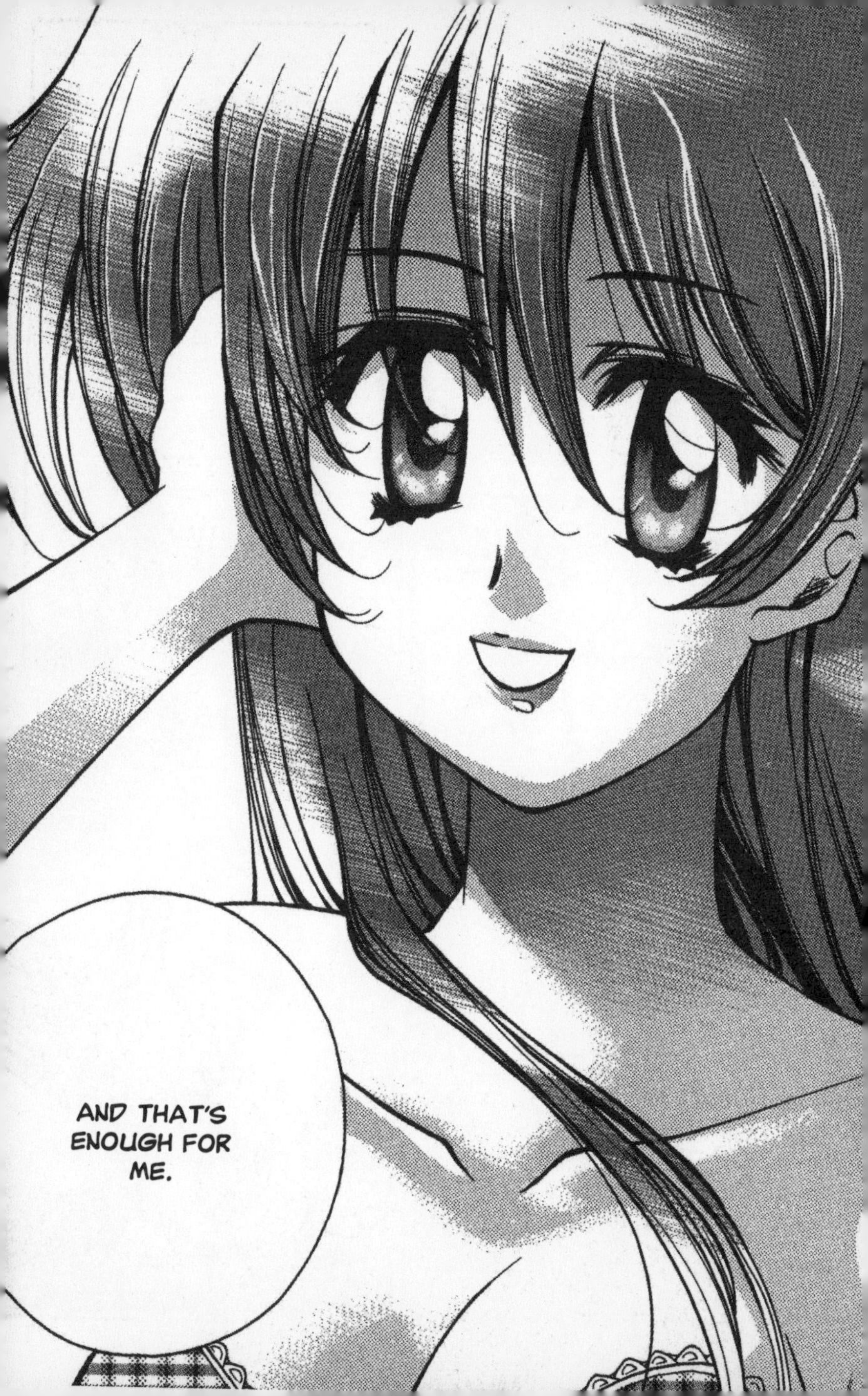
AND THAT'S ENOUGH FOR ME.

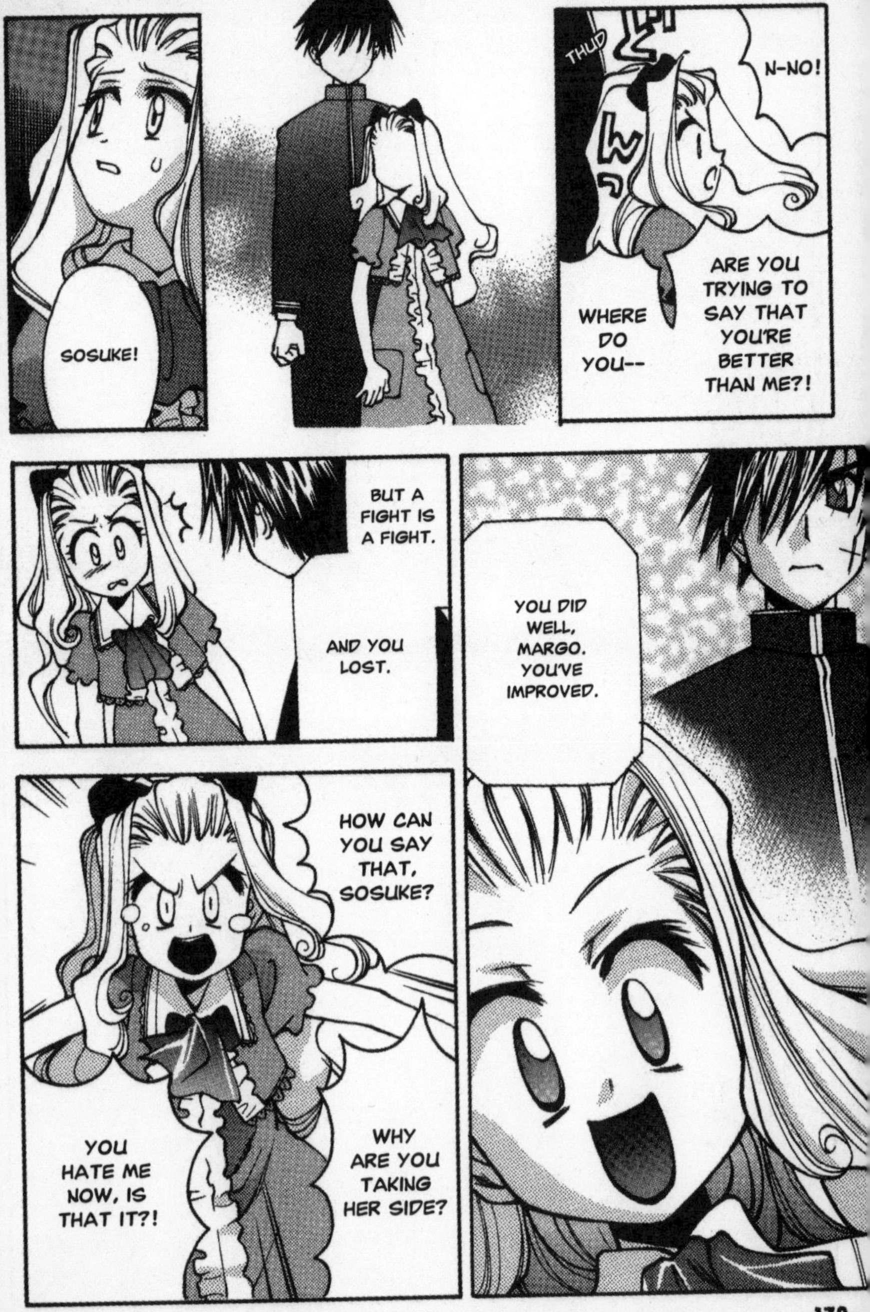
THUD
N-NO!
ARE YOU TRYING TO SAY THAT YOU'RE BETTER THAN ME?!
WHERE DO YOU--
SOSUKE!
YOU DID WELL, MARGO. YOU'VE IMPROVED.
BUT A FIGHT IS A FIGHT.
AND YOU LOST.
HOW CAN YOU SAY THAT, SOSUKE?
WHY ARE YOU TAKING HER SIDE?
YOU HATE ME NOW, IS THAT IT?!

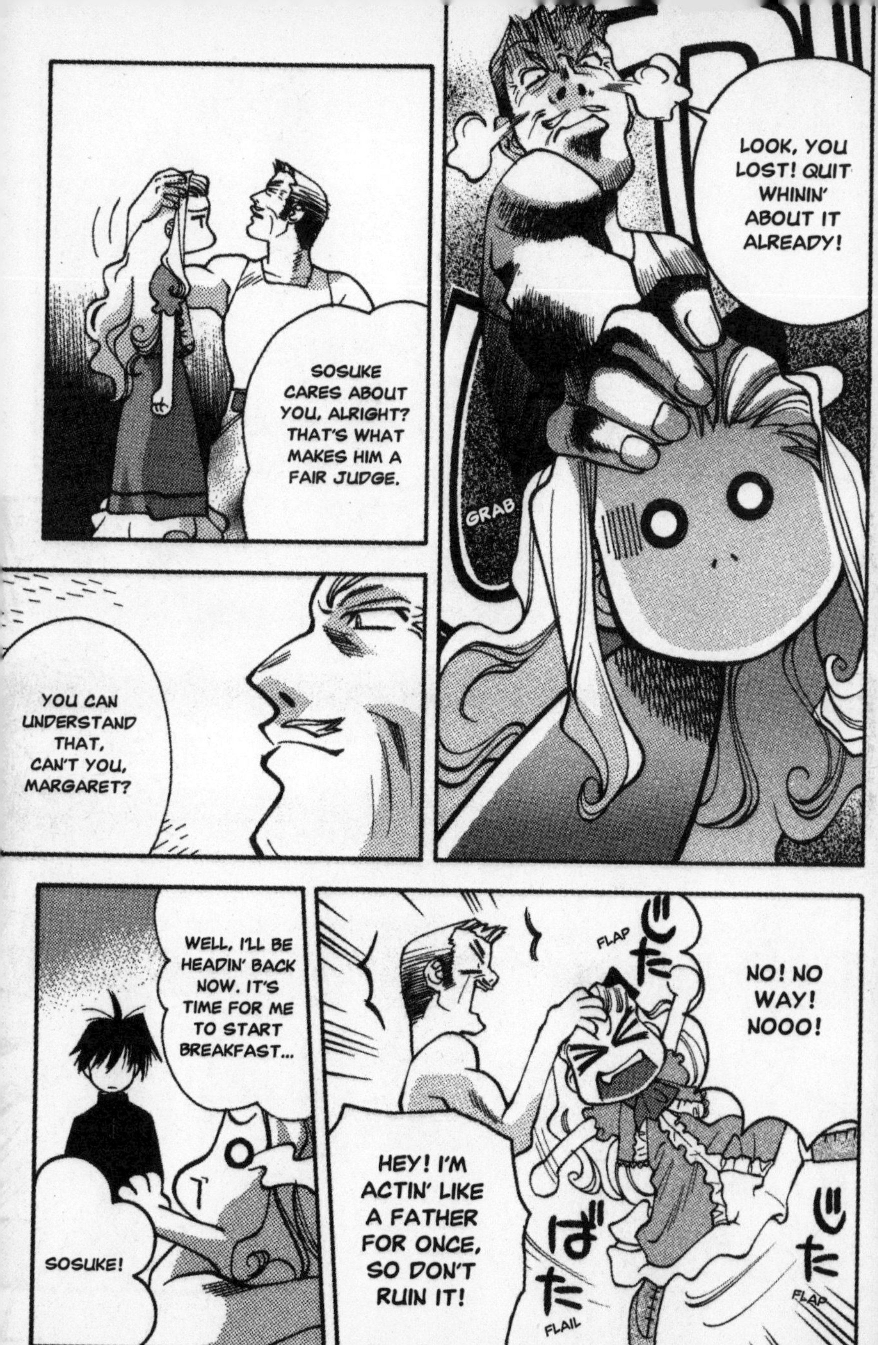
LOOK, YOU LOST! QUIT WHININ' ABOUT IT ALREADY!
GRAB
SOSUKE CARES ABOUT YOU, ALRIGHT? THAT'S WHAT MAKES HIM A FAIR JUDGE.
YOU CAN UNDERSTAND THAT, CAN'T YOU, MARGARET?
NO! NO WAY! NOOO!
FLAP
HEY! I'M ACTIN' LIKE A FATHER FOR ONCE, SO DON'T RUIN IT!
FLAIL
FLAP
WELL, I'LL BE HEADIN' BACK NOW. IT'S TIME FOR ME TO START BREAKFAST...
SOSUKE!

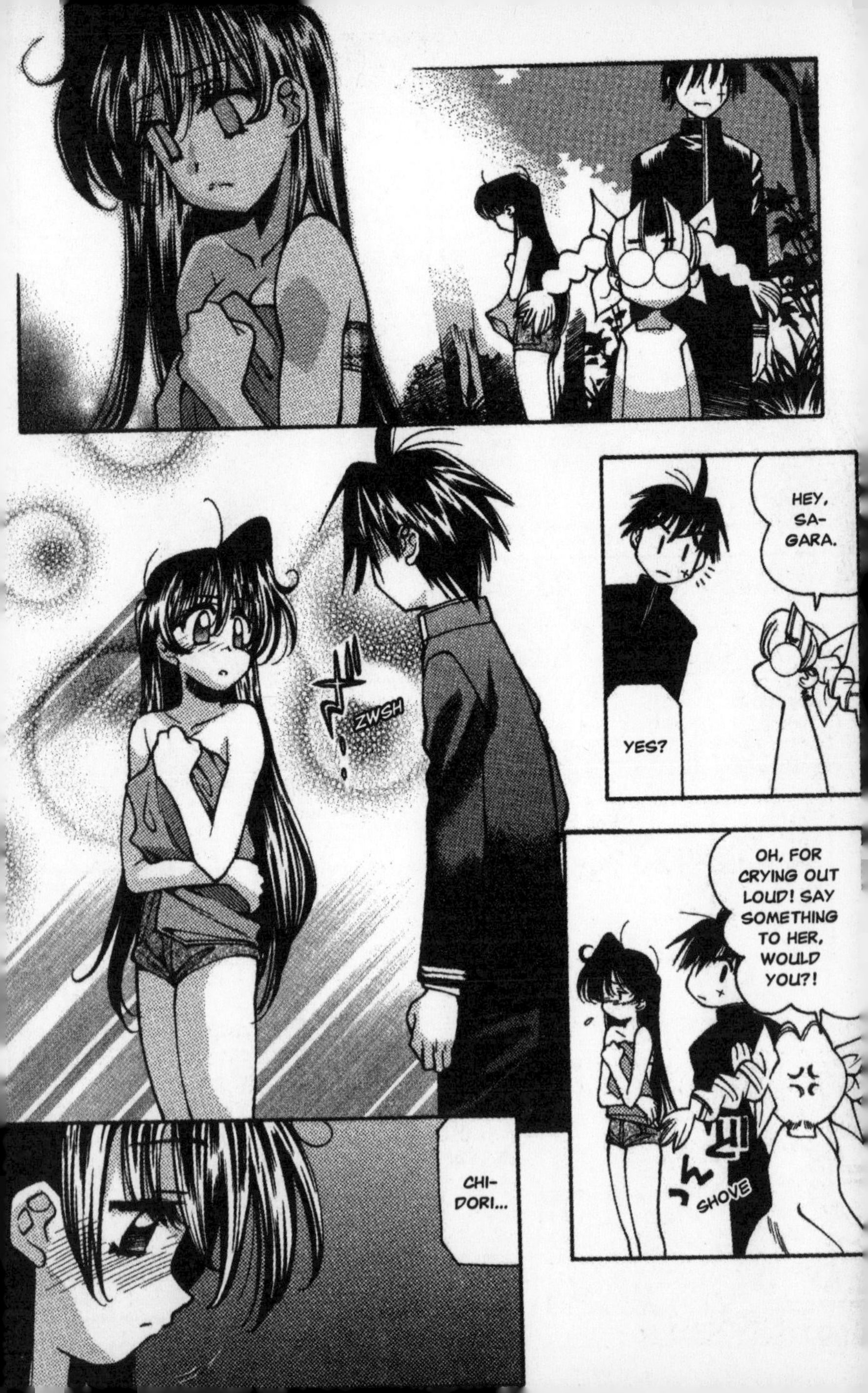
HEY, SA-GARA.
YES?
ZWSH
OH, FOR CRYING OUT LOUD! SAY SOMETHING TO HER, WOULD YOU?!
SHOVE
CHI-DORI...

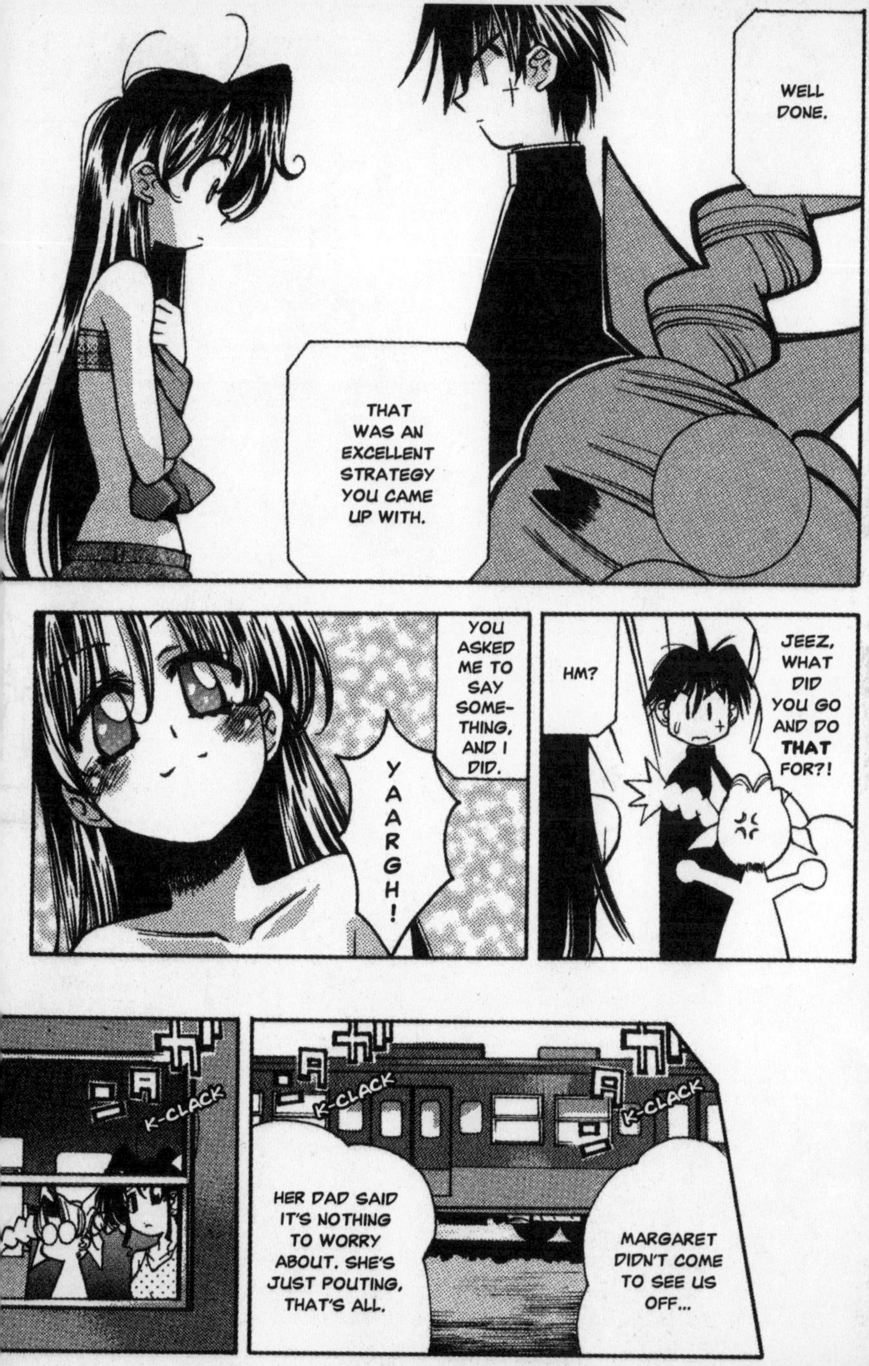
WELL DONE.
THAT WAS AN EXCELLENT STRATEGY YOU CAME UP WITH.
JEEZ, WHAT DID YOU GO AND DO THAT FOR?!
HM?
YOU ASKED ME TO SAY SOME-THING, AND I DID.
YAARGH!
K-CLACK
K-CLACK
MARGARET DIDN'T COME TO SEE US OFF...
HER DAD SAID IT'S NOTHING TO WORRY ABOUT. SHE'S JUST POUTING, THAT'S ALL.
K-CLACK

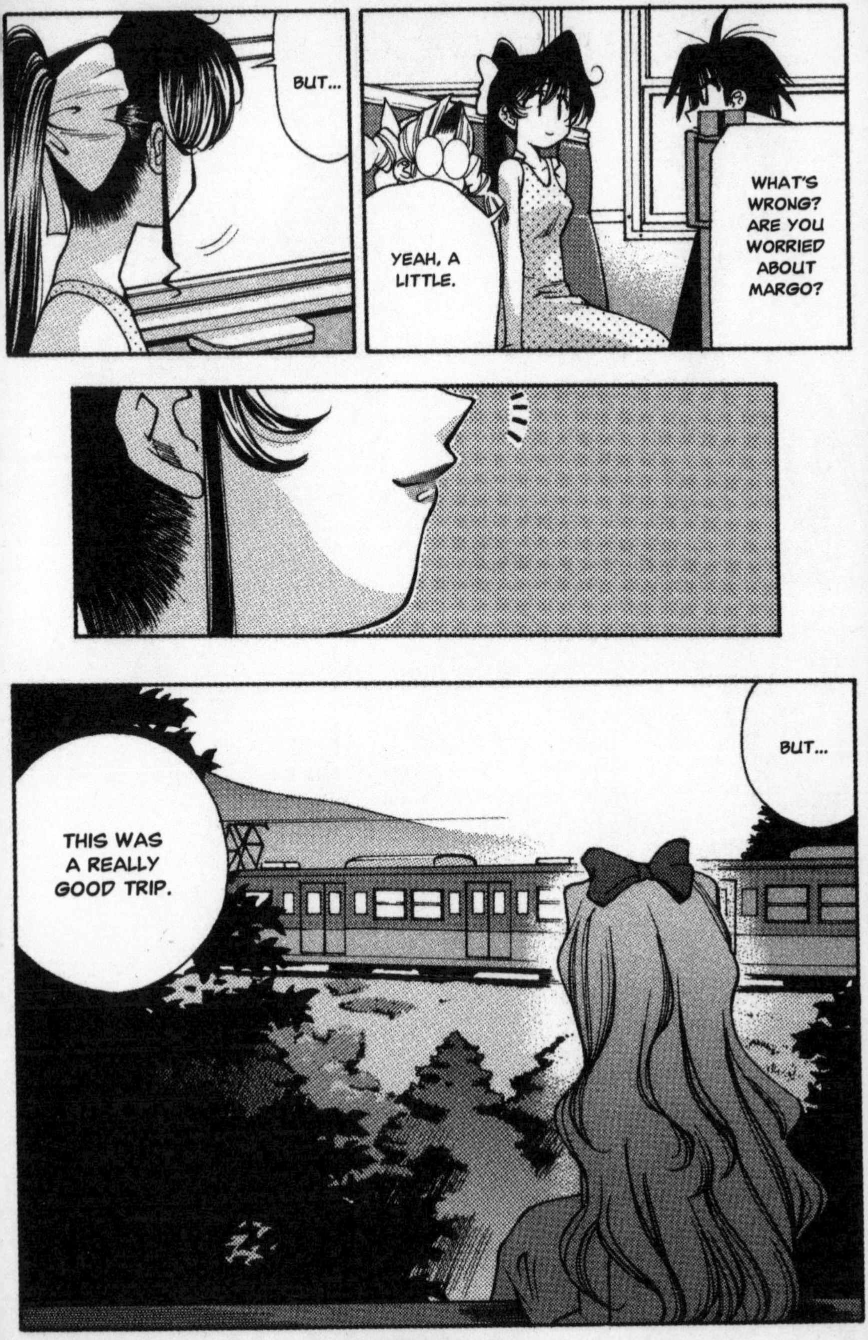
WHAT'S WRONG? ARE YOU WORRIED ABOUT MARGO?
YEAH, A LITTLE.
BUT...
BUT...
THIS WAS A REALLY GOOD TRIP.

CONTINUED IN VOLUME 4

FULL METAL PANIC! OVERLOAD! VOLUME THREE

© 2002 Tomohiro NAGAI • Shouji GATOU
© 2002 Shikidouji
Originally published in Japan in 2002 by
KADOKAWA SHOTEN PUBLISHING CO., LTD., Tokyo.
English translation rights arranged with
KADOKAWA SHOTEN PUBLISHING CO., LTD., Tokyo.

Editor **JAVIER LOPEZ**
Translator **AMY FORSYTH**
Graphic Artist **SCOTT HOWARD**

Editorial Director **GARY STEINMAN**
Creative Director **JASON BABLER**
Print Production Manager **BRIDGETT JANOTA**
Production Coordinator **MARISA KREITZ**

International Coordinators **TORU IWAKAMI & MIYUKI KAMIYA**

President, CEO & Publisher **JOHN LEDFORD**

Email: editor@adv-manga.com
www.adv-manga.com

www.advfilms.com

For sales and distribution inquiries please call 1.800.282.7202

ADV MANGA™

is a division of A.D. Vision, Inc.
5750 Bintliff Drive, Suite 210, Houston, Texas 77036

English text © 2005 published by A.D. Vision, Inc. under exclusive license.
ADV MANGA is a trademark of A.D. Vision, Inc.

ISBN: 1-4139-0327-4
First printing, December 2005
10 9 8 7 6 5 4 3 2 1
Printed in Canada

Full Metal Panic! Overload! Vol. 03

p. 56   *Anmitsu*

Anmitsu is a traditional Japanese dessert made of small cubes of agar jelly, served with sweet red bean paste and a variety of seasonal fruit. It is usually topped off with a sweet syrup.

p. 85   **Doraemon**

When Kyoko sees Sosuke produce all those guns from out of nowhere, she's suddenly reminded of Doraemon, the robotic cat from the future. The brainchild of Fujiko F. Fujio, Doraemon first debuted in 1970, and boasts such powers as the ability to pull an infinite number of things from its pocket.

p. 86   **Lord Dessler and the other side**

Lord Dessler is a character from the television anime *Uchuu Senkan Yamato*, also known as *Starblazers* or *Space Battleship Yamato* in the U.S. As one would gather from the reference, Dessler did in fact die in *Yamato*...before being resurrected in season two.

p. 132   **Sorry 'bout that!**

The reason for Kaname's startled look in this panel is that for some reason, Kurz decided to take a rather colorful approach to his apology, one that employs the kind of language that would appear in a samurai drama. Note also Kurz's sudden wardrobe change and folding paper fan—both of these call to mind Japanese *rakugo* storytelling, wherein the fan can be used as a prop and to punctuate comedic elements of the story.

FULL METAL PANIC OVERLOAD! 4

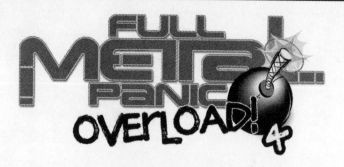

A STORM IS HEADED FOR TOKYO, AND CHIDORI AND THE OTHERS ARE RIDING IT OUT IN THE HALLS OF JINDAI HIGH. BUT WITH THE STUDENTS' SAFETY AT STAKE, SOSUKE DECIDES ITS TIME TO BRING OUT THE HEAVY ARTILLERY TO MAKE A FEW "MODIFICATIONS."

CAN JINDAI HIGH SURVIVE THIS ASSAULT *AND* WEATHER THE STORM? THE HIGH-CALIBER HIJINKS CONTINUE IN...

FULL METAL PANIC! OVERLOAD! VOLUME 4

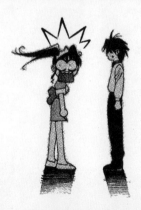

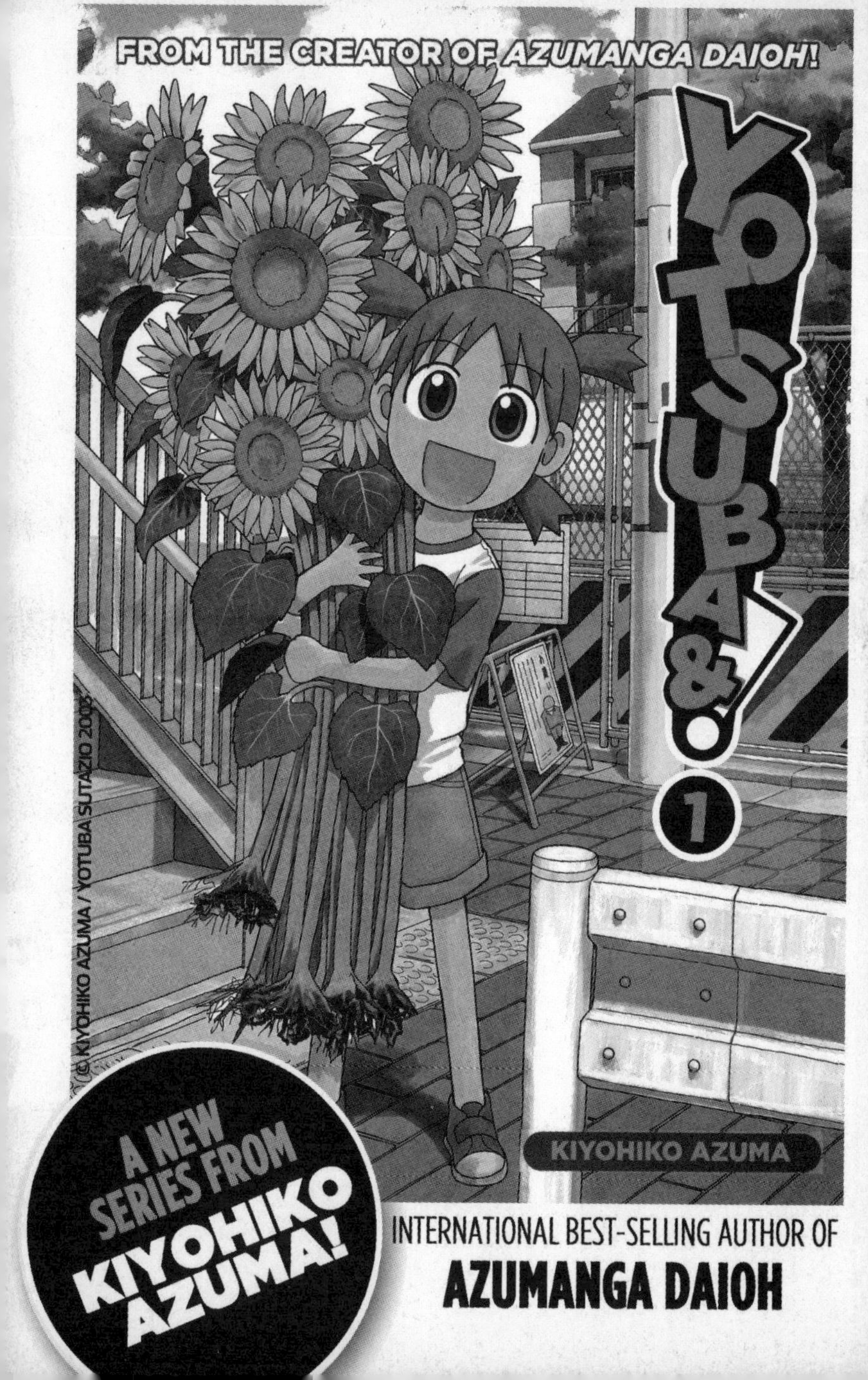
FROM THE CREATOR OF AZUMANGA DAIOH!
YOTSUBA&!
1
KIYOHIKO AZUMA
© KIYOHIKO AZUMA / YOTUBA SUTAZIO 2003
A NEW SERIES FROM KIYOHIKO AZUMA!
INTERNATIONAL BEST-SELLING AUTHOR OF
AZUMANGA DAIOH

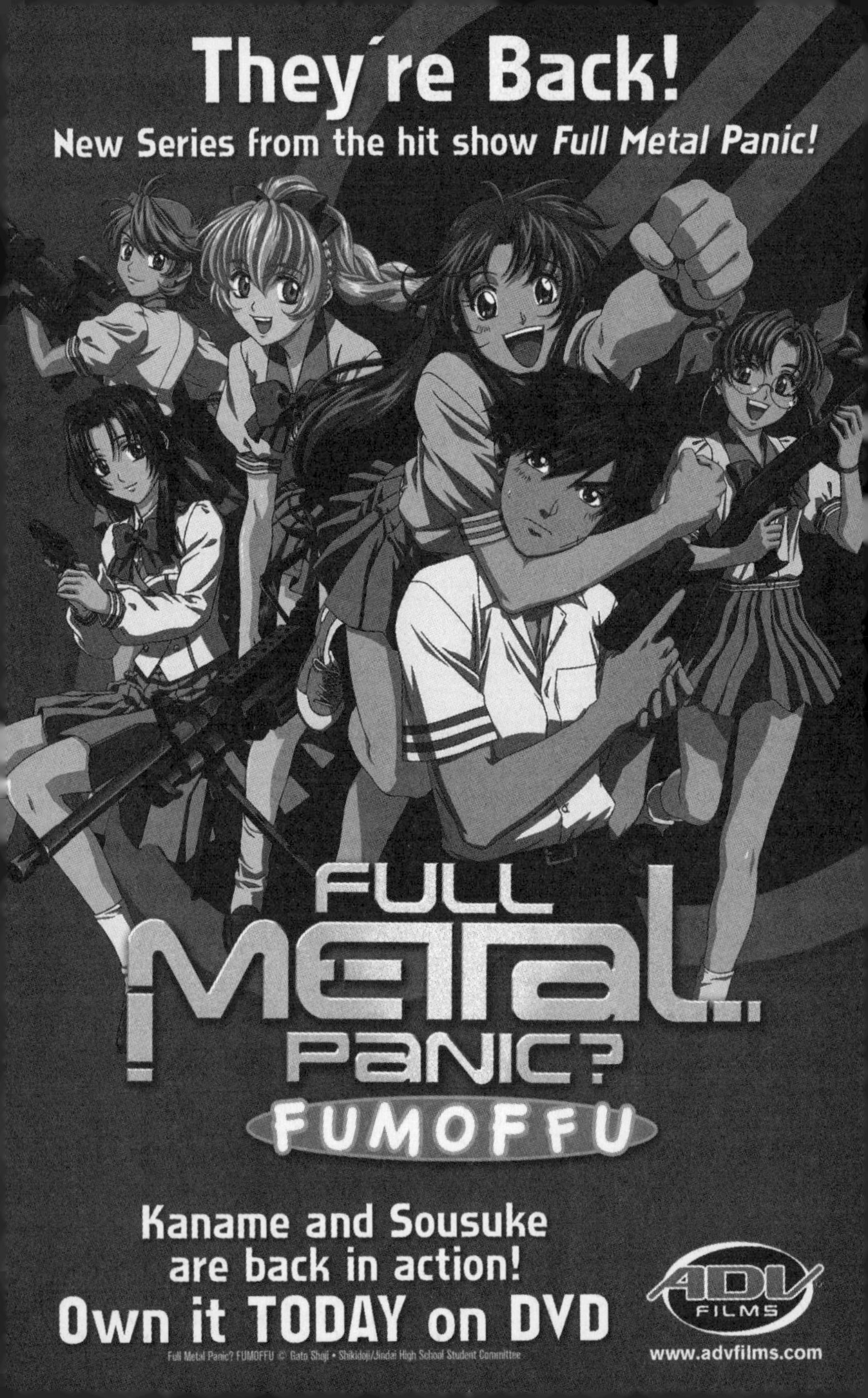
They're Back!
New Series from the hit show *Full Metal Panic!*
FULL METAL PANIC?
FUMOFFU
Kaname and Sousuke are back in action!
Own it TODAY on DVD
Full Metal Panic? FUMOFFU © Gato Shoji • Shikidoji/Jindai High School Student Committee
ADV FILMS
www.advfilms.com

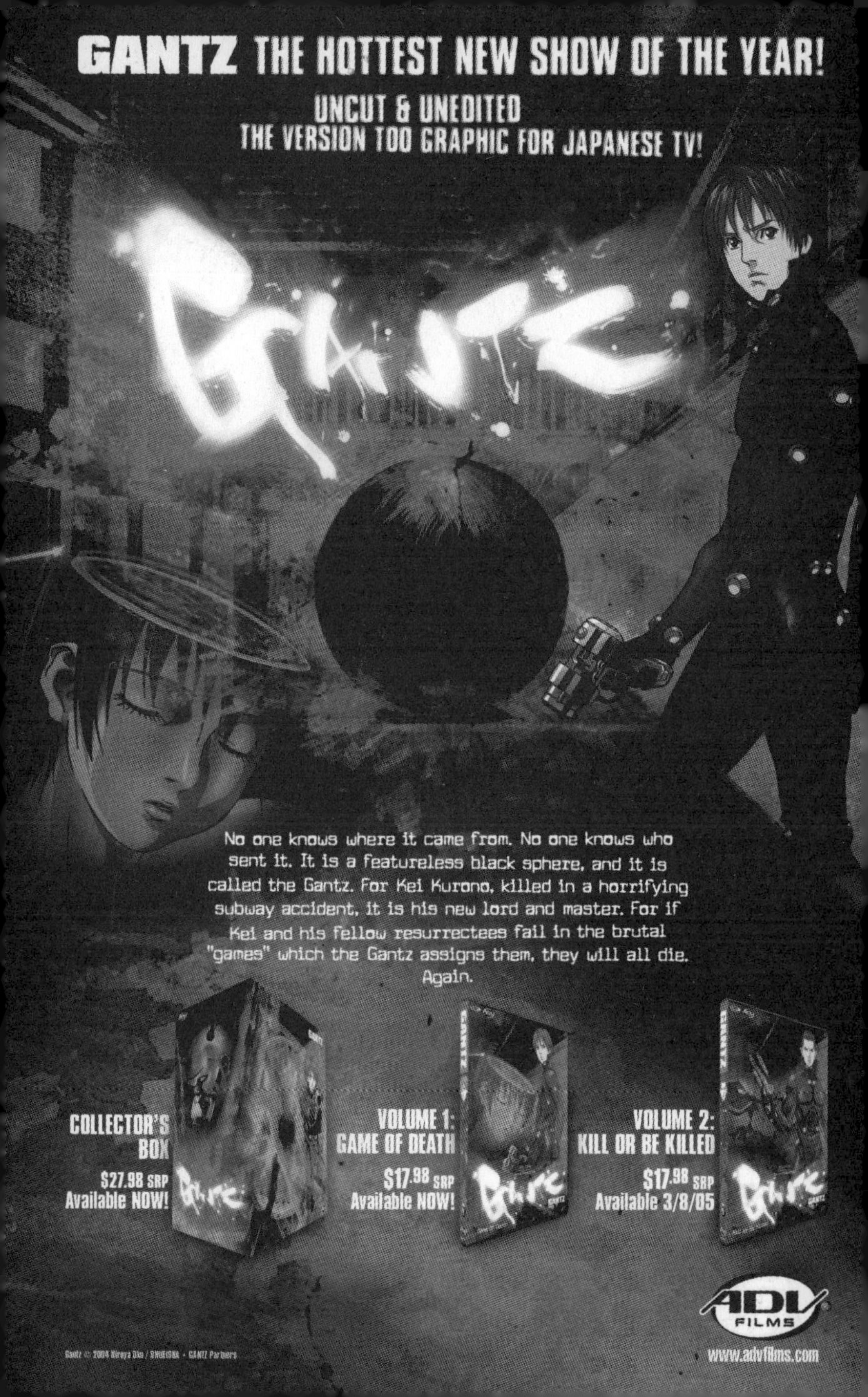

GANTZ THE HOTTEST NEW SHOW OF THE YEAR!
UNCUT & UNEDITED
THE VERSION TOO GRAPHIC FOR JAPANESE TV!
No one knows where it came from. No one knows who sent it. It is a featureless black sphere, and it is called the Gantz. For Kei Kurono, killed in a horrifying subway accident, it is his new lord and master. For if Kei and his fellow resurrectees fail in the brutal "games" which the Gantz assigns them, they will all die. Again.
COLLECTOR'S BOX
$27.98 SRP
Available NOW!
VOLUME 1: GAME OF DEATH
$17.98 SRP
Available NOW!
VOLUME 2: KILL OR BE KILLED
$17.98 SRP
Available 3/8/05
ADV FILMS
Gantz © 2004 Hiroya Oku / SHUEISHA • GANTZ Partners
www.advfilms.com

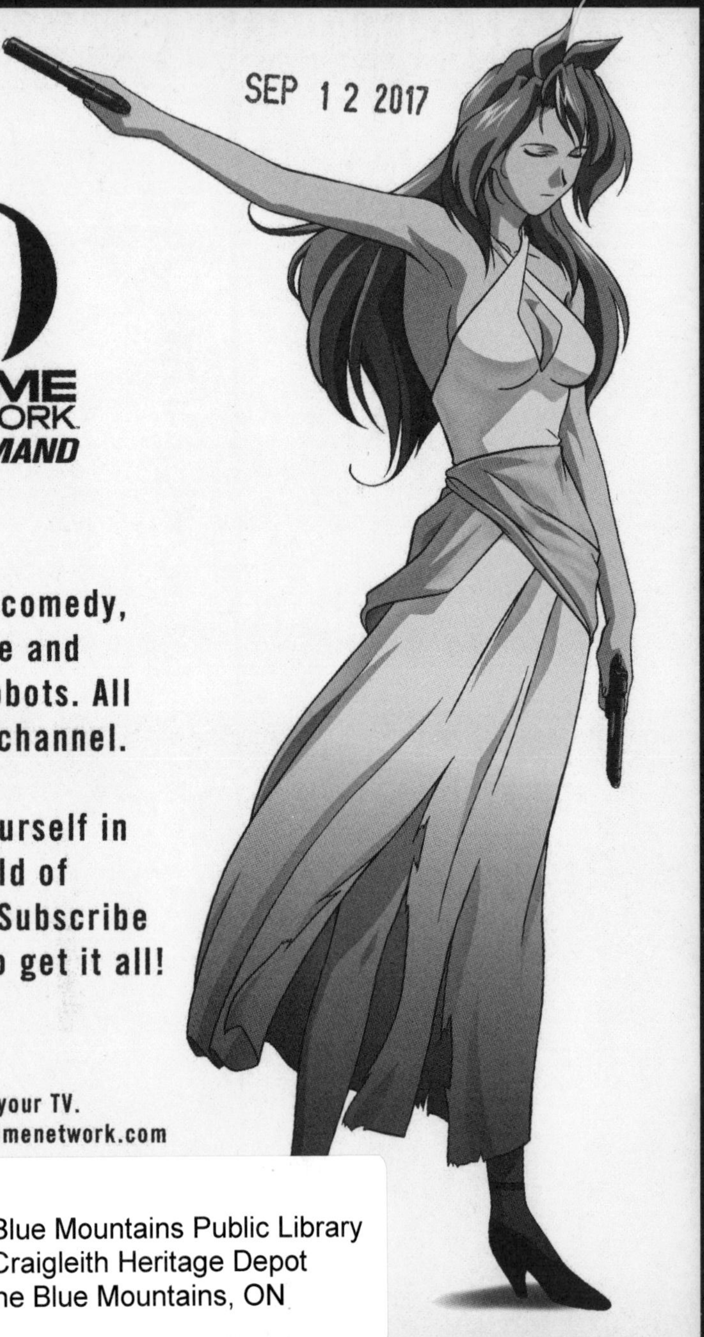